GREAT IDEAS IN

INFORMATION THEORY
LANGUAGE AND
CYBERNETICS

GREAT IDEAS IN

INFORMATION THEORY
LANGUAGE AND
CYBERNETICS

By
JAGJIT SINGH

Dover Publications, Inc., New York

Published in Canada by General Publishing Com-
pany, Ltd., 30 Lesmill Road, Don Mills, Toronto,
Ontario.
Published in the United Kingdom by Constable
and Company, Ltd., 10 Orange Street, London,
W.C. 2.

*Great Ideas in Information Theory, Language and
Cybernetics* is a new work, published for the first
time by Dover Publications, Inc., in 1966.

Standard Book Number: 486-21694-2
Library of Congress Catalog Card Number: 66-20417

Manufactured in the United States of America
Dover Publications, Inc.
180 Varick Street
New York, N. Y. 10014

PREFACE

ALTHOUGH recent work on the theory of language, information, and automata leans heavily on some rather difficult mathematics, to understand its main ideas we need only know simple elaborations of four commonplace principles. They are the principles of the race track, the slide rule, the chartroom, and the club (or old-school tie). The race-track principle is the bettor's rule for evaluating his betting odds. He assesses them according to the formula that while the chance of a "win" *or* "place" is the sum of individual chances of the respective events in question, that of a double haul is their product. The whole of probability calculus may well be built on these two addition and multiplication laws of compounding probabilities suggested by the bettor's intuition. The slide-rule principle is a way of transforming numbers so that multiplication of any two of them may be turned into addition of their transforms called logarithms. The chartroom principle is the basis of graphs designed to represent visually almost any state of affairs from the growth of automobile sales to the paths of projectiles. For a point on the graph line may stand for the number of automobiles sold or the height of a projectile above ground level at any instant, and the graph line as a whole their temporal successions during any given interval of time. While normally only such paper graphs and charts are in vogue, it is possible to represent more complex situations, where two or more variables are associated in a specified way, by "space" graphs and, with some imaginative effort, even by supergraphs in imaginary hyperspaces of higher dimensions. Finally, the club principle is the relationship that ties a member or individual to the club to which he belongs. We shall need its sublimate in logic, that is, the logical relation whereby an element or an individual is said to be a member of the class to which it may belong.

An element is said to belong to the class if and only if it possesses the prescribed attribute(s) qualifying it for membership. The theory of sets and classes, with all its manifold ramifications in diverse fields, is all but founded on this club or class-membership relation.

With an ideological equipment no heavier than that provided by a few simple refinements of the aforesaid four principles, which will be developed *ab initio* as required, the reader may confidently embark on an adventure in ideas destined to change the course of human civilization in an altogether new dimension. For they are now inspiring the so-called automation-oriented cybernetical revolution in contradistinction to the earlier industrial revolution. Thanks to the latter we have already learned partially to actualize the ancient dream of *perpetuum mobile*, an ever-flowing fount of physical power. For even though we now know enough about the nature of energy and physical power to realize that the dream is impossible, we also know that in the not too distant future we shall have in fusion-based nuclear reactors a substitute near enough to it to meet all the power needs of our planet. However, we do not live by brute physical power alone. We also use in good measure a very different sort of power—the power of our brains to understand our environment and use that understanding to mold it to our heart's desires. It is this cerebral power or intelligence that has already given us the means of amplifying some millionfold our muscle power. An astronaut, for example, moves five thousand times faster than a pedestrian can walk, so that the former's kinetic energy is $(5000)^2$ or twenty-five million times that of the latter. But we still do not know how to increase our mental prowess to anywhere near the same extent, despite the recent spectacular advances in computer technology. The reason is that human intelligence has not yet been sufficiently introspective to know itself. When at last we have discovered the physical structures and neurophysiological principles underlying the intelligence shown by natural automata such as the living brain, we shall have also acquired the means of simulating it synthetically. But before we can formulate these neurophysiological principles, we must study such artificial automata as we can make, which are at least capable in some rudimentary ways of imitating the intelligent behavior of the living brain such as its ability to compute, recognize audio-visual patterns, prove theorems, or play games. The stage will then be gradually reached when we shall find it possible to lever up our thinking power by equally large factors to match the extraordinary escalation of physical power we have already secured. This is why scientists all over the world are now straining the available resources of biophysics, biochemistry, mathematical logic and probability, microbiology, neurophysiology, and microminiaturization techniques of molecular electronics to make artificial automata capable of exhibiting somehow the intelligence of their living original. This book is a worm's-eye view of such multipronged probes into the nature of intelligence as the pooled wisdom of the afore-mentioned disciplines can give us at present.

We begin with a discussion of the symbolic processes of human language, the most overt manifestation of human intelligence, in order to prepare the ground for an account of the mathematical theory of "information" that an "intelligence" may produce or grasp. As will be shown, it is an abstraction that may be measured, communicated, stored, and processed. Indeed, by a mere reversal of its sign it may even be made structurally similar to the physicists' entropy. It is this structural similarity or isomorphism that provides the link between the two meanings of power—the power to do and the power to direct the doer. Thus information, like knowledge in the old proverb, *is* power in the dual sense used here. For it is the information-loaded punch tapes directing the computer in its programed computation as much as the information-soaked molecules called DNA that make man realize his biological heritage.

Although our account of how information may be measured or communicated effectively across media with speed and reliability (as in telephony and telegraphy) or stored and processed to serve prescribed goals (as in computers or automatically run industrial plants) occupies the first nine chapters, it is only a prelude to our main theme—the physical basis of the intelligence of the living brain. For there is an underlying similarity in the way in which artificial automata like computers and automated factories, on the one hand, and natural automata or living brains, on the other, function. Both employ devices, though of widely different materials and therefore of correspondingly different sensitivity and efficiency, which essentially measure quantities like temperature, pressure, rate of flow, voltage, and so on, and feed back their measurements into the network of electronic hardware in one case or of biological software in the other. While it is true that their study has also revealed that natural automata process their input information to suit their own ends in ways quite different from those of computers and control systems, it is only by preliminary peeps into these relatively simpler types of artificial automata that we can hope to gain some insight into the working of such high-complication automata as the living brain. This is why, after a rather longish preamble on information, computers, and control systems, the remainder of the book describes, in the light of our present-day knowledge, the actions of neural networks other than computers and control systems, whether made of living neurons like the animal brain or of their ersatz counterparts like artificial automata that can imitate (even though as yet crudely) some of the more difficult mental tasks the human brain takes in its stride, such as translation, chess playing, theorem proving, pattern recognition, and learning. If some of these newly contrived artificial automata seem but curious little playthings, it may be recalled that the power of steam to do useful work was also first demonstrated in Hero of Alexandria's toys long before it could be exploited in the steam engines of today. The great interest that these artificial automata have already aroused encourages the hope that the gap between the inevitable first faltering steps in making amusing toys and the final ones of fulfilling their engineering potential will not be as long as the one that intervened between Hero and Watt.

JAGJIT SINGH

New Delhi
September, 1965

CONTENTS

Chapter I

LANGUAGE AND COMMUNICATION

THE search for synthetic intelligence must begin with an inquiry into the origin of natural intelligence, that is, into the working of our own brain, its sole creator at present. Although the study of human speech and language is not the most direct approach to how the brain functions, there is perhaps a grain of truth in Fournié's surmise that human speech may well be a window through which the physiologist can observe cerebral life. He may have been led to it by Paul Broca's discovery of the fact that aphasia or loss of speech is caused by destruction of a certain relatively small area of the cortex in the dominant hemisphere of man.* This is not to say that speech is located there in the way the United States gold reserves are hoarded at Fort Knox, but that this small area is used as an essential part of a functional mechanism employed while the individual speaks, writes, reads, or listens to others who speak. For despite the damage to the area in question a man can still think and carry out other forms of voluntary activity even if the speech mechanism is paralyzed. In other words, the human engine continues to run although it has ceased to whistle.

Since Broca's discovery a great deal of work on cerebral mechanisms of speech has been done by neurophysiologists like Penfield, Roberts, and others. But the core of their work amounts to showing that although the brain of man in outward form is not so very different from that of other mammals like the dog or monkey, there is within it a further sophistication of cerebral organization that makes human speech possible. It is this unique cerebral endowment of man that confers on

* Just as Hippocrates identified the brain itself as the seat of consciousness at a time when the heart was looked upon as the repository of mind and spirit, from the observation that paralysis of one side of the body might result from an injury to the hemisphere on the other side.

1

him alone of all God's creatures the strange faculty of speech and language.   This is why a discussion of language is a convenient starting point for an exploration of our main theme, the nature and genesis of human intelligence.   Moreover, it is in any case the earliest manifestation of human intelligence and almost as old as Homo sapiens.

Long before man became Homo faber, a toolmaker, he was Homo logos, a talker.   The fossil remains of various manlike creatures of a million years ago are evidence enough of the major artifact of human prehistory—talk before tools.   There are, of course, no fossilized tape recordings or even cuneiform tablet transcriptions of these primitive prehistoric conversations.   But their handiworks, the chipped stone flakes and the like, bear eloquent testimony to the conversations their creators must have had.   For these could have been made only by the coordinated effort of teams of beings able to communicate with one another by means of a system of vocal sounds.   We should nowadays dignify such a system and call it a language because it was altogether much more sophisticated and refined than the symbolic cries and body movements of even the higher mammals that merely demonstrate but seldom convey any specific information by *abstraction*.   This is why it would be truer to attribute the uniqueness of man in the animal world not to any particular manifestation of his culture such as his political penchant, as Aristotle did, or to his toolmaking ability, as others have done, but rather to his capacity to speak some language.

His ability to speak a language in turn stems from two unique features of his biological make-up.   First, unlike all other creatures, who merely inherit various instinctually determined sound-making powers, man has a throat adequately equipped to produce a wide variety of arbitrary sound symbols.   Secondly, he alone in the animal world combines this laryngeal skill with sufficient abstraction-detecting cerebral powers to be able to correlate each one of his sound symbols with its own distinctive meaning.   Thanks to these twin gifts of nature, man is born with an innate urge to speak a language, although there is no particular language which is passed on to him genetically like the mating calls of carnivores, the distress cries of birds, or the courting dances of bees.

This inborn *capacity* to learn *any* language rather than the genetically transmitted, rigidly predetermined language patterns of the lower animals is the real mark of his humanness, because it enables him to use language in a way no other animal can.   By eliminating the need for any relation or resemblance whatever between the sound (word) symbol and its meaning, as in onomatopoeic words like "bow-wow," man finds a limitless ocean of communication possibilities opened up to him which are denied other animals handicapped by their severely limited laryngeal-*cum*-cerebral prowess. For example, the object you are reading now is called "book" in English, *livre* in French, and *kitab* in Hindustani; yet no one of these sound symbols has any greater claim to conjure up the object it denotes other than the initial but arbitrary choice of the group using the language. This initial freedom to associate any arbitrary sound with any object or idea, subject only to its acceptance by others of his group, enables man to organize the infinitely variegated range of sounds he can make into a system which is in fact the language of his tribe.

One great advantage of such a *free creation* of systematic sound patterns charged with meanings is that by mere talk man is able to transmit almost any kind of experience vicariously, thereby creating a basis for the cumulative development of civilization and culture. Language therefore is man's open-sesame to all the treasures of the earth he has since created or found for himself. Not that its powers are unlimited; rather, the limits of our language are in many ways the limits of our world, as Wittgenstein and Orwell have recently reminded us. Yet their reminder is at bottom a secularization for an irreligious but sophisticated age of the invocations to language which abound in the ancient sacred texts of all lands:

> In the beginning was the word, and the word was with God and the word was God.

The ancients even knew what we are at times still inclined to forget, that when the gods decide to confound a community, country, or commonwealth, they begin by interposing in its midst a language barrier, as in the disruption of the Adamites daring to scale the heavens on the Tower of Babel. The story is apocryphal. But its moral is particularly relevant today because, despite these days of easy communications, many countries are now afflicted with such a confusion of tongues that their most urgent reform is a comprehensive program of de-Babelization. Indeed, if we are to survive, de-Babelization of individual nations and countries must pave the way for a larger, if more arduous, linguistic integration on a planetary scale. For if lack of linguistic coherence *within* the nations is a source of great national unrest and tension, language differences *between* the nations are creating even greater havoc by giving rise to their own tangle of international misunderstandings. A classic instance of such a disaster-sparking misunderstanding has been cited by Stuart Chase in his *Power of Words*. Because of a mix-up in translation of a single word* in their reply to the Potsdam ultimatum of the Allies in July, 1945, the Japanese Cabinet was understood to have *ignored* the ultimatum, contrary to their real intention of *reserving comment* on it, with all the dire aftermath of Hiroshima and Nagasaki that we know. Likewise, some of the world's current misunderstandings with the Chinese may well be due at least partially to differences between the Chinese and the Western languages. In the latter there is a great deal of dichotomizing; terms go in pairs, with meaning reference to opposite extremes (good-evil, black-white, clean-dirty, strong-weak, and so on). In the Chinese there is much less dichotomizing and the language has few pairs of opposites. Consequently, what may seem to be a stark contradiction to a Western mind may not be so to a Chinese. Be that as it may, the influence of language on one's world view is indubitably great, even though its precise evaluation has yet to be made, despite philosophical wrangles over it since the days of the *Mahabharata* and the *Iliad*.

The great debate is still on and even today we have two antipodal evaluations. There is, on the one hand, a school of thought called linguistic philosophy which claims language to be an activity that is all but coterminous with human life. It solves the dilemma of Goethe's Faust—who wondered whether in the beginning there was the word or the deed—by identifying the two. On the other hand, there is the contrary view attributed to Antoine Roquentin, the hero of Sartre's *La Nausée*, that the word remains on the speaker's lips and refuses to go and rest upon the thing, making language an absurd medley of sounds and symbols beyond which flows the world—an undiscriminated and uncommunicable chaos. Between these two extremes there is no doubt many a halfway house where truth may lie. But it is not likely that we shall discover its precise location by mere philosophical disputation; quite the contrary. However, what philosophical debate fails to reveal may perhaps be shown if intelligence can be made to turn its gaze inward. For, if we can manage to hold a mirror before it to enable intelligence to look at itself, as the new science of cybernetics endeavors to do, its self-glance may illumine the interrelationship between the external world and the

---

* This word, *mokusatsu*, has two meanings: (1) to ignore and (2) to refrain from comment.

linguistic medium of its making through which it views that world. It is therefore well worth our while to examine what the new science of cybernetics is about.

Although cybernetics has now become a miscellany of loosely related activities, we shall use the term here to denote an inter-disciplinary inquiry into the nature and physical basis of human intelligence, with the object of reproducing it synthetically. Since human intelligence shows itself in the complexity of man's total conduct, such an introspective probe must naturally begin with the construction of mechanisms that will exhibit comparable complexity of behavior. But to construct the latter we must somehow specify in language the complexity we wish to embody in the machine. Consequently, the complexity of the system we attempt to define will inevitably be limited by our power of processing the information communicated in the language we use. Unfortunately, our information-absorbing powers, when we employ the language of our daily discourse, are notoriously limited. The only way of overcoming this handicap is to make machines that understand languages—machine codes—with far greater capacity to gobble and digest coded information fed into them than our own. As we shall see more clearly later,* several machine languages or codes of sufficient sophistication have recently been devised to permit description of highly complicated systems. There is thus a close but reciprocal tie-up between the complexity of a system and the language used to specify complexity for communicating it to the processing machine. Language and communication on the one hand and complexity of artificial intelligent systems on the other are, therefore, closely related. Advances in one, say, the power of language, enable the specification of more complex systems; whereas the construction of more complex systems that such specification allows leads to the invention of more powerful languages or machine codes. Thanks to parallel advances in machine codes and in the design of machines able to manipulate the information they embody, it has recently been possible to devise highly complex communication machines and control systems capable of imitating human behavior to some extent. Such, for example, are the machines which communicate with one another by means of a code or language very much as human beings do. There are others which store data put into them and thus exhibit what we call memory. This process has been extended to confer on these machines even the power to learn,

* See Chapters XII and XVI.

although the technique of building and employing such machines, as we shall see in Chapter XV, is still very rudimentary and imperfect. However, despite their imperfections, the study of all these kinds of machines has inevitably led to a new understanding of the mechanism of language, communication, memory, and learning in human beings.

The new understanding fostered by cybernetics is not only leading to the creation of improved technical devices (enabling a computer or even a summit leader to speak to its/his counterpart across the continent at the flick of a few switches) but is providing a basis for the design of what Hans Freudenthal calls "Lincos," a new language for cosmic intercourse. Beginning with a Lincos broadcast of such universal truths as "twice two makes four," it may be possible to develop sufficient vocabulary to converse even on God, love, Universal Mind and the like with celestial beings in other planetary worlds of the Milky Way and beyond.

The ability of cybernetics to take in its stride such a wide diversity of activities as the design of robots to guide satellites in their courses, pursue missiles, run refineries, or monitor telephone exchanges, on the one hand, and that of ersatz brains, intelligence amplifiers, and Lincos, on the other, stems from a basic unity pervading both types of control and communication mechanisms—the naturally occurring type found in animals as well as the artificially contrived one in man-made automata. It shows itself most strikingly in the rudimentary imitations of life embodied in the remarkable toys of electrophysiologists like Ross Ashby and Grey Walter. Ashby's creature, appropriately christened *machina spora*, for example, behaves as a "fireside cat or dog which only stirs when disturbed, and then methodically finds a comfortable position and goes to sleep again."* Actually it is merely a rig of electronic circuits similar to the reflex arcs within the spinal cord of an animal. Grey Walter's wandering tortoise, *machina speculatrix*, on the other hand,

> is never still except when "feeding"—that is, when the batteries are being recharged. Like the restless creatures in a drop of pond water it bustles around in a series of swooping curves so that in an hour it will investigate several hundred square feet of ground. In its exploration of any ordinary room it inevitably encounters many obstacles; but apart from stairs and rugs, there are few situations from which it cannot extricate itself.†

* *The Living Brain*, by W. Grey Walter, Penguin Books, Inc., 1961, p. 111.
† *Ibid.*, p. 114.

What the Ashby-Walter pieces of complicated electrical circuitry attempt to do is to simulate the mental activity of the brain, that is, its thinking process, in a rudimentary manner by substituting wire in place of nerve fiber, hardware in place of flesh, and electromagnetic wave in place of the mysterious pulse in the living nerve fiber. Although the purposive lifelike behavior of such simulacra and other servo systems devised for the automatic control of machinery and plant by no means warrants the assumption that the animal nervous systems function in the same way, their study is nevertheless an essential preliminary to our understanding of animal brains as well as of human behavior patterns such as speech and other habits. This is why cybernetics is now a confluence of many streams of knowledge—neurophysiology, biochemistry, computers, information theory, automation, mathematical logic, probability, linguistics, and psychology, to name only a few. This is also why it is likely to have even more momentous consequences for the future of mankind than the discovery of atomic energy, unless we happen to abuse the latter by blowing ourselves up in a fit of suicidal stupidity.

Indeed, cybernetics has already sparked what has been aptly called the *second* industrial revolution. In the first industrial revolution first steam-driven machines and then the internal combustion engine took over the physical work that man or his beasts of burden used to do. But man still had to perform all important control functions to guide the engines he set to work. In the second industrial revolution even such guidance has now begun to devolve in increasing measure on other machines. If the first revolution was the outcome of the efforts of a long succession of *application-oriented* engineers like Porta, Newcomen, Watt, and Boulton, the second sprouted from the labors of pure mathematicians like Leibnitz, Pascal, Babbage, and Boole. Charles Babbage made elaborate blueprints of automatic computers, showing a perspicacity and vision not unlike Leonardo's in foreseeing the day of airplanes. Both were far ahead of the technology of their times. Whereas the realization of Leonardo's dream had to wait for the invention of the internal combustion engine, that of Babbage had to wait for the emergence of electronics with its gift of electronic relays, vacuum tubes, magnetic tapes, and transistors. Once the new electronic tools to implement Babbage's ideas came to hand, it did not take long to automatize computation. Surprising as it may seem, automatization of computation immediately paved the way for automatizing industrial operations. The movement began with the chemical industry and soon spread to the telephone system and automobile production during the 1920's. It now bids fair to encompass all the remaining areas.

The reason electronics was able to advance automation so speedily is that for many years it was devoted almost entirely to the communication or transmission of information from one place to another. Besides wire and radio communication, it included sound recording, hearing aids, television, and other information-handling systems. In each of these applications the principal objective of the various pieces of equipment is to reproduce the input signal with as high fidelity as possible at the output device. From mere hi-fi transmission of information to its "processing" is but a step. Nevertheless, it was a major advance in that the electronic relays, vacuum tubes, transistors, and other similar control and communication devices which facilitate the processing of information are to the power machines they control what brain is to brawn. The control systems operate with low expenditure of energy and their mechanical efficiency is of no consequence, because their basic function is not to transform energy but to *process* information. The inputs of such systems are often the electronic counterparts of such animal sense organs as eyes and ears— thermostats, photoelectric cells, microphones, or stain gauges. The outputs are the analogues of an animal's muscles or communicating organs—loudspeakers, electric typewriters, and electric motors. Internally, the information being processed takes the form of the passage of electrical signals from one part of the system to another. It therefore follows that the functioning of the control devices depends primarily on proper flow or processing of information communicated by one part of the automatized system to another.

Control and communications systems attempt to do this in one of two ways or both. *Either* they merely transmit information with the least possible distortion, as in teletype, telephony, radio, and television, or they "process" the flow of such information from one part to another of an integrated whole in order to carry through a closely knit sequence of operations, whether industrial or computational, without human intervention at any intermediate stage. What then is this "information" with whose "flow" and "processing" the science of cybernetics and communication engineering are chiefly concerned?

In ordinary speech we use the word "information" as a synonym for news, knowledge, intelligence, report, and so on. It is an amalgam of so many vague and imprecise meanings that a scientist has to purify from the blend of its diverse connotations the one he requires for his purpose, very much as a chemist purifies a substance in order to study its behavior. In the communication engineer's purification of the term the stress is on the quantitative aspect of the *flow* in a *network* of an *intangible* attribute called *information*. It is measured (in a manner to be defined more precisely later) by its "news" value, that is, the extent of surprise it causes to the recipient. To understand the rationale underlying the surprise-value theory of information measure, consider a typical communications network. No matter whether it is a network of telegraph and telephone lines or of radio and television channels or even a mere living-room conversation, any such network will consist of at least three main parts:

(i) Transmitter or source.
(ii) Receiver.
(iii) Channel which conveys the communiqué from the transmitter to the receiver.

For example, in the case of a living-room conversation, the speaker is the source or transmitter, the air which carries his voice is the channel, and the listener is the receiver. Practical cases are generally much more elaborate, consisting of a number of sources and receivers in a complex network. The problems of transmission of information in such complex networks are somewhat analogous to those of electric transmission in a power grid using several interconnected generating stations to supply a number of towns. In both cases one seeks optimal schemes of distribution of the commodity flowing in the network on the basis of an appropriate criterion of efficiency of transmission. When the communiqué is tangible and therefore readily measurable, as in the case of an electric grid or a manufacturing belt, the problems encountered in the study of the communications system are of the types somewhat familiar to engineers and operational analysts. Such, for instance, is the case with an electric power network, where the criterion of efficiency is obviously the minimization of the heat loss *during* transmission. One way of accomplishing this (apart from using low-resistance transmission wires) is to increase the voltage at the input terminals of the line by installing a step-up voltage transformer and reducing the voltage to the prescribed level at the output terminals by another step-down transformer.

When, however, the flow in the network is an intangible like "information," as in the problem of the communications engineer concerned with sending messages by telegraph, telephone, radio, or otherwise, the criterion of efficiency naturally is the transmission of messages with minimum distortion at maximum speed and minimum cost. It happens that just as we may use a transformer to improve the efficiency of an electrical transmission system so also we may use what is called an encoder to improve the efficiency of a communication channel. The reason is that an encoded message is less liable to distortion by channel noise. Any communications system then may be symbolically represented as follows:

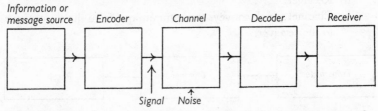

The information or message source selects a desired message out of a set of possible messages, just as a telegraphist selects one from a tray of messages awaiting transmission. The selected message may consist of written or spoken words or of pictures, music, and the like. The encoder codes the message or transforms it into the signal, which is actually sent over the communication channel from the encoder to the decoder. In the case of telephony, the channel is a wire, which carries the signal, a varying electrical current, produced by the encoder or the apparatus that transforms the sound pressure of source voice into the varying electrical current. In telegraphy the encoder codes the written words of the message into sequences of interrupted currents of varying lengths (dots, dashes, and spaces). In oral speech the information source is the brain, the encoder the voice mechanism that produces the varying sound pressure (the signal) which is transmitted through the air, the channel. In radio the channel is simply space and the signal the transmitted electromagnetic wave. Likewise, at the receiver's terminal a decoder is employed to transform the encoded message into the original form acceptable to the receiver. In other words, while the encoder transforms the intangible input commodity called "information" into a new form, the decoder performs the reverse operation to recover the encoded commodity in its pristine purity. In actual practice, however, there is no such pure recovery. One has always to contend with the vitiations of noise which in physical systems inevitably prevent perfect communication. These unwanted additions to the signal may be distortions of sound as in telephony, static as in radio, disfigurations in shape or shading of pictures as in television, or errors in transmission as in telegraphy. In all such communications systems the fundamental problem is to devise an appropriate measure of the "information" that they handle or process so as to use it to improve their "efficiency" in diverse ways such as enhancing the capacity of the channel to carry information to its optimal level and/or minimizing the adverse effects of noise vitiating its transmission.

Chapter II

WHAT IS INFORMATION?

TO discover a foothold for a metrical theory designed to serve the purpose described in the last chapter, consider any source of information. It produces messages by successively selecting discrete symbols from a given stock such as letters of an alphabet, words in a dictionary, notes of a musical scale, colors in a spectrum, or even the mere dash-dot twin of telegraphy. In other words, the message actually transmitted is a selection from a set of possible messages formed by sequences of symbols of its own repertoire. The communications system is designed to transmit *each* possible selection, not merely the one that happened to be actually chosen at the moment of transmission. To take a simple example, consider an ordinary doorbell. It is designed to communicate one or the other of a set of only two possible messages. Either (when pressed) it announces the arrival of a visitor or (when untouched) it denotes the absence of one. In more elaborate systems like the telephone or telegraph the set of possible messages is the aggregate of sequences of words in, say, the English vocabulary. No doubt many of these sequences will be meaningless gibberish without any matter. But here one may repeat with less punning and more literal truth what Locke said in a famous philosophical controversy: "No matter; never mind." For the technique of communication process pays no heed to the matter of the messages in question. The physical process of transmission such as the telephone or radio will transmit infantile twaddle as readily as a meaningful saying from the Talmud. Consequently, the metrical theory of information is not concerned with the semantic content of the set of messages from which it selects some particular one for transmission.

Because of the need, for our present purposes at least, to steer clear of meaning, "information" in this context is merely a measure of one's freedom of choice when one selects a message from the available set, many of which may well be devoid of meaning. If there are in all, say, *n* messages to select from and if each message is on a par with every other in that it is as likely to be chosen as any other, then the number *n* itself could be used as a measure of the amount of "information" present in the ensemble of messages available for transmission. Incidentally, the parity of the messages in the repertoire as expressed by the equal probability of their selection is important. For by choosing to adopt *n* as a measure of the information content of the communications system, we leave no room for any discrimination that the absence of parity would inevitably require.

But this way of measuring information, though simple, becomes awkward when we proceed from simpler communications systems to more complex ones. Suppose, for instance, we have a Morse key with its repertoire of just two messages—a dash and a dot. If we couple three such keys to produce a new complex, its repertoire will consist of $2 \times 2 \times 2 = 8$ different messages from which one could be selected, as is evident by a count of the various possible states of three Morse keys in unison listed below:

TABLE 1

State of keys	Morse key I	Morse key II	Morse key III
I	Dash	Dash	Dash
II	Dot	Dash	Dash
III	Dash	Dot	Dash
IV	Dot	Dot	Dash
V	Dash	Dash	Dot
VI	Dot	Dash	Dot
VII	Dash	Dot	Dot
VIII	Dot	Dot	Dot

If we choose to measure the information content of a system by the number of messages in its stock, the measure of each Morse key in isolation will be two, and that of three in combination, eight. But the measure is inappropriate in that it is natural to expect the information content of the united system to be the sum of its individual components, that is, $2 + 2 + 2 = 6$, instead of their product, $2 \times 2 \times 2 = 8$, as is actually the case. Fortunately this hiatus between actuality and anticipation is not difficult to bridge. For there is a neat way of transforming products of numbers into their sums by recourse to the logarithms we all learned at school. As is well known, the logarithm of a product of any set of numbers is the sum of their individual logarithms. In particular, $\log (2 \times 2 \times 2) = \log 2 + \log 2 + \log 2$. This additive property of logarithms stands us here in very good stead indeed. For by simply choosing to measure the information of each of the Morse keys by log 2 instead of plain 2, we ensure that the information measure of the complex of all the three together is the sum of their individual components:

$$\log 2 + \log 2 + \log 2 = \log 2 \times 2 \times 2 = \log 8.$$

This is why mathematicians prefer to measure the information content of a communications system having a stock of, say, *n equally likely* messages by log *n* instead of *n*, leaving the arbitrarily free choice of the logarithmic base open to suit any convenience. Number 2 seems to be the obvious choice as a base because it is the minimum number of messages that even the most rudimentary communications system like a doorbell or Morse key has to have in its repertoire. The information measure of such systems having a twofold or binary stock of messages therefore becomes $\log_2 2$, that is, unity. We are thus led to a natural unit of measurement of the information content of communications systems, namely, that of a system with equally likely binary choices. It is called a *bit*, a portmanteau word contracted from the phrase "binary unit." Its chief merit is strict conformity to our intuitive anticipations. For as we saw, if the information content of a single binary communications system like our doorbell or Morse key is one "bit," then that of a union of *m* such systems is *m* bits. Verily the logarithmic stitch at the outset saves nine at the end.

A serious limitation of our measurement scheme, however, is the assumption of equiprobability of all the messages in the system's stockpile, an assumption made to ensure their mathematical parity. For it greatly oversimplifies the actual situation encountered in most communications systems. Even in the simple case of the doorbell cited above, the probability of its being pressed announcing the presence of a visitor is much less than that of his absence, otherwise the householder would go crazy! As for the Morse key of our earlier illustration, with its assumed equiprobability of a dash or a dot, there is nothing to prevent us in any actual case from signaling on the average, say, nine dots for every dash, exactly as certain letters of the alphabet like *e*, *t*, *o* are used more frequently than others such as *v*, *k*, *x*. Consequently we have to amend the information measure proposed earlier, namely, $\log_2 2$, to express the system's overwhelming preference for a dot to a dash. A possible clue to the required revision is the fact that a measure of the lack of parity between the messages in a communications system's kit bag may as well be the probability of their respective selection. Thus in the case of our Morse key with its heavy odds in favor of a dot we may denote the relative parity of the two messages by the probability of their selection, that is, $\frac{9}{10}$ or 0.9 for a dot, and $\frac{1}{10}$ or 0.1 for a dash. The system can now be described by two numbers or rather two proper fractions, viz., 0.9 and 0.1, the respective probabilities of a dot and a dash instead of the single number 2 when both of them were equally probable. Obviously, on the logarithmic principle we have already found so appropriate, the information contributed by a dot is $\log_2 (0.9)$ and that by a dash, $\log_2 (0.1)$ bits. The total information of the system as a whole is then merely the sum of the two components, each contribution being "weighted" by its own probability of selection:

$$-(0.9 \log_2 0.9 + 0.1 \log_2 0.1) = 0.476 \text{ bits.*}$$

The decline in the system's information content from one bit to about half its value with mere loss of parity between the two messages in its repertoire is again to be expected. For with the system's pronounced predilection for a dot it is now easier to predict the outcome than previously when both the choices were assumed to be equally likely. Naturally the easier the prediction, the less the freedom of choice and consequently the less the information conveyed by the message. This is why any phrase or sentence in a text such as an old cliché that can be guessed with certainty is redundant and a greetings telegram on a wedding night conveys no great information. The amended scheme of measurement therefore conforms to our intuitive anticipation in this respect as well. Consequently its further generalization to cover a system with more than two, say, n messages, each with its own distinct probability $p_1, p_2, p_3, \ldots, p_n$ of selection, is in order. Its information measure is simply the analogously weighted sum of each contribution typified by $\log_2 p_i$, namely,

$$-(p_1 \log_2 p_1 + p_2 \log_2 p_2 + \ldots + p_n \log_2 p_n) \text{ bits.} \qquad (1)$$

It is obvious from expression (1) that the information content of a

---

* The negative sign at the beginning of the expression is added to make it positive since, as it happens, logarithms of all proper fractions like 0.9 and 0.1 are negative numbers.

message repertoire is a function of the probabilities of the occurrence of the messages included therein. By merely changing the probability pattern of any given message source or ensemble we alter completely its information content. Consider, for example, an ensemble of three messages M_1, M_2, M_3 with 1/2, 1/3, 1/6 as their respective probabilities of occurrence. With this scheme of probabilities the information content of each message and the probability of each message would be as follows:

TABLE 2

Message	M_1	M_2	M_3
Probabilities of message	1/2	1/3	1/6
Information content of message	$-\log_2 1/2 = 1$	$-\log_2 1/3 = 1.58$	$-\log_2 1/6 = 2.58$

The weighted sum (I_1) of the information content of these three messages is then the measure of the information of the message ensemble as a whole. I_1 is simply:

$$1/2(1) + 1/3(1.58) + 1/6(2.58) = 1.46 \text{ bits.}$$

But if we altered the probabilities of occurrence of M_1, M_2, M_3 to the new values, say, 2/3, 1/4, and 1/12 respectively, it is easy to verify that the information content of the same message ensemble now turns out to be 1.18 bits:

TABLE 3

Message	M_1	M_2	M_3
New probabilities of message	2/3	1/4	1/12
Information content of message	$-\log_2 2/3 = 0.58$	$-\log_2 1/4 = 2$	$-\log_2 1/12 = 3.58$
Weighted sum or information content of message ensemble as a whole	2/3(.58)	+ 1/4(2)	+1/12(3.58) = 1.18 bits

Obviously therefore, the probability pattern of the message ensemble is the very warp and woof of its information content. To each such pattern there corresponds a unique value of the information content of the ensemble. But among all the possible probability patterns there is one and only one that maximizes it. It is the equality pattern, that is, the case when all n messages are on a par. When this is the case, they are all equiprobable and each probability p is $\frac{1}{n}$ so that the sum (1) becomes $-\frac{n}{n} \log_2 \frac{1}{n}$ or $\log_2 n$, as it should. It is clearly the maximum value that a system with n messages in its repertoire can possibly have. For when all choices are equally probable and none prevails over any other, a person is, of course, completely free to choose among the various alternatives. As soon as one or more messages become more probable than any other, the freedom of choice is restricted and the corresponding information measure (1) must naturally decrease.

So far our informative function (1) has behaved in accordance with our intuitive anticipations. It is additive as we required, that is, we can add the information measures of individual messages to derive that of the ensemble by weighting each individual contribution by its own probability of occurrence. It also attains its maximum value when all the messages are equiprobable, again as we expected. But there is yet another aspect in respect of which it conforms to our expectation, namely, that its value does not depend on how the message ensemble is treated. Take, for instance, the ensemble of three messages M_1, M_2, M_3 with respective probabilities of occurrence 1/2, 1/3, and 1/6 considered earlier. As we showed, its information content was 1.46 bits. We obtain the same value even if we treated the ensemble as a packet of two subensembles. We could, for example, substitute for the original ensemble (M_1, M_2, M_3) with its probability pattern (1/2, 1/3, 1/6) another ensemble (M_1, M_2') with probability pattern (1/2, 1/2) where the single message M_2' is really a subsystem composed of two messages M_2, M_3. If we did so, the subsystem M_2' consisting of M_2, M_3 would have its probability pattern altered from (1/3, 1/6) in the original set to (2/3, 2/6) in the subset to make its sum equal to 1. We could now proceed in two steps. First, when we deal with the original set or ensemble as made up of M_1 and M_2' we treat M_2' as if it were a *constituent* of the original set. In the second step we treat M_2' as a set in its own right with its own subconstituents M_2 and M_3. Carrying out the first step we find that the probability pattern of the ensemble $(M_1, M_2' = M_2 + M_3)$ is (1/2, 1/3 + 1/6) or (1/2, 1/2) so that its information content I_2 is $-(1/2 \log 1/2 + 1/2 \log 1/2) = 1$ bit. Likewise, the information content I_3 of M_2' with its probability pattern $(2/3, 2/6)$ is $-(2/3 \log 2/3 + 2/6 \log 2/6) = 0.92$ bits. This shows that

$$1.46 = 1 + 1/2(0.92)$$
$$I_1 = I_2 + I_3$$

In other words, the information content of the ensemble does not depend on how we partition the system. We could compute the information content of each individual message in the ensemble and then compute the weighted sum, or alternatively divide it into subsets of messages and compute the information content of each subset before deriving the weighted sum.

A scheme of information measurement that lives up to our intuitive anticipations in so many different ways may naturally be expected to be of great value in communication theory concerned with the exchange of "information." This is indeed the case. Consider, for example, any one of the languages whereby most of the information we use is communicated. The repertoire of "messages"* of that language, in the most elementary sense, is its alphabet, consisting in the case of English of 26 letters plus the blank space between adjacent words—in all 27 symbols. If each of the 27 symbols were equally probable, the information content of the English alphabet as a communications system would be $\log_2 27$ or 4.76 bits per letter. But this is far from the true value, as the different letters do not, in fact, occur with equal frequency in the language. By actual count we find that the frequency of letters like $a, b, c, d, e, \ldots$, is $6, 1, 2, 3, 10, \ldots$, per cent respectively. In other words, the respective probabilities $p_1, p_2, p_3, p_4, p_5, \ldots$, of these letters are $0.06, 0.01, 0.02, 0.03, 0.1, \ldots$. Substituting them in (1) we find that the information content of the English alphabet is about 4 bits per letter on an average, a value lower than the 4.76 calculated earlier under the assumption of equiprobability of selection of all symbols.

The real value of information yielded by each letter is even lower still. For the English language allows us far less freedom of choice than that assumed in our calculation. In making it we have completely ignored an important property of all languages called "redundancy." It is this redundancy that makes language intelligible in

---

* Although a "message" in ordinary parlance is any sequence of intelligible sentences, in our present context, where we pay no heed to its semantic content, we may consider each letter as a sort of elementary "message" and an ordinary message as an assemblage of such elements.

the midst of noise, that is, any distortion vitiating a message during its transmission. But for its existence we could never solve a crossword puzzle, which after all is a deliberate mutilation of intelligible words by the poser to enable the solver to guess them. Such guesses succeed only because of a correlation or linkage between successive letters of the alphabet. Thus the probability of the letter *u* following *q* is a certainty but that of *x* following *j* is zero. Likewise, while the probability of *n* following *tio* is very high, that of *k* following *oug* is slender. Although we still do not know enough about the occurrence of letter complexes like *qu*, *tion*, *ou*, and so on, the probabilistic influence of one letter spills over onto its immediate successor and even well beyond to its more distant neighbors. Obviously, the more we heed the constraints on our freedom of choice imposed by this spillover, the less the information conveyed per letter. While we cannot yet evaluate precisely the *actual* information content per letter because of lack of adequate data concerning the diffusion of probabilistic influence of individual letters over their neighbors, we do have a short cut to an approximation or at any rate a lower bound, thanks to an ingenious game. It is played by first selecting a sentence and then requiring an "opponent" totally ignorant of it to guess the letters (including blanks) one by one. After each guess, the answer "yes" is given if it succeeds; otherwise the letter itself is intimated before the player proceeds to the next guess.

In an actual game played with a sentence of 129 letters, 89 were guessed correctly and 40 had to be intimated. Since every guess answered by "yes" or "no" represents one bit of information, 89 successful guesses yielded 89 bits of information. In the remaining 40 letters which had to be intimated, a total of 40 × 4 bits were communicated, the information content per letter without regard to redundancy being 4 bits as computed earlier. It therefore follows that 129 letters of the sentence carried in all $(89 + 40 \times 4) = 249$ bits, or an average of $\frac{249}{129} = 1.93$ bits per letter.

The real information content of the English alphabet thus seems to be about 2 bits per letter, if we take into account all the constraints due to redundancy. As we saw before, the information content per letter is 4.76 bits if we consider all letters to be equally probable, that is, when we have maximum freedom of choice. We may therefore adopt the ratio between the two rates, $\frac{2}{4.76} = 0.42$, as a measure of the relative freedom of choice actually available vis-à-vis the maximum attainable with the same number of symbols. In other words, the English language in its choice of symbols to form a message is about 42 per cent as free as it could possibly be with the same alphabet. Unity minus relative freedom, that is, $1 - 0.42 = 0.58$, may appropriately be adopted as a measure of redundancy; this fraction of each message is redundant in the sense that if it were missing, it could be readily guessed because of the accepted statistical regularities underlying our use of the alphabet. Since the redundancy of English is, as we observe, about 58 per cent, only 42 per cent of the letters we choose in writing are under our free choice, the remainder being controlled by the statistical constraints of the language. It is just as well that it has only about 42 per cent of real freedom. If it had 100 per cent freedom, this would be license, with its inevitable nemesis, a serious impairment of intelligibility.

The fact that the information content of the English alphabet (ignoring its redundancy) is about four times that of an ordinary Morse key (wherein the dots and dashes occur with equal frequency) merely means that any actual "message" (a sequence of symbols of its repertoire) transmitted by Morse code contains about four times as many symbols as the corresponding message in plain letters of the alphabet. The reason is that an ordinary letter happens to carry about four times as much information as a dash/dot of telegraphy. The situation has an exact parallel in arithmetic where numbers, though normally written in the decimal notation, could also be written in any other. In fact, the only reason we use the ten digits 0, 1, 2, 3, 4, 5, 6, 7, 8, 9 to write numbers is the physiological accident that gave us ten fingers on our two hands. If we had had only two fingers we might have adopted the binary notation, in which we work with only two digits, 0 and 1. It is remarkable that we can express any number whatever in binary notation using only these two digits. Thus, the number two would be written in binary notation as 10, three as 11, four as 100, five as 101, six as 110, and so on. For 10 in the binary notation is $(2)^1 + 0(2)^0 = 2$ in the decimal notation. Likewise, 110 in the binary notation is $1(2)^2 + 1(2)^1 + 0(2)^0 = 6$ in the decimal notation. A binary "millionaire" would be a very poor man indeed, for the figure 1,000,000 in the binary scale is a paltry

$$1(2)^6 + 0(2)^5 + 0(2)^4 + 0(2)^3 + 0(2)^2 + 0(2)^1 + 0(2)^0 = 64$$

in the decimal notation. Nevertheless, the binary notation is potentially as capable of expressing large numbers as the decimal. The only difference is that it is a bit lavish in the use of digits. In the language of the information theory, the binary notation with its repertoire of two digits 0 and 1 both equally probable carries an information content of $\log_2 2$ or one bit. The decimal notation, on the other hand, with its stock of ten digits again all equally probable has an information content of $\log_2 10 = 3.32$ bits. It therefore follows that in writing any given number the binary notation is about 3.32 times as prodigal as the decimal notation simply because each digit in the latter is loaded with that many times more information than in the former—exactly as in writing a message, the dash-dot symbolism of teletype is about four times as lavish as the English alphabet and for the same reason. Incidentally, as we shall see more clearly later, it could be made only twice as lavish if we made full use of redundancy in our language.

Chapter III

INFORMATION FLOW OVER
DISCRETE CHANNELS

HAVING devised a measuring scheme for handling the basic problem of communications engineering, namely, the transmission of information over any given channel, it is time to proceed to the problem itself. This consists simply of evaluating the operating efficiency of a communications channel, that is, matching its actual performance against its optimum potential. A natural measure thereof is the ratio of the *actual* rate of flow of information to its ultimate *capacity*. But what is a channel over which information flows and what is its capacity?

A channel is any physical medium such as a wire, a cable, a radio or television link, or magnetic tape, whereby we may either transmit information or store it as in a memory device like a tape. The transmission and/or storage takes place by a code of symbols which may be pulses of current of varying duration as in telegraphy, light flashes as in navigation, or radio signals of different intensity, polarity, and so forth. Thus, in teletype, signals are transmitted by a code of two symbols made out of the presence or absence of a current pulse for a given duration which is the same for both. These two symbols enable a modern printing telegraph system to transmit any given English text by means of what is commonly called the Baudot code. In this system five impulses are transmitted for every letter, any one of which may be either a current pulse or a gap. That is, in each of the five impulses the circuit is either closed (current present) or open (current absent). With such a code it is possible to obtain $2 \times 2 \times 2 \times 2 \times 2 = 2^5 = 32$ different permutations, of which twenty-six are assigned to letters of the alphabet and five to other functions such as space, figure shift, or letter shift, leaving one spare. The five impulses making up the code are sent to the line successively by means of a rotating distributor or commutator and are distributed at the receiving end by means similar to those of the five receiving devices. These devices, through any of several selecting mechanisms, determine which one of the letters of a typewriting machine is to be printed. The essential point is that the system works with only two symbols of equal duration, namely, a current pulse of unit duration (S_1) or its absence for the same period (S_2).

In telegraphy, signals are transmitted by a code of four symbols made out of short and long pulses of current separated by intervals of no current. The short and long pulses are termed, respectively, dots and dashes. The dot is a very short signal lasting barely $\frac{1}{24}$ second when made by hand on a Morse key. The dash is about three times as long. The space between components of a single letter is equal to one dot, and that between letters is equal to one dash; the space between words is twice one dash. The scheme thus yields four symbols which we may designate S_1, S_2, S_3, S_4 for coding the alphabet:

(i) S_1: a dot, that is, a pulse of current of unit duration $(\frac{1}{24}$ second$)$ followed by a gap or circuit closure of unit duration so that total duration of S_1 is two units.

(ii) S_2: a dash, that is, a pulse of current of three units' duration followed by an interruption of unit duration, the whole lasting four units.

(iii) S_3: a letter space, that is, a break of three units' duration.

(iv) S_4: a word space, that is, a gap or circuit closure of six units' duration.

In other words, the four symbols S_1, S_2, S_3, S_4 last two, four, three, and six units of time respectively. As is well known, these four symbols enable us by means of Morse code to transmit any given message in ordinary English over telegraph wires.

Despite the great diversity of communications devices and the plethora of attendant codes with which they function, all that we need consider to make an abstract mathematical model capable of taking any communications situation in its stride is the *bare existence* of a set of discrete symbols consecutively catalogued S_1, S_2, ..., S_n and their corresponding durations t_1, t_2, ..., t_n. For, as we shall presently show, such an abstract scheme embodies all the essential features common to every communications system required to define and evaluate its optimum capacity for transmitting information.

Consider, for instance, the simplest communications model, the teletype, which operates with only two symbols S_1, S_2 of identical duration t seconds. This equality of durations of the symbols with which the system works is very helpful, as it vastly simplifies the evaluation of capacity of the channel. Thanks to it we can divide *any* given interval of time T seconds into equal subintervals each lasting t seconds. Clearly the division yields $m = \dfrac{T}{t}$ such subintervals, each of which *could*, if we so desired, accommodate a symbol. With two symbols S_1, S_2 we could transmit $2 \times 2 = 4$ *different* messages in the first two of these m subintervals, as the table below clearly shows:

TABLE 4

First subinterval	Second subinterval
S_1	S_1
S_2	S_1
S_1	S_2
S_2	S_2

Likewise, in the first three subintervals we could with the same choice of two symbols per subinterval transmit $2 \times 2 \times 2 = 8$ *different* messages as listed below:

TABLE 5

First subinterval	Second subinterval	Third subinterval
S_1	S_1	S_1
S_2	S_1	S_1
S_1	S_2	S_1
S_2	S_2	S_1
S_1	S_1	S_2
S_2	S_1	S_2
S_1	S_2	S_2
S_2	S_2	S_2

Obviously the permutation possibilities increase geometrically as we tag on successive subintervals, so that by the time we have reached the mth subinterval at the end of our time-tether T we have a choice of $2 \times 2 \times 2, \ldots\, m$ times or 2^m messages from which to select one for transmission over our channel. It therefore follows that we have in theory a choice of $N(T) = 2^m$ different messages from which to select any one for transmission. This is merely a way of saying that we could transmit over our channel $\log_2 N(T) = \log_2 2^m = m$ bits of information during T seconds. The capacity of the channel therefore is $\frac{m}{T} = \frac{T}{tT} = \frac{1}{t}$ bits per second. Recalling that t, the duration of a symbol S_1 or S_2, is $\frac{1}{24}$ second, the capacity of the channel is 24 bits per second. This is the capacity if we operate with a *single* pulse. But as in actual practice a teletype system operates with five pulses in unison, the capacity is five times as much, that is, $5 \times 24 = 120$ bits, because, as we have already seen, the information content of any complex is merely the sum of its individual components. Not that the teletype channel will always be transmitting information at 120 bits per second—far from it. It is merely the maximum possible rate we could ever reach under ideal circumstances. Whether or not it actually does so depends, among other things, on the source of information which feeds the channel.

When, however, we proceed to consider the case of a system with many symbols of unequal duration, a new complication arises. The equality of symbol durations permitted an exact division of the given interval T into equal aliquot parts into which all symbols in the system's repertoire could be as neatly fitted as a hand to the glove. This hand-to-glove fit enabled us in turn to enumerate all the permutation possibilities of messages in a relatively straightforward manner. But the inequality of symbol durations blocks our earlier breakthrough. For each duration is now a law unto itself and there is at first sight no way of curbing its waywardness. Take, for instance, the case of telegraphy with its four symbols S_1, S_2, S_3, S_4 of durations two, four, three, and six units respectively. We have here an *embarrass de choix* of aliquot parts into which the main interval T during which information is to flow could be split, but no clue as to our escape from the multilemma we face.

Fortunately, mathematicians have a ready tool to resolve difficulties of this kind. The tool is the theory of *finite difference equations*. These may be considered mathematical step ladders enabling us gradually to descend from a complication of any magnitude to that one degree lower or vice versa. Thus if $N(T)$, the number of different messages or message choices that can be accommodated in the interval T, is *not* known, we try to compute it on the assumption that the choices for the next lower intervals are *known*. Consider, for instance, the case of a channel using only two symbols S_1 and S_2 of durations 1 and 2 units respectively, as it illustrates very well the step-ladder principle. We need to compute the number $N(T)$ of messages that can be accommodated within an interval of T units of time. Since we do not happen to know $N(T)$, we assume that we *do* know the number corresponding to time intervals of next lower durations, that is, $(T - 1)$ and $(T - 2)$ units. Let these be $N(T - 1)$ and $N(T - 2)$ respectively. Given any message in the interval $(T - 1)$, we can generate from it *one and only one* by tagging on at the end symbol S_1 of duration 1 to turn it into that of duration T. Addition of S_2 which lasts two units is out of bounds as it will not yield a message of duration T but one of $T + 1$. A *parallel* or concurrent way of building a message of duration T is the addition of symbol S_2 (of duration 2 units) to any one of the messages lasting $(T - 2)$ units. Here the addition of S_1 is ruled out as it only turns it into one of duration $T - 1$ but not T. Thus $N(T)$ is simply the sum of messages of durations $(T - 1)$ and $(T - 2)$. In other words,

$$N(T) = N(T - 1) + N(T - 2). \qquad (1)$$

This is the step ladder we have been in search of. It enables us to climb completely out of the complications caused by the inequality of symbol durations in the system's repertoire. In the case we have considered, if T is 1, the number $N(1)$ of messages is clearly 1, as only S_1 of unit duration can be accommodated therein. For $T = 2$, $N(T)$ is 3 for we can accommodate in two units of time any of the following three and no others:

$$S_1, S_1S_1, S_2.$$

Having computed these two values of $N(1)$ and $N(2)$, we could successively determine $N(3)$, $N(4)$, $N(5)$, ..., by means of the step-ladder equation (1). Thus,

$$
\begin{aligned}
N(3) &= N(2) + N(1) = 3 + 1 = 4 \\
N(4) &= N(3) + N(2) = 4 + 3 = 7 \\
N(5) &= N(4) + N(3) = 7 + 4 = 11 \\
N(6) &= N(5) + N(4) = 11 + 7 = 18 \\
N(7) &= N(6) + N(5) = 18 + 11 = 29
\end{aligned}
$$

and so on.

In short, to evaluate any $N(T)$ we merely add the two immediately preceding values. However, such a step-by-step climb is likely to be tedious and we should prefer to have a tangible expression yielding the value of $N(T)$ for any value of T we care to choose. The theory of finite difference equations enables us to do exactly this. What is more, it can handle on the basis of the same ladder principle not only the relatively oversimplified case of two symbols of duration 1 and 2 but indeed that of *any* finite number of different symbols having diverse durations. We can by means of it evaluate precisely for any given communications system $N(T)$, the number of messages that could theoretically be fitted in any time span of T units. It therefore follows that the system can transmit $\log_2 N(T)$ bits of information during time T. Consequently the theoretical *rate* of information flow over the channel is $\dfrac{\log_2 N(T)}{T}$ bits per second.

Naturally the value of this rate* depends on that of T. Thus for the two-symbol channel we considered earlier we tabulate below the values of the rate of flow for diverse values of T:

TABLE 6

Value of T	$N(T)$†	Information in bits $\log_2 N(T)$	Rate of flow in bits per unit of time $\log_2 N(T)/T$
1	2	3	4
1	1	0	0
2	3	1.58	0.79
3	4	2.00	0.66
4	7	2.78	0.69
5	11	3.45	0.69
6	18	4.17	0.69
7	29	4.85	0.69
8	47	5.55	0.69
9	76	6.24	0.69
10	123	6.94	0.69

† Values in this column are obtained by simply adding the preceding two in accordance with our difference equation (1).

It will be seen that while the value of the rate of flow shown in column 4 fluctuates a good deal for the first three values of T, it begins to stabilize itself as we climb to higher values of T. Indeed, continuing the table to very large values of T leads approximately to the same value of the rate of flow, viz., 0.69. Thus, if we computed it for a sufficiently large value of T, say, 10,000 units, we should find that any

* Unlike the teletype case where the rate is independent of T.

larger value of T yields practically the same rate. In more precise mathematical language, the rate of flow, $\dfrac{\log_2 N(T)}{T}$, tends to a definite limit as T approaches infinity. This limiting value is the capacity of the channel, the ultima Thule, which the information flow cannot transcend. It happens that such a limiting value exists not merely for the two-symbol case we have just considered but also for more complex channels operating with a wide diversity of discrete symbols of varying durations.

Chapter IV

CODING THEORY

IF the capacity of a communications channel is the ultimate limit which the actual rate of information flow can never surpass, how closely may it be attained and by what means? The answer is provided by two famous theorems of C. E. Shannon about coding—coding because, as will be recalled, a code is to a communications channel what a transformer is to electrical transmission, that is, a means of improving its operating efficiency. Just as to obtain maximum power transfer from a generator to a load a transformer matching the load resistance must in general be introduced, so also there has to be an appropriate code matching the statistical structure of the language used in transmission. That is why it is no mere accident that coding theorems should be so intimately linked with the optimum utilization of channel capacity.

Although a source or transmitter may transmit a message in its original form* without coding, even as a grid may transmit power without recourse to a transformer, it has in practice to be enciphered by a code into a form acceptable to the channel. The exigencies of the channel often require coding because it is only in a coded form that the signal can actually travel over it. A case in point is the dash-dot sequence of telegraphy into which a message must be transformed before transmission and from which it must be decoded back into the original text upon arrival. In general, the transmitter or message source feeds the message into an encoder before transmission and the decoder restores it to its original form on emergence from the receiver. Obviously, given a communications system and the type of symbols it can handle, any code constructed with them could be arbitrarily

* As for example in ordinary living-room conversation or, for that matter, telephonic conversation wherein the transmitter merely changes the pattern of the audible voice into an equivalent pattern of electrical currents on the telephone wires.

chosen to encipher the message, though all such codes will naturally not yield the same rate of flow of information over the channel. Some will step it up more than others. The problem of optimum utilization of the channel capacity is therefore essentially one of matching the code to the channel in such a way as to maximize the transmission rate.

Take, for the sake of definiteness, the case of telegraphy where the channel can transmit only current pulses of two durations, say, a short pulse (dot) and a long one (dash). Various combinations of these may be used to code different letters of the alphabet, the usual Morse code being only one among the many possible alternatives. But in choosing one, to secure a higher rate of information flow, we must ensure that the most frequently occurring or most probable signals are short while the rare ones are long. Thus in Morse code the most frequently occurring letter, e, is denoted by the shortest signal, a mere dot, and the rarely occurring ones like z are denoted by relatively longer signals. Codes which depart from this ideal inevitably lessen the rate of information flow. Shannon's first theorem ensures in the case of noiseless channels the actual realization of the channel capacity within any preassigned tolerance, no matter how narrow, by guaranteeing the existence of an appropriate code that precisely matches the channel with the language used in transmission.

Suppose, for example, our channel could transmit only two symbols like a current pulse (denoted by 1) and a gap or circuit closure (denoted by 0) of equal duration, say, $\frac{1}{24}$ second as in teletype. As we saw before, its channel capacity would be 24 bits per second. What code would match such a channel most efficiently, that is, secure us an actual rate of information flow that is arbitrarily close to 24 bits per second, if we had to transmit messages in ordinary English? To devise such a code we begin by cataloguing all possible messages in English that we may ever have to transmit, somewhat as a telegraph directory will list 27 different stock phrases for greeting telegrams, except that in our case their number would be legion. This inordinate multiplicity of messages, however, is a complication without relevance here, as Shannon's theorem applies to the wider list as readily as to the restricted one of the telegraph directory. Confining ourselves therefore to the latter only, let us number them successively $M_1, M_2, \ldots, M_{27}$. There is no reason why their actual incidence should be the same, quite the contrary. Thus M_{16} showering "heaven's choicest blessings on the young couple" would be far more frequent than M_9, wishing a mere "merry Christmas," and M_9, in turn, more frequent than M_{24}, conveying "best wishes" for success in elections, if only because marriages are celebrated daily while Christmas comes but once a year and elections, thank heavens, only once every four or five years.

If we compiled statistics of the actual frequencies of these 27 types of messages, we could even say how often each message did in fact occur. Dividing the actual frequency of occurrence of each kind of message by the total number included in our message count, we obtain its relative frequency, which is merely another name for the probability of its occurrence provided the count is fairly large. However, since the actual number of messages in the list is immaterial to Shannon's argument, we may further simplify our exposition by reducing the number of message *types* in our repertoire from 27 to only, say, six. We may find by an actual poll of messages received for transmission that the relative frequencies or probabilities of these six types of messages, M_1, M_2, M_3, M_4, M_5, M_6, are respectively:

TABLE 7

Message	M_1	M_2	M_3	M_4	M_5	M_6
Probability	$\frac{1}{16}$	$\frac{4}{16}$	$\frac{2}{16}$	$\frac{3}{16}$	$\frac{5}{16}$	$\frac{1}{16}$

all probabilities totaling, of course, to unity. We now arrange them in decreasing order of their probability beginning first with the most frequent, M_5, and ending with the least frequent, M_1. The new order would then be

TABLE 8

Message	M_5	M_2	M_4	M_3	M_6	M_1
Probability	$\frac{5}{16}$	$\frac{4}{16}$	$\frac{3}{16}$	$\frac{2}{16}$	$\frac{1}{16}$	$\frac{1}{16}$

We next divide the rearranged series into two parts so as to make the sum of probabilities of messages in each part as nearly equal to one another as possible, as shown below:

TABLE 9

Message	M_5	M_2	M_4	M_3	M_6	M_1
Probability	$\frac{5}{16}$	$\frac{4}{16}$	$\frac{3}{16}$	$\frac{2}{16}$	$\frac{1}{16}$	$\frac{1}{16}$
FIRST PARTITION						
Sum of probabilities	$\frac{9}{16}$		$\frac{7}{16}$			
Code	0		1			

To all messages in the first part, M_5 and M_2, we assign the symbol 0 and to those in the second, M_4, M_3, M_6, M_1, the symbol 1. They are the first-place digits in our coding scheme. To assign the code digits in the second place we do unto each part what we did to the parent series, that is, split each again into two groups to make the probability sum of messages included therein as near equal as we can. As before, we assign the digit 0 to the messages in the first group and 1 to those in the other. They are the second-place digits of our code:

TABLE 10

Message	M_5	M_2	M_4	M_3	M_6	M_1
Probability FIRST PARTITION	$\frac{5}{16}$	$\frac{4}{16}$	$\frac{3}{16}$	$\frac{2}{16}$	$\frac{1}{16}$	$\frac{1}{16}$
Sum of probabilities		$\frac{9}{16}$			$\frac{7}{16}$	
Code (first digit)		0			1	
SECOND PARTITION						
Sum of probabilities	$\frac{5}{16}$	$\frac{4}{16}$	$\frac{3}{16}$		$\frac{4}{16}$	
Code (second digit)	0	1	0		1	

Proceeding in this manner we find that we can perform just two additional encores of this sort:

TABLE 11

Message	M_5	M_2	M_4	M_3	M_6	M_1
Probability	$\frac{5}{16}$	$\frac{4}{16}$	$\frac{3}{16}$	$\frac{2}{16}$	$\frac{1}{16}$	$\frac{1}{16}$
FIRST PARTITION						
Sum of probabilities		$\frac{9}{16}$			$\frac{7}{16}$	
Code (first digit)		0			1	
SECOND PARTITION						
Sum of probabilities	$\frac{5}{16}$	$\frac{4}{16}$	$\frac{3}{16}$		$\frac{4}{16}$	
Code (second digit)	0	1	0		1	
THIRD PARTITION	nil	nil	nil			
Sum of probabilities	—	—	—	$\frac{2}{16}$	$\frac{2}{16}$	
Code (third digit)	—	—	—	0	1	
FOURTH PARTITION	nil	nil	nil	nil		
Sum of probabilities	—	—	—	—	$\frac{1}{16}$	$\frac{1}{16}$
Code (fourth digit)	—	—	—	—	0	1

No additional partition beyond the four listed in the above scheme is possible as each subgroup now consists of a single message incapable of any further divisions. But this is as far as we need go because by this time each message gets its full allotment of symbols required to make the optimal code:

TABLE 12

Message	M_5	M_2	M_4	M_3	M_6	M_1
Code						
First digit	0	0	0	1	1	1
Second digit	0	1	0		1	1
Third digit	—	—	—	0	1	1
Fourth digit	—	—	—	—	0	1
Complete code	00	01	10	110	1110	1111
Message	M_5	M_2	M_4	M_3	M_6	M_1

The above code is optimal, at any rate reasonably so, because we are able to assign the shortest code 00 to the most frequent or probable message M_5 and the longest codes 1110 and 1111 to the rarest or least probable, M_6 and M_1, thus matching the length of the coded message to the probability of its occurrence. It has the additional merit of being *separable* or *uniquely decipherable* because, unlike English, it does not require any spacing. As we know, common English words need to be spaced. For example, if two separate words "as" and "sign" are transmitted together without spacing they form a different word, "assign," which is not implied by the two individual words. But if in our coded vocabulary of six messages we transmitted any two coded messages, say, 110 and 00, without separation as 11000, they will automatically separate into 110 and 00 as no other possible separation yields a "meaningful" message included in our vocabulary. Thus all possible separations of 11000 such as 1 and 1000, or 11 and 000, or 1100 and 0, and the like, are out of bounds or meaningless as none of them is a recognized code for any message in our scheme. This automatic separability of the code stems from the fact that no encoded message can be obtained from any other by addition of more symbols at the *end* of it. Thus if we added any more symbols to the code 01 for M_2, such as 011, 010, or 01111, we would not obtain a code for any other message in our repertoire. It can be shown that separability is an inherent attribute of all codes generated by the binary fission process we have just outlined but the *optimal* condition depends on the extent to which the probabilities of the messages actually yield the desired successive equiprobable partitioning. If the message probabilities are such that the sum of the probabilities of the two subgroups into which the parent group is divided are not reasonably equal at each stage, the desired code may not be an optimum code. But even an approximate fulfillment of this requirement leads to reasonably efficient encoding procedures.

The binary fission process, however, does have another serious drawback when we have to deal with not merely a limited repertoire of a few stock phrases of a telegraph directory but the all but infinite varieties of our daily commerce. For we may not always be able actually to carry out the successive partitions described above to derive the optimal separable codes. The process could, nevertheless, be always carried out in principle. Thus, suppose we have *any* number (n) of messages each with its own definite relative frequency or probability of occurrence even though we may not happen to know it. We could then *imagine* the series of messages arranged in order of their decreasing probability so as to divide it into two groups of as nearly equal probability as possible, exactly as we divided the series of six messages of our earlier illustration. If the message whose code is required lies in the first group, the first digit of its code is assigned 0; otherwise it is assigned 1. We continue the successive division of each subgroup into two sub-subgroups of nearly equal probability, and the particular sub-subgroup in which the message falls determines the second binary digit of the code, that is, 0 if it falls in the first sub-subgroup, otherwise 1. This process is repeated as often as is necessary till it automatically halts when each of the broken fragments of our initial series consists of a single message (see Fig. 1). We can thus, at least in theory, always devise such an ideal code although we have to pay a price for it in that the more nearly ideal it is, the longer is likely to be the delay *in the act of coding*.

However, the assumption that the binary partition at each stage yields equiprobable subgroups is gratuitous. Strictly speaking, for it to materialize, the probability pattern of the messages in our repertoire has to be of a rather special kind. Indeed, each message probability has to be a fraction like $\frac{1}{2}$, $\frac{1}{4}$, $\frac{1}{8}$, $\frac{1}{16}$, and so on. To the

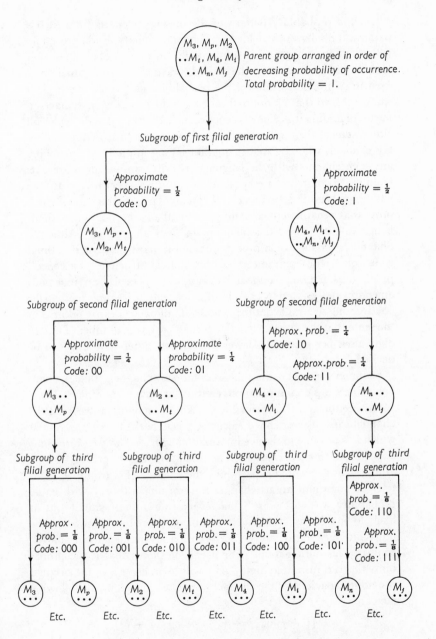

Fig. 1 Shannon-Fanno binary fission process.

extent the probability pattern of the messages departs from such a pattern, the subgroups yielded by Shannon's binary fission procedure will result in subgroups of substantially unequal probabilities after each division. As a result the desired code may not be optimal. But even in such cases, whatever the probability pattern of messages, it can be proved that an optimal code *does exist* even if we may have no means of finding it. The existence of such an optimal code under all circumstances then is the kernel of Shannon's first theorem for noiseless channels whereby we are guaranteed an optimal code matching any such channel with the language used in transmission despite its inability to construct one in practice. In this respect it is of a piece with those beautiful "existence" theorems of pure mathematics which prove that a mathematical entity exists or at any rate ought to without being able to clothe the phantom in flesh and blood. Although Shannon's binary fission process does not in most cases yield optimal codes otherwise guaranteed by his non-constructive "existence" proof, it is not an irremediable handicap. For by an ingenious amendment suggested by D. A. Huffman it leads to a simple method for constructing separable optimal codes. Huffman codes are optimal in the sense that the average length per message or the number of binary digits used per message is fewer than in any other code that can be devised.

Shannon's second coding theorem for *noisy* channels, that is, channels subject to signal mutilations en route, is even more remarkable, if yet more ethereal. For, roughly speaking, it too guarantees that the channel capacity as defined earlier is precisely the maximum rate at which it is possible to receive information with *arbitrarily high reliability despite all the vitiations of noise*. The result is indeed surprising because at first sight one would expect quite the reverse. For example, if our teletype communications channel transmitting a 0 or 1 with equal probability was so "noisy" that every transmitted symbol was as likely to be right as wrong, it is not difficult to see that there would be no communication whatever. More rigorous mathematical analysis confirms this anticipation. For it can be shown that if the probability that a transmitted digit 0 or 1 will be in error is p, the original pre-noise capacity C of the channel would be reduced by the following factor:

$$[1 + p \log_2 p + (1 - p) \log_2 (1 - p)].$$

For $p = \frac{1}{2}$, which is the case when the transmitted digit is as likely to be right as wrong, the factor is easily seen to be zero with consequent complete extinction of the channel transmission. Nevertheless, even though the effect of "noise" on the transmission capacity is ruinous to a varying degree, the situation is not quite irretrievable. We can always manage by a simple stratagem to safeguard transmission over the channel against the depredations of noise. The most obvious recipe for reliable transmission in the presence of noise is repetition of the message a sufficient number of times to ensure reliable reception. One could, for example, repeat each symbol in a signal an odd number of times and decide at the receiver by a majority vote what was transmitted. Naturally, the more numerous the repetitions, the better the reliability. But too many repetitions for too high a reliability bring their own nemesis in that total reliability entails almost total extinction of transmission. There are, no doubt, a large number of halfway houses that secure a measure of reliability by an appropriate amount of repetition or redundancy. But the essential dilemma of reliability through redundancy remains—that the more we have of it, the less is the associated rate of information flow. It is precisely because Shannon's second theorem resolves this dilemma, albeit only theoretically, that his feat is a tour de force as beautiful as it is unexpected.

Shannon's proof of his theorem on noisy channels is merely a mathematical formulation of our instinctive practice when obliged to talk in the midst of loud noise. In such a situation we tend to avoid using similar-sounding words which are likely to be confused with one another. We do so by recourse to a restricted vocabulary of as widely antihomophonic words as possible so that each has little chance of being mistaken for another. We can then ensure that a word even after some mutilation by noise does sound sufficiently different from all others in our repertoire to be recognized for what it really is. A similar procedure can be adopted while transmitting messages over a noisy channel.

Consider, for example, the transmission of information over a teletype channel by means of a code of two symbols, 0 and 1. If we choose to make a code of four-symbol-long sequences, the code vocabulary will consist of a total of $2 \times 2 \times 2 \times 2 = 2^4 = 16$ "words" or permutations of 0's and 1's. Some of these permutations are more alike and therefore more prone to confusion with one another than the rest. A case in point is the permutation 0000 which has a greater risk of confusion with 0001 than with, say, 1111. For the permutation 0000 is more widely disparate from 1111 than from

0001 in that the former, 1111, can result from the original transmission of 0000 only by four consecutive errors while the latter, 0001, results from a single one.   By choosing only widely disparate sequences like 0000 and 1111, which have a small probability of being mistaken for one another and rejecting those like 0001 which are similar to those already chosen and therefore have a high probability of confusion with them, the chance of error can be greatly reduced.   Now as the length of the sequence is increased from 4 to n, the number of possible permutations increases exponentially to $2 \times 2 \times 2 \ldots n$ times $= 2^n$. Shannon has shown that if the sequence length n is increased indefinitely, the number of permutations which have a large probability of being confused with others and have therefore to be omitted, becomes a vanishingly small proportion of the total number.   Thus by increasing our "word" length sufficiently the proportion of quasi-"homophonic" or similar "words" which we must discard to avoid error can be made as small as we like.   This is a way of saying that sufficiently long sequences or code groups enable us to transmit information even over a noisy channel at a rate arbitrarily close to its capacity but with an arbitrarily small error.

Unfortunately, Shannon's proof of the existence of such optimal codes, though logically impeccable, is non-constructive.   It does not enable us to find the optimal code in any given concrete case.   Despite fourteen years that have elapsed since it was discovered, we still have not begun in practice to take advantage of the theorem's promise. Even in the case of the simplest non-trivial channel it is not yet known in complete detail how to reach the theorem's promised El Dorado—an optimal code.   As a result most research workers in the field, instead of attempting to evolve such codes, have diverted their attention to constructing error-detecting codes which safeguard the transmitted message against various kinds of mutilations interjected by noise.   We shall give an account of their efforts in the next chapter.

Chapter V

RELIABLE TRANSMISSION AND REDUNDANCY

SINCE reliability-through-redundancy reduces radically the rate of transmission in a noisy channel, an attempt to make a matching optimal code that combines high reliability with high information flow would seem like eating one's cake and having it too. Nevertheless, buttressed by the assurance of Shannon's theorem which guarantees a way of doing both, even if it does not actually lead to it, attempts have been made to reach the goal in stages. As a first step the enormous complexity of the problem is mitigated by a relaxation of its aim. The problem is no longer a search for optimal codes but those *near*-optimal ones which secure fairly high reliability by low enough redundancy while still yielding a reasonable rate of transmission. For the sake of simplicity, assume that our linguistic medium is basic English, with a total vocabulary of 512 words. Suppose further that the probability of occurrence of all the words in the language is the same. Both assumptions are, of course, not true. The actual basic vocabulary exceeds our chosen number (512) by two to three hundred words and their probabilities of occurrence are far from alike. No matter; we have made these assumptions so as not to encumber our exposition of basic principles with inessential detail.

Starting with our vocabulary of 512 words we may enumerate them successively as $1, 2, 3, \ldots, 512$, as would be the case if we itemized each word in our basic dictionary. Suppose, again for the sake of simplicity, that our channel can transmit only two symbols: a current pulse denoted by 0 and a current gap or a circuit closure denoted by 1, both of the same duration, say, $\frac{1}{24}$ second. How many symbols must the code assign to each word to be able to encompass all the words in our dictionary? For example, if we assigned two symbols per word, we could have only $2 \times 2 = 2^2$, or four different permutations of 0

39

and 1, that is, 00, 01, 10, and 11, with which to encipher barely the first four words of our dictionary. With three symbols per word, we could secure $2 \times 2 \times 2 = 2^3$ or eight different permutations of 0 and 1—000, 001, 010, 011, 100, 101, 110, and 111—adequate only for eight words of the dictionary. But as the different permutations with longer sequences of 0 and 1 begin to multiply geometrically like the grains of wheat demanded by King Shirman's Grand Vizier* as a reward for his invention of chess, it is easy to see that with an alphabet of barely two symbols, 0 and 1, we can generate as many different permutations as we need to cover any dictionary, no matter how large. This is the mere molehill of truth in the mystic's mountain of a maxim: *Omnibus ex nihil ducendis sufficit unum* ("One suffices to derive all out of nothing") or its equivalent "Give me a naught and one and I will make the world"—a formidable mystical counter to Archimedes's famous boast. Whatever power the maxim may claim stems from the fact that terms derive their meaning from the contrast between themselves and their negations. That is, to have any meaning every term must have its own denial, so that to every thesis denoted by 1 there corresponds its antithesis represented by 0. If not, we make our criteria of meaning either so stringent or so loose that either *nothing* at all *can* or *everything must* fall under it. In both cases there is no communication and therefore no language and the world it can create.

But to revert to our basic dictionary of 512 words, we need only nine symbols per word to encompass it all. For a stretch of nine symbols would yield $2 \times 2 \times 2 \ldots$ (nine times) $= 2^9$, or 512 distinct permutations, just enough for our 512-word dictionary. In general, for any number (N) of different words in our repertoire, we need only guess how many times 2 has to be multiplied by itself to make the product equal to N. Suppose the required number is x. Clearly $2 \times 2 \times 2 \ldots$ (x times), or 2^x different permutations of 0 and 1, must equal N, the total number of words in the dictionary. This yields the equation $2^x = N$, which leads to $x = \log_2 N$. In the case of our basic English of $N = 512$ words, x is thus $\log_2 512$ or $\log_2 2^9$ or simply 9.

---

* The allusion here is to the well-known legend of the Grand Vizier who asked for one grain of wheat in the first square of a chessboard, two in the second, four in the third, eight in the fourth, sixteen in the fifth, and so on till the sixty-fourth. The poor king never suspected, till it was too late, that the total number of grains required to fill even the single last square in this manner would exceed the total world production of wheat during two millennia at its present rate of production.

Now if the channel were free of noise, such a binary or two-symbol code which transmitted words of our basic English dictionary in sequences of nine symbols (or $\log_2 N$ in the general case of an N-word dictionary) would yield a transmission rate of one bit per $\frac{1}{24}$ second, the optimal value. But when noise intervenes to ruin the transmission redundancy must be introduced. That is, more than nine symbols (or in the general cases more than $\log_2 N$ symbols) must be employed to encipher each word. How many more depends, of course, on the channel capacity and our desire to limit redundancy to a scale small enough not to lower inordinately the rate of information flow.

The simplest device for introducing limited redundancy is the so-called "parity" check whereby we use only one extra symbol above the bare minimum we actually need. Thus in our current illustration of coding basic English we should use ten symbols instead of nine, the tenth being a checking symbol added at the end to obtain "parity." This is merely a way of saying that we add in the tenth (last) place a 0 or 1 so chosen that the number of 1's is always even. Obviously the choice of an even sum is arbitrary. We could make it odd if we so desired. But in what follows we shall for convenience adhere to the even-parity convention throughout. With this convention, if any word in our basic dictionary is assigned, for example, the code 000101011 containing four (even) 1's, we add at the end the checking symbol 0. On the other hand, in the case of a word represented by the symbol sequence, say, 101011010 containing five (odd) 1's, we add the checking symbol 1. In either case the choice of the checking symbol is determined by the need to make the sum of 1's even.

The incorporation of such parity checks will evidently throw up immediately a single error in the main symbols. We merely count the number of 1's in the transmitted signal to see if their total is even. If not, there has been an error *somewhere*. But clearly such a parity cannot pinpoint the erroneous symbol itself. Its further handicap is that two or any *even* number of errors remain undetected through mutual compensation. Both handicaps, however, can be overcome by a sophisticated interlocking of several parity checks employed at the same time, as we shall now proceed to show.

Take first the problem of locating the erroneous symbol when it is assumed that there cannot be more than a single error in the transmission of a symbol sequence representing a word. If we have only a one-symbol sequence to transmit, obviously we can represent only two words, one by the solitary sequence symbol 0, and the other by 1.

Since for the sake of reliability in transmission we have to introduce a parity check designed to make the sum of 1's even, it follows that when we have to transmit the word denoted by 1, we should actually signal the double sequence 11; and for the word represented by 0, the double sequence 00. In this way alone can we ensure that the sum of 1's in the transmitted signal is even.

Now suppose we actually received 01. We know, of course, immediately that an error has occurred. But where? With only one error we could have received 01 in two alternative ways. First, while intending to transmit 00 we might actually have received 01 so that the first digit is right but the second wrong. Secondly, while intending to transmit 11 we might actually have received 01, with the first digit in error but the second right. It therefore follows that with a single parity check we cannot say which of the two digits is in error. To do so we have to introduce a second parity check properly dove-tailed with the first. In other words, we have to transmit yet an additional symbol—in all a triple sequence of digits. Consequently when we wish to ensure reliability in the transmission of a single symbol used for "information," we must use two more for "check." But this opens up new possibilities among which we must make a choice, because our earlier requirement of a parity check, that the sum of the 1's be even, no longer yields an unambiguous answer. For when we wished to transmit the solitary-sequence word 1, a single parity check unequivocally required that we actually transmit 11 to make the sum of 1's even. But with two parity checks for the trans-mission of the same single information digit 1, we have before us two alternatives, either 110 or 101, either of which makes the sum of 1's even. Obviously our earlier parity condition, namely, that the sum of the 1's be even, which uniquely determined the choice of the checking symbol, fails us now. The reason is that while with a single parity check a single condition suffices to make our choice, with a double check we require a double condition. If, instead of our previous condition that the sum of the digits be even, we take this double con-dition to be

(i) the sum of the first and second digits is even;
(ii) the sum of the first and third digits is even;

we obtain a clear unequivocal answer. Thus our earlier dilemma between 110 or 101 for the transmission of the single information digit, 1, is now completely resolved. Neither of these two sequences satisfies the afore-mentioned double condition. Instead our choice must fall on 111 as this is the only sequence wherein the sums *both* of the first and second *and* of the first and third digits are even. Indeed, if we write out the various alternatives that the introduction of a second parity check generates, we shall find that we can locate the erroneous symbol, provided there is not more than one error in the whole triple sequence of symbols transmitted.

Consider, for example, the transmission of the single information symbol, 1, with the double parity check specified above. As we saw, the double-parity condition that the two sums of first and second as well as of first and third digits be even requires that we actually transmit 111. Now suppose that with the input signal 111 a *single* error occurs somewhere. The output signal at the end of the transmission channel can then be only one of the following three:

TABLE 13

	Position and type of symbols			Unsatisfied conditions	Location of the erroneous symbol
	Informa-tion symbol	First checking symbol	Second checking symbol		
Either	1	0*	1	First sum fails	First checking symbol
or	1	1	0̲	Second sum fails	Second checking symbol
or	0̲	1	1	Both sums fail	Information symbol

* The symbol in error is underlined.

Consider now the second alternative when the information symbol is 0. To transmit it under a double parity check we should need to signal 000. Again with a single error only one of the three alternatives shown in Table 14 can arise.

It therefore follows that a double parity check of the type described above suffices not only to reveal the error but also to reveal its whereabouts. The underlying principle is simply this: with a sequence of three binary symbols (one for information and two for check) we can have in all $2 \times 2 \times 2 = 2^3$ or eight possible different permutations. Four of these are employed for ensuring the reliable transmission of the information symbol 0 and the others for that of 1. Out of the set

TABLE 14

	Position and type of symbols			Unsatisfied conditions	Location of the erroneous symbol
	Informa-tion symbol	First checking symbol	Second checking symbol		
Either	0	1*	0	First sum fails	First checking symbol
or	0	0	1	Second sum fails	Second checking symbol
or	1	0	0	Both sums fail	Information symbol

* The symbol in error is underlined.

of four permutations reserved for the reliable transmission of 1 we have one, namely, 111, for the actual true transmission and the remaining three—101, 110, 011—for revealing a single error, if any, and its location.   In all three cases the underlined symbol is in error and its location is indicated by the failure of the first, second, or both the parity sums used as checks.   Likewise, of the remaining four permutations one, 000, is used for true transmission and the remaining three—010, 001, and 100—for detecting and locating the single error that might occur.

Indeed, the principle of single, double, triple...parity checks is general.   Suppose we had any sequence of, say, nine symbols to transmit as we need to do for our basic dictionary of 512 words.   To ensure their reliable transmission we would require a number of parity checks, say, k.   We thus have to transmit in all a sequence of $(9 + k)$ symbols of which nine are for information and k for checks.   Now each sequence of $(9 + k)$ may either be right or may have one error in any of its $(9 + k)$ places, two errors having been ruled out by definition as impossible.   It therefore follows that each sequence would need $(9 + k + 1)$ checks: one check to indicate that the sequence is all correct, and one check to reveal the single error if it happened to occur in any of the $9 + k$ places of the transmitted sequence.   But as we saw, a single parity check yields two (2^1) indications, namely, error present or absent; a double check four (2^2) indications: one to show error absent and three to locating the error in any of the *three* places of the transmitted sequence.   Continuing, it would seem that a triple parity check should give rise to 2^3 indications, a quadruple check to 2^4 indications, and so on to our k-parity check

with its 2^k indications.   Consequently we need merely determine k so
that its 2^k different indications are at least equal to the total number
of parity checks required, or $9 + k + 1$.   In other words, we choose
k to make

$$2^k \geqslant 9 + k + 1.$$

By trial we find that k must be at least four, our 2^k remaining short of
$9 + k + 1$ for any lesser value.

However, while the *number* of parity checks we require in any given
case is easy to determine, specification of the different parity conditions
underlying these checks is much more difficult.   For as the number of
symbols permitted in a sequence mounts, the permutation possibilities
increase so prodigiously that their paper-and-pencil enumeration one
by one is out of the question.   We have to invent a new and more
versatile approach that can take any sequence of symbols in its stride.
This is exactly what R. W. Hamming did when he employed the ideas
of *finite* geometry to solve the problem of inventing self-correcting
codes.

That Hamming could apply the ideas of finite geometry in such a
new context at all is due to the great power latent in the basic concept
of a point that underlies all geometries.   A point is quite literally a
mathematician's bottled djinn.   When he removes the cork from the
bottle in which Euclid first imprisoned it in his innocent-looking
epigram—that a "point" is that which has position but no magnitude
—he releases a veritable giant which unlike its counterpart in the
Arabian Nights is benevolent enough to support almost any mathematical structure.   Nearly all its miraculous sustaining powers stem
from a single amazingly simple fact that any sequence of two, three,
four, five, or more numbers can be made to act as a locum tenens for
some "point" in a space of two three, four, five, or correspondingly
higher dimensions.   Such "spaces" are, of course, pure figures of
speech.   But their immense powers of evocative imagery stand us
in excellent stead when we wish to handle or manipulate very long
sequences of 0's and 1's in an intelligible manner.

Consider, for example, Hamming's exploitation of this property of
a point to invent self-correcting codes.   As we saw, a binary code for
transmission of messages is merely a sequence of 0's and 1's such as
11, 101, 111010, and so on.   Each one of these sequences could then
be made to deputize for a point in some space of appropriate dimensions.   Thus all two-symbol sequences of 0's and 1's can be made to

represent points in a two-dimensional space like the surface of this page. But as there are in all only four two-symbol-long sequences— 00, 01, 10, and 11—the "geometry" of our "space" is naturally circumscribed by this peculiarity. Indeed, the four two-symbol sequences listed above may be represented by the four corners of the unit square *ABDC* in Fig. 2, with the rest of the square dissolved into

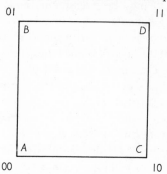

Fig. 2   Code space consisting of the four corners *A*, *B*, *C*, *D* of the unit square *ABCD*.

sheer nothingness. For the geometry we require to represent the totality of our four sequences is not that of the entire Euclidean plane or even that of the whole square but rather the finite geometry of its four corners *A*, *B*, *C*, *D*—which are indeed only four names of the four two-symbol-long sequences in question: (00), (01), (1,0), and (1,1) respectively. All the infinity of the points of the Euclidean square or plane excepting these four must therefore be excluded from the assemblage of points of our "space" representing only the four sequences in question.

So far we have merely used the property of a point as a location center or site indicator to act as a repository of a sequence of symbols or digits like 0 and 1. But to make further headway we need to define an analogue of geometric distance too. In geometry, we define distance between any two points *A* and *B* as the number of times we have to interpose consecutively a standard measuring rod like a foot-rule in order to reach *B* starting from *A*. In trying to reach *B* from *A* we have normally to follow the "shortest" route that the geometry of our space permits. Thus if *A* and *B* are two locations on earth— say, New Delhi and New York—we may carry the standard measuring rod along the "shortest" route permitted by the two-dimensional "space" formed by the surface of our globe, that is, by always remaining thereon, or alternatively along the "shortest" route in the three-dimensional space in which that globe is embedded, that is, by burrowing through it like Jules Verne's subterranean explorers. In both cases we measure the "distance" by sticking to the "space" of our choice, either the surface of the earth's outer shell or the entire globe itself including the interior enclosed by the globular shell. In other words, the mode of transport of our standard footrule from one place to another to measure the distance between them is dictated by the exigencies of the "space" in which we choose to embed the points in question. What then is the exigency that determines the way of measuring the "distance" between any two points when our space is merely the set of only four corners A, B, D, C of our square with the rest of its contents blown out of existence? Obviously our usual notion of "reaching" one place from another breaks down here because our "space" of four disjoint points is no longer a continuum where every pair of points has an infinity of neighbors in between. The only way in which "reaching" one point from another in a "space" of a limited or finite number of points can be given a meaning is to count the number of standard transformations that must be performed on a "point" or its equivalent symbol sequence to lead to another. Thus consider the point A, alias symbol sequence 00, and another point B, which is another name for the sequence 01 (see Fig. 2). To "reach" B from A in our new situation all that we need do is transform the second digit of A from 0 to 1—only one transformation. We may therefore take 1 as the measure of distance between A and B:

TABLE 15

Point	Symbol	Number of standard changes required	Distance
A	0̲0̲	1	1
B	0̲1̲		

Similarly, to "reach" $D(11)$ from $A(00)$ we need *two* transformations because both the zeros have to be changed into 1's. We may adopt 2 as a measure of their distance:

TABLE 16

Point	Symbol	Number of standard changes required	Distance
A	00	2	2
D	11		

We observe that in doing so we assign to the standard transformation of symbol 0 into 1 or vice versa the role somewhat analogous to that of the footrule transport in spanning the distance between two locations. On this analogy a legitimate measure of "distance" between any two points of our "space" of the four corners A, B, C, D is merely the number of standard changes in the symbol sequence of one required to yield another. Thus, as we noted earlier, the distance between A and B is 1 because we need to make only one change in the symbol sequence (00) of A to turn it into (01), that of B. Likewise, the "distance" between AD is 2 because two changes must be made in the symbol sequence (00) of A to obtain (11), that of D. Can you figure out the distance between BC, BD, DC, and AC, the remaining four pairs that can be obtained by picking out of four points two at a time?*

To recapitulate the idea of this rather longish detour: if we are transmitting two symbol sequences like 00, 01, 10, and 11, our entire code "space" is the assemblage of four "points," the four corners of the unit square $ABDC$ in Fig. 2. The "distance" between any two points in this code "space" is merely the number of changes we need make in the symbol sequence of one to turn it into that of the other. This is the only way in which we can "reach" one point of our "space" from another while submitting to its peculiar exigencies. This idea of code "space" and "distance" is now so general that it may readily be applied universally to sequences of any length whatever. For example, consider three-symbol-long sequences with which, as we saw earlier, we had to operate to transmit reliably single-symbol words. The totality of eight three-symbol sequences—000, 010, 100, 110, 001, 011, 101, 111—now form the eight corners A, B, C, D, E, F, G, H of a unit cube as in Fig. 3. This set of eight "points" is our code "space" and their mutual "distances," taken in pairs, may be derived by counting the number of changes required to be made in the symbol

* A glance at Fig. 2 shows that they are 2, 1, 1, 1 respectively.

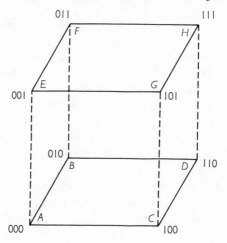

Fig. 3 Code space consisting of the eight corners of the unit cube *ABDCEFHG*.

sequence of one point to lead to that of the other. Thus obviously the distance *AH* is 3 as three changes are needed to turn the sequence ($\underline{000}$) of *A* into (111) that of *H*. Likewise, the "distance" between *E* ($\underline{001}$) and *C* (100) is 2 and that between *C* ($10\underline{0}$) and *G* (101) is only 1. Obviously the code "space" idea with its attendant notion of "distance" would also work with sequences longer than three symbols in precisely the same way even if we cannot embody the idea in a diagram like those of Figs. 2 and 3, which picturesquely describe the code "spaces" of two- and three-symbol sequences respectively. Indeed, all the Grand Vizier-like proliferation of permutation possibilities as the sequence length increases are brought under proper control with these ideas of "distance" and code "space."

Thus any sequence of *n* symbols will yield 2^n different permutations with two symbols 0 and 1. All these sequences are the "corners" of a unit *n*-dimensional "cube." Distances between any two corners can be measured by merely counting the number of symbol changes in the sequence of one corner to derive that of the other. This is, indeed, the only equivalent of "reaching" one corner from another while conforming to the structure of our code "space." Thus, with a nine-symbol sequence required for communicating our basic dictionary of 512 words, our "code" space is a unit nine-dimensional "cube" with $2^9 = 512$ "corners," each corner being a locum tenens for a word in the basic dictionary. For example, if the nine-symbol sequence (0̲1̲1̲011011) is one corner (word) and (110111001) is another, their mutual "distance" is 4 as may be verified by counting the underlined symbols in the former sequence. We need only change the underlined ones there to obtain the latter.

But if we associated each of the 512 corners of our nine-dimensional "cube" with a word in our 512-word basic dictionary and thus made every corner meaningful, even a single error would not be detectable. For a single error in transmission will clearly change a given corner (word) to another corner (word) at a distance of one unit away from it. Since the transmitted signal, even if erroneous, is meaningful under this scheme, wherein minimum distance between any two meaningful corners is 1, no single error would be detectable. To detect it we must ensure that when one meaningful corner (one associated with a word in our dictionary) undergoes a single error in transmission, the resulting corner will be meaningless, that is, not associated with any word. The receipt of a meaningless corner (word) is a sign that an error has occurred somewhere. It therefore follows that any corner C associated with a word in our vocabulary should have all corners which are at a distance one unit away from C, unattached to any word, that is, meaningless. This merely means that the minimum distance between any two meaningful corners (those associated with words in the vocabulary) should be 2 if a single error is to be detectable. Thus for our basic dictionary of 512 words, what we need is not a nine-dimensional cube but a ten-dimensional one. This latter cube has $2^{10} = 1024$ corners of which we choose every alternate one for representing 512 words, keeping the other half free or unattached. Consequently, when any meaningful corner attached to a word suffers a single error in transmission, it changes itself into an unattached corner one unit away and thus reveals the error. By keeping in this way the minimum distance 2 units between every two corners associated with words in our vocabulary we can detect a single error though we are not able to correct it.

To correct an error we must also be able to locate it. This evidently requires that the minimum distance between any two corners associated with words should be 3. For if we keep all meaningful corners three units apart and a single error results, a meaningful corner turns after transmission into one only unit distance away. Since the nearest meaningful corner to the one in question is three units away, the transformed meaningless corner reveals the identity of the intended corner. It is the nearest *permissible* or *meaningful* corner to the one received. There will always be only one if every meaningful corner is at least three units apart from every other.

In sum, the basis of such error-detecting and error-correcting schemes is keeping a certain minimum distance between every two corners associated with words in our vocabulary. As we have seen, the distance scale for various requirements is as follows:

TABLE 17

Minimum required distance between two meaningful corners associated with words in vocabulary	Capacity of the code
1	Error cannot be detected.
2	Single error can be detected but not corrected.
3	Single error can be detected as well as corrected.
4	Single error can be corrected plus double error detected.
5	Double error can be corrected.

We may illustrate the afore-mentioned basic ideas of Hamming underlying these codes by an example. Consider the transmission of three-symbol-long sequences. There will in all be $2^3 =$ eight such sequences which we may denote by the eight corners A, B, D, C, E, F, H, G of our three-dimensional cube as shown in Fig. 3. If we associate each of these corners with a word, that is, assign a meaning to the eight three-symbol-long sequences that the eight corners represent, we have enough corners or sequences to represent in all a repertoire of eight words. But as a single error in the transmission of any word, say, that denoted by B, will send it to a corner one unit away, that is, either to A, D, or F, and since each of these corners is meaningful having a word of our repertoire associated with it, receipt of A, D, or F in lieu of B cannot be recognized as an error. But if, on the other hand, we took care to keep every pair of corners associated with a word in our repertoire at least two units apart, a single error in the transmission of a word corner will send it to a corner which is unattached to any word and will thus be immediately detected even if not located. Consequently, if we choose to associate a word with, say, corner A, then all corners one unit away from it, namely, B, C, and E, must remain unattached or meaningless. For if we keep all these corners free, then in case the corner A happens to undergo a single error in transmission, it will be received as B, C, or E and thus be immediately recognized as an error. We recall that none of these corners has any word in our repertoire associated with it (see Fig. 3). However, D, which is two units away from A, can be associated with a word. But if we do so, then the corners H, B, and C which are but one unit away from D must remain free. Again, since F is two units away from D, a word can be associated with it, but again the three corners H, E, and B which are only a unit away from it must remain free. Next, since G is two units away from F, it too can be associated with a word but the three corners one unit apart from it, E, H, and C, must remain free. In this way, if we associate four words in our repertoire with the four corners A, D, F, and G and keep the other four, B, C, E, and H, free, we have a scheme of coding which can detect a single error though only by halving the stock of words it can take in its stride. But despite the sacrifice it still cannot locate the single error if and when it does occur. For corner A may with a single error in transmission become corner B one unit away. But so also can another meaningful corner D, which too is one unit away from B. It therefore results that when we receive B after transmission we do know that an error has occurred, because corner B is meaningless, but we cannot infer whether it is a mutilation of A or D for it can be either. If the error is to be detected we must remove this ambiguity. We can do so only by keeping meaningful corners still further apart from each other. Thus in our present case we find that only two corners, A and H, are three units apart. Hence we now decide to associate the words in our repertoire only with these two corners, A and H, and keep all the remaining six, B, C, D, E, F, G, completely free. Under this scheme, corner A after transmission may with a single error appear as either B, C, or E. If so, the only meaningful corner one unit away from any of these three corners is A, the other meaningful corner H being two units away. Likewise, if we intend to transmit corner H, it may with a single error in transmission turn into D, F, or G. But if so, H is the only meaningful corner near to it, the other meaningful corner A being two units away from each of them. Thus by keeping every pair of meaningful corners at least three units apart we succeed in detecting as well as locating a single error if and when it occurs, even though the number of words in our repertoire that can be coded falls from the initial eight words to only two.

This is exactly what we observed earlier by independent reasoning without the evocative imagery of Hamming's geometric language. We showed that to ensure reliable transmission of a single-symbol sequence yielding a two-word vocabulary we need to transmit sequences of three symbols, two symbols being added for two parity checks. A glance at Table 18 shows how the two parity sum checks

TABLE 18

Transmitted signal		Received signal		Erroneous symbol in received sequence	Parity checks: (i) Sum of first and second digits even (ii) Sum of first and third digits even
Meaningful corner in code space	Associated symbol sequence transmitted	Symbol sequence received	Associated corner in code space		
A	000	1̲00*	*C*	First digit	Both parity sums fail.
A	000	01̲0	*B*	Second digit	First parity sum fails but not second.
A	000	001̲	*E*	Third digit	Second parity sum fails but not first.
A	000	000	*A*	Nil	Both parity sums satisfied
H	111	0̲11	*F*	First digit	Both parity sums fail.
H	111	10̲1	*G*	Second digit	First parity sum fails but not second.
H	111	110̲	*D*	Third digit	Second parity sum fails but not first.
H	111	111	*H*	Nil	Both parity sums satisfied.

* Symbols in error are underlined.

given earlier are identical with those of Hamming outlined above. It is thus clear that Hamming's geometrical approach leads, in practice, to the same parity checks we found by our trial-and-error technique. But Hamming's geometrical reasoning provides a method that can readily be applied to more complex situations where we have to work with considerably longer sequences of symbols. For obviously the coding problem of how many code words at most can be included in a vocabulary built up by n-symbol sequences subject to a single-error detection, has its geometric analogue. It is simply this. What is the largest number of corners in an n-dimensional cube such that no two corners thereof are closer than two units apart? The answer is easily obtained by analogical reasoning. First consider the problem for $n = 2$. As shown in Fig. 2 there are in all four corners A, B, D, C with six mutual distances $AB = BD = DC = CA = 1$ and $AD = CB = 2$. In other words, a two-dimensional cube (that is, a square) has 2^2 corners of which at most 2^1 are two units apart. For $n = 3$, a glance at Fig. 3 shows that there are indeed two distinct squares $ABDC$ and $EFHG$ superposed on each other like two consecutive floors of a building. Obviously the cube has 2^3 or eight corners, with the distance between at most four pairs (2^2) of them two units apart. We may therefore conclude that an n-dimensional cube has 2^n corners of which at most 2^{n-1} corners are two units apart. Therefore for single-error detecting schemes with code words each n symbols long, we can have at most 2^{n-1} intelligible or meaningful sequences. The remaining 2^{n-1} corners have to be kept free or unattached to any of the words in our vocabulary.

Our coding theory shows how heavily it has to lean on redundancy for reliable transmission. Thus for our basic dictionary of 512 words we require a minimum of nine symbols per sequence. But as a nine-dimensional cube has only $2^9 = 512$ corners, it has no spare corner available to make any error detection possible, every pair of meaningful corners being at least one unit apart. Merely to detect a single error we need to proceed to ten-symbol-long sequences, but even so we do not have any means of correcting the error if it occurs. As we showed earlier, we need to prolong the sequence by k symbols to devise error-detecting as well as error-correcting codes where,

$$2^k \geqslant 9 + k + 1,$$

so that k must at least be 4 in our present case. We thus need to operate with 14-symbol-long sequences to have sufficient parity checks to take care of only our basic repertoire of barely 512 words. In the geometric language we have used so far, we would have a 14-dimensional cube which has $2^{14} = 16,384$ corners in all. Of these we associate the 512 words of our basic dictionary with 512 corners suitably spaced, leaving the remaining 15,872 free. Such a large measure of redundancy inevitably levies its toll on the rate of transmission. This is why an iterated scheme of coding recently devised by P. Elias has evoked widespread interest. His scheme achieves as high a degree of reliability as one could desire, yet does not result in the arbitrarily low rate of transmission that our earlier but rather naïve assumptions seemed to suggest. It does not, it is true, achieve a rate of transmission equal to the channel capacity. Nevertheless, it has two interesting features. First, for a fixed rate, the reliability can be increased at the cost of coding delay. Secondly, for a fixed delay, the reliability can be increased at the cost of transmission rate. In a quite real sense Elias's scheme achieves its goal by introducing redundancy very much as a natural language like English does.

In view of Hamming's classic exploitation of the ideas of *finite* geometry to evolve error-detecting and error-correcting codes, it is no mere accident that the new concept of *group* has also been made to carry grist to the coding mill. For the latter is the umbilical cord that ties finite geometry to the theory of permutation groups, that is, *sets* of permutations that form a *group*. It may seem a tautology to say that a set is a group; but the word "group" is used here not in its lay meaning of a mere aggregate or assembly of entities but in the technical sense of a collection of entities that possess the additional property of *self-closure*. This is a way of saying that if we have a set of numbers, sequences, operations, or symbols and a *rule* for combining any two of them, the set becomes a group, *if* the result of their combination is an entity also belonging to the set. Consider, for example, a set of six different permutations of three cards such as the ace, two, and three of spades. Since there are six and only six distinct ways in which three cards can be permuted, any combination of two shuffles, that is, two shuffles successively applied, will inevitably yield one of the six shuffles of the set itself. By combining any two or more of the six shuffles, we cannot generate any new shuffle not already included in the original six of the set. In other words, the set of six shuffles is closed. Any collection of entities like the set of six shuffles of three cards, whose elements combine in such a way that any two or more of them in unison are equivalent to some single item of the set, is known as a *group*. The essential point is that the elements of the group can be combined according to some law, and any combination of them produces an element belonging to the set itself. It is therefore completely self-contained or closed.

It often happens that the elements of the original group may be divided into two or more distinct *subsets* in such a way that the elements included in each subset satisfy the property of self-closure separately. In such a case, each subset possessing the group property in its own right is known as the *subgroup* of the original group.   Thus, in the case of the six shuffles of the three cards cited earlier, the six shuffles can be so divided into two subgroups of three shuffles each, that each of the subgroups will possess the group property in its own right.

The reason group theory applies so readily to coding problems is that the set of all messages formed by taking sequences of binary digits 0, or 1, forms a *group*.   Consider, for example, sequences consisting of binary digits, 0 or 1, formed by taking any number of digits, say, three at a time.   Obviously there will be in all $2 \times 2 \times 2$ or eight such different three-digit-long permutations of 0's and 1's:

$$000, 010, 101, 111, 001, 011, 110, 100 \qquad (1)$$

If we devise a rule whereby any two permutations may be combined to yield another, we can test whether or not our set of eight permutations is a group in the sense defined above.   The simplest rule of combination is to add the digits in the corresponding positions of the added sequences, divide each sum by 2, and adopt the remainder (which will naturally be either 0 or 1) in the corresponding position of the derived sequence.   Thus if we add the two sequences 011 and 110 in this manner, their "sum" is obviously 121, which after casting out the divisors of 2 from each digit, becomes 101.   The "sum" of two sequences 011 and 110 according to our addition rule is therefore a new permutation 101 of the digits 0 and 1.   Obviously 101 is also a member of the set of eight permutations with which we started. Indeed, no matter which two of these eight permutations we combine in this manner, the end product will obviously be some one or other of the totality of eight sequences simply because there can be no other three-digit sequence of 0's and 1's.   The set of eight permutations of three-digit-long sequences is self-contained.   It is therefore a group under the combination or addition rule we have specified.   The rule is known as "addition modulo 2" because it is the remainder obtained by dividing the sum of added digits by 2 in the prescribed manner that yields the digit in each position of the combined sequence.   The remainder is invariably either a 0 or a 1, which is exactly as it should be since they are the only two digits we are allowed to permute. Naturally what holds for binary sequences of three digits is equally true of sequences of any length—four, five, ten, or n digits.   The set of sequences becomes progressively more numerous but continues to remain self-contained in that the combination or "sum" of any two sequences yields another of the set itself.   Consequently the set, S, of all binary sequences of length n, that is, a total of 2^n such sequences, form a group under "addition modulo 2."

Now it happens that the eight permutations or sequences of the main group of three-digit sequences can be divided into two subsets each of which possesses the group property of being self-contained in its own right.   Thus the subset of the first four of the eight permutations listed in (1) above, namely,

$$000, 010, 101, 111$$

possesses the group property.   As may be readily verified, the "sum" or combination of any two of these four permutations is one of the four permutations of the subset itself.   Thus the addition of the second and third of the subset yields 111 which also belongs to the subset, and so on for all the six pairs taken out of these four, two at a time. Likewise, the subset of the following four permutations of our original set of eight,

$$001, 011, 010, \text{ and } 000,$$

also possesses the group property of being self-contained in its own right.   Each of these two subsets of four sequences is therefore a subgroup of the main group of eight.

D. Slepian was the first to show the equivalence of the ideas underlying Hamming's parity-check codes and the group theory.   He showed that the main group S of all possible n-digit-long permutations of binary digits 0 and 1 contains subsets each of which is a subgroup of S.   These subsets form codes which are known as systematic *group codes*.   Slepian's technique for determining such error-correcting group codes is a landmark in coding theory.   By a still more remarkable confluence of the ideas of finite geometry and group theory, R. C. Bose and Ray-Choudhari gave a constructive method for finding codes that correct any prescribed number e of errors in n-digit-long messages by using at most $e \log_2 (n + 1)$ parity checks.   The result of their work has been a major improvement in sending messages on what are known as "toll grade" telephone circuits.   Under a recent coding scheme of R. C. Bose, for example, an error would occur as rarely as once every three hundred years, whereas with ordinary transmission an error normally occurs once a minute.

R. C. Bose has, indeed, plumbed the depths of coding theory even further.   He has shown that certain coding problems are intimately linked with the problems of combinatorial mathematics handled by finite geometry and group algebra.　For he has reduced the whole gamut of statistical problems—from error-correcting codes to balanced block designs and "confounding" in the theory of experimental designs—to a geometrical problem of astonishing sweep, versatility, and power.　Bose calls it the "packing" problem because all the problems it subsumes amount to packing or finding the maximum number of distinct points in a finite abstract space (like our code space) so that no preassigned number, say, n of them, are "dependent." For example, if n is 3, no three of them should be on the same straight line as otherwise only two of them would determine the line on which the third also lies and they would not be independent of one another. If n is 4, to ensure their independence no four of them should be on a plane, and so on.

In spite of the profound work done by leaders like Hamming, Slepian, Elias, Bose, and others, or perhaps because of it, many new problems in coding theory have arisen and have yet to be solved.　As Slepian himself has remarked, our understanding of group codes is still "fragmentary."

Chapter VI

CONTINUOUS CHANNELS

WE have so far considered communication of messages built out of discretely identifiable elements such as the dash-dot of telegraphy or teletype. They could be typified by sequences of binary digits 0 and 1 in the same way that a written text is a collection of letters, a melody a musically expressive succession of single notes, and a halftone picture a juxtaposition of discrete spots. But messages like music and pictures may also be more than mere rows of distinct letters or strings of discrete notes and spots. They are often a continuum of sounds and colors, each merging insensibly with its neighbor, not unlike the speaking voice with its continuous variation of pitch and energy, or the imperceptible shadings of red into violet or orange-yellow in a Renoir rainbow.

We have therefore to extend our theory of communication of information to take account of continuous messages as well as those built of discrete elements. Such extension of results from discrete systems to systems with continuously varying parameters is quite frequent in mathematics and physics. It is usually secured by dividing the continuously varying parameter of the problem throughout its range into a finite number of equal discrete parts, just as we reduce the *measurement* of the length of a continuous rod to a mere *count* of discrete fragments by breaking it up into a number of separate pieces of some standard size. This reduction of the measurement of a continuum to a mere count of an ensemble of discrete fragments is, no doubt, an approximation as the division of a length into a number of standard pieces often leaves a residue which is awkward to handle and has to be ignored. But as the residual leftover cannot exceed any of the standard bits into which the rod is broken, the awkward remainder can be made negligibly small by sufficiently decreasing the size of the

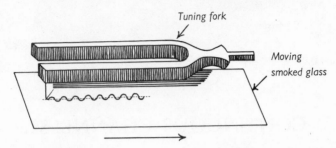

Fig. 4 Trace of the vibrating tuning fork on the moving smoked glass underneath.

standard bit. This principle of sufficiently microscopic fragmentation of the continuous parameter into a number of discrete equal parts makes the passage from the discrete to the continuous natural and smooth. Indeed, the approximation itself becomes exact as we make the standard bit infinitesimally small, though to avoid certain pitfalls otherwise inevitable in handling infinity the limiting process has to be steered under a rigorous mathematical discipline all its own.

In our present case one particularly fortunate circumstance facilitates the transition from the discrete to the continuous. It is that any continuous signal such as any continuous sound or succession of sounds can be represented by a curve, and this representative curve, though continuous, may in turn be specified by means of a *finite* number of *discrete* measurements *with as great fidelity as we desire*. To understand the full import of this statement requires a slight digression, but it is well worth making as it takes us to the heart of the problem of communication.

When we make a curve represent a sound or a signal, all that we do is to graph the amplitude of the sound or signal against time. Con-

Fig. 5 Straight line made on smoky deposit when the tuning fork is still.

sider, for example, a musical note emitted by an ordinary tuning fork when we strike one of its prongs with a hammer. The prongs begin to vibrate as we may actually see from their fuzzy outline. It is because of this vibration of the prongs, communicated to our eardrums through the air surrounding them, that we hear its sound. We may easily obtain a time graph of these vibrations by attaching a light gramophone needle to the end of one prong of the fork and running a piece of smoked glass under it as shown in Fig. 4. If, in a perfectly straight line and at a steady speed, we move the glass underneath the fork prong when the fork is still, the point of the needle would naturally scratch a straight cut through the smoky deposit of the glass

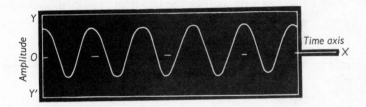

Fig. 6 Wavy furrow on smoked glass traced by the vibrating tuning fork (curve simplified).

like the line in Fig. 5. But when the fork is vibrating, the needle plows a wavy furrow through the smoke deposit and thereby yields an imprint of its vibrations (see Fig. 6). This wavy furrow is the time graph or the sound curve of the note we have been in search of. For obviously each complete wave corresponds to a single complete cycle of the to-and-fro motion of the needle point and so to a complete cycle of the vibrating prong of the tuning fork. Moreover, each point of the wave measures against time the corresponding amplitude, that is, the distance of the prong from its central position of equilibrium when it is at rest.

The most remarkable feature of our sound curve is the extreme regularity of its waves. All of them are of precisely identical shape, a visual reminder of the recurrence of the movement pattern of the prong at regular intervals. But a tuning fork once struck will not go on vibrating for ever. At the outset a fairly loud note is produced but this gradually declines as the vibrations dissipate their energy into the surrounding air. What declines, however, is its *intensity* or *loudness*, not its *pitch*, which continues to be the *same* throughout until the very end when the note whimpers into silence. This feature too shows itself in the sound curve. The height to which the wavy furrows rise —counterparts of the amplitude or the distance up to which the prongs move away from their central position of rest—progressively diminishes as the sound diminishes in strength but the waves remain always of the same time length or duration (see Fig. 7). In this respect the vibrating fork behaves exactly like an oscillating pendulum and for the same reason—the restoring force that tends to pull the moving system, the prong or the pendulum bob, is directly proportional to the distance the vibrating particle has moved away from its central position of rest. The farther it is from its central position, the greater the restoring force. As a result, once the bob is set in motion, its ampli-

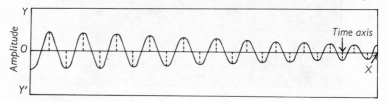

Fig. 7   Diminishing amplitude of the successive waves while the period of pulsation or pitch remains the same.

tude of motion (the height to which it rises in each swing) gradually diminishes till it comes to rest, but not the *period* of its one complete swing, which remains the same till the end despite progressive diminution of the amplitude of successive swings. In exactly the same way the vibrating prongs of the tuning fork continue to keep constant time *in diminuendo*. This constancy of the period of one complete cycle of vibration of the prong is the tuning fork's signature tune. The period itself, of course, is normally only a small fraction of a second. But to avoid having to deal with small fractions we express it inversely as a "frequency" of vibration, i.e., the number of complete vibrations or cycles of to-and-fro movements that it executes in a second. Actual experiment shows that a tuning fork which is tuned to, say, middle C of the pianoforte executes 261 vibrations in a second regardless of whether the sound is loud or soft.

The extreme simplicity of the shape of the sound curve of a tuning fork, even though an almost ideal source of pure musical tone of one single frequency, is, however, an oversimplification of a situation that, in reality, is much more involved. When we set the tuning fork going

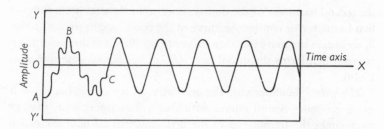

Fig. 8 Sound curve of the clang and main tones taken together.

by hitting it with a hammer, we also hear at the outset a number of additional "clang" tones of higher frequencies. No doubt the latter tones die away quite rapidly but for the short duration that they last they make the *initial* part of our sound curve considerably more complex than the regular pattern of waves of Fig. 6. The initial part of our sound curve would be of the more complicated type shown in curve *ABC* in Fig. 8. One complication is that its wavy pattern is not quite apparent at first sight. But it can be shown that this more intricate sound curve, the outcome of both the "clang" and the main tones, is the sum of two distinct curves of simpler forms. One of them is, of course, the regular curve of the fundamental frequency of 261 cycles per second pertaining to the main tone we have already seen in Fig. 6. The other is an equally regular curve but one whose frequency is twice that of the first like the dotted curve in Fig. 9. If we consider the 261-frequency curve of the main tone, that is, the continuous curve in Fig. 9, as our first fundamental *harmonic*, the curve of the "clang" tone corresponding to twice this frequency, that is, the dotted curve in Fig. 9, is called the *second harmonic*. If we superpose

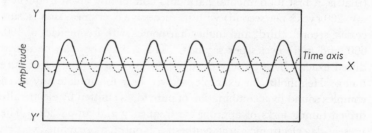

Fig. 9 The continuous curve is the clang tone, and the dotted curve is its second harmonic.

the second harmonic or the dotted curve of the "clang" tone onto the first harmonic or continuous curve of the main tone as shown in Fig. 9, we obtain the more intricate curve of Fig. 10. It is this superposed curve which forms the initial part *ABC* of our actual note shown in Fig. 8.

The principle underlying the generation of the second harmonic is quite general. Sound curves with frequencies three, four, five, or more times the frequencies of the first fundamental note are called successively third, fourth, fifth, and higher harmonics. In musical language they are one, two, three or more octaves higher than the first fundamental note or harmonic. The generation of higher har-

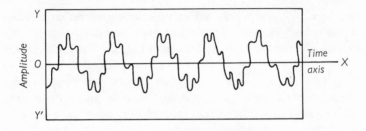

Fig. 10 The superposed curve obtained by adding the corresponding ordinates of the continuous and dotted curves of Fig. 6 at each instant of the time axis.

monics serves a very useful purpose. For we find that what is true of the initial part of the more complicated sound curve of the tuning fork of our illustration is equally true of the sound curve of any sound, no matter how complex, whether the voice of a soprano or the honk of a motor horn. We can build them all up by blending a pure tone (that is, a first fundamental harmonic note of any given frequency, say, 200 cycles per second) with its successive overtones (that is, successive second, third, and higher harmonics with frequencies of 400, 600, and more cycles per second). This is why they can be reproduced exactly by a battery of tuning forks or other sources of pure tones. Helmholtz, for example, showed how to simulate any given complex sound by a combination of pure tones emitted by electrically driven tuning forks of appropriate frequency and amplitude. The present-day electronic music synthesizer is only a more refined version of Helmholtz's original apparatus. More recently Professor Dayton Miller has built up groups of organ pipes, which produce the various vowels when sounded in unison; other groups say "papa" and "mama."

Such reconstruction of any sound from a pure tone and its corresponding overtones with frequencies two, three, or any other integral multiple of octaves higher than the pure tone itself is based on a mathematical theorem known as Fourier's theorem after its discoverer, the famous French mathematician J. B. J. Fourier. He showed that any curve, no matter how complicated, can be built up by the superposition of an appropriate number of simple harmonic curves such as the wavy furrows of our tuning fork. The theorem tells us that we need only use waves of certain specified frequencies. If, for instance,

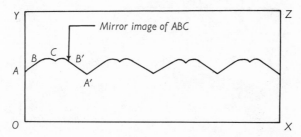

Fig. 11

the original curve repeats itself regularly 200 times every second, we need only employ curves which repeat themselves regularly once, 2, 3, 4, or more times as much every second. That is, we use wavy curves of frequencies 200, 400, 600, 800, and so on, cycles per second. This is almost self-evident since unless all the component waves which blend to make the given curve march in step with the fundamental frequency of 200 cycles per second, the composite curve cannot exhibit the prescribed rhythm. In other words, the frequencies of all the component waves must be exact multiples of 200 cycles per second. Waves with any other frequencies such as 145 or 219 will obviously be out of step with the rhythm of 200 cycles per second of the original curve.

Even if the sound curve shows no regularity or rhythm so that it does not repeat itself at all, we may still make it part of a longer curve which does repeat itself. We may, for example, build it up by first continuing the given curve into its mirror image as in Fig. 11 and thereafter repeating the two joined pieces at regular intervals. Thus the original non-regular sound curve *ABC* may be deemed to continue itself into its mirror image *CB'A'*, and this synthetic curve *ABCB'A'* be taken to repeat itself in a regular rhythm as shown in Fig. 12. Taking *ABCB'A'* as our original curve, we can build it up out of simple harmonic constituents such that the first has one complete half wave within the range of the original curve *ABC*, the second has two complete half waves, the third has three, and so on. The constituents which contain fractional parts of half waves need not be employed at all.

This possibility of building up any sound curve by a blend of an appropriate number of simple harmonic curves or wavy furrows is the lucky circumstance to which we alluded earlier. Its value lies in the

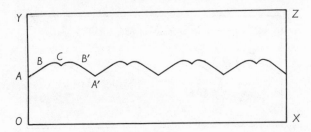

Fig. 12

fact that, while for an *exact* blend we need an infinite number of harmonics or overtones with frequencies an integral multiple of octaves higher than the original tone, for blends that meet even our onerous hi-fi requirements they need not actually be infinite. Of course, they have to be fairly large but mere largeness is no insurmountable difficulty so long as it falls short of the actual infinite. The reason is that no physical communications system can transmit waves of unlimited frequency. There is always a limiting frequency beyond which it cannot transmit. Thus very satisfactory telephone channels are limited to a maximum frequency of 4000 cycles. Even though the human voice contains higher frequencies, the frequency limit of 4000 cycles of such telephonic channels permits the human voice to be transmitted with reasonable similitude. Communications systems whose limiting frequency extends to ten or twelve thousand cycles are adequate even for hi-fi radio transmission of symphonic music. In the case both of telephone and hi-fi radio the respective limiting frequency which cuts out the higher harmonics of the original message source is, thanks to Fourier's theorem, no serious bar to *fidèle* communication. This is why Fourier's theorem is the main bridge which makes possible the transition from the discrete to the continuous in the realm of communications. It does so by reducing any sound or symphony to a simple count of its component overtones, thereby uncovering the factual basis of Leibnitz's mystical statement that has delighted musicians ever since, that "music is a veiled exercise in arithmetic by the soul unaware of its counting." Indeed, it not only unveils the "soul's" unconscious counting but also provides the link that unites the domains of time, line and color of which Oswald Spengler spoke in his book *The Decline of the West*. Perhaps he had Fourier's formula in mind as "one of the forms of the higher analysis" when he wrote: "The history of the modern orchestra, with all its discoveries of new and modifications of old instruments is in reality the self-contained history of one tone-world—a world moreover that is quite capable of being expressed in the forms of higher analysis."

But to revert to our sound curve. Having broken the continuous sound or signal curve* into a finite number of harmonics with a limiting frequency of, say, W cycles per second by recourse to Fourier's theorem, we have next to consider how to transmit across a communications channel the information it contains. Taking our cue from the procedure followed earlier in transmitting the information content of messages built up of a succession of discrete digits like 0 and 1, we have first to reduce somehow our continuous curve (or its equivalent, the several but *finite* sets of harmonics of which it is a blend) to a string of *discrete* and *finite* measurements. Fortunately this is precisely what Shannon's famous sampling theorem enables us to do. It shows that any sound curve extending over any duration T but band-limited in frequency to W cycles per second can be *completely* specified if we sample its amplitude or ordinate at intervals of $\frac{1}{2W}$ second. It therefore follows that all we need do is to sample it at $2W$ points every second or at $2WT$ distinct points in all during the life span T of our curve completely to encompass it.

---

* In general, a signal curve, like the sound curve, is a time graph of some continuously varying quantity such as electric current through a photoelectric cell, temperature, sound pressure, and so on. It will be recalled that a communications channel like the telephone transmitter merely changes the pattern of the voice (sound curve) into an equivalent pattern of currents (signal curve) on the telephone wires.

Such a long preamble to the apparently trivial conclusion that a continuous curve may be defined by a specified number of ordinates spaced at regular intervals may seem rather odd. But the theorem is nevertheless very remarkable. For, ordinarily, a continuous curve can be only *approximately* characterized by stating any finite number of points through which it passes, since the interpolation between any two adjacent sampled points is always more or less arbitrary. For complete information we should need to specify the curve at every point of the time continuum over which it ranges. But if the curve is built up out of harmonic constituents of a limited number of frequencies, as any complex sound may, by resort to Fourier's theorem, be built up out of a limited number of pure tones, then a finite number of amplitudes or ordinates of the curve equally spaced at intervals of $\frac{1}{2W}$ second suffice for its *exact* representation. This *exactitude* of representation is the real core of Shannon's sampling theorem. Its great merit is that it provides the second bridge (Fourier's theorem was the first) which we need to reduce the character of the communications problem for continuous signals from a complicated situation where we would have to deal with an infinite number of values to a considerably simpler situation where we deal with a finite (though large) number of discrete values. The transition from the continuous to the discrete is therefore complete in principle.

The actual problem of communicating the information content of any sound or signal curve therefore resolves itself into transmitting in all $2WT$ *discrete measurements* of its ordinates or amplitudes. As we have seen, this suffices to retain sufficient detail of the curve for the desired degree of fidelity in transmission. But when we have to transmit each single measurement, we face yet another rub not encountered in the transmission of discrete messages. In transmitting messages built up of discrete symbols like 0 and 1 across a noiseless channel, we had at each stage only two possible choices (because there were exactly two distinguishable states, or levels, of the symbols transmitted): either 0 or 1. On the other hand, when we transmit a measurement across a noiseless channel, we no longer have only two or a finite number of choices before us; we face instead a whole infinity of them. For we can distinguish on a noiseless channel an infinite number of levels of measurement at each act of its transmission. That is, what is transmitted can be only one value out of an infinite continuum of possible values. It therefore results that while transmitting each one of the

$2TW$ sampled measurements of our curve we have an infinity of choices open to us at each stage. This is merely a way of saying that the capacity of a noiseless channel is infinite. In actual practice, of course, there is always some noise. But, even so, if the transmitter power S of the signal is unlimited, we can still distinguish an infinite

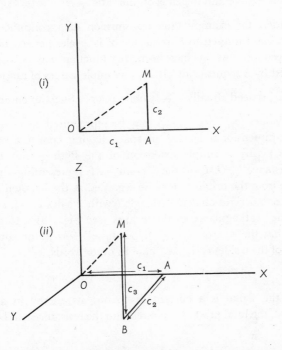

Fig. 13 (*top*) In the two-dimensional right-angled triangle OAM, the square of the hypotenuse $OM^2 = OA^2 + AM^2 = c_1^2 + c_2^2$.

(*bottom*) In the three-dimensional analogue of the "right-angled triangle" $OABM$, the square of the hypotenuse $OM^2 = OA^2 + AB^2 + BM^2 = c_1^2 + c_2^2 + c_3^2$.

number of levels of measurement while transmitting each one of the $2TW$ sampled amplitudes or ordinates of our curve. Accordingly the capacity of our channel remains infinite.

Only when the signal power S is limited and some noise is present do we have a finite capacity for our channel. What the capacity will then be depends on the statistical structure of the noise as well as the nature of the power limitation. Suppose noise is of the simplest statistical type called by Shannon "white thermal" noise* with power N. Can we calculate the number of distinguishable levels of amplitudes under these circumstances? In other words, given S and N, can we compute the number of choices the channel allows us when we transmit any single amplitude measurement? The answer is in the affirmative and depends on the ratio $\frac{S}{N}$.

Consider, for example, the transmission of a continuous signal function band limited to a frequency of W cycles per second lasting for T seconds. As we have seen, the function can be completely described by a sequence of $2WT = n$ sample values of amplitude c_1, $c_2, \ldots, c_n$, spaced equally $\frac{1}{2W}$ seconds apart. Such an ensemble of n sample values $(c_1, c_2, c_3 \ldots, c_n)$ may be represented as a "point" M in an n-dimensional Euclidean space having coordinates $(c_1, c_2, c_3, \ldots, c_n)$. By a simple extension of the Pythagorean theorem, the "distance" OM of the "point" M representing the signal function from the origin O may be regarded as the hypotenuse of an n-dimensional right-angled "triangle" with n sides $c_1, c_2, c_3, \ldots, c_n$ along the rectangular coordinate axes (see Fig. 13). It therefore results that the square of the "hypotenuse" OM is the sum of the squares of the n sides $c_1, c_2, \ldots, c_n$. In other words,

$$OM^2 = r^2 = c_1{}^2 + c_2{}^2 + c_3{}^2 + \ldots + c_n{}^2.$$

Now if the signal is a current dissipating its energy in a 1-ohm resistance, the total power† P poured into the resistance can be shown to be

$$P = \frac{1}{2WT}(c_1{}^2 + c_2{}^2 + c_3{}^2 + \ldots + c_n{}^2),$$

so that the distance r from the origin O to the signal point M is

$$r^2 = 2WTP.$$

Since r^2 is proportional to the average power of the signal, all signals having a power P or less will lie within an n-dimensional sphere of radius r. This remarkable relation between signal power P and dis-

---

* That is, a noise whose energy is distributed uniformly over the entire signal band and for which the amplitude distributions are "normal."

† This follows from the fact that power, that is, energy dissipated per second by an electrical current c flowing through a 1-ohm resistance, is c^2.

tance r of the signal "point" M from O enables us to calculate the number of distinguishable levels of amplitudes given both the average power of the signal as well as noise impeding its transmission. For noise of power N during transmission has merely the effect of creating a fuzzy sphere of uncertainty of radius $\sqrt{2TWN}$ about the signal point. The signal point M may after transmission thus find itself anywhere within a sphere of radius $\sqrt{2TWN}$ around M. Now if the signals are restricted to an average signal power S, the set of allowed signal points will be contained within a sphere of radius $\sqrt{2TW(N+S)}$. Assuming that signal points lying within the same noise sphere cannot be distinguished, the greatest number of distinguishable signal points will be equal to the number of noise spheres which can be accommodated within the signal-plus-noise sphere. The number m of distinguishable levels we are in search of is therefore approximately the relative volumes of the two spheres. Since the spheres in question are n-dimensional, their volumes are proportional to the nth power of their radii. Hence

$$m = \left[\frac{\sqrt{2WT(N+S)}}{\sqrt{2WTN}} \right]^n$$

$$= \left(1 + \frac{S}{N} \right)^{\frac{n}{2}} = \left(1 + \frac{S}{N} \right)^{\frac{2WT}{2}} = \left(1 + \frac{S}{N} \right)^{WT}$$

Having computed m, the distinguishable choices open before us, we find by the analogy of our earlier reasoning that the information content of the signal function is

$$\log_2 m = \log_2 \left(1 + \frac{S}{N} \right)^{WT} = WT \log_2 \left(1 + \frac{S}{N} \right) \text{ bits.}$$

Since this information is communicated during an interval of time T, the channel capacity C or the maximum rate of transmission of information reckoned in bits per second is

$$C = \frac{WT}{T} \log_2 \left(1 + \frac{S}{N} \right) = W \log_2 \left(1 + \frac{S}{N} \right) \tag{1}$$

In the special case when $\frac{S}{N} = 1$, $C = W$. That is, the channel capacity in bits per second is just the band width of the facility in cycles per second when the signal to noise power ratio is unity.

Equation (1) is the famous Shannon-Hartley law. It stipulates that it is possible to transmit, by the best possible coding, only $W \log_2 \left(1 + \dfrac{S}{N} \right)$ bits per second and to recover them at the receiving end with as little error as desired. But it is an optimal rate which cannot be exceeded, no matter how clever the coding, without a definite loss of reliability.

This concludes our account of coding theory. As we have seen, its chief benefit is the demonstration that it is possible to communicate information over noisy channels both discrete as well as continuous with arbitrarily high reliability by recourse to optimal codes having an appropriate degree of redundancy. Its relevance to the problem of animal intelligence lies in the fact that all multicellular organisms must with great reliability communicate to internal organs information about the external environment in which they are placed. The question whether communication over the natural nerve network of animals can be accomplished as reliably as that on the artificial channels we have hitherto considered is, of course, vital for animal survival. While we know from such actual survival that the answer is in the affirmative, we also need to know how it is secured. As we shall see in Chapter XII, von Neumann has shown that in principle sufficient redundancy can likewise be injected into neuron networks to ensure as high a reliability as we desire, even if the constituent neurons themselves are statistically unreliable and liable to malfunction.

Chapter VII

INFORMATION AND ENTROPY

AS will be recalled, we measured the information content of a message in any given ensemble of messages by the logarithm of the probability of its occurrence. This way of defining information has an earlier precedent in statistical mechanics where the measure of entropy is identical in form with that of information. It is, therefore, no mere accident that there is a deep-rooted connection between the two. To start with, both information theory and statistical mechanics are statistical. We have already seen that the probability of a message in a set of messages is merely the relative frequency of its occurrence in a large number of trials. Statistics of the incidence of messages in repeated trials are thus the very stuff of their information content. In statistical mechanics, too, as the name implies, we try to deduce the behavior of bodies by applying statistical considerations to crowds of molecules of which they are made.

Now whenever we are confronted with crowds of entities, whether of men, messages, or molecules, there are two ways of dealing with them. *Either* we specify the attribute(s) under consideration of each and every individual in the crowd, *or* we specify the over-all statistical average(s) of their individual attribute(s). The former is said to define the internal structure or *microstate* of the crowd and the latter its outer façade or *macrostate*. A case in point is the age attribute of a class of pupils. Its *microstate* is defined by the actual age of each one of its individuals. Its *macrostate*, on the other hand, may well be defined by the average age of the entire class. Obviously, to any given *macrostate* of the class, that is, its average age as a whole, there corresponds a whole gamut of possibilities of its *microstates*, that is, the various age patterns yielding the same average. Fixing the average age of the class in no way determines the actual age distribution of its individuals any more than the average depth of a river provides a basis for deciding whether to ford it or swim it.   Nevertheless, when the number of individuals in the class becomes very large, the specification of its macrostate by means of the average age of its members may well be the only way open to our limited intelligence to grasp anything of their age attribute.   This difficulty created by the sheer bulk of numbers in a crowd is almost infinitely accentuated in statistical mechanics, where the crowds of molecules constituting the bodies under study are so enormous that any attempt at a detailed description of the welter of their individual motions only creates a tangle impossible to unravel.   Statistical mechanics therefore cuts the Gordian knot by trying to grasp the motion of the entire assembly of molecules by a statistical study of the group, as for instance, by calculating the *average* energy of the aggregate of molecules and identifying it with the measure of its temperature.

Just as to each single *macrostate* of a crowd defined by the average values of one or more of its attributes there correspond in general several *microstates* of the crowd, so also to each macrostate of the motion of the molecules of the body as defined by the average speed of its molecules (or what amounts to the same thing, by its temperature), there correspond many microstates of its molecular motion. No wonder then that in a body consisting of billions upon billions of molecules there are a large number of *different microstates* of motion, each of which may pertain to one *macrostate* having the *same* average speed per molecule.   To our gross senses the body in any one of these different microstates will appear to remain at the same temperature. But behind the façade of the stability of its average speed or temperature there lurks a continual whirl of transitions from one microstate to another which mere measurement of the body temperature is unable to reveal.   The number of different microstates which correspond to a single given macrostate defined by any temperature T is known as its *thermodynamic probability*.   The underlying rationale for calling it "probability" is the truism that the greater the number of microstates corresponding to the macrostate defined by temperature T, the greater the odds that any microstate chosen at random will display the outward feature of that macrostate, that is, exhibit the temperature T.

Consider, for example, a body all of whose molecules are moving with the same speed and in the same direction as the body itself. This completely regimented motion, in which a knowledge of the speed of any one molecule leads to that of the speed of all the molecules, belongs to a *macrostate* which has only a single *microstate*. It is like the class of pupils all of whose members are of one and the same age, so that a knowledge of the age of any one of them suffices to tell the age of all the others, including their average. This state of the *highest internal order* or *organization* in the motion of the molecules has the *lowest* thermodynamic probability, there being only *one* microstate among the myriads possible. On the other hand, when the state of motion of the molecules in the body is highly *disorganized* or anarchic, with each molecule in the chaotic whirl a law unto itself, the number of microstates leading to one and the same macrostate is much more numerous so that its thermodynamic probability becomes exceedingly great. This state of great thermodynamic probability obviously yields much less information about the actual structure of the internal motions simply because there are now so many more alternatives to choose from. Thermodynamic probability of a body thus provides us a measure of information about the state of its internal motions even if it does so in a negative way. For since a large number of microstates, that is, large thermodynamic probability, goes hand in hand with large disorder and little regimentation in its internal make-up, thermodynamic probability (or rather its logarithm called entropy) is really an index of molecular chaos that prevails within. It is, nonetheless, a useful one for we require it for a quantitative determination of the trend of natural processes when crowds of molecules of which bodies are made are left on their own.

Entropy thus serves two closely related purposes. First, it is what Eddington called time's arrow, that is, a pointer of the drift of natural processes. Secondly, it reveals to us quantitatively the statistical structure of internal motions very much as information theory does that of our message ensemble. Moreover, it does so in an analogous way. For we take entropy as the logarithm of thermodynamic probability of a macrostate just as we measure information of a message by the logarithm of the probability of its occurrence. The reason in either case is to secure additivity. It will be remembered that recourse to the logarithmic form enabled us to ensure that the information content of any complex of messages is the sum of its individual components. For exactly the same reason we measure the entropy of a body in any macrostate by the logarithm of the number of its corresponding microstates, that is, its thermodynamic probability. Take, for example, a body like a cylinder of gas whose macrostate with temperature T has S distinct microstates of its internal molecular motion. If we have another cylinder of gas also at temperature T but having S' microstates of motion corresponding to it, the two cylinders when connected to form one system will obviously have SS' different microstates. For each one of the microstates of the first cylinder may be combined with any one of the second to yield a permissible microstate of the larger system formed by taking the two together. It therefore follows that if the entropy (E) of the first cylinder is measured by log S instead of only S and that of the second

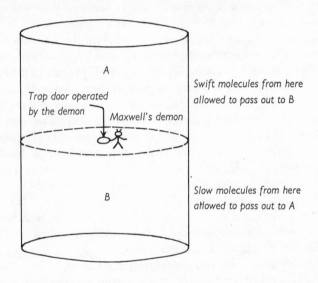

Fig. 14

(E') by log S' instead of only S', then that of the two together, log SS', is simply log S + log S' or the sum of the individual entropies E and E' of the two systems, as required.

Obviously, information and entropy are two sides of the same coin in that internal order or organization, and therefore greater knowledge or information of the system's internal make-up, goes hand in hand with *low* thermodynamic probability or rather its logarithm, which we have chosen to call entropy. Since in any given system, the greater the number of microscopic states corresponding to any assigned macrostate, the greater will be its entropy, it follows that entropy is a measure of our *ignorance* of its ultra-microscopic structure.

In other words, entropy is information *in reverse gear*, for which reason L. Brillouin coined the term "negentropy" by contracting the phrase "negative of entropy."

This remarkable resemblance between information and entropy was first noticed by L. Szilard in his resolution of the paradox of Maxwell's demon which J. C. Maxwell had enunciated in his *Theory of Heat* in 1871. Maxwell began his argument by postulating "a being whose faculties are so sharpened that he can follow every molecule in its course, and would be able to do what is at present impossible for us. Let us suppose that a vessel is divided into two portions, *A* and *B*, by a division in which there is a small hole, and that a being who *can see the individual molecules* opens and closes this hole so as to allow only the swifter molecules to pass from *A* to *B*, and only the slower ones to pass from *B* to *A*. He will thus without expenditure of work raise the temperature of *B* and lower that of *A* in contradiction to the second law of thermodynamics" (see Fig. 14).

Since the demon's sorting activity results in concentrating swifter molecules in *B* and the slower ones in *A*, and since, moreover, temperature is merely a measure of the average speed of the moving molecules in a region, clearly *B*, the new niche of the faster molecules, will be at a higher temperature than *A*, the rendezvous of the sluggards. But such *effortless* segregation of the molecules of a gas into a warm and cold region could provide a basis for constructing a *perpetuum mobile*. For we could now make heat flow from the warmer *B* region of the vessel to the colder *A* and obtain mechanical work in the bargain, exactly as in the operation of a steam engine. But there is obviously a catch somewhere. The bargain is too good to be true as we know from the cumulative frustrations of those generations of engineers who have sought in vain to solve the problem of power for human needs on this power-hungry planet of ours. Indeed, the second law of thermodynamics which forbids all such *effortless* gains* is an embodiment of precisely this engineering impotence of ours. What then is the fallacy in Maxwell's reasoning? Is it the impossibility of such sorting demons or even of automata like self-acting miniature spring valves that Maxwell invoked?

Nothing is easier than to dodge Maxwell's paradox by affirming the impossibility of such beings. But if we did so from the very beginning instead of trying to demonstrate it, we would miss an insight into the

* We cannot get anything for nothing, not even an observation, as D. Gabor has recently reminded us.

deep connection that ties information and entropy.   To begin with, is it actually possible for the demon or any automatic device to "see" the individual molecules?   Although to decide the question we would need to probe rather deeply into the meaning of "seeing" at the molecular level, we may for our present purpose simply remark that an entity registers its existence in any "ego," whether an animate being or an inanimate automaton, by the electromagnetic radiation (of which radiant light is but a minute fragment) that it emits.   To be more precise, it is not the radiation emitted by an object that enables it to be seen but the *difference* between what it receives and emits.   For an object not only emits radiation but also receives it from others.   It is just the *difference* between radiation emitted and absorbed that makes observation of it possible.   If all objects in an environment radiated as much as they received from their neighbors, nothing could be observed there.   Now a Maxwell demon at the trap door separating the two regions *A* and *B* of our vessel would be in such an unobservable environment, where nothing could be perceived simply because he is in an enclosure where all radiation is in a state of equilibrium.   That is, every molecule of the enclosure radiates as much to the walls as it receives from the walls so that it simply fades out of the observer's ken as he has no means of distinguishing them. The demon then must be provided with a means of "seeing" the approaching molecules such as an electric torch of microscopic dimensions.   The torch is a source of radiation not in equilibrium and provides the *difference* in electromagnetic radiation required to observe the molecule.

Armed with such a microscopic torch, a source of some form of radiation not in equilibrium with its environment, the demon can "see" an approaching molecule and obtain the information he needs to decide whether or not to open the trap door.   The *decrease* in the state of "mixed-upness" of the vessel which the demon's sorting into swift and slow molecules brings about is really negentropy derived from the information that the illumination of the demon's torch yields.   But as under quantum mechanics the energy of the illuminating photon must exceed a minimum, depending on the frequency of the radiation used for observation, the demon experiences a small ' recoil every time he lights the torch to emit the speed-probing photon, exactly as a rifleman does when he fires a bullet.   As a result the demon is himself subject to a series of small random motions until, as Norbert Wiener has remarked, he falls into a "certain vertigo" that makes him incapable of clear perception. In other words, he no longer remains a Maxwell demon.

The longish detour we have followed in exorcising Maxwell's demon, rather than denying outright the existence of such a molecular homunculus capable of sorting and ordering, has a purpose. It points to a novel way of reconciling an apparent conflict between the second law of thermodynamics and the process of biological evolution. For the latter, with its continual emergence of ever new forms of life from inanimate matter via the "subvital" autocatalytic particle of protein all the way up to man as an increasingly complex crescendo of self-sustained chemical reactions, does seem to tend towards increasing organization and "patternedness" of matter. On the other hand, according to the second law of thermodynamics, matter continues to drift towards a state of increasing chaos and "mixed-upness." The physicist claims that the conflict is illusory. The march of our universe as a whole towards its heat-death doom of total disorder does not preclude the rise of order and organization here and there in some localized regions with an overcompensating loss of order elsewhere. He therefore views the irruption of biological order in myriad forms of life as a transient blossom in a vast erosion of free energy of which the most conspicuous manifestation is the enormous and continuous outpouring of stellar radiation in empty space. A tiny fraction of the immense downpour of sunshine from our own sun, for example, suffices to provide the wherewithal of all the biological order that reveals itself in the phenomenon of terrestrial life. Some biologists, however, are inclined to the view that the thermodynamic principle of order is fundamentally different from the biological principle of organization, just as the alphabetical word order of a dictionary is very different from that of *Roget's Thesaurus*. Thus if we connect two gas cylinders at different temperatures, in course of time they arrive at exact thermal equilibrium in accordance with the second law. From the physicist's point of view there was greater order or organization before the two cylinders were connected, for the swift-moving molecules were in one and the slow-moving ones in the other. After the two are connected, there is a complete shuffle between the slow and the fast-moving molecules resulting in greater chaos. But, as J. Needham has suggested, a biologist may well consider that the system has passed from asymmetry to symmetry. Needham concedes, of course, that it is a far cry from this simplest possible case of symmetry to the extraordinarily complex patterns of symmetry produced by animate beings. Nevertheless, he believes that "this apparently jejune idea" may be the first crude premonition of a "profound truth." A case in point is the spontaneous formation of crystals. As is well known, in all such processes there is a decrease in the over-all free energy or order in accordance with the second law of thermodynamics. In the physicist's sense of the term the disorder has, no doubt, increased. But "the biologist, as a student of patterns, cannot but say that there is more order and organization in the well-arranged crystal than in its homogeneous mother-liquor." No possible conflict between thermodynamical order and biological organization can therefore arise, as the two concepts are quite different and incommensurable. "Only as the time process goes on," Needham continues, "only as the cosmic mixing proceeds, only as the temperature of the world cools, do the higher forms of aggregation, the higher patterns and levels of organization, become possible and stable. The probability of their occurrence increases. The law of evolution is a kind of converse of the second law of thermodynamics, equally irreversible but contrary in tendency. We are reminded of the two components of Empedocles' world, $\phi\iota\lambda\iota\alpha$, friendship, union, attraction; and $\nu\epsilon\hat{\iota}\kappa\sigma$, strife, dispersion, repulsion."

Both points of view, however, though valid, seem to skirt the paradox rather than resolve it. The difficulty is not one of proving that there is available a vast reservoir of free energy in the form of sunshine, a small proportion of which serves as the ultimate motive power of all life on earth. It is rather *how* any given assembly of molecules which is expected when left to itself to become more and more shuffled and disordered does under certain circumstances begin to exhibit greater pattern and organization even though it is of an altogether different kind from that envisaged by the physicist. In other words, the riddle of biophysics is to discover how the fortuitous concourse of myriads of blind and chaotic molecules while obeying the laws of physics and chemistry become at the same time integrated into organic wholes capable of entropy-decreasing animated activity. The problem therefore is to trace the very real differences in the behavior of animate and inanimate matter to their objective foundations in some kind of spatio-temporal relationships. Recent researches in biophysics and biochemistry have endeavored to unmask these relationships with remarkable success. They have shown that life is a vast chain of chemical reactions catalyzed by minute substances called enzymes essentially similar to any ordinary chemical reaction in the laboratory sparked by a catalyst. The complexity of life processes that still baffles us lies in the vastness of the chain of interrelated chemical reactions but not in the nature of the individual reactions per se. Thus to account for the whole metabolic process of a single cell we require a thousand species of enzymes. The isolation of all the enzymes involved in the functioning of any particular type of cell is therefore even now an enormously complex task though by no means as hopeless as earlier biologists imagined. But all the complexity springs from having to dovetail into one consistent pattern a vast number of interrelated chemical reactions that are otherwise quite ordinary. They take place according to the usual physiochemical and thermodynamical laws and like all laboratory reactions are accompanied by certain transformations of matter and energy. Nor is there anything peculiar about this energy or matter. It is plain energy of everyday physics having no affinity with Bergsonian *élan vital* or Shavian life force, even as matter is ordinary commonplace matter.

Thus a living cell extracts the free energy it requires to maintain its inherently unstable and improbable organization by recourse to a sort of miniaturized combustion process in exactly the same way as an internal combustion engine provides us power from the chemical bonds of the fuel it burns. The only difference is the exceedingly low temperature at which it is carried out, so that life is quite literally an infinitely attenuated flame. The mechanisms of these subdued and smoldering fires of cellular combustion that sustain the processes of life have been studied in detail and found to conform in every respect to the fundamental laws of physics and chemistry including both laws of thermodynamics. Whether the cells obtain the energy they need directly from sunlight by the process of photosynthesis as do the chloroplasts of green plants, or by respiration, that is, oxidation of prefabricated complex chemical fuels such as carbohydrates, proteins, and fats as in the mitochondria of animal cells, the same well-defined molecule—adenosine tri-phosphate (ATP)—carries the free energy extracted from foodstuffs or from sunlight to all the energy-consuming processes of the cell. In both processes of energy recovery—whether in the photosynthetic phosphorylation of the plant cells or the respiratory glycosis and Krebs citric acid cycle of the animal cells— the energy-loaded electrons are carried through a series of "electron-carrier" molecules of the mediating enzymes. Although all the "carriers" have not yet been fully identified, there is little doubt that the existence of disentropic phases within living matter, that is, phases leading to decrease of entropy, is due to a kind of sorting of energy-rich electrons by a large diversity of specific enzymes, which seem to be Maxwell demons of some sort decreasing entropy by a much more complex variant of the activity of their precursor of 1871.

Just as the Maxwell demon acted on the basis of information regarding the velocity of the gas molecule, the enzyme demons of the biochemist act on the basis of genetic information of great specificity that they receive at birth in a coded form. It has recently been shown that the chief carrier of the genetic information that tells the enzyme concerned what to do in the process of protein build-up is a substance called DNA (deoxyribonucleic acid) containing nitrogen and phosphorus. Its key components are four molecular units or bases which, strung together in long chains, form DNA. Since the proteins that the enzymes help synthesize are made up of some twenty amino acids, it follows that the genetic information coded in a DNA molecule in the four-letter alphabet of its four basic components must be translated into another language whose messages are written in a twenty-letter alphabet of amino acids. The translation is achieved by permuting groups of three or four nucleotides, that is, chains of some of the four DNA bases, to obtain different sequences, each corresponding to a particular amino acid. Such an arrangement enables the four-letter DNA alphabet to spell out the entire dictionary of protein structures written in the twenty-letter alphabet of amino acids. The information encoded in the DNA molecule in this universal genetic language is conveyed to the sites in the living cell where proteins are actually assembled by means of another allied substance, ribonucleic acid, commonly called RNA. On the basis of information supplied by messenger RNA at the cellular assembly sites amino acids are sorted out and brought into proper alignment to be linked together into protein molecules in a series of chemical reactions of great specificity. The proteins so manufactured, many of which are themselves enzymes, become the mediating agencies whereby the cell synthesizes a host of other molecules—purines, carbohydrates, fats, pigments, sterols, and the like—necessary to its structure and function. The precise mechanism of protein synthesis is, no doubt, exceedingly complex and is not yet fully understood. But its underlying principle does seem to be a cyclic transformation of information into negentropy and of negentropy in turn into information somewhat akin to the actions of Maxwell's demon. It will be recalled that by lighting his molecular torch Maxwell's demon poured negative entropy into the cylinder to obtain the information he needed to carry out the segregation of the swifter gas molecules from the sluggards. Guided by this information, he opened or shut the trap door as required and rebuilt negative entropy thereby completing the cycle

$$\text{negentropy} \rightarrow \text{information} \rightarrow \text{negentropy}.$$

The somewhat analogous activity of the cellular enzymes suggests that they are threshold egos trading information (knowledge) for negentropy (power), thus demonstrating anew that knowledge is power as much *within* a molecule of life as it is *without* in the life of man.

Chapter VIII

AUTOMATIC COMPUTERS— ANALOGUE MACHINES

THE concept of information described in earlier chapters was developed by communications engineers who were concerned merely with the transmission of messages from one place to another. Whether they dealt with wire or wireless communications or for that matter with any other information-handling system like tape recording, public address, or television, the principal objective of the various gadgets devised was to reproduce the input signal with as high fidelity as possible at the output device. But, as we remarked in Chapter I, from mere hi-fi transmission of information by coding to its "processing" is but a step. The simplest machines that process the information they receive instead of merely transmitting it in its original purity are the automatic computers. Since the living brain is also a neurophysiological machine (though of infinitely greater complexity) that processes the information transmitted within it by the different sensory modalities such as vision, hearing, or touch, it is but natural that the study of computers should provide at least a foothold for a first glimpse into the nature of human intelligence. As we shall see more clearly in Chapter X, the principles underlying the organization of computers have suggested various types of mechanisms that are at work in the functioning of the animal nervous system even if they as yet elucidate its mystery in a relatively minor way. Thus the servomechanism principles made familiar by the inventions of analogue computers described in this chapter have been found to be at work in the reflex arcs of the animal nervous system, in the prevention of runaway excitation phenomena such as occur in epileptic seizures, or in the regulation of sensitivity to select aspects of the sensory input data. Likewise, digital computers, the subject of the next chapter, have suggested possible choice mechanisms that may be employed by the living brain in perception and selective attention, or what the psychologists call "set." This is why we take up now the theory of automatic computers, the first artificial automata that modern technology has enabled us to build, as a prelude to that of natural automata. Automata or automatic computers, as the name implies, are concerned with computation. Even those automata which are used to control processes, such as directing anti-aircraft fire or running an oil refinery, are really computers in that the control function in question is fundamentally the outcome of a computation. Thus the power of the anti-aircraft gun predictor to direct the gun's aim stems from its ability to compute the future rendezvous of the aircraft and the shell it fires by solving a pair of simultaneous equations. In all such cases, whether of pure computation or control via computation, the input is the data of the numerical problem to be solved, and output is the solution arrived at after manipulation of the information fed into it. There are just two ways of feeding a computer with input information. First, it may obtain such information by means of a device which translates numbers into physical quantities measured on specified *continuous* scales such as lengths, angular rotations, voltages, currents, magnetic states, forces, torques, deformations, flow, and so on. After operating with these quantities it measures some physical magnitude which gives the result. Secondly, it may employ a contrivance which operates with numbers directly in their digital form by counting *discrete* events like electrical pulses or discrete objects like the teeth of a gear wheel, as is the case, for example, with the ordinary desk calculating machines commercially known as Brunsviga and Marchand. We shall deal with digital computers in the next chapter and confine ourselves here to computers of the former type.

An example of a computer that operates with continuous magnitudes may be seen in the engineer's slide rule. Here, to multiply two numbers x and y, we read on the first scale the length corresponding to the logarithm of the number x and, by sliding to the required extent a second scale alongside the primary one, add to it the length corresponding to the logarithm of the other number y. We then read the number corresponding to the combined lengths to obtain the product xy, making use of the basic law of logarithms according to which the logarithm of any *product* (xy) is the *sum* of the logarithms of the individual multiplicands x and y, that is,

$$\log (xy) = \log x + \log y.$$

In general, continuously variable physical quantities such as distance between marks on a foot rule, angles through which a disk is rotated, electric currents in wire networks, or the quantity of light transmitted through optical media are used to represent numbers, and various mathematical operations are performed on them by means of specially contrived components exploiting some known physical law. Thus Ohm's law, $c = \dfrac{v}{r}$, connecting the current (c) flowing through a wire, its resistance (r), and voltage (v) across its terminals may be used to derive the quotient of two numbers v and r by simply measuring the current flow c through it or alternatively the product cr by measuring the voltage v. Appliances like slide rules and electrical networks, which perform mathematical operations such as multiplication and

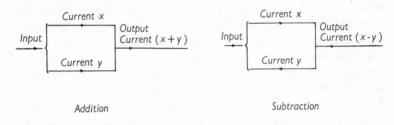

Addition   Subtraction

Fig. 15

division by reproducing analogous physical situations implementing the operation in question, are known as analogue computers.

Now any numerical computation, no matter how complex, is basically a series of additions, subtractions, multiplications, and divisions performed on numbers according to a predetermined plan. Consequently, if we devise on the analogy principle organs or components capable of performing on the representative numbers measured by the physical quantities these four basic operations of arithmetic, we can in theory solve any numerical problem by a sufficiently ingenious arrangement of such components and their proper orchestration. Since it is not difficult to realize these four arithmetical operations by mechanical, electrical, optical, and other means, it is possible in theory to make analogue machines capable of performing any kind of computation, even though, as we shall see later, we may not in every case be able to implement the theory in practice. The construction of analogue computers is therefore the art of assembling and orchestrating components that carry out the four fundamental operations of arithmetic already mentioned.

Components that execute addition and its inverse subtraction are quite easy to make. Thus we may add or subtract two numbers x and y by representing them as currents in wires and then merging them in parallel or antiparallel directions (see Fig. 15). Multiplication (xy) of two currents as well as division is more difficult; but various kinds of electrical circuitry yielding both can be devised.* If, on the other hand, we choose to represent numbers by the angles through which certain disks are rotated, instead of addition ($x + y$) and sub-

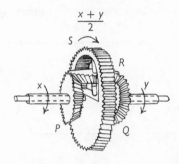

Fig. 16   Differential gear (adding mechanism).

traction ($x - y$), the operations $\dfrac{x + y}{2}$ and $\dfrac{x - y}{2}$ are offered because they emerge prefabricated out of a readily available mechanism, the so-called differential gear universally used on the back axle of an automobile. A glance at Fig. 16 showing the arrangements of its main parts indicates how it can yield the semi-sum or difference of any two numbers. It will be seen that two input shafts P and Q both mesh with a third gear R which can turn freely about an axis fastened to the inside rim of a fourth larger gear S. As a result, when we turn the shaft P by x and shaft Q by y the gear S turns by $\dfrac{x + y}{2}$. The same

* Thus currents may be multiplied by feeding them into the two magnets of a dynamometer thereby producing a rotation. The rotation is then transformed back into current which is the product of two input currents. The transformation mechanism is rather complex. It employs a rheostat to turn the rotation into resistance which is then connected to two sources of fixed but different electrical potentials.

device generates the semi-difference $\dfrac{x-y}{2}$, if only we turn the input shaft Q in the opposite direction.   Likewise, instead of multiplication xy and division $\dfrac{x}{y}$ a mechanical analogue computer uses an entirely different operation called integration.   The reason is that the product xy of two numbers x and y can be expressed as the sum of two integrals, and a very simple device—a wheel turning on a surface—enables us to accomplish integration.   To understand how such a mechanism performs this recondite mathematical operation, consider first a wheel provided with a counter which counts the number of turns it makes about its axis.   If we let such a wheel roll without slipping over a plane

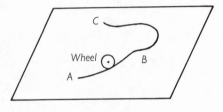

Fig. 17

surface like the floor of a room, along any curve such as ABC in Fig. 17, the number of turns the wheel makes obviously will indicate the length of the curved path it traverses.   This is precisely how an automobile milometer works.   By merely counting the number of turns the automobile wheel makes (which it converts into miles by multiplying the number of turns by a conversion factor) it measures the length of the curve the wheel traces as the automobile meanders along a winding roadway.   A rolling wheel with a counter thus provides us with a physical analogue of the simplest form of *integral*, the length of the curve ABC, which incidentally is the sum of the lengths of a very large number (n) of very small quasi-straight bits of lengths $ds_1, ds_2, ds_3, \ldots,$ ds_n into which the curve ABC may be sliced.   Thus the number of turns of the wheel equals the sum

$$ds_1 + ds_2 + ds_3 + \ldots + ds_n.$$

The smaller the elementary bits into which we fragment the curve, the straighter and more numerous they become.   We may denote the quasi-infinite sum of such elementary bits by the symbol S and write

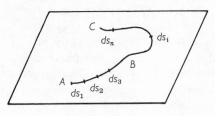

Fig. 18

it as Sds_i as an abbreviation of the phrase "sum of bit lengths typified by ds_i where i runs successively through all the integers 1 to n."

When the number of bits is increased indefinitely, with each bit length becoming vanishingly small, the limiting infinite sum is called the integral and is abbreviated as $\int ds$, where the integral sign $\int$ is merely a distortion of the summation symbol S, and ds is the length of any typical infinitesimal straight-line slice, all of which in the aggregate span the full curve ABC.

If further we make the wheel turn on a plane platform that itself rotates, we obtain what is called an *integrator*. For the new mechanism can be made to compute any kind of integral whatever. Thus consider a wheel W turning vertically around a long horizontal axle T that stretches across a rotating platform P from side to side but crossing exactly its center of rotation (see Fig. 19). The platform P rotates horizontally about a vertical shaft S. By merely turning a screw Q going through the support of the platform P it is possible to shift the center of the platform in relation to the edge of the wheel. If we turn the platform a little, the wheel pressing on it will also

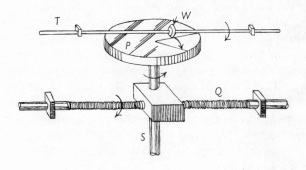

Fig. 19   Mechanical integrator.

correspondingly turn. But as the turning in the wheel induced by the turning of the platform is directly proportional to the distance of the resting wheel edge from the center of the platform, it follows that a small turning dx of the platform superimposed on a turning y of the screw causes the wheel to turn $y\,dx$. Consequently the total turning of the wheel when the platform undergoes a succession of several infinitesimal turnings $dx_1, dx_2, dx_3, \ldots$, corresponding respectively to the screw Q turning synchronously $y_1, y_2, y_3, \ldots$, is the sum

$$y_1\,dx_1 + y_2\,dx_2 + y_3\,dx_3 + \cdots.$$

This sum is precisely the integral $\int y\,dx$. A mechanical integrator is therefore merely a wheel turning on a rotating platform whose center can be shifted by turning another screw so that with an input

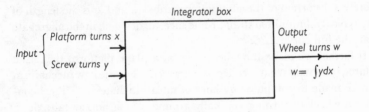

Fig. 20

of x turns of the platform and the concomitant y turns of the screw we have an output of w turns of the wheel measuring the integral $\int y\,dx$. (See Fig. 20.) The wheel-and-platform integrator we have described is a purely mechanical device. But we can make its electrical counterpart easily enough. All we need do is to replace the input variable x of the mechanical integrator by the universal variable, time, which continues to flow at all times and everywhere independently of us. In other words, an electrical integrator can be constructed provided we wish to derive the time integral of any given function. To understand how we may obtain such an integral, consider an electrical capacitor which stores up electrical charges. As current flows into it, the voltage or potential difference across the capacitor changes. But the change in voltage (dv_1) during any short period of time (dt_1) is proportional to the current y_1 and to the length of time it flows, so that

$$dv_1 = y_1\,dt_1.$$

It therefore follows that after the lapse of several such successive time intervals, say, $dt_1, dt_2, dt_3, dt_4, \ldots, dt_n$, the voltage difference will be the sum

$$y_1 \, dt_1 + y_2 \, dt_2 + y_3 \, dt_3 + \ldots + y_n \, dt_n.$$

As before, if the intervals of time $dt_1, dt_2, dt_3, \ldots$, considered are infinitesimally brief, the sum is the integral $\int y \, dt$.

Now it can be proved that the product xy of any two numbers x and y can be expressed as the sum of two integrals, though the proof will not be reproduced here:

$$xy = \int x \, dy + \int y \, dx.$$

Consequently, to obtain multiplication we require two integrators and one adding device. Integrators can be built to yield division $\left(\dfrac{x}{y}\right)$ too but we have to resort to a rather different artifice for the purpose.

Since, as we remarked before, any numerical problem, however complex, can be resolved into a series of basic arithmetic operations of addition, subtraction, multiplication, and division performed in a predetermined order, analogue computers to solve such problems can be built by proper sequencing in tandem of components like differential gears, wheel-and-platform integrators, electrical networks, and other simulators which perform these basic operations. To make such a chain of components actually work, however, we have to employ yet other kinds of catalytic devices called amplifiers and servos. If the components are electrical, such as circuits and other electro-mechanical appliances, we need amplifiers to make up the huge losses of input power used to drive them. If, for instance, a computer component transmits, say, one-tenth of its incoming power to its next neighbor in the chain, by the time the sixth component is energized its power punch is attenuated by a factor of $\left(\frac{1}{10}\right)^6$, or a millionfold. Clearly, with such prodigious enfeeblement en route, no amount of initial power input will suffice to activate the final components in the chain unless it is replenished on the way by means of amplifiers. The amplifiers used in the computers are in principle similar to their counterparts in communications engineering, though they have a more sophisticated design. In mechanical computers built out of components like wheels and gears, since the amplifiers' electrical output cannot be directly used, we have to employ its mechanical counterpart to

secure the required uplift.   Such a device is called a "servo," meaning
a mechanical slave.   It is a power-boosting invention initially called
for by the need to manipulate increasingly unwieldly rudders of ships
as ships began to grow in size.   Marine designers therefore built
steam steering engines to turn the rudders, arranging their control
valves admitting steam to the appropriate engine cylinder in such a
way as to keep the ship automatically on a fixed course, come wave,
wind, gust, or gale.   There is nothing mysterious in this type of self-
steering mechanism.   For it functions in exactly the same manner as
the erstwhile helmsman that it displaced.   As we know, the helmsman
at the ship's wheel estimates by means of a compass the deviation
between the ship's actual and desired course and uses this information
to turn the wheel to the precise extent required to correct the deviation.   The ship's self-steering servomechanism likewise uses signals

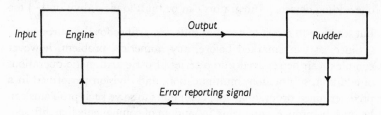

Fig. 21   Servo steer.

reporting the deviation or angular difference between the actual and
prescribed course to modify the output of the engine activating the
rudder exactly to the extent required to rectify the reported error (see
Fig. 21).   In other words, the output of the steering engine is made to
influence its own input so as to steer the ship automatically on its
prescribed course.   This feature whereby the output of a system is
used to control the source of its driving power in such a way that power
is throttled, on the one hand, if its output rises beyond a determined
point but is amplified, on the other, if the output lags, so that the
system regulates itself automatically at the prescribed level, is the
heart of all control systems simulating purposeful or teleological
behavior.   It is called "feedback" by communications engineers;
"servo system," "closed-loop" or "closed-cycle control system" by
systems engineers; "homeostasis" by physiologists; "reflex neural
circuit" by neurologists; "*petitio principii*" by logicians; "vicious
circle" by psychologists, and "boom and slump cycle" by econo-

mists. It appears even as the first act of creation in the following metaphysical limerick:

> Said a fisherman at Nice,
> "The way we began was like thees
> A long way indeed back
> In chaos rode Feedback
> And Adam and Eve had a piece."

Its underlying rationale is that physiological processes such as those that help keep constant our body temperature, blood pressure, or glucose concentration in the blood stream are as good examples of

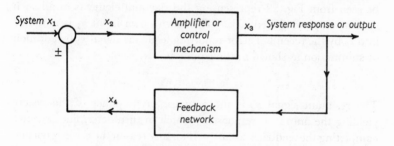

Fig. 22   Feedback mechanism.

feedback principle in action as a thermostat controlling a furnace to steady the room temperature, a computer guiding a missile to its zigzagging quarry in the sky, or a servo steer navigating a ship on its prescribed course.   In all these cases feedback adapts the behavior of the system to its desired goal by using incoming error-reporting signals to correct the error caused by outside random disturbances.

Although a powerful tool in the design of control systems, the feedback principle is not without a serious pitfall in that systems based thereon are often liable to uncontrolled oscillations or hunting.   Consider the case of ship's servo steer itself.   Because of the inevitable time lags on the one hand, between the actual state of the rudder and arrival of the input signal reporting this state to the steering engine, and, on the other, between the arrival of the signal and the completion of the rectifying action it initiates, it is quite likely that by the time the ship's rudder reaches the desired alignment it has acquired sufficient momentum to overshoot the mark.   The error then is reversed and the steering system applies the correction, but because of the time lags it may overshoot again in the opposite direction. A system liable to overshoots of this kind behaves in one of two ways. Either the amplitude of each overgo progressively diminishes and tends to die out, thereby settling the system into a stable state, or it goes on increasing, throwing the system off balance in a frenzy of violent yawing. It is the latter eventuality that often comes to pass, unless the system is cured of it by minimizing the time lags as well as dissipating the system's surplus momentum by means of some kind of braking or damping device.

In general, there has to be quite a precise tie-up between the output response of a servo system and its error-reporting input signal, as will be seen from Fig. 22 representing the essential elements of all such systems employing feedback. The servo's own input x_1 is modified into x_2 by the receipt of error-reporting feedback signal x_4 by addition or subtraction as shown in the equation

$$x_2 = x_1 + x_4$$

The resultant signal x_2 is the actuator or amplifier of the system yielding the output or response x_3 which in turn determines x_4, thus completing the feedback circuit. If for any reason the error-reporting incoming signal x_4 fails to modify its own input x_1 to the precise extent required to ensure its stability, it may spark an orgy of uncontrolled oscillations that makes the system utterly useless for any self-regulation. The phenomenon "intention tremor" wherein the patient's hand merely ends in violent to-and-fro swings in a vain attempt to pick up a cigarette is a case in point of such a failure of feedback due to an injury in the cerebellum. To avoid similar oscillatory swings in electrical and mechanical feedback systems we need a very refined sophistication of the principle, one we cannot go into here. Suffice it to remark that H. Nyquist first developed it to evolve the design of electrical feedback amplifiers. The advanced state of electrical communications theory permitted rapid advances in the art. As is often the case, these advances were applied back to the mechanical servo systems so that we now have a vast armory of devices. For example, servos may accept weak mechanical signals in the form of shaft rotations and retransmit them as powerful mechanical motions. Alternatively, they may take in weak electrical signals and transform them into mechanical motions, thus performing a dual amplifying-*cum*-conversion function changing electrical data into mechanical. Servos can also be made in sizes and powers ranging all the way from the Lilliputian transistors operating light dials to Brobdingnagian transformers lashing giant guns into a crescendo of fury but with a deftness as great as that of Arturo Toscanini's baton. This is why feedback principle is a new milestone in the theory of servo systems and automation. It has already led to automatic control processes that not only keep ships on their courses and guide missiles to their quarries in the sky but also enable us to run chemical plants, oil refineries, or steel, textile, and paper mills, as well as to process office data concerning sales, inventory, production, and payroll—all without human intervention.

As we mentioned before, all these control processes are the outcome of elaborate computations. Most of the computations handled by analogue machines in common use fall into three main categories. One group solves finite equations, both algebraic and transcendental, and in typical instances makes use of cams, linkages, gears, or variable electrical elements to establish the required connection among the given variables. A second group evaluates integrals and derivatives by means such as wheels rolling on surfaces of various shapes, or charges and currents in electrical circuits, or the quantity of light transmitted through specially prepared optical media. The third group solves partial differential equations and may employ elastic membranes, electric currents in conducting sheets of polarized light.

Despite the great diversity of problems that analogue computers enable us to solve, there are three serious limitations in the way of their further development. First, the accuracy of an analogue computer is limited by the accuracy with which physical quantities can be measured. In practice it can rarely reach a precision of about one part in 10,000 and has often to make do with much less—sometimes 50 to 100 times less precise. While this level of exactitude is adequate in some cases there are many others where it is not. Secondly, there is a definite physical limit to the extent to which the various components in an analogue computer chain can be cascaded. If it is a mechanical computer, longer and ever longer links of gears, shafts, cams, wheel-and-platform integrators, and other gadgets must be strung together. If, on the other hand, it is an electrical computer, more and more amplifiers must be provided to rejuvenate the continually fading actuating power. In the former case, the inevitable looseness in the gears and linkages, though acceptable in simple setups, will eventually cumulate to the breakdown point where the total "play" in the machine will exceed the significant output quantities, making it utterly useless. In the case of electrical computers, the random electrical disturbances called "noise" inevitable in electrical circuits, will similarly snowball to such an extent as to drown the desired signals although the breakdown stage in electrical structures is reached much later than in mechanical systems. As a result, electrical analogue computers can be built to far more complicated designs than mechanical machines. Nevertheless, each type has its own limiting complexity beyond which it will not work. For example, the Radio Corporation of America's analogue computer, Typhoon, which simulates the flight of a guided missile, closely approaches this limit, being perhaps the most complicated analogue device existing. Thirdly, an analogue computer's dependence on specific physical situations to simulate complicated mathematical functions, as with the wheel-and-platform integrator, has the consequence that when one has been found to reproduce a mathematical relation it has little or no application beyond that relation. As a result, analogue computing devices are simpler but inevitably less versatile. For more versatile computers that can take in their stride any mathematical problem and can handle equally well two vastly different situations such as the flow of heat in a cylinder and the determination of an optimum inventory pattern for a warehouse, we have to make machines that do not have to search for physical simulations to represent the mathematical operations they perform. Such machines are the digital computers which operate with numbers directly in their digital form by counting *discrete* objects or events. In essence, they attempt to reduce control and computation to a still more basic elementary level. As we saw, analogue computers reduce control functions to computation and the latter to arithmetic. Digital computers carry this reduction a stage further by resolving arithmetic, in turn, to mere counting. They thus provide a new rationale for the *double-entendre* of the verb *compter* in Anatole France's aphorism: "People who won't count do not count." This extension of the normal meaning of "count" is not peculiar to French and English. It is common to most other languages in implicit recognition by the human race of the pre-eminence of *counting* in its affairs.

Chapter IX

AUTOMATIC COMPUTERS—
DIGITAL MACHINES

AS we remarked in the last chapter, a digital computer operates with numbers directly in their digital form by counting discrete events or objects such as electrical pulses or gear teeth instead of *measuring* continuous magnitudes like distances, currents, voltages, angles, rotations, and the like, as in analogue machines. In doing so it scores several advantages over its analogue rival, among which two are pre-eminent. In the first place, not having to rely on specific physical situations to simulate mathematical operations it is certainly much more versatile even though the simplest digital machine is likely to be a good deal more elaborate than its analogue counterpart. In the second place, while the accuracy of the latter inevitably depends on that of the construction of the continuous scale on which the physical quantity is measured, that of the former relies only on the sharpness with which a discrete set of events like electrical pulses or wheel teeth can be distinguished from one another. Since it is easier to distinguish a set of discrete events than to construct a fine continuous scale, the former, that is, the digital machine, is preferable for high-precision work. Further, since it is simpler still to distinguish two discrete events than ten, digital machines constructed on the binary scale are superior to those on the decimal scale of our daily use. A digital machine on the binary principle is therefore merely an assemblage of components such as switches or relays each one of which is capable of only two states instead of the myriads that the analogue type can assume. One advantage of the simplification is that the component can be made to compute as well as decide, as will be apparent later on. This ability to decide is a particularly valuable asset in an automatic computer. For it is obviously a machine which is designed to turn out the final answer with as little human interference as possible after the initial input of data. This means that after the initial insertion of the numerical data the machine must be able not only to perform the computation but also to decide among the various contingencies that may arise during the course of the calculation in the light of blanket instructions inserted at the beginning with the numerical data.   In other words, a digital computer is also a logical machine capable of making a choice between "yes" and "no," the choice of adopting one or the other of two alternative courses open to it at each contingency that may arise during the course of the computation.   Since both its number vocabulary and its range of choices at each stage are binary, its structure need be only a bank of relays or switches each capable of two conditions—say, "on" and "off," one of which may denote the number "0" or the choice "no" and the other the number "1" or the choice "yes."   All that we have to do to make the bank of relays function in the desired manner is to ensure that at each stage the relays are able to assume positions determined by the position of some or all relays of the bank at a previous stage by incorporating a clocking device* for progressing the various stages.

The arrangement envisaged is possible because the fundamental rules of any arithmetical calculation, namely, addition and multiplication, are formally identical with those of the logical calculus, as we shall presently show.   It is because of this identity that the apparatus designed to mechanize calculation is also able to mechanize acts of logical choices, that is, decisions.   To show the identity of the logical and arithmetic calculi, consider first arithmetic.   As we explained in Chapter II, the binary system of representing numbers by using only two digits, 0 and 1, is fully as effective as the decimal system of our daily use even though it is about 3.32 times as lavish in the number of digits used to express any given number.   If we write numbers in the binary notation, we can add or multiply any two numbers by repeated applications of the following basic rules:

I.   *Addition Rules:* $0 + 0 = 0$; $0 + 1 = 1$; $1 + 0 = 1$; $1 + 1 = 10$. If we remember that while adding one to one, we get a "one" which should be "carried" to the next place, we can summarize the addition rules in Table 19 of arithmetical addition.

To read the result of the addition of any two numbers, say, 0 and 1, take the row 0 and column 1; these are easily seen to intersect at 1.

---

* There are asynchronous computers requiring no clocking arrangements but we shall not deal with them here.

The same rule applies in reading all the subsequent tables described in this chapter.

TABLE 19

Arithmetical Addition		
+	0	1
0	0	1
1	1	10

Consider now the rules of ordinary multiplication. They are as follows:

II. *Multiplication Rules:* $0 \times 0 = 0$; $0 \times 1 = 0$; $1 \times 0 = 0$; $1 \times 1 = 1$. Obviously they too can be summarized in a similar table of arithmetical multiplication:

TABLE 20

Arithmetical Multiplication		
×	0	1
0	0	0
1	0	1

There are no doubt specific rules of arithmetical subtraction and division. But both can be reduced to addition and multiplication. Thus subtraction may be turned into addition by what is called complementation. Consider, for instance, any ordinary subtraction like $542 - 123 = 419$. We may substitute for the subtrahend 123 its nines complement, that is, the number 876 obtained by subtracting from nine successively the three digits 1, 2, 3. The original *difference* ($542 - 123$) may then be obtained from the *sum* of the minuend and the complement ($542 + 876$). The latter sum is 1418. We notice that this sum is the same as the actual difference 419 except that the last digit 1 on the extreme left needs to be shifted to the units place. That is, 1418 becomes 419 by adding 1 to 8 as indicated by the arrow. In the digital computer operating with only two digits 0 and 1 the summit in our new scale of reckoning is 1 instead of nine so that we have to employ complements of 1 instead. Consequently, to subtract any binary-digit number from another, we *add* to the latter the complement of one in respect of the former with the endaround "carry" as before. Thus the difference $(1011 - 100) = 0111$ is the *sum* $(1011 + 011) = 1110$, which, with the end digit 1 carried around as indicated, becomes 0111, the desired difference. Note that one's complement of 100 is the number 011, obtained by changing 1 into 0 and 0 into 1 in the original number.

Division is iterated subtraction just as multiplication is iterated addition. By trial-and-error subtraction procedures we may actually execute any given division. It therefore follows that all the four basic arithmetic operations may be reduced to only two—addition and multiplication—or even only one, with multiplication becoming merely repeated addition. In consequence, all arithmetical operations may be reduced to patterns of alternative actions organized in highly repetitive sequences and governed by strict rules embodied in the afore-mentioned tables of addition and multiplication.

To see the close affinity between these rules of arithmetic and those of the logical calculus we may remark that in logic we deal with meaningful statements or propositions, not numbers. Nevertheless, since all such statements are either true or false, they too can be assigned truth values which can be handled in a manner very similar to that of the manipulation of numbers. Thus let us assign the truth value $T = 1$ when a proposition is true, and $T = 0$ when it is false. Every proposition such as "Socrates drank the hemlock"—which we may denote by the letter A for facility of subsequent reference—will then have the truth value 0 or 1. Obviously every proposition like A yields another, its contrary or not-A, usually symbolized as $\bar{A}$ or $\sim A$. By definition $\bar{A}$ merely affirms the denial of A so that if the truth value of A is 1, that of its denial, not-A or $\bar{A}$, is 0, and vice versa.

If we have another proposition, say, "Voltaire wrote *Gulliver's Travels*" (which we may denote by B), we can form a compound proposition from A and B in various ways. First, we may produce a compound proposition S which is considered true provided *either A or B or* both are true. In this case $S*$ is the logical *sum* of A and B and the process of obtaining it is the analogue of numerical addition. Second, we may obtain another compound proposition P which is considered true if, and only if, *both A and B* are true. $P\dagger$ is known as

* S is also known as the disjunction of A and B and is written as $S = A \vee B$ or $A + B$.

† P is also known as the conjunction of A and B and is written as $P = A . B$ or $A \wedge B$.

the logical product of A and B and the process of obtaining it is the counterpart of arithmetical multiplication. In the instances we have chosen, S, the logical sum of A and B, is the compound proposition:

$$S \begin{cases} \textit{Either} & \text{"Socrates drank the hemlock"} \\ \textit{or} & \text{"Voltaire wrote } \textit{Gulliver's Travels.''} \end{cases}$$

P, the logical product of A and B, is, on the other hand, the compound proposition:

$$P \begin{cases} \text{"Socrates drank the hemlock"} \\ \qquad\qquad \textit{and} \\ \text{"Voltaire wrote } \textit{Gulliver's Travels.''} \end{cases}$$

Since we know that A is true and B false, S will be true but P false. Consequently when the truth value of A is 1 and of B zero, that of S will be 1 and of P zero. In the same way we can easily work out the truth values of S and P, given those of A and B in any other case. In general, as mentioned earlier, for S to be true *only one* of the two constituents A and B need be true, whereas for P to be true *both A* and B have to be true. This rule suffices to evaluate the truth values of S and P, as we shall now show.

Suppose both A and B are true so that the truth values of both are 1. Since S is true when either A or B or both are true, the truth value of S is 1. This leads to the summation rule:

$$1 + 1 = 1.$$

If both A and B are false, then obviously their logical sum S too is equally false so that the summation rule now is

$$0 + 0 = 0.$$

But if only one of the two, namely, A or B, is true, then S is also true, because S is true when *either* of them is true. This leads to the summation rules:

$$0 + 1 = 1; \quad 1 + 0 = 1.$$

TABLE 21

Logical Addition		
+	0	1
0	0	1
1	1	1

We may summarize these summation rules in the table of logical addition (Table 21).

Consider now the product proposition P. Since P is true only when both A and B are true, its truth value is 1 if and only if that of both A and B is 1. In every other case P is not true and therefore its truth value is 0. This leads to the product rules:

$$1 \times 1 = 1; \quad 0 \times 1 = 0; \quad 1 \times 0 = 0; \quad 0 \times 0 = 0.$$

They may be summarized in the table of logical multiplication:

TABLE 22

Logical Multiplication

x	0	1
0	0	0
1	0	1

In defining both the notions of logical addition and multiplication of any two given propositions A and B, all that we have done is to link them by means of a conjunction—the conjunction "or" for their logical sum and the conjunction "and" for their product. But we could also couple them by means of other connectives like "if," "if and only if," "or else," and others of similar character. One of the chief tasks of logic in its study of the structure of propositions and of the general conditions of valid inference is the analysis of the properties of such logical connectives and the evaluation of truth values of compound propositions made up by stringing together a number of elementary propositions by means of them. This is the reason underlying Tweedledee's witticism: "Contrariwise, if it was so, it might be; and if it was, it would be; but as it isn't, it ain't. That's logic."

Take, for instance, the connective "if" used by Tweedledee. It is the basis of the fundamental notion of logic called *implication*. When we say that a proposition A implies another proposition B, we mean, in ordinary parlance, that "*if A is true, then B is true*," a statement which may be abbreviated as, "*B if A.*" But what if A is *not* true? In that case we, the lay folks, do not care whether B is true or false. But not so the logician. He is less concerned with the truth or falsity of elementary propositions than with their mutual relations. For his motto is the verse:

> "Not truth, nor certainty. These I forswore
> In my novitiate, as young men called
> To holy orders must abjure the world.
> 'If . . ., then . . .,' this only I assert;
> And my successes are but pretty chains
> Linking twin doubts, for it is vain to ask
> If what I postulate be justified
> Or what I prove possess the stamp of fact."

This renunciation of truth and certainty is the price the modern logician has had to pay to purge logic of the proverbial cantankerousness both Bacon and Newman obviously had in mind when the former attributed to it the power to make men contentious and the latter recollected an acquaintance's complaint that the Oriel Common Room stank of "logic." For centuries men have used logic to confute one another like Omar's two-and-seventy jarring sects; it is only recently that they have realized that the "if-then" tack of modern logic is the only way of eliminating controversy and obtaining universal assent in at least some spheres of human activity. The logician no longer asks anyone to believe in the truth of his premises. He merely asks them to agree that certain stated conclusions really do follow from them. This way of persuading may seem to be evasive, skirting as it does the truth of the matter, but it has one merit over such other alternatives as persuasion by brain washing, intimidation, invocation of sacred texts, or confusing the issues by trickery. Unlike all its other rivals it lacks completely the property of doublethink in that a logical argument cannot now be used to establish false statements just as readily as to establish true ones. This is why when the logician takes over our everyday notion of implication for further refinement he cannot afford to neglect the contingency when A happens to be false. He faces it squarely by subsuming the two cases—the case when A is *false* and B is *true* as well as the case when A is *false* and B is *false*—in the same notion of implication. Accordingly, when he says that A implies B or when he writes its symbolic shorthand $A \rightarrow B$, he excludes only the last-mentioned of the following four possible cases, namely, the coincidence of the truth of A and the falsity of B:

"B if A" or "A implies B" or "$A \rightarrow B$" means any of these three cases, but *not* the fourth.

> Case I: A true, B true;
> Case II: A false, B true;
> Case III: A false, B false;
> Case IV: A true, B false;

which is to say that the implication rules are

$$1 \to 1 = 1; \quad 0 \to 1 = 1; \quad 0 \to 0 = 1; \quad \text{and } 1 \to 0 = 0.$$

They too may be summarized in an analogous table of logical implication:

TABLE 23

Logical Implication		
$\to$	0	1
0	1	1
1	0	1

From the manner in which we have defined the extended notion of logical implication it is obvious that $A \to B$ merely means that though A is a sufficient condition for B, it is *not* necessary. For while A true suffices to ensure the truth of B, A false will imply a false B as readily as a true one. One curious consequence of this extension of our usual notion of implication is that a *false* proposition implies *any* proposition. Another is that $A \to B$ does *not* necessarily imply $B \to A$. Thus if $A \to B$, we may have the conjunction of A *false* and B *true*, case II of the four listed above, which is the one contingency expressly excluded if $B \to A$ is deemed to hold. However, since $A \to B$ requires the exclusion of case IV (A true, B false) and $B \to A$ that of case II (B true, A false), the simultaneous validity of $A \to B$ and $B \to A$ means either that A and B are both true or both false. In other words, A and B both have the same truth value 0 or 1. This

TABLE 24

Logical Equivalence		
$\equiv$	0	1
0	1	0
1	0	1

is why A and B are said to be equivalent and the notion of equivalence defined by the identity of their truth values is more restrictive than that of implication. For it is the outcome of a double implication, namely, $A \to B$ as well as $B \to A$, holding together, that is, "B if A" and "A if B," which may be compressed into the single expression

"*B if and only if A*" and written symbolically as $A \equiv B$ or $A \leftrightarrow B$. Hence the equivalence rule governing the use of the new connective "if and only if." While both 0's and both 1's combine to yield 1, the other two couplings, namely, 0 and 1 and 1 and 0, yield 0 as shown in the table of logical equivalence (Table 24).

Finally, the connective "or else" must be distinguished from the connective "or" used earlier to define the logical sum of A and B. The former is the exclusive "or" in the sense of the Latin *aut* (A or B but *not* both A and B) whereas the inclusive "or" of the logical sum has the sense of the Latin *vel* (A or B or both) so that the possibility of both A and B being true simultaneously is admitted. It therefore follows that the rules of the *aut* or exclusive sum, symbolized $A \mid B$ to distinguish it from the *vel* or inclusive sum $A + B$, would be as shown in Table 25.

TABLE 25

Logical Sum (exclusive)		
/	0	1
0	0	1
1	1	0

All the results of the various logical operations like addition, both inclusive and exclusive, multiplication, implication, and equivalence, shown in the afore-mentioned tables may be summarized in a single master table.

TABLE 26

Propo- sition A	Propo- sition B	A and B Logical product	A or B Logical sum (in- clusive)	A or else B Logical sum (ex- clusive)	B if A Implica- tion	B if and only if A Equivalence
		$A . B$	$A + B$	$A \mid B$	$A \rightarrow B$	$A \equiv B$
1	1	1	1	0	1	1
0	1	0	1	1	1	0
1	0	0	1	1	0	0
0	0	0	0	0	1	1

The table shows that all the rules of logical addition, multiplication, implication, and the like, can be mathematized by an appropriate mathematical symbolism so as to make the rules of logical reasoning formally similar to those of numerical computation in the binary scale, e.g.,

$$0 + 1 = 1; \quad 1 + 1 = 1; \quad 1 \times 1 = 1; \quad 1 \times 0 = 0; \quad 1 \to 0 = 0, \text{ and so on.}$$

This process of symbolizing logic confers on it great power. For logic deals with rules whereby we can derive from a given set of elementary propositions, called premises, another set, called valid conclusions. Now we may be able to obtain directly without the help of a symbolic notation conclusions of the simple kind which are referred to in textbooks of logic by a syllogism in Barbara like

> All men are mortal,
> Socrates is a man,
> Therefore, Socrates is mortal.

But when we are confronted with long concatenations of propositions, it is impossible to see the structure of their complicated relations without recourse to symbols. Take, for example, the proposition "*Either* not-both *A* and *B or* both of *A* or not-*B* and of not-*A* or *B*, is always true." If we try to analyze it in its linguistic form as written, it is difficult to see why it should necessarily be always true no matter what the truth values of its elementary constituents *A* and *B*. But if we use the symbolic language of logic we have been employing in writing the above tables, the proposition becomes the expression

$$\overline{A \cdot B} + (A + \bar{B}) \cdot (\bar{A} + B) \tag{1}$$

Now the truth value of *A* and *B* may be 0 or 1. If we take the truth value of *A* to be, say, 1 and that of *B*, say, 0, and substitute them in expression (1), we have

$$\overline{1 \cdot 0} + (1 + \bar{0}) \cdot (\bar{1} + 0). \tag{2}$$

Recalling that denial of a true proposition is falsity and vice versa so that $\bar{1}$ is 0 and $\bar{0}$ is 1 and applying the rules of logical addition and multiplication already cited, expression (2) becomes

$$\bar{0} + (1 + 1) \cdot (0 + 0) = 1 + (1) \cdot (0) = 1 + 0 = 1.$$

In fact, no matter what combination of truth values of *A* and *B* we choose to adopt, the truth value of the expression turns out to be 1 in every case, even when both *A* and *B* happen to be false. The compound proposition in question whose symbolic rendering is expression (1) is therefore always true as already stated. Any logical expression like (1), which is always true independent of the truth of the elementary propositions it contains, is called a *tautology*. Its logical antithesis or negation is called *contradiction*. The latter is therefore a logical expression that is always false no matter what the truth value of its constituent elementary propositions. Thus $A \cdot \bar{A}$, which asserts the truth of A as well as of not-A at the same time, is obviously always false. It is therefore a contradiction in terms. A less obvious instance of contradiction is the expression not-$(\overline{A \cdot B} + A)$, which too is always false. Thus suppose both A and B to be true. It follows therefore that the truth value of $\overline{A \cdot B}$ is 0 and that of $(\overline{AB} + A)$ is 1 so that the truth value of not-$(\overline{AB} + A)$ is 0. It can be shown in like manner that no matter what truth values we may choose to assign to A and B, that of the expression, not-$(\overline{AB} + A)$, is always zero.

To test whether any given logical expression is a tautology/contradiction or not, all we need do is to make a table presenting all possible combinations of its truth values. To do so we may proceed as follows. If the expression contains only one proposition A, we write

TABLE 27

A	1	0

(3)

If it contains two propositions A and B, we write

TABLE 28

A	1	1	0	0
B	1	0	1	0

(4)

If it contains three propositions A, B, C, we write

TABLE 29

A	1	1	1	1	0	0	0	0
B	1	1	0	0	1	1	0	0
C	1	0	1	0	1	0	1	0

(5)

Each of the Tables 28 and 29 and others of like pattern are formed from the previous one by rewriting each column of the previous one twice, first with a 1 below it and the second time with a 0 below it. After writing the table it is easy to evaluate the truth value of the given expression corresponding to each possible combination of the truth values of the constituent elementary propositions like A, B, C, and so on. Thus to evaluate $(A \cdot B) \to A$ we begin with Table 28 and use it to compute the truth values of A, $A \cdot B$, and thence $(A \cdot B) \to A$. These truth values follow from the definitions of logical multiplication and implication already given. The result is as shown below:

TABLE 30

A	1	1	0	0
B	1	0	1	0
$A \cdot B$	1	0	0	0
A	1	1	0	0
$(A \cdot B) \to A$	1	1	1	1

It will be seen that no matter what the truth value of A and B, that of $(A \cdot B) \to A$ is always 1 so that the expression is a tautology. We

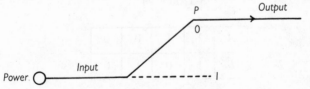

Fig. 23   Inversion switch. Current flows only if switch is in the open position denoted by 0 and is inhibited when it is in the closed position denoted by 1.

may similarly construct truth tables to prove that the expression $A + \bar{A}$, $\overline{A \cdot B} + (A + \bar{B}) \cdot (\bar{A} + B)$ and $\overline{AB} + A$ are always true.

Such symbolic evaluation of the truth values of long chains of elementary propositions by means of truth tables is grist to the computer mill because, as Shannon was the first to show, symbolic logic

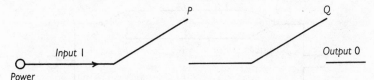

Fig. 24 Logical product circuit. Current flows if and only if both *P* and
Q switches are closed.

devised by logicians to illumine the process of logical deduction can in
fact be applied to automatic switching circuits used by communications engineers. Indeed, to each logical connective like "not,"
"and," "or," "implies," and so on, used to link elementary propositions there corresponds a circuit which is the physical embodiment of
corresponding logical processes such as negation, multiplication, addition, implication, and equivalence. Thus a simple inversion switch
P shown in Fig. 23, where the current flows only if it is open or "off,"
implements negation, that is, yields a proposition which holds only if
its denial is false. Likewise, two simple switches *P* and *Q* joined in
series as in Fig. 24 embody the logical idea of multiplication, for
both propositions, namely, "switch *P* is closed" and "switch *Q* is
closed," have to be true if current is to flow from the input *I* to the
output *O*. On the other hand, a union of two switches in parallel as
in Fig. 25 is an analogue of logical addition of the afore-mentioned
two propositions, for either one or the other or both suffice to let the
current flow in the channel. The dual control switch in a home that
enables one to put on or off a light both from upstairs or downstairs
is a slightly amended version of the parallel circuit embodying logical
addition. As we saw, the parallel circuit of Fig. 25 allows current
flow when either switch *P* or *Q* or both switches *P* and *Q* are closed.
But a household switch is an arrangement whereby either *P* or *Q* but

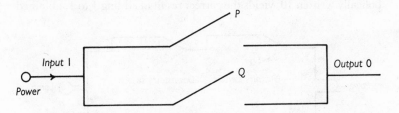

Fig. 25 Logical (inclusive) sum circuit. Current flows if either *P* or *Q* or
both switches are on.

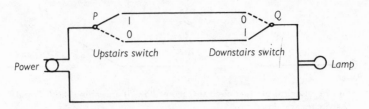

Fig. 26   Logical (exclusive) sum circuit.   Current flows if only one of the two switches *P* or *Q* is on.

not both can light the lamp.   Thus consider Fig. 26 where *P* denotes the upstairs and *Q* the downstairs switch.   If we use the symbols 0 and 1 to represent the off and on positions of the two switches and the lamp, we have the following four alternatives:

TABLE 31

Physical Indication	Symbolic Representation
P off and *Q* off = lamp off	$0 + 0 = 0$
P on and *Q* off = lamp on	$1 + 0 = 1$
P off and *Q* on = lamp on	$0 + 1 = 1$
P on and *Q* on = lamp off	$1 + 1 = 0$

In other words, the circuit is an embodiment of the exclusive or *aut* logical addition.   Incidentally it also represents arithmetical addition except that in the case of $1 + 1$ it yields 0 instead of 10.   To turn it into a binary (arithmetic) adding appliance all that we need therefore do is to provide a place for the "carry" digit 1 that is missing in our scheme.   We do so by including in the circuit a *second* lamp which lights if and only if both *P* and *Q* are on as in Fig. 27.   The joint indication of both, that is, the second lamp on and the first off, symbolically written 10, yields the correct result of adding 1 to 1, obtained

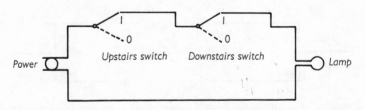

Fig. 27   Carryover circuit.

by putting on both switches. The amended arrangement therefore may be used as a binary adding machine.

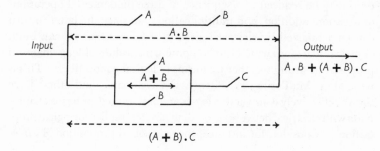

Fig. 28

Of the afore-mentioned five circuits materializing some of the basic logical operations, the first three, namely, the negation (Fig. 23), multiplication (Fig. 24), and addition (Fig. 25) circuits are fundamental. For we can build out of them others to implement *any* logical operation or their combination. Consider, for example, the logical operation of implication denoted by the symbol [→]. It can be shown that the proposition "$A \to B$" is equivalent to $\bar{A} \vee B$. For if we form the truth table corresponding to these two propositions in the manner described earlier, we find that both are true or false together no matter what may be the truth values of their elementary components A and B. See Table 32:

TABLE 32

Truth Table of "$A \to B$" and $\bar{A} \vee B$

A	1	1	0	0
B	1	0	1	0
$\bar{A}$	0	0	1	1
$A \to B$	1	0	1	1
$\bar{A} \vee B$	1	0	1	1

Likewise equivalence, which is double implication, may be defined in terms of these three operations. For $A \equiv B$ means in effect that

$A \rightarrow B$ and $B \rightarrow A$. Consequently $A \equiv B$ is merely the conjunction $\bar{A} \lor B \cdot \bar{B} \lor A$. Since all logical operations as well as their combinations may be reduced to a sequence of three fundamental operations of negation, addition, and multiplication, and since the latter in turn can be actualized by electrical circuits, it follows that we can build electrical machines which can compute truth values of long chains of propositions strung together by means of logical connectives. This is why, as A. M. Turing, W. Pitts, J. von Neumann, and others have shown, effectively constructive logics are best studied in terms of automata with electrical networks providing physical replicas of logical propositions. Consider, for instance, the compound proposition $A \cdot B +$

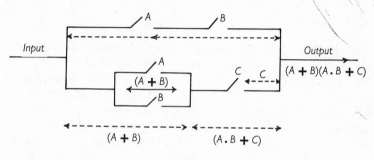

Fig. 29

$(A + B) \cdot C$. Its physical representation is the electrical network shown in Fig. 28. Viewed from the input end, the circuit is evidently the *sum* of two *products* $A \cdot B$ and $(A + B) \cdot C$ yielding the expression $A \cdot B + (A + B) \cdot C$. But the same circuit may also be viewed differently from the output end. It is then seen to be the *product* of two *sums* $(A + B)$ and $(A \cdot B + C)$. (See Fig. 29.) It therefore follows that both expressions $AB + (A + B)C$ and $(A + B)(A \cdot B + C)$ are equivalent in respect of their truth value, as we may also verify directly by evaluating the truth tables of both expressions in the manner previously described. This is one elementary instance of how a purely logical problem may be evaluated by resort to switching circuits. Another is the well-known Kalin-Burkhart logical truth calculator, which is merely a piece of complicated electrical circuitry that translates various kinds of connectives like "and," "or," "if," "if and only if," etc., into their electrical counterparts like switches in series or parallel and other similar outfits. The problem it is required to solve may be of the type given by Irving M. Copi in his *Symbolic*

Logic: "If old Henning wants to retire, then he will either turn the presidency to his son or sell the business. If old Henning needs money, then either he will sell the business or borrow additional capital, but old Henning will never sell the business. Therefore, if he neither turns the presidency over to his son nor borrows additional capital, then he neither wants to retire nor needs money." With the letters R, T, S, N, and B denoting respectively retiring, turning, selling, needing, and borrowing, the problem boils down to evaluating the truth value of the compound proposition:

$$[R \rightarrow (T + S)] \cdot [N \rightarrow (S + B) \cdot (\bar{S})] \rightarrow [(\bar{T} \cdot \bar{B}) \rightarrow (\bar{R} \cdot \bar{N})] \qquad (6)$$

As will be observed, expression (6) involves five elementary propositions (and their negations) linked together with connectives like [$\rightarrow$], [$+$], [$\cdot$], and so on. To evaluate its truth value we may adopt the procedure described earlier to test whether or not a given logical expression is a tautology. In this case, however, we have to start with a longer truth table of 32 columns to obtain all possible combinations of the truth values of five propositions. If we form such a table, we may easily derive the truth value of each bracket like $(T + S)$, $[R \rightarrow (T + S)]$, and so forth, appearing in expression (6) by repeated application of rules of logical addition, multiplication, implication, and negation. A glance at Table 33 at the end of this chapter shows how the truth value of the total expression (6) may be derived from piecemeal evaluation of its components for each one of the possible 32 combinations in question. It will be seen that the truth value of expression (6) is always 1, so that it is a tautology. The logical truth calculator merely turns this column-wise bracket-by-bracket scanning into a routine and evaluates the truth value of each combination by recourse to suitable switching circuits.

Because electrical circuits can be devised to carry out the operations of logical addition, multiplication, denial, implication, equivalence, and so on, and because of the formal *identity* of the operations of addition and *multiplication* in logic and arithmetic in the binary notation we have already noted, the apparatus devised to perform logical operations can also be made to do those of arithmetic. Such devices, that is, automatic digital computers, simulate "thinking" by making calculations in a manner entirely analogous to that of any ordinary computation of our daily life. If we analyze the process of cogitation that such a computation entails, we may distinguish a number of stages. To start with, our brain calculates by recalling the results of

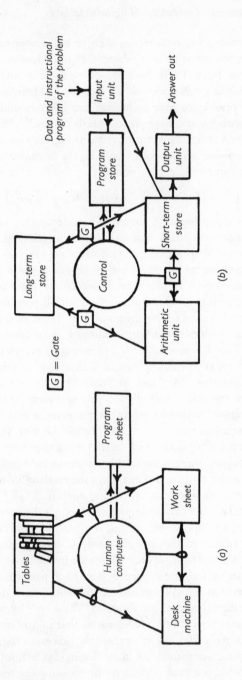

Fig. 30

multiplication and addition tables learned by heart in early childhood. It then remembers the partial answers of each such calculation either by retaining them in the head or by recording them on paper if they exceed the brain's retention capacity. In all this it also exercises a strict control over the sequence of calculations to be performed, deciding at each step what to do next. There are, no doubt, various short cuts to computation such as consulting logarithmic tables for multiplying and dividing large numbers or alternatively employing ordinary desk machines for all the four basic operations of arithmetic. But, even so, the benefit derived from these methods is not fully realized because of our own all too human incapacity to work as fast as a machine. For example, a mechanical desk machine that we may press into service adds, subtracts, and multiplies much faster than it takes us to read an answer off it and note it down on a work sheet. In a fraction of the time it takes us to hunt through a book of tables for a particular number, say, the logarithm of 567, a machine can scan the table and sense the coincidence of 567 with its logarithmic associate. It follows that if we could also entrust to a machine the progressing of the various stages of computation, in addition to each basic arithmetical operation involved in the computation, we could give our usual computational techniques a new appearance. This possibility was first clearly foreseen over a hundred years ago by Charles Babbage though its full realization came only in our own day barely twenty years ago. Babbage saw that of the two functions of the human computer programing—planning the sequence of computational work and executing the program—only the former requires intelligence and therefore cannot be delegated to a machine. But if a program can be made sufficiently explicit and detailed, then the second function of slavishly following it could be done better and faster mechanically.

A glance at Fig. 30, depicting the parallel ways in which a human and a digital computer function, shows how closely the two resemble each other. In place of the program sheet according to which the human computer proceeds and the work sheet on which he records his interim results, the digital computer has respectively a program store and a register. Instead of the desk machine for doing basic arithmetic it carries an arithmetical unit, and in lieu of the sets of tables the human computer consults or carries in his head, it has another more permanent store called memory. The human computer himself yields place to a control system, which, when one operation in the program sequence is complete, "informs" the program store and receives from it the next instruction to be carried out. This is secured by suitably operating a number of logical control organs called gates. But besides program store, register, memory, and arithmetic unit—the respective counterparts of the human computer's work plan, work sheet, sets of tables, and desk machine—a digital computer has to incorporate two additional organs not needed by the human computer. They are the input and output units. The former is required to translate the data or information from the outside world in a language intelligible to the machine, and the latter to reconvert the result produced by it in a form that we of the outside world can understand. Now the language of the digital computer is determined by the fact that it is essentially an assembly line of

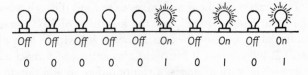

Off	Off	Off	Off	Off	On	Off	On	Off	On
0	0	0	0	0	1	0	1	0	1

Fig. 31

switches or relays each one of which is capable of exactly two states, "on" or "off," which we may designate as the "energized" or "stimulated" state and the "de-energized" or "unstimulated" state. If we denote the former by 1 and the latter by 0, any input signal in such a machine is merely a row of 0's and 1's. That is, the alphabet of the machine language in which its "words" are written is the set of binary digits 0 and 1.

As we have seen in Chapter II, numbers may be written in the binary notation that uses only two digits, 0 and 1, instead of the ten digits of the familiar decimal notation. Thus the number 21 in the decimal notation is the number 10101 in the binary notation. (We may recall that it is merely the number $1(2)^4 + 0(2)^3 + 1(2)^2 + 0(2)^1 + 1 = 16 + 0 + 4 + 0 + 1 = 21$ in the usual notation.) It may therefore be represented by a sequence of, say, ten relays or electric lamps of which the first, third, and fifth from the right are on and the rest off as shown in Fig. 31. Incidentally we choose ten lamps to enable the same setup to represent larger numbers when required. Otherwise, for the number 21 itself five lamps would do. But rows of 0's and 1's or their physical counterparts like rows of lit and unlit lamps or rows of on and off relays suffice to provide a common lingua franca for writing not merely numbers but also instructions specifying the operations to be performed on those numbers. For its "words," which are mere chains of 0's and 1's, can be stored in the computer memory, which is composed of a large number of memory boxes like mailboxes. To do so each memory box includes a row of electric lamps (or relays) wherein a "word" is stored by keeping an appropriate number of lamps on and the remainder off. In this way we can manage to place in the memory box the information-loaded word to be memorized almost as mail is put into a mailbox. The mailbox analogy extends even to the point of assigning to each memory box an "address" which again is a number like the postbox number. Thus if a computer has 128 memory boxes, each a set of lamps or relays, their respective addresses might be numbered successively from 0 to 127. This enables us to make a "word" or chain of 0's and 1's represent an instruction in addition to a number. All we need do is to adopt a code that will tell the machine whether a word stored in its memory is a number or an instruction. For example, we may adopt the following code: that if a word is an instruction, the three digits farthest left will be all 0's; the next three digits, the fourth to sixth, will denote the operative part of the instruction; the seventh digit will be 0, and the last seven the address of the operation in the instruction. The reason for reserving three digits for the specification of the operation in the instruction is that there are in all eight possible permutations of three binary digits, each of which can serve as a code for eight different operations like addition, multiplication, division, or transfer from one memory box to another, and so forth. Thus we may represent addition by 000, subtraction by 001, division by 101, and so on. The last seven digits yield $2^7 = 128$ numbers from 0 to 127 and thus can be used to denote 128 addresses of the memory boxes of our foregoing illustration. For example, the seven-digit sequence 0010101 denotes the memory box address 21, and so on. Under such a code a fourteen-digit word like 000, 101, 0, 0010101 means the instruction, "Divide the present content of the register by that of the memory box number 21," though the chain of 0's and 1's looks like a number. A similar code suffices to write even a blanket type of instruction which is somewhat more elaborate. For it does not specify any particular operation but only a ramification of possibilities among which the machine is required to choose in the light of results of its earlier computation. Thus the machine may be made to do one thing if the result of a computation happens to exceed, say, 50, and quite another otherwise. In other words, the machine itself decides what to do next depending on the result of its own computation one stage earlier. The machine therefore makes the decision on the basis of its present stage, information about which is "fed back" into its controls. This is, indeed, our old friend feedback in yet another guise. It has been utilized to spiral computer programs to increasingly dizzy if more sophisticated heights.

Having devised a way of translating the program instructions both specific as well as blanket into the machine's language, all that is required is to arrange them in a sequence and process each successively under the guidance of a master clock making each instruction nominate its own successor. This may take the form that the successor of an instruction at address x will be the command at address $x + 1$ unless the machine is otherwise ordered that it is to be found at another address y. Once the complete program of instructions as to what the machine is to do at each stage of computation is written out in the binary alphabet 0 and 1 of the language the machine can comprehend, it is no great matter to embody it in computer hardware. For there are many physical outfits that can record the input information in computer language for feeding into the machine. Earlier we mentioned the electric lamp and the relay whose unlit or "off" position denoted the digit 0 and lit or "on" position the digit 1. But there are many others. A location on a punched card can represent 0 if no hole is punched there and 1 if a hole is punched; a location on a magnetic tape can represent 0 if it is not magnetized and 1 if it is magnetized. A punched paper or magnetic tape may therefore be used as an embodiment of input instructions. If we use punched paper tape for the purpose, an electromechanical device ensures that a hole in the tape will be interpreted by the computer as 1 and its absence as 0. In the case of a magnetic tape, another appliance exists that interprets a magnetized location as 1 and a non-magnetized spot as 0. After the program is taped out, the paper or magnetic tape is run through the computer. The tape reader translates the holes or magnetic spots into 0's and 1's according to the pattern impressed thereon. The computer then calculates the result and offers it naturally in its own language, which may be recorded by making the computer punch a paper tape. Thus with an input tape which is recording received information the computer yields an output tape of "processed" information. The latter is then put into a machine that

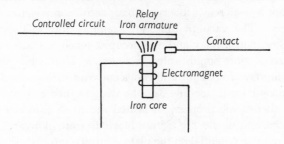

Fig. 32

does the reverse of punching, that is, looks at the paper tape and translates the message punched thereon back into the language of our daily intercourse.

Although we have explained the functioning of computers by means of such simple components as lamps and relays, they are in practice subject to several crippling limitations. First, a memory or "store" built out of them would occupy a great amount of space even if it had no more than a score or two of memory boxes. Secondly, they consume a great deal of power which finally appears as heat and must be drained off lest the computer melt. Thirdly, a memory box of electric lamps is very awkward to manipulate physically although this particular handicap is less serious in the case of relays whose reaction time is much less. For the latter can be turned on or off in less than a hundredth of a second as against a second required to reach and turn a light switch by hand. For these reasons vacuum tubes, crystal

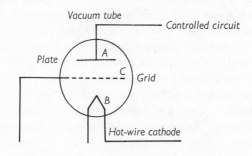

Fig. 33

diodes, transistors, ferromagnetic cores, and so forth, are better suited than lamps or even relays to serve as basic active components of digital computers.   The vacuum tube, for example, acts 1000 or 10,000 times faster than a relay and also occupies much less space because it employs a more sophisticated technique.   Thus while the relay depends for its action on the ability of a current swirling round an iron core to magnetize it (see Fig. 32), the vacuum tube employs the less tangible thermionic property of heated metals to emit electrons to obtain a current flow.   Fig. 33 is a block diagram of a vacuum tube where a positive potential on the plate A attracts electrons emitted by the hot-wire cathode B thus allowing current to flow in the controlled circuit.   It can also be inhibited by keeping the grid C at a suitable positive potential so that it traps all the electrons emanating from the cathode before they can reach the anode A.   A transistor in all essentials is a still tinier version of the vacuum tube wherein the crucial grid-to-cathode distance BC of about 10^{-1} to a few times 10^{-2} cm is further reduced by a factor of 10.   But even a transistor is by no means the ultimate in miniaturization.   Thanks to superconductivity of certain materials, whose electrical resistance vanishes completely at temperatures near absolute zero, or $273.1°$ C. below the freezing point of water, it is possible to make a yet more compact device wherein the counterpart of the grid-to-cathode distance is diminished by another factor of 10^2 to 10^3.   Perhaps a better idea of the relative compactness of these various kinds of components available for assembly into a computer can be given by quoting the number of components of different kinds that may be packed in any given space rather than the size of the operative cathode-to-grid distance in the case of a vacuum tube and its counterparts, the so-called "whisker electrodes" of a transistor and the thickness of the superconducting film in a cryotron. A cubic foot of space which could barely house a few hundred vacuum tubes could comfortably accommodate a few thousand transistors and some million cryotrons.   Despite the enormous range of sizes of these three types of components, their reaction times are pretty much the same, about one to twenty microseconds.

Unfortunately memories built out of such swift-acting components have drawbacks. They are expensive and yet have rather low storage capacities.   Because quick-in-the-uptake memories, despite their high cost, do not lead to extensive memory capacities,* most

---

* This may not be true of computers built with cryotrons but none such exist at present as swift-acting cryotrons have been invented only very recently.

machines at present carry a short-term store of small capacity made up of swift components (vacuum tubes) and a long-term store of great capacity built out of slow-acting parts (relays), with a few stores of intermediate capacities in between these two extremes. Thus arise hierarchies of memories of various levels that a large-scale modern high-speed digital computer contains. For instance, it may incorporate a sequence of four or more kinds of stores: a large and a small store with two or more buffer stores of capacities N_1, N_2, N_3, N_4 "words"† and of reaction times t_1, t_2, t_3, t_4, respectively, so that these capacities become more extensive as the reaction times become less exacting. That is, the larger the storage capacity (N), the greater the reaction time (t) of the components of which it is made. The N- and t-sequences therefore march in step. As the former progresses with $N_1 < N_2 < N_3 < N_4$, the latter advances with $t_1 < t_2 < t_3 < t_4$, ensuring that N_1 words are required at reaction time t_1, N_2 at t_2, and so on. The reaction time t_1 of the first level corresponds to the basic switching time of the machine. It is the smallest store the machine can have, usually having a capacity of at least three or more words and reaction time of 5 to 20 microseconds. The memory organs in use in the second level have memory capacities N_2 ranging from 10^3 to 10^4 words, with reaction time t_2 about 5 to 10 times that of the previous level, t_1. The capacities of the higher levels increase geometrically by a factor of 10 at each step with reaction times rising even faster. As a general rule, memories appearing earlier in the hierarchy which require the fastest components are built out of certain electrostatic devices and magnetic core arrays. For the later levels of the memory hierarchy magnetic drums, magnetic tapes, and relays are mostly in use at present.

It is the lightning speed with which even the slowest of these components acts that is the chief asset of the digital computer. Without it the machine would be much worse at its job than a human calculator, considering the myriads of basic arithmetical operations the machine has to perform before it can answer the simplest problem put

---

Their use as computer components depends on our ability to solve a number of unexpected problems that have cropped up though the cryotron principle still looks reasonably promising.

† If each word is a sequence of, say, p binary digits 0 or 1, the capacities would be $N_1 p$, $N_2 p$, $N_3 p$, $N_4 p$ "bits" or pieces of yes-no information in which memory capacities are usually measured. For obviously a word sequence of p binary digits carries p bits of information.

to it.   Thus, to obtain a single addition of only two numbers like 5676 and 4198, it may have to perform some thirty or more separate additions of binary digits 0 and 1 including "carryover" additions. For more complex problems the total number of elementary arithmetic operations would run into millions and more.   While the electronic speed of operation of the individual components enables the computer to handle them all in a few minutes or hours, the programing of such enormous numbers of individual computations may seem at first sight to be a hopeless affair.

Fortunately the situation is made a good deal easier by resort to a type of recurring or iterative process which has merely to be repeated many times with different numerical data.   Once such a routine has been found and programed, it is possible to make the machine do it over and over again as often as required, supplying the machine with numerical data for each encore of the same basic computational theme.   Consider, for example, the evaluation of the square root of any number N.   The usual method of square-root extraction we learned at school is not very suitable for mechanization.   But there exist iterative schemes which yield progressively a more exact approximation x_{i+1} from a less exact approximation x_i.   It is simply the formula

$$x_{i+1} = \frac{1}{2}\left(x_i + \frac{N}{x_i}\right). \tag{7}$$

Thus suppose we require the square root of $N = 4$.   We know, of course, that it is 2.   But if we did not know it and made any wild guess by taking it (x_1) as, say, 4, then our formula (7) provides us a much closer approximation:

$$(x_2) = \frac{1}{2}\left(4 + \frac{4}{4}\right) = \frac{5}{2} = 2.5.$$

From $x_2 = 2.5$, we may obtain a still better approximation (x_3) by a second application of the same formula, namely,

$$x_3 = \frac{1}{2}\left(\frac{5}{2} + \frac{4}{\frac{5}{2}}\right) = \frac{41}{20} = 2.05.$$

From x_3 we may derive a yet closer approximation (x_4) by another repeat performance of the same routine, so that

$$x_4 = \frac{1}{2}\left(\frac{41}{20} + \frac{4}{\frac{41}{20}}\right) = \frac{3281}{1640} = 2.0006.$$

Thus even if we start initially with a grossly inaccurate estimate, as we have done, we begin to converge upon the actual result in barely four to five iterations. Although we cannot usually foresee and program how many iterations will be necessary to obtain an answer of the prescribed level of accuracy, the machine can itself be made to determine the number of encores it need perform. For if the machine at the end of each iteration is made to square the answer and subtract it from N, then the result is obviously zero only when the answer is the actual square root $\sqrt{N}$ we are in search of. So long as the answer continues to be non-zero, the machine can easily be made to recognize the fact, and programed to continue the iteration until the difference shrinks to zero. Finally, when the difference does vanish, the machine can be instructed to stop the iterative process and proceed to execute the next instruction taped in the program.

Iterative routines are the warp and woof of computer programs. For the machine finds it much easier to execute such routines than more familiar methods of computing a required result. The routines, no doubt, often involve many more arithmetical operations than the computations, but in view of the rapidity with which digital computers execute them (e.g., a million additions per hour) such proliferation of arithmetical operations is no longer an obstacle. As a result there has come to the fore a machine's-eye view of computation very different from the usual one. First, as we have seen, the machine prefers iterative routines even if they involve far more numerous elementary operations than the more familiar and direct methods of computation we know. This is one instance where a roundabout way is quicker than a crow flight. Secondly, there has occurred an inversion of means and ends. What were formerly considered as means of achieving certain mathematical ends have in this machine age become ends, and vice versa. For example, it was usual to consider a problem as "solved" if we managed to obtain a set of linear simultaneous equations leading to the postulated result even if the number of equations happened to be too large to be soluble in any practical way. Thus, suppose we wanted to find the values of x and y for which the quadratic expression

$$(4x - 3y - 5)^2 + (6x + 7y - 19)^2 \tag{8}$$

is minimum. Since this is the sum of two square terms, it cannot possibly be negative. Consequently, the minimum value is zero, which it assumes for just those values of x and y for which both expressions $(4x - 3y - 5)$ and $(6x + 7y - 19)$ taken separately vanish. In other words, quadratic expression (8) attains its minimum value for such values of x and y as satisfy the two simultaneous equations

$$4x - 3y - 5 = 0$$
$$6x + 7y - 19 = 0. \tag{9}$$

But if quadratic expression (8) had been a sum of fifty squares of fifty linear expressions, each containing fifty variables, its minimum value *mutatis mutandis* would be given by those values of variables which are solutions of a set of fifty linear equations. We could still regard the

TABLE 33

Truth Table for Evaluating the Truth Value* of

$$\underbrace{[R \to (T + S)]}_{a} \cdot \underbrace{[N \to (S + B)] \cdot \bar{S}}_{b} \to \underbrace{[(\bar{T} \cdot \bar{B}) \to (\bar{R} \cdot \bar{N})]}_{c}$$

Elementary Proposition	Truth Value													
	Column Number:													
	1	2	3	4	5	6	7	8	9	10	11	12	13	14
R	1	1	1	1	1	1	1	1	1	1	1	1	1	1
T	1	1	1	1	1	1	1	1	0	0	0	0	0	0
S	1	1	1	1	0	0	0	0	1	1	1	1	0	0
N	1	1	0	0	1	1	0	0	1	1	0	0	1	1
B	1	0	1	0	1	0	1	0	1	0	1	0	1	0
$T + S$	1	1	1	1	1	1	1	1	1	1	1	1	0	0
$R \to (T + S)$ (or a)	1	1	1	1	1	1	1	1	1	1	1	1	0	0
$S + B$	1	1	1	1	1	0	1	0	1	1	1	1	1	0
$N \to (S + B)$ (or b)	1	1	1	1	1	0	1	1	1	1	1	1	1	0
$a \cdot b$	1	1	1	1	1	0	1	1	1	1	1	1	0	0
$\bar{S}$	0	0	0	0	1	1	1	1	0	0	0	0	1	1
$a \cdot b \cdot \bar{S}$	0	0	0	0	1	0	1	1	0	0	0	0	0	0
$\bar{T}$	0	0	0	0	0	0	0	0	1	1	1	1	1	1
$\bar{B}$	0	1	0	1	0	1	0	1	0	1	0	1	0	1
$\bar{T} \cdot \bar{B}$	0	0	0	0	0	0	0	0	0	1	0	1	0	1
$\bar{R}$	0	0	0	0	0	0	0	0	0	0	0	0	0	0
$\bar{N}$	0	0	1	1	0	0	1	1	0	0	1	1	0	0
$\bar{R} \cdot \bar{N}$	0	0	0	0	0	0	0	0	0	0	0	0	0	0
$\bar{T} \cdot \bar{B} \to \bar{R} \cdot \bar{N}$ (or c)	1	1	1	1	1	1	1	1	1	0	1	0	1	0
$a \cdot b \cdot \bar{S} \to c$	1	1	1	1	1	1	1	1	1	1	1	1	1	1

problem as solved because a set of fifty linear equations is in principle soluble by recourse to the well-known determinant method. But such a solution is a mere figure of speech, as the actual values of fifty unknowns of a set of fifty linear equations are buried as deep under the dead weight of fifty-one fifty-order determinants as in the original fifty equations, it being no simple matter to evaluate even a single one of them. Under such circumstances, because of the computing facilities now available it is more feasible to think the other way around, that is, to regard the solution of the simultaneous equations being reduced to the minimizing of a quadratic form. In other words, given any set of simultaneous equations like the two shown

TABLE 33 (Contd.)

TRUTH TABLE FOR EVALUATING THE TRUTH VALUE* OF

$$\underbrace{[R \to (T + S)]}_{a} \cdot \underbrace{[N \to (S + B)}_{b} \cdot \bar{S}] \to \underbrace{[(\bar{T} \cdot \bar{B}) \to (\bar{R} \cdot \bar{N})]}_{c}$$

						Truth Value											
						Column Number:											
15	16	17	18	19	20	21	22	23	24	25	26	27	28	29	30	31	32
1	1	0	0	0	0	0	0	0	0	0	0	0	0	0	0	0	0
0	0	1	1	1	1	1	1	1	1	0	0	0	0	0	0	0	0
0	0	1	1	1	1	0	0	0	0	1	1	1	1	0	0	0	0
0	0	1	1	0	0	1	1	0	0	1	1	0	0	1	1	0	0
1	0	1	0	1	0	1	0	1	0	1	0	1	0	1	0	1	0
0	0	1	1	1	1	1	1	1	1	1	1	1	1	0	0	0	0
0	0	1	1	1	1	1	1	1	1	1	1	1	1	1	1	1	1
1	0	1	1	1	1	1	0	1	0	1	1	1	1	1	0	1	0
0	1	1	1	1	1	1	0	1	1	1	1	1	1	1	0	1	1
0	0	1	1	1	1	1	0	1	1	1	1	1	1	1	0	1	1
1	1	0	0	0	0	1	1	1	1	0	0	0	0	1	1	1	1
0	0	0	0	0	0	1	0	1	1	0	0	0	0	1	0	1	1
1	1	0	0	0	0	0	0	0	0	1	1	1	1	1	1	1	1
0	1	0	1	0	1	0	1	0	1	0	1	0	1	0	1	0	1
0	1	0	0	0	0	0	0	0	0	1	0	1	0	1	0	1	0
0	0	1	1	1	1	1	1	1	1	1	1	1	1	1	1	1	1
1	1	0	0	1	1	0	0	1	1	0	0	1	1	0	0	1	1
0	0	0	0	1	1	0	0	1	1	0	0	1	1	0	0	1	1
1	0	1	1	1	1	1	1	1	1	1	0	1	1	1	0	1	1
1	1	1	1	1	1	1	1	1	1	1	1	1	1	1	1	1	1

*The truth value of each elementary expression may be worked out by the application of the rules of logical addition, multiplication, negation, and implication described in the text.

in (9), we can derive a quadratic expression like (8) by simply adding the squares of their left-hand sides. The problem of solving the equations is then simply that of finding those values of the variables which minimize the quadratic expression so derived. In a similar manner the older method of solving a differential equation was to approach the solution through a sequence of functions each of which satisfies the equation but not all the initial or boundary conditions. However, in view of the computing facilities now provided by computers, the final solution is approached through a sequence of functions each of which satisfies all the boundary conditions but not the differential equation. The reason is that many forms which appear unduly complex according to the older point of view are very suitable for the new methods of numerical computation by calculating machines. Then again it is likely that the digital computer may also induce a more fundamental revision of the outlook of the mathematical physicists. For example, such physicists have hitherto adhered to the hypothesis of continuity of space and time not so much because of its logical validity, which a deeper analysis of Zeno's paradoxes has shown to be fictitious, but because of its mathematical convenience in that differential equations are usually more tractable than difference equations, at least analytically. But the increasing use of digital computers to solve such equations, which it does by turning them into difference equations, may well lead to the abandonment of the hypothesis or at least erode its main justification, that of mathematical facility or expediency. All this, however, is a small change in the transvaluation of old mathematical values required for the next significant advance in computer theory. For what exists today is merely "an imperfectly articulated and hardly formalized body of experience" underpinned by formal logic. Its debilities, in particular those of formal logic, begin to be evident when we compare the artificial automata with their natural counterpart, the human brain. A deeper mathematical study of both bids fair to inaugurate a mathematical revolution far more profound than the invention of the decimal system or the calculus, as we shall see in the next four chapters.

Chapter X

THE COMPUTER AND THE BRAIN

THE feats of control and communication that computers nowadays perform have earned them the nickname of "giant brains." The sobriquet is well deserved because of their ability to imitate, with a speed, skill, and accuracy far beyond the powers of any genius alive, certain processes of thought, though of a routine, repetitive, and rudimentary kind. But in reality a fair comparison of the powers and debilities of these artifacts vis-à-vis their natural model, the living brain, would show that the "giants" are yet in many ways mere playthings beside the "midget" they aspire to simulate. Consider, for instance, the basic component of the human nervous system, the nerve cell or the neuron, which is to the brain what a vacuum tube or a transistor is to the computer. It is still a marvel of compactness and economy. For reasons that will be apparent later on, it beats in respect of size its artificial analogues, the vacuum tube and the transistor, the basic components of computers, by a factor of a hundred to a thousand million. Even if we succeed in replacing the transistor with the more miniature superconducting cryotron—a promising possibility beginning to open up and yet to be fully realized —the lead factor will still be a hundred thousand to a million. This is why artificial imitations of living brains tend to be much more lavish in the use of space than their natural prototypes, though making up for their extravagance by being enormously swifter. But the swiftness in turn entails another handicap in that they require a lot of power to activate them. Whereas the energy dissipation by a typical neuron is barely one-billionth of a watt, a quantity so vanishingly small as to be for all practical purposes a synonym for zero, a typical vacuum tube would dissipate 5 to 10 watts and a transistor one-tenth of a watt. Once again the neuron is a more efficient unit outpacing its synthetic rivals by factors as high as those already encountered.   It is true that a superconducting cryotron in future computers may perhaps consume as little as one hundred thousandth to one millionth (10^{-6}) of a watt. But even so, the natural neuron would still be ahead of it a few ten thousand times.   Because of the prodigal per capita rate of consumption of both space and power by the computer components, the artificial automata reach their packing peaks much earlier than the natural ones.   For example, the giant computer, ENIAC, which is an assembly of about 18,000 vacuum tubes, already weighs 30 tons and gobbles up 150 kilowatts of power, a formidable pack for a repository of only 700 "bits" of information.   On the other hand, the human brain, which contains at least a few billion neurons and is therefore *functionally* a millionfold as *large*, having a memory capacity of about 1,000,000-000,000,000 or 10^{15} bits, weighs barely a pound and is compact enough to be lodged comfortably within the human skull, consuming in all about 10 watts.   Even the average human brain like that of Goldsmith's village schoolmaster therefore accommodates within a liter of volume a million times more bits of information than the present population of the world.   Had this finding of modern cybernetics been known in his day, Goldsmith would no doubt have been more respectful of the master's mental prowess in his description of the "rustics rang'd around" gaping at their idol's head:

> And still they gaz'd, and still the wonder grew
> That one small head could carry all he knew.

Obviously the giant electronic "brains" of today have a long way to go before they match the performance of even the village master's head. This is why computer-machine theoreticians and mathematicians like Norbert Wiener, Walter Pitts, and A. M. Uttley have joined hands with neurophysiologists like A. Rosenblueth, W. S. McCulloch, and D. A. Sholl to plumb the secrets of the brain's amazing economy and wisdom.

Neurophysiologists have shown that the material basis of both its wisdom and its economy is the network of the neural communications system which keeps the organism informed of the state of affairs in its external and internal environment so that it may adapt itself in time to the changing vicissitudes of its habitat for survival in a hostile world notoriously red in tooth and claw.   "To beware one must be aware" has been the leitmotif of life ever since its emergence.   During the eons of its slow climb out of the Pre-Cambrian mud and slime it has gradually perfected a mechanism of acquiring awareness of the potentially dangerous or beneficial situations in its surroundings. Such a mechanism is what Sir Charles Sherrington has called the "enchanted loom" of neurons or nerve cells, whose function is to transmit messages from the sense organs to the central nervous system and from the latter to the muscles and glands. The incoming or "afferent" messages are decoded and the outgoing or "efferent" messages framed or coded in the brain and its offshoot, the spinal cord, the nerves merely acting as conducting channels between the periph-

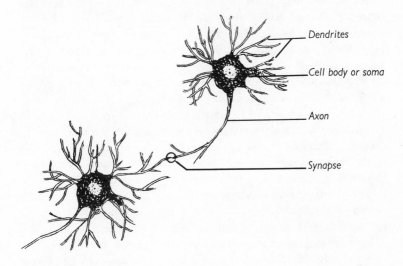

Fig. 34

eral outposts of the body and the central nervous system within. The whole purpose of the nervous system is thus to bring afferent neurons into touch with efferent ones in order to bind one part of the organism to another in such a way that what the environment is doing to the organism at one place may evoke an appropriate response in other parts, such as stimulating or restraining movement in the muscles or secretion in the glands even though they may be situated elsewhere. This is why the nervous system has often been viewed as a sort of mammoth automatic telephone exchange whose key function is to effect the correct neural connections by switching and reswitching communication lines from one to another. Although the unique unmodifiable circuitry demanded by such a model is not supported by anatomical and neurophysiological evidence, it is nevertheless beyond dispute that the afore-mentioned binding or coordinating action of the brain on which we depend for our sensation, motion, understanding, perception, and consciousness is the outcome of myriad messages flashed back and forth along the neurons. What then is this wonder stuff of a neuron, which is the very warp and woof of the Cartesian *cogito ergo sum* that makes us what we are?

If we observe a neuron with the naked eye, it appears as a long cord of whitish, translucent material. The large nerve trunks such as the sciatic in man may be half an inch in breadth, though the ultimate branches are scarcely visible thin gossamer threads. Under the microscope the gossamer thread is seen to be made up of a number of fibers about one thousandth millimeter in diameter, each of which acts as an independent channel. Consequently a nerve of medium size may contain several thousand fibers of different lengths varying from a few hundredths of a millimeter to a few meters. The reason is that while some are connected to inside glands close at hand, others have to reach the distant sense organs on the outskirts of the body such as eyes, ears, limbs, skin, and muscles all the way from top to toe. This is why there are many kinds of neurons classified variously according to situation, shape, size, number and length of branches, and so on. But despite their diversity, they are basically alike in that they consist of two essential parts, first, the soma or nerve-cell body and, second, its offshoots or branches which are nerve fibers (see Fig. 34). Although the soma of a neuron may ramify into one or several branches, one and only one of them is distinguished as the axis cylinder process or axon, the others being called dendrites or end feet. What distinguishes the axon from the others is that when the neuron itself "fires" it is the axon that carries the *outgoing* nerve impulse away from the soma. Its other dendrites, on the other hand, convey towards the soma the *incoming* impulses sent by other neurons in its vicinity. Again, although a single axon conducts the impulse away from the soma, it can convey it to several other adjacent neurons. The reason is that as we approach its terminal the axon branches freely into several terminal structures or end bulbs which impinge on the dendrites of other adjacent neurons across some intervening junctional material. This junction is called a synapse. The synaptic arrangement by which communication is established between contiguous neurons varies considerably in detail in different situations. In some cases the axon of one neuron and the dendrites of the next both break up into

a finely interlaced mass of separate branches, comparable to the inter-
lacing of branches of trees growing close together.   More often there
is a plexus or basket of fine axon branches surrounding the body of the
second neuron and terminating in small buttons or end bulbs applied
closely to the cell body or its dendrites.   However, in all the various
anatomical arrangements the function of the different types of
synapses is fundamentally the same.   In each case under certain con-

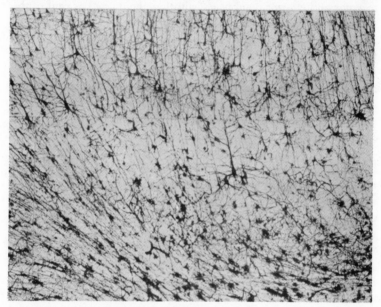

Fig. 35   Sensory motor cortex of cat (section).   (From *The Organization
of the Cerebral Cortex*, by D. A. Sholl, Methuen & Co. Ltd., London, 1956,
Plate 3.)

ditions an electrochemical disturbance or impulse fired in a neuron is
carried at a fixed speed along its axon across synapses to the cell
bodies or somas of *one or more* adjoining neurons.   In other words, a
neuron is a single-lane channel of an axon with one or more outlets
into its neighbors delivering to them the impulse it originates.

It is by means of the passage of such an impulse along its axon
across synapses with other adjacent neurons that it tends to stimulate
or inhibit them.   This general description applies to the "inter-
nuncial" or central neurons that link one neuron with another.   But,
with one modification to be presently explained, it holds for sensory

(afferent) and motor (efferent) neurons as well.   In the former case its cell body is excited by an external stimulus, for example, light impinging on a retinal receptor cell or pressure on a special-purpose capsule in the skin.   In the latter, the impulse originating in the cell body travels along its axon to its end bulbs terminating in a muscle fiber or a gland and thus tends to activate or inhibit the muscle contraction or gland output.   There are perhaps 100 million of these receptor and effector neurons constituting about one per cent of the ten billion neurons in the brain.   The passage of neural impulse in all the three is unidirectional in accordance with Sherrington's law of forward movement, so that a synapse acts like a valve blocking any backflow in the reverse direction.   Further, since the glial cells that largely fill the space between parallel neurons insulate one from another like a sheath of insulated cables in a casing, the electro-chemical impulses along parallel neurons continue to pass independently without getting into each other's way or short-circuiting.

A mesh of billions of neurons interlinked with one another in the afore-mentioned manner is naturally an amazing piece of biological circuitry that we are yet far from understanding.   Fig. 35, which is merely a small section of the sensory motor cortex of a cat, gives a glimmer of the complexity of neural connectivity in a tiny corner of the brain.   It shows the cell bodies or somas of the cortical neurons with their dendritic branches interconnected by thin fibers, the axons, which unfortunately do not show because of the staining method used in making the picture.   Since, however, this method stains only about one-seventieth of the neurons, the neural network shown has to be multiplied seventy times in order to get an idea of the real intricacy of the neural interconnections in the region under view.   In the cerebral cortex of man, which is an even more extensive convoluted sheet of neural fields, a single axon of a neuron may influence as many as five thousand others and each neuron on the average holds within its own dendritic grasp about 100 somas of other neurons.   The ten billion neurons of the human nervous system thus form a meshwork with about one thousand billion internal synapses.   There are therefore several hundred times more neural connections in the living brain than there are people on the earth.   It is indeed a marvel that such a complex neural circuitry continues to function excellently every day of man's life, from guiding him to suck his mother's breasts at birth to helping him to learn all the skills of his later life, while at the same time regulating the blood circulation, respiration, digestion, and all the myriad physiological processes of his body. It is no doubt this astronomical multiplicity of connections that confers on the animal nervous system the ability to receive along parallel neural pathways a vast diversity of messages at one time and to pick up and process simultaneously the large amount of information brought by them. Such synchronous handling of information by the brain enables it to attend to several things simultaneously. The brain therefore scores yet another advantage over artificial automata, which by and large function serially, executing program instructions successively but only one at a time. Another advantage of myriad parallel lines of neurons is that their existence secures through lavish redundancy immeasurably

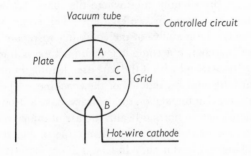

Fig. 36

greater security against possible damage to any part of the nervous system. Thus recent learning experiments conducted on octopuses have shown that even if 90 per cent of the five and a half million neurons in the inferior frontal and subfrontal lobes of their brain are destroyed, the animals still manage to retain their capacity to learn a tactile discrimination between two nearly similar objects. In fact, they may be taught some of the simpler tasks in tactile discrimination with even as few as 35,000 neurons left. There are reasons to believe that such replication or redundancy of machinery in the nervous system is the general rule in all animals including Homo sapiens. This is in sharp contrast with artificial automata, where replication and redundancy have perforce to be avoided in view of their comparatively extravagant consumption of both space and power. As a result they are infinitely more prone to total damage even by stray injury to or malfunction of a few components. Obviously, computers cannot possibly safeguard themselves against such eventualities by abundance of redundancy on any scale comparable to that adopted by natural automata unless the size of their basic component, the transistor, is reduced at least a billion times. Perhaps with the use of the cryotron or some other device we will reach the ultimate in miniaturization of computer componentry, securing a thousandfold reduction in their present size. The neuron will then still continue to outstrip it by a factor of one hundred thousand to a million. Any further significant diminution is extremely unlikely because of the very nature of the materials (chiefly metals) used as computer hardware. Their employment requires that the metals be packed rather closely and yet be separated at certain critical points by a vacuum as, for example, in the vacuum tube where the space AB between the electrodes must be a vacuum (see Fig. 36). This entails yet another debility, namely, the inability of the computer to repair itself when damaged. If perchance a computer vacuum tube is fractured, the vacuum is destroyed and with it the part itself,leading in most cases to a permanent and total breakdown of the machine. The biological materials in natural automata, on the contrary, have a strong tendency to restore themselves to normal health in case of injury or any other ordinary malfunction. A ruptured membrane or blood vessel, for instance, will quickly heal itself. In fact, if living materials had been even partially as refractory to self-restoration as the computer componentry, life could never have survived the hazards of its origin and subsequent career. The vastly greater economy, wisdom, initiative, memory, safety, synchrony, stability, and self-healing capacity of the natural automata vis-à-vis their artificial simulators therefore stem in the last resort from the over-all superiority of biological materials over the computer hardware.

Nevertheless, despite all the advantages of the human brain, the basic ingredient of which it is made, the neuron or nerve cell, is quite a humble sort of entity. It is no different from that present in almost any other animal, be it the lowly rat or even the lowlier squid, cuttlefish, and octopus. The neuron in all these animals conducts an impulse whose initiation and passage make up a complex process. Although the process has several aspects—physical, chemical, mechanical, and electrical—its most overt manifestation is the propagation of an electrochemical disturbance in the axon. In its normal unstimulated or resting state the axon may be regarded as an extended cylinder of intracellular fluid of special composition enclosed in an outer sheath of an exceedingly thin lipoid protein film or membrane hardly a thousandth of a millimeter wide. When the fiber is stimulated the membrane breaks down and becomes highly and selectively permeable at the point of stimulation. The result is that the original state of ionic electrical equilibrium is disturbed and local currents consisting of the influx of sodium ions followed by the outgo of potassium ions begin to flow. The region of disturbance affects the next portion of the axon, and so on all along the nerve fiber. Thus, while the nerve impulse normally originates in or near the soma or body of the nerve cell, its propagation occurs all along the axon. It is true that the initial stimulation that sparks the impulse has to be of sufficient intensity or otherwise it will not "fire" at all. But once the stimulus exceeds the sparking threshold characteristic of the neuron, the impulse generated is independent of the details of the process that gave rise to it, very much as a pianoforte note remains the same regardless of how the key was struck. In other words, although a neuron undergoes a series of complicated changes before it transmits an impulse on receipt of a stimulus, the final upshot is an "all-or-none" affair analogous to the binary or two-way behavior of a switch, relay, or vacuum tube which too, for all effective purposes, is either on or off. The natural neuron therefore acts on the digital principle much as the artificial components in digital computers do. But it scores over the latter an important advantage in that the neuron cell acts on a molecular level in contrast to the grossly molar dimensions of its "hardware" analogues. The reason is that the cell membrane of the axon, whose rupture starts the electrical impulse and thus provides the basis of its digital action, is only a thousandth of a millimeter, an almost molecular magnitude as the "large" protein molecules go. On the other hand, the corresponding "grid-to-cathode" distance *BC* of Fig. 36 in the case of the vacuum tube is 10 mm, and even the "whisker-electrodes" distance in its tinier version, the transistor, 1 mm. The *linear* dimensions of the crucial neural part is thus shorter than that of the artificial components by a factor of at least 10^3. It therefore results that a neuron is more economical of space usage than the corresponding artifacts by a factor of $(10^3)^3 = (10)^9$, or a thousand million. For the same reason its power dissipation is equally low.

While these advantages of economy of space and power consumption are primarily due to the molecular dimensions of the neural materials (the axon membrane), there are other advantages whose bases are quite different. Thus a neuron is much more versatile in that it can also respond to such continuously varying attributes of external environment as heat, light, sound, and pressure as well as to physical and chemical changes brought about by the blood stream and other humoral media within the organism. A neuron has therefore also to transmit the values of continuously varying quantities such as blood pressure, temperature, sugar content, and the like. A neuron that has to do so still transmits nothing but individual "all-or-none" impulses. But it manages to encode the continuously varying magnitude in question by means of a process of frequency modulation. What really happens is this. After the neuron has transmitted the first impulse by a rupture of its membrane, it has to recover itself before it is loaded to "fire" again. The rupture of the neuron's membrane is healed and the neuron comes back to its resting state recharged to trigger a second impulse. All this takes a finite though small time, called the recovery time. If another stimulus were to be applied before the lapse of the recovery time, it would have practically no effect. But the recovery time itself is a function of the environment in which the neuron happens to find itself. By correlating the magnitude of its recovery time with the value of the continuous variable in the stimulating environment the neuron is in effect able to report the latter. Thus, consider a neuron exposed to the stimulus of a continuously varying pressure. Since the pressure is uniformly present at all times, the stimulating influence is a continuous one. But although the stimulus is acting permanently, the neuron fires intermittently because of its need to recover after each coup. How intermittently it actually does fire depends on the ambient pressure to which it is exposed. For example, it may happen that whereas under high pressure its recovery time is, say, 10 milliseconds, under low pressure it will prove to be 15. In other words, the former value of the pressure is given away when the neuron transmits an impulse every 10 milliseconds, or with a frequency of $\frac{1000}{10} = 100$ impulses per second, and the latter by a pulse frequency of $\frac{1000}{15} = 66$ per second. The pulse frequency therefore is *not* the actual value of the pressure but manages to mirror it by marching in step with it. Although the alternative of amplitude modulation is also capable of reporting the pressure, nature seems to have preferred frequency modulation. The reason is its greater imperviousness to distortion by "noise," that

is, background random but unintended effects. For whereas in amplitude modulation the weaker the signal the greater its sensitivity to
noise, in the case of frequency modulation the weaker the signal the
longer the interval between signals, and vice versa, so that it acquires
a natural immunity to noise.

A neuron armed with relatively noiseproof frequency-modulation
capacity thus becomes a dual-purpose component. For despite a
genuine built-in "all-or-none" behavior it also acquires the capacity
to report continuously varying magnitudes in addition to discrete
numbers. But it secures the discrete-into-continuum transition by a
method all its own. A computer, if it operates with continuous
magnitudes, exploits some physical law for computation. For
example, an analogy machine exploits a physical law to express continuous magnitudes. The digital computer, on the other hand, uses
rows of "on" and "off" electric bulbs, relays, tubes, transistors, or
what have you, to express numbers in the positional (binary) system
where the position of the digit is of greater significance than its own
intrinsic value. Although, like the relay and tube, the neuron is
digital in action, either "firing" or "quiescent," it discards the much
more efficient and compact positional system of expressing numbers in
favor of the more primitive method of counting. It counts the
frequency of pulse transmission and modulates the continuously
varying value of pressure it has to report by correlating it with the
pulse count it has made. The reason for the neural preference for the
primitive counting method to the more sophisticated positional system
of denoting numbers lies in its greater safety against error. For
example, in writing a large number like a million we require seven
digits in the decimal system and about twenty in the binary system of
notation. Consequently a succession of twenty binary digits or
equivalently twenty neural "firings" would suffice to express the
number. But a single error occurring in the twentieth place or anywhere close to it would almost completely vitiate the entire result.
On the contrary, if it were transmitted the hard way by counting a
million "firings" one by one, a few errors would affect the result only
marginally. Because of the hypersensitivity to error of the positional
system adopted in the artificial automata, where even a single error
may spell disaster to the final outcome, artificial automata are in need
of elaborate error-detecting procedures called "debugging" before
they can be trusted to yield reliable results, or for that matter any
result. The natural automata, however, are not at all allergic to a

few errors and malfunctions because of their lavish resort to redundancy through counting and replication by means of parallel neural networks. Perhaps, as von Neumann has surmised, there are other deeper reasons for nature's choice of the counting method besides its obvious safety, such as the greater simplicity of encoding-decoding facilities required by counting than those demanded by the positional method. But there is more substance in the matter than meets the eye at first sight. It seems that the nervous system resembles any artificial automaton in that both incorporate a logical part in which arithmetical processes play no role *and* an arithmetical one whose essential function is computation with possibly some others wherein the two intertwine. But the chains of logical and arithmetical operations and of their mélange which are employed in the computer are far longer than those used by the brain, with the result that its computational precision is greatly inferior to that of the machine. Thus any artificial computer having to work under conditions of complexity even remotely approaching that facing the human brain would require 10- to 12-decimal precision at least. For the chains of computation are long, and rounding errors or approximations made during its course add up. At each step of the computation the computer has necessarily to round off the last digit, with the result that as the steps proceed apace the last digit becomes less and less precise. It can be shown that after 100 such steps the last digit becomes worthless. A stage then arrives when the next-to-last digit begins to be affected till after $(100) \times (100) = (100)^2 = 10,000$ successive steps, the last two, and after $(100)^3$ or $1,000,000$ steps, the last three digits are totally unreliable, and so on for the last four, five, and other digits. The computer must therefore carry more digits than are actually significant to safeguard against serious but inevitable deterioration of precision in the course of a long calculation. But with the frequency-modulation method of reporting numbers resorted to by the nervous system, any such precision (10 to 12 decimals) is altogether out of the question. The reason is that the pulse frequencies employed in the modulation process have a limited range between 50 to 200 pulses per second. As a result the method can reach an accuracy of barely two to three decimals. It is indeed a marvel that the human brain can perform all the complex tasks it does on such a low level of precision. No known artificial automaton can operate reliably and significantly on so crude a computational basis. Since the longer the calculation the lower the accuracy of the end result, the computer has to safeguard itself by operating on a much higher level of precision than the brain. But the brain apparently overcomes the handicap of its computational clumsiness by resort to a vastly superior logic. As von Neumann has surmised, the brain is somehow able to trade a deterioration in arithmetic for an improvement in logic. He has suggested that besides counts or statistics of pulse frequency-modulating magnitudes other statistical attributes of such trains of pulses such as correlation coefficients of various kinds might also be transmitting information. If so, it would seem that the language of the brain is not the language of mathematics as we know it today. In this respect we may well be as ignorant as the Greeks, who located the mind in the midriff. It is therefore likely that whatever language the brain is using is much less involved and structurally simpler than the languages of arithmetic and logic we consciously use. For otherwise it could hardly be equal to the complex tasks it takes so comfortably in its daily stride. This is no mere inference from a hypothetical premise. There is steadily accumulating direct neurological evidence in its favor. Thus the retina of the human eye performs a considerable reorganization of the visual image as perceived by the eye, all of which is accomplished at the point of entry of the optic nerve by means of only three successive synapses, that is, in three consecutive logical steps. Its transcription in the logical language we normally use would certainly involve many more steps.

The discovery of the language of the brain is therefore the next big significant advance in cybernetics. It is an essential preliminary to the construction of computers able to practice at least a part of the brain's wisdom and economy. For the present, we seem to be still far from making such a discovery. Indeed, we cannot even begin theorizing about the matter unless we have by direct observation mapped out in much greater detail than at present the activity of the human brain. As we have seen, the cerebral hemispheres are the rendezvous of innumerable stimulations of different quality and intensity carried along billions of neural channels and varied streams of humoral media both from outside as well as from within the organism. How they all meet, collide, and interact to weave meaningful patterns which are ceaselessly coming into being and passing away, never staying still even in our deepest slumbers, is a mystery with many layers of complexities. To name a few: First, the influence of humoral media—the secretions of glands, the hormones, the blood stream, and the like—on the nervous system is in itself a tangled skein of many complications. Secondly, the working of the elementary unit of the nervous system, the neuron, is a riddle we have barely begun to divine. Thirdly, to the complexity of its structure and function there supervenes yet another dimension of intricacy because of the sheer bulk of numbers of such units assembled in the nervous system. There is no artifact wherein the number of components runs

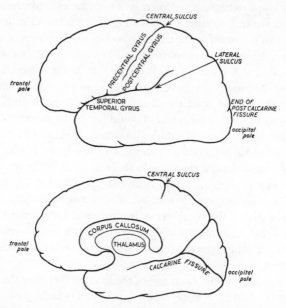

Fig. 37   The surface of a human brain, showing some of its many parts. *Top:* Lateral surface of a left hemisphere. *Bottom:* Medial surface of a right hemisphere. (From *The Organization of the Cerebral Cortex*, by D. A. Sholl, Methuen & Co. Ltd., London, 1956.

into millions and billions as is the case with the human brain. We may recall that the human brain is a neural network of some ten billion neurons, each on the average linked with a hundred others. Even if we somehow succeeded in specifying the details of each one of these 10^{12} connections, we would then have to face the staggering task of analyzing the performance of such a network. We could hardly even hope to map the entire topology of the neural network in the living brain in order to understand in this analytical manner how the neural elements are organized into a whole and how the whole in turn functions as the coordinated sum of all its parts. Fourthly, unlike the computer, the brain is not an assembly of a number of units to which particular subtasks are assigned, such as the storing of information (memory unit), computation (arithmetic unit), implementing of programed instructions (control unit), and so on, yielding on the basis of input data the desired output computation or control function. Nor is it like any of the so-called "thinking" machines, which can

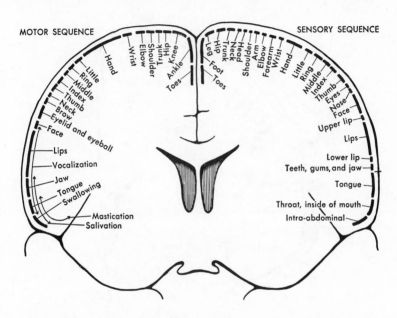

Fig. 38 Cross-section of the cerebrum through the sensorimotor region with the motor and sensory sequences indicated. The lengths of the solid bars represent an estimate of the average relative cortical areas from which the corresponding responses were elicited. (Reprinted with permission of The Macmillan Company from *The Cerebral Cortex of Man*, by Wilder Penfield and Theodore Rasmussen, p. 24. Copyright 1950 by The Macmillan Company.)

recognize patterns, play chess, translate books, or elucidate even some aspects of the nature of human reasoning by means of highly complicated scanning devices. While the internal circuitry of all these machines is well understood, the neural circuitry of the brain is still a complete mystery in spite of all the latest neurophysiological researches. Most of them are concerned with the gross anatomy of the brain and do not shed much light on its internal functioning.

Thus we have discovered that certain regions of the brain have well-defined functions; in particular, stimulation of points in the post-central gyrus causes the subject to feel sensations, while stimulation of the pre-central gyrus causes motor action (see Fig. 37). We have also found that the body is precisely mapped on these regions so that the response is quite specific.

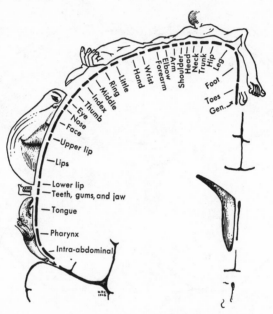

Fig. 39 Sensory homunculus. The right side of figurine is laid upon a cross-section of the hemisphere, drawn somewhat in proportion to the extent of sensory cortex devoted to it. The length of the underlying block lines indicates more accurately the comparative extent of each representation as in Fig. 38. Compare with Fig. 40. (Reprinted with permission of The Macmillan Company from *The Cerebral Cortex of Man*, by Wilder Penfield and Theodore Rasmussen, p. 44. Copyright 1950 by The Macmillan Company.)

These somato-sensory receiving as well as somato-motor radiating areas in the human cerebral cortex are strikingly illustrated in Penfield's diagrams wherein their relative sizes and positions are represented by the appropriate areas of a homunculus (see Figs. 38, 39, and 40). However, these areas cover only the terminals of the afferent and efferent neurons which form barely one per cent of the bulk of neurons that go to make up the human cerebral cortex.

Moreover, the mappings of these afferent and efferent neurons give no hint of how the brain itself functions since they serve only to shift the input and output terminals from the receptor and motor organs onto the brain surface. As a result the deeper interaction within the brain between the input and output on its periphery is still an unsolved riddle. For example, we do not yet know how memory and higher

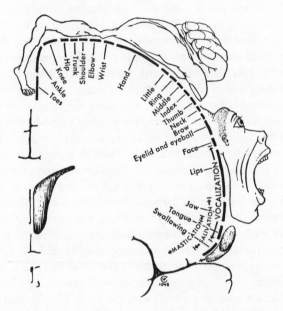

Fig. 40   Motor homunculus.   The right side of the figurine is laid upon a cross-section of the hemisphere.   Compare with Fig. 39.   (Reprinted with permission of The Macmillan Company from *The Cerebral Cortex of Man*, by Wilder Penfield and Theodore Rasmussen, p 57.   Copyright 1950 by The Macmillan Company.)

functions are distributed in the over-all fine structure of the brain. The brain apparently carries all its immense store of information, some 10^{15} bits, without any storage organ and recognizes the vast diversities of shapes, forms, and patterns without any of the highly complicated scanning devices used by heuristic* or learning machines to make even the most primitive discriminations such as distinguishing a vertical bar from a horizontal one.   It seems to take all the functions

* That is, machines which seek their goals by trial and error instead of prior programing as in digital or analogue computers.   See also Chapters XV and XVI for further elucidation.

in its stride in an over-all gestalt or intuitive fashion.   Apparently all the neurons of the cerebral cortex are in constant activity, and cortical integration consists of complex patterns of neural interactions but not conduction of neural impulses over fixed specific circuits for specific tasks.   This is shown by the amazing plasticity or "equipotentiality" of brain tissue which enables its residual parts to take over the functions of those extirpated.   Indeed, large sections of the brain may be removed with no apparent permanent loss of function.   While at first glance, therefore, this immense network of neurons, the living brain, resembles the electronic computers and heuristic or learning machines in that they are all structures of small basic components repeated over and over again (neurons, relays, vacuum tubes, transistors, scanning cells, and so on), and while they appear to simulate animal behavior in some respects, the attempt to model the brain as an amplified digital computer or a heuristic machine is not likely to succeed except to a limited extent.   The rub is that the computer-brain parallel is a mighty paradox.   The computer and the brain are in many ways as far apart as the poles and in others as close as twins. To resolve the paradox we have to discover a much profounder and subtler logical theory than that underlying the computing machines. Only then shall we begin to understand high-complication automata like the central nervous system and be able to make a significant advance towards overcoming at least some of the more serious limitations of present-day computers and heuristic-*cum*-learning machines. Meanwhile we have to press on with the study of (idealized) neural networks, which too is of great value in many ways.   For example, it helps elucidate certain aspects of brain function even if to a limited extent, showing how other processes of cogitation besides computation such as pattern recognition, chess playing, and machine translation may be mechanized or artificially simulated.   A beginning in this direction has been made by recent studies of neural networks by W. S. McCulloch, W. Pitts, J. von Neumann, S. C. Kleene, A. M. Turing, D. M. Mackay, A. M. Uttley, A. Rosenblueth, and others. They are mainly concerned with the behavior of an assembly or network of neurons as a whole, treating each component as a "black box" with an assumed (idealized) all-or-none *modus operandi*.   We shall deal with these investigations in the following chapters.

Chapter XI

NEURAL NETWORKS—
McCULLOCH AND PITTS

AS we saw in Chapter IX, Shannon was the first to show how such abstract logical operations as addition, multiplication, negation, implication, and equivalence could be implemented physically by recourse to electrical switching circuits. The basis of the suggested implementation is the fact that to each combination of abstract logical propositions linked by connectives like "not," "and," or "or," there corresponds a circuit formed by connecting basic components such as the inversion or negation, addition, and multiplication switches shown respectively in Figs. 23, 24, and 25 in Chapter IX. W. S. McCulloch and W. Pitts suggested the parallel idea of representing them by means of networks of neurons. Consequently chains of logical propositions may be embodied in either electrical hardware or its neural counterpart, biological "software." The former are automatic computers and the latter (idealized) models of nervous systems. It is therefore no accident that these two types of automata, the artificial and the natural, are alike in some respects. But because of the radical difference in the two kinds of materials used in their make-ups they also differ in many significant ways. In the last chapter we noted some of the coincidences and contrasts of their respective behaviors. The theory of neuron networks is designed to take account of both as a prelude to the understanding of high-complication natural automata, the living brains of animals including our own.

The obvious starting point of any such theory is the fact that a biological organism or natural automaton receives stimuli via its sensory receptor organs and performs responsive actions through its effector organs. In other words, responsive actions are evoked by their sponsoring stimuli as, for example, salivation by the smell of food or pupillary contraction of the eye in bright light. This means in

145

effect that the organism itself may be treated as a machine which with a prescribed system of input stimuli yields a correlated system of output responses.

Indeed, the receptor and effector organs of animals are in many ways analogues of various gadgets that modern technology employs for the automatic operation of machines. Thus receptor neurons are to biological systems what transducers are to control and communications systems of modern technology. These transducers are devices that process information mostly by converting one form of energy into another. Thus they measure temperature, pressure, rate of flow, voltage, illumination, chemical concentration, and so on, and feed their measurements into artificial circuits rigged up for the automatic control of plants and factories. Likewise, their biological counterparts, the receptor organs or neurons, convert the particular form of energy to which each is attuned into the electrical energy of the nerve impulse. Cases in point are rods and cones in the retina for the conversion of light energy, thermal receptors in the skin for that of heat, and mechanoreceptors in muscles for that of pressure, into electrical energy of the nerve impulse. The specialized receptor of the neuron is either an outgrowth of the nerve cell or in intimate contact with one. How the input stimuli such as light, pressure, or heat are converted into nerve impulses is a question that has begun to be studied only recently. Recent experiments with the Pacinian corpuscle, a specialized ending of the nerves of touch, have shown that incoming stimuli give rise to a generator current by transfer of ions (that is, charged atoms or molecules) across the receptor membrane. It is this generator current that triggers off the nerve impulse, which incidentally has been studied far more thoroughly than its sponsor, the generator current itself. It somehow gives rise to the signal which in the receptor nerve fibers travels from the periphery to the nerve centers conveying information about color, shape, texture, sound, temperature, and so forth. Just as the receptor sparks the signal, which travels from the periphery to the nerve center conveying information about the environment, so the effector carries the commands for contraction of muscles or for glandular secretions or other appropriate responses that the organism evokes to adapt itself to its changing environment both internal and external. Except for the fact that signals in one case carry information and in the other orders, there is no basic difference between the two kinds of fibers of the receptor and effector neurons. Although the mechanism that converts the input stimuli into nerve impulses in the receptor or the incoming nerve impulses into output responses in the effector is still quite a mystery, we may as a preliminary sidestep their complexities and make a simplifying assumption. Thus we may merely assume that any sort of stimulation leading to a given response has a definite representation in the internal state of the organism or automaton. This definite though unspecified internal state naturally occurs *after* the administration of the stimulus but *before* the evocation of the correlated response. There is therefore an inevitable time lag between the input stimulus and the output response. Hence arises an important difference between ordinary logic and the automata designed to represent it. For while time plays no role whatever in logic, no real nervous system, or its model the neuron network, can avoid abiding by a definite time schedule.

The need to heed the temporal sequence of neuron networks may seem to make their theory even more complicated than logic, a subject already notorious for its refractoriness. Fortunately, however, the introduction of the additional complication of time is not without compensation. It effectively bars various kinds of more or less overt vicious circles which have plagued logic ever since the paradoxes of Epimenides and Zeno and continue to plague it as the work of C. Burali-Forti, Bertrand Russell, D. König, J. Richard, and others clearly shows. By providing itself with a definite time lag while embodying the content of logical propositions which it symbolizes, the representative automaton or the neuron network acquires a built-in safeguard against such pitfalls. The inclusion in neuron-network theory of the additional complication of time lag thus has its compensation, though in including it we have to make some patently unrealistic assumptions to mitigate some of its rigors. Our main assumptions are two. First, the travel time of an impulse along the axon of a neuron is assumed to be constant for all neurons. Thus if a neuron "fires" at any time t, that is, if an impulse of nerve current enters it at any time t, the impulse reaches its exit in an interval of time which is the same for all neurons in the network. Although this time interval is actually a few milliseconds, we may for the sake of simplicity adopt it as our unit of time. Accordingly an impulse originating at the entrance of a neuron at time t reaches the exit at the end of its axon or "dies" at time $t + 1$. The second assumption of nerve-network theory is that neurons can fire only at discrete moments of time and not continuously at *any* time. This is a way of saying that if we set our clock appropriately and adopt the travel time of a neuron as our unit of reckoning, then neurons in our network can fire only when t equals 1, 2, 3, or any other whole number but not when t is $2\frac{1}{2}$ or $\frac{3}{4}$ or any other fractional number. As mentioned earlier, both assumptions are contrary to fact. They have, nevertheless, to be made to keep the neuron firings in phase and prevent the analysis from becoming intractable.

If to these two assumptions concerning the action time of neurons we graft a few others governing the linkage of one neuron to another in the network, we acquire a basis sufficient to erect thereon a theory of neural networks or idealized models of nervous systems. Naturally the rules of linkage must ensure that the influence of the input stimuli or of changes in environment at the sensory organs of the organism will be passed on to its effector organs via neural channels. It therefore follows that there must be at least two kinds of neurons: one whose *entrance* is on the sensory organ receiving the incoming stimulus, and the other whose *exit* is on the effector organ executing the outgoing correlated responsive action. The former are known as receptor neurons and the latter as effector neurons. But in order that the gap between the two may be bridged conveniently over wider distances within the organism, there has to be yet a third type of neuron mediating between them. This is the central or inner neuron, whose *entrance* is the exit of a sensory neuron and whose *exit* is the entrance of an effector. Of course, there are degrees of such sort of innerness. For there may well be inner neurons interposed between two others which are themselves *inner* in the sense that their entrance does not happen to be a sensory organ nor their exit an effector. Despite the differences between these three kinds of neurons, they are all alike in that while they have only one entrance they may have one or more exits or end bulbs. The reason is that the neural impulse can flow only along its single axon which ramifies into one or more outlets. In sum, neuron networks are assemblies of three types of neurons having the following attributes:

(*a*) *Receptor* neurons receive impulses from the environment and send impulses to other neurons. Their entrance therefore is the sensory receptor organ, shown in Fig. 41 by a small square, which under suitable conditions in the environment causes the neuron to fire. That is, the stimulus initiates an impulse which travels in unit time to all of its one or more end bulbs.

(*b*) *Central* or inner neurons somehow receive impulses from neurons and pass them on to others. Their entrance consequently is a

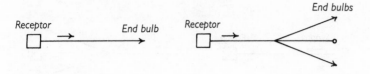

Fig. 41   *Left:* Receptor neuron with one end bulb.   *Right:* Receptor neuron with three end bulbs.

synapse, that is, a junction whereon impinge the exits or end bulbs of other (adjacent) neurons (see Fig. 42).   The impulse originates at the synapse and travels in unit time to all its own exits or end bulbs terminating on other neurons.

(c) *Effector* neurons receive impulses from neurons and send them to effector organs.   Accordingly their entrance is a synapse as with the central neuron, but their exits instead of end bulbs are effector organs, indicated in Fig. 43 by diagonalized squares.   It is these organs that finally carry out the response initially sparked by the input of the sensory receptors and cause changes in the environment such as the contraction of muscles by effector nerve cells in animals.   As before, the nerve impulse travels to the effectors in unit time.

It will be observed that while the exits of receptor and inner neurons are end bulbs, those of the effector neurons are effector organs.   Obviously effectors of any given neuron are all of one piece in the sense that they have to carry into effect the correlated response when the neuron is fired.   The end bulbs of the receptor and central neurons, on the other hand, have for greater versatility of performance to be of two kinds in order that they may either excite or inhibit the impulse in the adjoining neuron on which they terminate.   Those which tend to excite the adjacent neuron on which they impinge are called excitatory and denoted by arrowheads [→], while those which tend to inhibit it are called inhibitory and denoted by unshaded

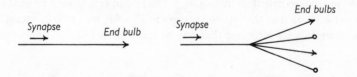

Fig. 42   *Left:* Central neuron with one end bulb.   *Right:* Central neuron with four end bulbs.

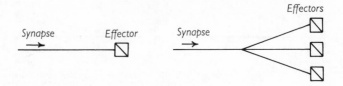

Fig. 43   *Left:* Effector neuron with one effector.   *Right:* Effector neuron with three effectors.

circles [o].   Thus of the three end bulbs of the receptor neuron shown in Fig. 41 two are excitatory and one inhibitory.   Likewise, two of the four end bulbs of the central neuron shown in Fig. 42 are excitatory and the remaining two inhibitory.

With the completion of these preliminaries regarding neural attributes, the rule governing the formation of networks is simply stated: "Each end bulb of a neuron impinges on the soma or body of exactly one neuron, no more, no less."   Accordingly each end bulb can contact one and only one synapse, though on the other hand each synapse is contacted by at least one if not more end bulbs.   The situation is similar to that prevailing in a polygamous society where every wife (end bulb) has one and only one husband (synapse), though every husband has at least one wife and in all likelihood a whole harem. For example, a receptor neuron with one end bulb and an effector neuron with one effector must be joined together as in Fig. 44.   But if the receptor neuron has three end bulbs, then all the three must share the same synapse of the single effector available, as in Fig. 45. In either case, if the receptor neuron fires at time t, it reaches its end bulb(s) on the synapse of the effector neuron at time $(t + 1)$ and evokes the appropriate response by the effector organ at time $(t + 2)$. That is, the response would occur after a lag of two units of time. But whether or not it actually occurs at all depends on another feature of the synapse called its threshold.   The reason is that for a neuron in a network such as the effector neuron in Fig. 44, 45, or 46 to fire, it is *necessary* but *not* sufficient that one or more of the adjoining neurons

Fig. 44   Synapse with one end bulb.

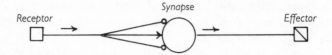

Fig. 45 Synapse with three end bulbs.

whose end bulbs impinge on its synapse fire. The adjoining neural firings *suffice* to trigger the neuron in question *if and only if* the sparking activity exceeds its synaptic threshold. Accordingly the threshold of a synapse is merely a whole number h specifically associated with it in the following manner: The synapse fires at any time t if and only if $(e - i)$ exceeds h, where e is the number of excitatory end bulbs (arrowheads) contacting it and dying at time t, and i that of the corresponding inhibitory ones (circles). Since e and i are always whole numbers, h too is naturally a whole number though it may be positive, negative, or zero. Thus consider the synapse shown in Fig. 46 with its assigned threshold number $h = 2$. As will be seen, the synapse is a junction of three end bulbs (two excitatory and one inhibitory) of the receptor neuron r_1 and one excitatory end bulb of the second receptor r_2. The synapse fires if and only if the number of excitatory end bulbs dying exceeds the inhibitory ones by at least two, the synaptic threshold. This means that both the receptors r_1 and r_2 must fire together before the effector e can be activated. For either by itself yields an excess of only *one* excitatory end bulb over the inhibitory ones against the required excess or threshold of two.

By using suitable receptors and effectors interlinked by means of central or inner neurons and assigning suitable thresholds at their synapses, McCulloch and Pitts showed that we can in theory construct nerve networks satisfying any given input-output specifications. The "functioning" of such a network may be defined by singling out some

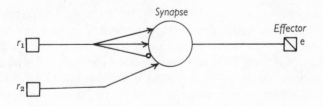

Fig. 46

of the input of the entire system and some of its outputs and then describing what original input stimuli are to cause what ultimate (output) responses. The most important result of the McCulloch-Pitts theory is that *any* such "functioning," no matter how complex, provided it can be defined at all logically, strictly, and unambiguously in a finite number of words, can also be realized by such a formal neural network. The result derives its great (theoretical) importance from the fact that it debunks once and for all a major limit law of neurophysiology that had all along been assumed as a matter of course. For it has often been claimed that the activities and functions of the human nervous system are so complicated that no synthetic or ersatz mechanism could ever possibly perform them, not merely here and now but forever. Specific functions which by their very nature exhibit this debility have even been named in order to "prove" that they are per se incapable of mechanical and/or neural realization despite their complete logical description. The McCulloch-Pitts theory puts an end to all this. It proves that anything that can be exhaustively and unambiguously described or put into words is *ipso facto* realizable by a suitable finite neural network.

This is not to say that the *theoretical* possibility of realizing *in principle* every completely and logically describable input-output specification of natural automata will tell us *in practice* how to build the network in flesh and blood or even in electrical hardware. All that it does tell us is that

(i) *if* we could get enough neuron cells of various kinds; and
(ii) *if* they were small enough to be accommodated within the limited space available to the organism; and
(iii) *if* each cell had enough end bulbs; and
(iv) *if* we could put enough end bulbs at each synapse; and
(v) *if* we had enough time to assemble them, and so forth,

then we could make robots that would behave in *any* completely and unambiguously specified way under prescribed environmental circumstances. The unending conjunction of "ifs" in the preceding sentence may look like a new variant of the old saying: "If pigs had wings, they would fly." Indeed, it is so. For on the basis of the McCulloch-Pitts results alone we shall never, for many reasons, be able actually to make robots imitating the human nervous system. First, we know no means of acquiring the many billions of cells required for the purpose. Secondly, even if we did somehow manage to acquire them, the brain resulting therefrom would be of an absurdly large size. Thirdly, there is not time enough to assemble the neurons even if we could make them. For at the ultrarapid pace of putting one cell into position per second, 10 billion cells would take some five centuries to assemble. While the neuron-network theory therefore does not shed any light on these ultimate problems of neurophysiological practice, the theory is nevertheless of great heuristic value in pointing a way to what Arthur Clarke calls the "edge of the possible." It is in this respect similar to Shannon's two coding theorems described earlier in Chapter IV which proved the existence of optimal codes while giving no clue as to how to obtain them. Likewise, the McCulloch nerve-network theory tells us what is *in principle* possible without indicating how to implement the principle in practice.

The principle it proves is just this: if we start with some (n) receptor neurons $r_1, r_2, r_3, \ldots, r_n$ and some (m) effectors $e_1, e_2, e_3, \ldots, e_m$ and some (usually many) central neurons, there exists a neural network conforming to any preassigned input-output prescription by assembling (on paper) these three types of neurons in a suitable manner and assigning appropriate threshold numbers to the various synapses of the network. In fact, as will be apparent later, corresponding to any given input-output specification there are usually several ways of assembling the neurons, yielding many alternative networks. Any such network of neurons embedded in a supporting and protecting structure or body is the robot of science-fiction writers ranging all the way from the Great Brains of Olaf Stapledon to the Black Cloud of Fred Hoyle. For by connecting with the supporting body power devices of various kinds activated by the effectors we may make them perform any of those marvelous feats that make us gape in wonder. Thus some of these power devices may enable it to change the shape of its body, either grossly or in relatively local parts. These power devices which change the shape of the body or move its parts relative to one another could be constructed of contractile material like the muscles of animals, if that becomes technically feasible, or of course could be made of engines and motors with accessory wheels, pulleys, and levers as in the case of Ashby's *machina spora* or Walter's *machina speculatrix*. Or again power devices may enable it to transmit energy in the form of radio signals to the environment without any apparent mechanical bodily changes. Examples are the emission of light by a firefly or of electricity by an eel. Or yet again some of these power devices could be used to move the robot parts in order to self-repair any non-lethal injury or damage to its own external or internal mechanism such as fixing its own fractures (flat tires) or faulty neural connections at the synapses. All these problems of robot engineering and neurophysiology such as how to embed the networks in stable structures or how to maintain their power supplies and other metabolism, though interesting, are entirely bypassed by the nerve-network theory. In fact, in a gravitation-free environment there may well be no need to provide any of these supporting structures of bone and muscles or casings and enclosures, so that pure intelligence could conceivably emerge almost unencumbered by such protective armors. It is this perfectly logical conception that is the basis of Fred Hoyle's surmise that intelligent life may well exist in diffuse gaseous clouds using radio signals to maintain neurological control over all its parts. Indeed, his Black Cloud is such an intelligent being itself. A (logical) network of (idealized) neurons is merely an abstract schema wherein the attempt to trap intelligence without its material trappings of supporting structures and armors is carried yet a stage further than even in the Black Cloud, indeed, to its ultimate conclusion in order to produce what may aptly be called disembodied intelligence. The exclusive concern of the exercise is merely to prove *in principle* the equivalence between abstract intelligence exhibited by an automaton and neural networks. Surprising as it may seem, it does so in a remarkably simple manner.

As we have seen, the binary alphabet of 0 and 1 suffices to write any text. No doubt the more elaborate the text, the greater the vocabulary required for writing it. But there is really no end to the vocabulary that we can make with the binary symbols 0 and 1. Thus a two-digit sequence in binary language yields $2^2 = 4$ different "words," three digits yield $2^3 = 8$ different "words," four digits $2^4 = 16$ different "words," and so on in an avalanche of increasing geometric progression. Consequently, using an appropriate number of digits we could transcribe in our binary alphabet any specified stimulus as well as response. In other words, any given input-output specification for an automaton is merely a table of two parallel rows of sequences of binary digits wherein the top row is a codified description of the input stimuli and the bottom one that of the correlated responses. Consider, for instance, a simplified automaton having in all four distinct input stimuli and two distinct output responses. To represent the former in our binary code we need four different "words." Obviously two binary digits suffice to yield $2^2 = 4$ different permutations of 0's and 1's, each one of which could be made to denote one or another of the four given inputs. For the two outputs two single-digit "words," namely, 0 and 1, suffice. Now suppose further that input stimuli denoted by 00 and 01 evoke the output response denoted by 0, and that the stimuli denoted by 10 and 11 call forth the response 1. Then the input-output specification for this particular automaton is as shown in Table 34.

TABLE 34

Input stimuli	00	01	10	11
Output response	0	0	1	1

To obtain a neuron network or model of the automaton conforming to the afore-mentioned input-output specification we observe that *two* receptor neurons, each capable of two states—either firing (stimulated) denoted by 1, or quiescent (unstimulated), denoted by 0—suffice to represent all four given stimuli. Accordingly the network should consist of two receptor neurons, r_1 and r_2. Similarly, its two output responses would need only one effector neuron, whose unstimulated state, denoted by 0, calls forth the output response 0 and stimulated state, denoted by 1, the second output response 1. We have next to decide how the two receptors r_1 and r_2 are to be connected to the single effector e_1 in order that the two inputs 00 and 01 are correlated with the output 0 and the remaining two 10 and 11 with the output 1. A glance at the nerve net drawn in Fig. 47 shows that if we assign to the effector synapse the threshold 1 and provide the receptor r_1 with two end bulbs, one excitatory and one inhibitory, and the receptor r_2 with only one excitatory end bulb, all three of them impinging on the body of the effector e_1, we obtain a net that satisfies all the input-output specifications of Table 34.

Thus, consider the case when neither r_1 nor r_2 fires at any time t, corresponding to the input 00. None of the excitatory and inhibitory end bulbs therefore die at the synapse at time $t + 1$ so that the effector e_1 remains quiescent at time $t + 2$, corresponding to the output response 0 as indeed our specification requires. Next, if at time

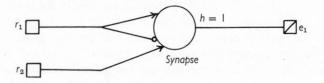

Fig. 47 Neural network implementing input-output specification shown in Table 34.

t, receptor r_1 fires but not r_2, corresponding to the second input stimulus 01, only one excitatory and one inhibitory end bulb die at the synapse at time $t + 1$. Since the excess of excitatory end bulbs over the inhibitory ones dying at the synapse falls below its threshold (1), the effector e_1 remains unstimulated, again evoking the response 0. On the other hand, if at time t either r_2 fires alone or both r_1 and r_2 fire simultaneously, as is the case respectively when the input stimuli are 10 and 11, the excess of excitatory end bulbs over the inhibitory ones dying at time $t + 1$ at the synapse is 1, its threshold, so that the output response in both cases is 1 as required.

Consider again the case of a more elaborate automaton having eight different kinds of input stimuli and an equal number of output responses. Clearly, to represent $8 = 2^3$ different inputs in our binary code we need three-digit "words" like 000, 001, 010, 011, 100, 101, 110, 111. This means that the neural network or model would require three receptor neurons r_1, r_2, r_3, each capable of two different stimulated or unstimulated states. Likewise, eight different output responses too would need three-digit (binary) words so that the number of effector neurons required is also three. We wish to draw a neural network joining the three receptors r_1, r_2, r_3 to the three effectors e_1, e_2, e_3 satisfying the input-output specifications given in Table 35.

TABLE 35

Input stimuli	000	001	010	011	100	101	110	111
Output responses	100	101	110	111	000	001	010	001

A glance at the neuron network drawn in Fig. 48 shows that corresponding to each particular input stimulus, such as 101 shown in

Table 35 occurring at time t, the network will evoke at time $t + 2$ the correlated response 001 shown underneath its sponsoring stimulus (101).

What is true of the simple automata drawn in Figs. 47 and 48 with input-output specifications as shown in Tables 34 and 35 is equally true of more complex ones which may require any number (n) of digits to denote the stimuli and any other number (m) of digits to write the responses. Since the stimuli require n binary digits for their complete representation, their total number must be 2^n. Similarly m binary digits for the output responses mean that there are in all 2^m different outputs to represent. The network must obviously contain n receptor neurons whose two possible conditions, stimulated and

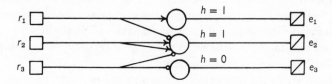

Fig. 48 Neural network implementing input-output specification shown in Table 35.

unstimulated, would yield 2^n different input stimuli. Likewise, the network would require m effector neurons to obtain 2^m different output responses. There are, of course, many ways of correlating the given (2^n) input stimuli with the specified (2^m) output responses, depending on which particular input of the possible 2^n is to evoke which particular response of the total 2^m possible responses. Thus consider the first item of the total aggregate of 2^n given input stimuli. We may require it to evoke *any one* of 2^m possible responses. Consequently, to each input stimulus there correspond 2^m distinct ways of choosing a response. What is true of the first stimulus is equally true of the second, third, fourth...and the last 2^nth input in our list of stimuli so that we can have in theory $(2^m)(2^m)(2^m) \ldots [2^n$ times] $= (2^m)^{2^n}$ different ways of correlating 2^n inputs with 2^m outputs. Each of these different ways is a possible input-output specification for an automaton. It therefore results that with n receptor neurons and m effectors we can in theory obtain $(2^m)^{2^n}$ different automata of $n \times m$ degree of complexity. Thus the neural network shown in Fig. 48

corresponding to the input-output specification of Table 35 is one particular instance of $(2^3)^{2^3} = (8^8)$ possible automata we could have with an outfit of three receptors and three effectors suitably interlaced with or without some central neurons. Indeed, J. T. Culbertson has given perfectly general rules whereby we could draw a neuron network corresponding to any given (finite) input-output specification.

In short, the automaton's input-output specification is a sort of dictionary that gives the meaning (output response) of every possible input-stimulus "word" in its repertoire. The automaton or network itself is merely a scanning device that consults the dictionary each time an input stimulus is received from the environment to discover the associated "meaning" or response. Given any finite dictionary of input stimuli and their associated meanings or output responses, we can, following Culbertson's general rules, always make (on paper) a scanning device or neural network capable of consulting the dictionary and producing the listed meaning or response for each input "word" denoting its associated stimulus.

However, as the number of neurons in the network increases, its complexity begins to get out of hand. It is here that a simple conceptual tool called the "connection matrix" and devised by Heinz von Foerster proves very useful. Consider, for instance, the nerve net of 33 neurons shown in Fig. 49. Even though one necessary detail of the network, namely, whether a connection is inhibitory or excitatory, has been omitted, it is quite tedious to trace in the diagram the connection of any one neuron with another. A more readable representation of the connectivity situation in such cases is obtained by constructing a square matrix with exactly as many rows and columns as there are neurons in the network (see Fig. 50) and indicating for each neuron along the abscissa all its efferent (outgoing) contacts by placing a dot at the appropriate height along the ordinate. Thus, since the eleventh neuron in the network of Fig. 49 has two efferent contacts, one each with the twenty-fourth and twenty-fifth neurons, the eleventh abscissa has two dots, one each against the twenty-fourth and twenty-fifth ordinates in the connection matrix drawn in Fig. 50, to represent the network of Fig. 49. Obviously the connection matrix drawn in this manner provides a one-to-one mapping of connections in the nerve net. Further, once drawn it also yields immediately all the afferent (incoming) contacts of each neuron if one enters the matrix at the appropriate ordinate and reads the

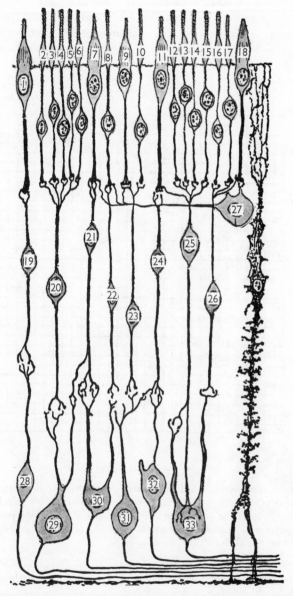

Fig. 49   Nerve connections in the outer layers of a human retina.   (From
Bradley M. Patten, *Human Embryology*, 2nd ed., McGraw-Hill Book Company, Inc., New York, 1953, p. 405. Copyright 1953. Used by permission.)

dotted values along the abscissa, e.g., the twenty-third neuron has afferent contacts one each with the ninth and tenth neurons.

By recourse to connection matrix we may derive a number of results concerning neural networks. First, with n neurons we can build

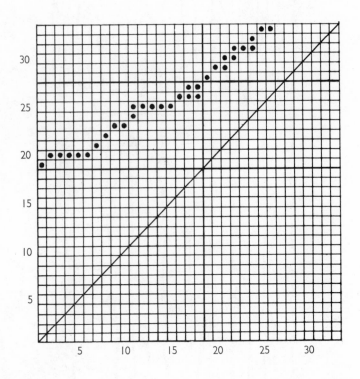

Fig. 50　Connection matrix of nerve connections in the outer layers of a human retina. (From "Some Aspects in the Design of Biological Computers," by Heinz von Foerster, in *Proceedings of the Second International Congress on Cybernetics, Nomur, September 3–10, 1958,* Association Internationale de Cybernetique, 1960, p. 247.)

exactly 2^{n^2} networks. For there are in all $n \times n = n^2$ little squares in the connection matrix. Each of these squares may or may not have a dot. In preparing the corresponding connection matrix we have thus to make in all n^2 yes-or-no binary decisions each of which will define a different net. Q.E.D. With barely three neurons the number of possible networks is

$$2^{3^2} = 2^9 = (8)^3 = 512.$$

But even with six neurons the number of networks rises fantastically to the hundred-billion mark:

$$2^{6^2} = 2^{36} = (10)^{11}.$$

Actually the number of possible networks is higher still because our connection matrix oversimplifies the situation in one respect. It merely indicates whether a connection between any two given neurons in the network is present or not. To obtain a fuller description of the organization of the net we require a specification of the kind of connections provided, whether excitatory or inhibitory. In other words, we have to decide not merely whether any given little square of the matrix is to be dotted or not but what kind of dot it is to have if it is dotted at all. Thus, given that a square is to have a dot, we may decide to put the positive symbol $[+]$ if the contact is excitatory, and otherwise the negative symbol $[-]$. The connection matrix is therefore now made by deciding whether each of $n \times n$ little squares is to be filled or not and, if so, with which of the two symbols $[+]$ and $[-]$. Since the earlier binary decisions have now become tertiary, the number of possible networks is 3^{n^2}. We could further increase the number of possible decisions with respect to different connections and thus provide for other features such as the synaptic thresholds hitherto ignored. For example, with k possible decisions or different ways of filling each little square of our matrix corresponding to k different types of connections in the network, we can have in theory k^{n^2} different networks. If we choose a number m such that

$$k^{n^2} = 2^{m^2} \tag{1}$$

it is obvious that the number of possible networks with n neurons having k different types of connections is the same as that of networks with m "modified" neurons having only two types of oversimplified connections considered earlier. If we so "modify" the neural behavior, equation (1) shows that the number m of "modified" neurons is given by

$$m^2 = n^2 \log_2 k; \quad \text{or,} \quad m = n\sqrt{\log_2 k}.$$

An interesting corollary follows from this relation. Since m is only slightly larger than n, the complexity of a nerve net is not substantially increased by permitting fanciful variations in the neural connections. It is the number of neurons which really catapults the complexity.

The heuristic value of the connection matrix depends on the fact that it practically turns the evaluation of neural networks into a

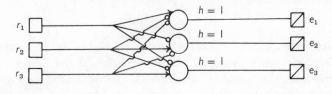

Fig. 51

systematic routine. Take, for instance, the network consisting of three effectors and three receptors drawn in Fig. 51. If all the thresholds are unity, one may verify that e_1 is fired if and only if r_1 alone is fired, and so on for the remaining two effectors e_2 and e_3. We may also derive the same conclusion more readily from the corresponding matrix:

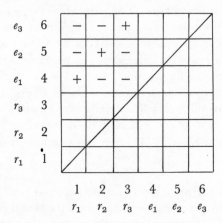

Since there are in all six neurons, consisting of three receptors and three effectors, our connection matrix consists of 6×6 little squares, the first three abscissas and ordinates representing the three receptors and the remaining three the effectors. Further, since the first receptor r_1 has one excitatory end bulb on e_1 and one inhibitory end bulb each on e_2 and e_3, the first abscissa "1" has been assigned the

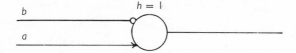

Fig. 52 Single-output network implementing negation. The network fires when $a.\bar{b}$.

symbol $[+]$ against the ordinate 4 corresponding to the effector e_1, and the symbol $[-]$ against ordinates 5 and 6 corresponding to effectors e_2, e_3. All we need do is to look at all its afferent or incoming connections shown in the matrix corresponding to its ordinate—5 in this case. It is clearly $[-, +, -]$ so that to fire it we have to fire the second receptor r_2 alone. All other inputs of the receptors will merely inhibit e_2.

While connection matrix, no doubt, simplifies evaluation of networks, even this artifice does not suffice to curb the rising crescendo of complexity as the number of neurons in the network increases. One way of handling such an exponential avalanche of network possibilities is to confine ourselves to much simpler single-output automata, that is, neuron networks having several inputs but only *one* output, which is stimulated under a given set of input stimulations but remains quiescent under all the others. The reason is that such simpler single-output networks or automata belong to a certain category of elements called "universal" in the sense that we can make any more complex network with multiple outputs by merely assembling a suitable number of single-output networks. The complexity of the network problem is thus greatly simplified. For example, the outputs of certain of the simpler single-output networks may be connected by lines, wires, or nerve fibers to some of the inputs of the same or other networks to yield more complex systems with multiple outputs. This naturally requires consideration of several single-output networks simultaneously and introduces a new difficulty. For the

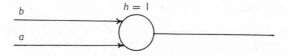

Fig. 53 Single-output network implementing logical addition or disjunction. The network fires when either a or b or both fire.

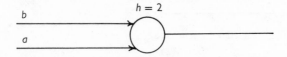

Fig. 54 Single-output network implementing logical multiplication or conjunction. The network fires if and only if both *a* and *b* fire.

time lag of response in all of them may not be the same. We resolve it, however, by assuming that all their respective time lags are integral multiples of a common value, which we may adopt as our unit of time. The assumption may not be correct for an actual nervous system. It is nevertheless partially justified so long as only a finite number of single-output automata are considered for assembly. We therefore postulate that the time lags of all our single-output networks are discrete so that they are restricted to only integral values like 1, 2, 3, . . ., 10, and so forth.

Since our object is to consider single-output networks with a view to their subsequent synthesis into more complex neural structures, we describe here three basic networks or organs which suffice to make all the others. As will be recalled from Chapter IX, of all logical operations such as negation, addition, multiplication, implication, or equivalence, only the first three are fundamental in that all others can be reduced to a combination of two or more of these three only. The corresponding electrical circuits implementing these three operations were shown in Figs. 23, 24, 25 in Chapter IX. It is therefore no wonder that neural counterparts of these three switching circuits are precisely the basic single-output universal elements we are in search of. They are drawn in Figs. 52 to 54. In Fig. 52 the neuron *b*, if fired, inhibits the action of neuron *a* so that the latter stimulates the output response if and only if *b* does *not* fire. In other words, it implements the conjunction of *a* and not-*b*, that is, $a\bar{b}$. In Fig. 53, because the synaptic threshold is 1, the output response is stimulated

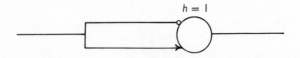

Fig. 55 Permanently grounded or "dead" network.

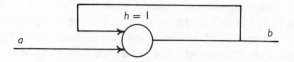

Fig. 56 Permanently "live" network.

when *either* neuron *a* *or* neuron *b* *or* both are fired. It therefore embodies logical addition. In Fig. 54, where the synapse has the threshold 2, the output response is evoked if and only if both neurons *a* and *b* are fired simultaneously. It therefore realizes logical multiplication. In all three cases the output obviously occurs after unit delay.

Besides these three basic single-output universal organs there are two others which we will have occasion to use. The first, shown in Fig. 55, is permanently "grounded" or "dead" in that its output is never stimulated. The second, drawn in Fig. 56, is, on the contrary, always live or active because it is stimulated at all times if its input has been ever (previously) stimulated. The former is also designated in network diagrams by the symbol //⊢ and the latter by /ı/⊢ instead of being drawn in full as in Figs. 55 and 56. The utility of these supplementary perpetually "dead" or ever "live" components is that they may be incorporated in the basic organs of Figs. 52 to 54 to yield others. Thus the network of Fig. 52, implementing *ab̄*, yields only *b̄* by itself if we make its *a*-terminal permanently live as in Fig. 57. The network thus inverts *b*. That is, the output response is stimulated after unit delay if and only if *b* does *not* fire. More specifically, if *b* fires at time *t*, the output of the network stays quiet at *t* + 1; but if *b* is quiet at time *t*, the output fires at *t* + 1, which is precisely what an inversion or negation network ought to do.

We choose three basic universal organs implementing negation, addition, and multiplication because we can reduce any complex of

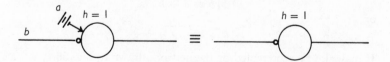

Fig. 57 Negation network.

logical operations to a combination of only these three.   Indeed, the reduction can be carried a stage further.   Thus since $ab \equiv$ not $- [\bar{a} + \bar{b}]$, it follows that the multiplication organ of Fig. 54 is equivalent to a system built of the remaining two, the addition and negation networks.   Or alternatively, since $a + b \equiv$ not-$(\bar{a} \cdot \bar{b})$, the addition organ of Fig. 53 may be constructed out of the negation and multiplication organs of Figs. 52 and 54.   Although the afore-mentioned two reductions may tempt us to try also the third, namely, building the negation organ of Fig. 52 out of the addition and multiplication organs of Figs. 53 and 54, it is not possible to do so unless we resort to what von Neumann has called "the double-line trick."   The trick in question consists in representing propositions on a double line instead of a single one.   We assume that of the two lines at all times one and only one is stimulated.   There are thus always two possible states of the line pair: the first line stimulated and the second quiescent, and the second line stimulated and the first quiescent.   Other states, such as having both lines stimulated or both quiescent, are considered inadmissible or out of bounds.   We let one of these two (admissible) states correspond to the stimulated single line of the original system, that is, to a true proposition, and the other state to the unstimulated single line, that is, to a false proposition.   With these stipulations it is possible to show that any one of the three basic organs of negation, addition, and multiplication may be built up out of the other two.

The afore-mentioned reduction of the basic organs to only two is by no means the end.   It can be advanced to a still higher state where the number of basic organs is only one.   To do so we have to invent an even more basic organ wherewith to synthesize any of the three basic organs drawn in Figs. 52 to 54.   Such a universal organ is the embodiment of the so-called "Sheffer stroke" function introduced by K. A. Brueckner and G. Gell-Mann for the purpose here in view. It is simply the expression "either not-a or not-b," that is, the logical sum $\bar{a} + \bar{b}$ or its equivalent, not both a and b, that is, $(\overline{a \cdot b})$.   In symbols, it is simply written as:

$$a \mid b \equiv \bar{a} + \bar{b}$$

or

$$a \mid b \equiv (\overline{a \cdot b})$$

It may also be represented by the network drawn in Fig. 58.

With this definition we can represent logical negation, addition, and multiplication as follows:

Negation: $(a \mid a) \equiv \bar{a} + \bar{a} \equiv \bar{a}$ (i)

Addition: $[(a \mid a) \mid (b \mid b)] \equiv (\bar{a} \mid \bar{b}) \equiv \bar{\bar{a}} + \bar{\bar{b}} = a + b$ (ii)

Multiplication: $[(a \mid b) \mid (a \mid b)] \equiv [(\bar{a} + \bar{b}) \mid (\bar{a} + \bar{b})] \equiv [\overline{\bar{a} + \bar{b}}]$
$$\equiv a \cdot b \quad \text{(iii)}$$

The respective networks representing the three operations in question
are drawn in Figs. 59 to 61. A glance at these diagrams shows that
while the output of the organ of Fig. 59 occurs after one unit delay,
that of Fig. 60 or 61 occurs after a delay of two units.

A little consideration makes all the afore-mentioned equivalences
(i) to (iii) obvious, although they may also be proved by means of
the truth-table technique already explained in Chapter IX. Consider,
for example, equivalence (iii) derived from $[\overline{\bar{a} + \bar{b}}] \equiv a \cdot b$. If we

TABLE 36

SHEFFER STROKE TRUTH TABLE

a	1	1	0	0
b	1	0	1	0
$\bar{a}$	0	0	1	1
$\bar{b}$	0	1	0	1
$a \cdot b$	1	0	0	0
$a \mid b$ or $\overline{(a \cdot b)}$	0	1	1	1
$a \mid b$ or $\bar{a} + \bar{b}$	0	1	1	1
$\overline{(\bar{a} + \bar{b})}$	1	0	0	0

work out the truth values of each of the two expressions on both sides
of the equivalence as in Table 36, we find that they are both alike for
all the four possible combinations of the truth values of their constituent
propositions a and b.

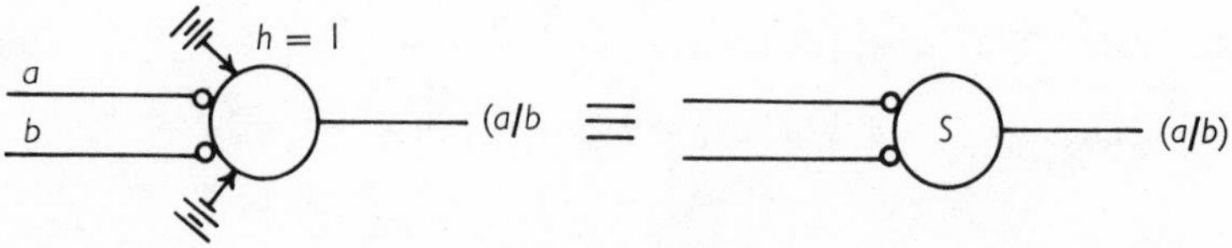

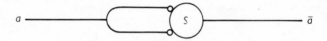

Fig. 58

A comparison of the truth values of $a \cdot b$ and not-$(\bar{a} + \bar{b})$ or $(\overline{\bar{a} + \bar{b}})$ shows that both are alike in every case, whence their complete equivalence. Likewise, $\bar{a} + \bar{b}$ is seen to be equivalent to not-$(a \cdot b)$ or $(\overline{a \cdot b})$.

Yet another universal basic organ for which we will have some use later is the so-called "majority" organ of von Neumann. It is so-called because it is merely a single-output three-input device whose

Fig. 59   Sheffer stroke representation of negation.

outcome is decided by a majority vote of the three inputs a, b, c. That is, the output is stimulated if and only if at least two of the three inputs are stimulated. The network is therefore of the form shown in Fig. 62. In symbols, $m(a, b, c) \equiv ab + bc + ca \equiv (a + b) \cdot (b + c) \cdot (c + a)$. To implement logical addition or the conjunction "and" by means of the majority organ all we need do is permanently ground one of the three neurons, say, c, as shown in Fig. 63. Since c is permanently dead, both a and b must fire simultaneously for

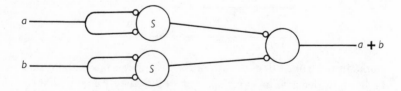

Fig. 60   Sheffer stroke representation of logical addition.

Fig. 61   Sheffer stroke representation of logical multiplication.

the output to be stimulated.   It therefore embodies logical multiplication.   On the other hand, we obtain logical addition, that is, the
disjunction "or," if we make one of the three neurons, *c*, permanently
live.   For in that case *either a or b or* both suffice to activate the output (see Fig. 64).   All three basic universal organs of Figs. 52 to 54
based on the three fundamental logical operations of negation, addition, and multiplication, or their revised versions of Figs. 59 to 61

Fig. 62   Von Neumann's majority organ.

reared on the "Sheffer stroke" operation of Fig. 58 or the majority
organ of Fig. 62 have a certain property in common.   In each* a
stimulus of one of the inputs at the left may be traced through the
machine until at a certain time later it emerges as a stimulus of the
output on the right.   In other words, no pulse ever returns to or "feeds
back" into a neuron through which it has once passed.*   A neuron
network having this property is called "circle-free" by McCulloch

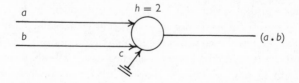

Fig. 63   Majority organ yielding logical addition by permanently
grounding *c*.

* The permanently live network of Fig. 56 is the sole exception.

and Pitts. While the theory of circle-free networks or automata is extremely simple, the simplicity is a serious handicap as it restricts greatly the scope and versatility of such networks. Those permitting feedback circles or loops, on the other hand, suffer no such debility. By enabling the state of the network's output to depend on the state of its input in the indefinitely remote past, the network can be made to accomplish feats of memory. For example, the feedback circuit of Fig. 56 is a kind of elementary memory machine. Once stimulated by *a*, this organ remains permanently stimulated, sending forth a pulse in *b* at all times thereafter. More complicated networks constructed on these lines can be made to perform all manner of operations like counting, simple arithmetic, and even a series of unlimited inductive processes encountered in intuitionistic logic, as we shall see more

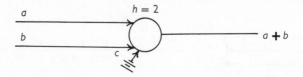

Fig. 64 Majority organ yielding logical multiplication by making *c* permanently "live."

clearly later. Indeed, the use of feedback loops yields networks which realize a large portion of intuitionistic logic. Although the limitation of size inevitable in finite networks of this kind precludes the realization of all of intuitionistic logic, there are ways of evading it. For instance, Turing has shown that by providing our automata with an unlimited memory such as an infinite tape and scanners connected to afferent organs along with suitable efferent organs to perform motor operations and/or print the tape, all intuitionistic logic becomes precisely equivalent to the logic of such constructable machines. In particular, he has shown that all computable numbers in the Turing sense can be computed by some such network. We shall deal with the subject in more detail in Chapter XIII. Meanwhile we may remark that the three basic elements founded on Sheffer stroke or any of its counterparts we have already described suffice to make a network capable of realizing any given (finite) input-output specifications. Consequently if we do not need to worry about the practical problems of actually assembling all the neurons in the network, there is in principle no difficulty in making a formal neural network imitating any real or imagined mode of behavior that can be completely and unambiguously described.

Whether any existing mode of behavior such as that of the natural automata like the living brains of animals can really be put "completely and unambiguously" into words is altogether a different matter. For while some partial or limited aspects of the neurophysiological behavior of animals can certainly be so described even though at great length, it is by no means obvious that the same is true of their totality. The doubt arises because of the refractory nature of all reality, including neurophysiological reality, which often defies verbal description. There are innumerable classes, categories, patterns, and modes which refuse to be trapped in any linguistic net of our making. No matter how illuminating our attempted description of them we never quite succeed in eradicating all the penumbra at its fringe. A case in point is that of life itself, the commonest category on earth. Even its clearest verbal definitions shade insensibly into obscurity at the boundaries. All this is inevitable because whereas language is based on our grossly molar experience of *macro*-events, their actual outcome is the result of a play of myriads of *micro*-events we can hardly ever observe individually. Nearly all the present difficulties of quantum mechanics stem from this basic gap between our experience or awareness of macro-phenomena and the actual micro-phenomena that lead to that awareness. In trying to understand the nervous system of animals we face difficulties of the same kind. The language we use in describing the nervous activity of animals is derived from our experience with digital computers, whose components, despite all the micro-miniaturization we have achieved with the invention of transistors and cryotrons are, as we saw in Chapter X, still a long way from the *micro*-componentry of the animal nervous system. This is why it is very likely that our attempts to understand the functions of the living brain via neural networks built on elaborate verbal descriptions of its behavior patterns will soon reach a dead end if they have not already done so. Consider, for instance, one specific function of the brain among the millions it performs during the course of its life, the visual identification of analogous geometrical patterns. Any attempt at an "unambiguous and complete" verbal description of the general concept of analogy, the basis of our visual faculty, will inevitably be too long to be of much use for even drawing (on paper) neuron networks having the wide diversity of visual responses the natural automata normally exhibit as a matter of course.   No one in our present state of knowledge dare hazard a guess whether such an enterprise would require thousands or millions or any larger number of volumes.   Faced with such a descriptive avalanche, one is tempted to substitute the deed for the description, treating the connection pattern of the visual brain itself as the simplest definition or "description" of the visual analogy principle.

In view of the serious difficulties encountered in the description of high-complication automata like the nervous system there is no more profit in pursuing further the McCulloch-Pitts line of argument.   It serves a definite purpose in establishing the equivalence between logical principles and their embodiment in a neural network.   But the equivalence in practice merely comes to this, that while in the simpler cases the logical principles might furnish a simplified expression of the network, in cases of extreme complexity such as natural automata exhibit, the reverse might very well be true.   This is why for a better understanding of the central nervous system we require a new mélange of logic and neurology wherein logic perhaps will have undergone a metamorphosis towards neurology to a much greater extent than the other way about.

Chapter XII

NEURAL NETWORKS— VON NEUMANN

ONE way of reorienting neural-network theory towards neuro-physiology is to attenuate the rigidity of some of its underlying assumptions to secure greater conformity to neurophysiological reality. Among other assumptions there is one which is obviously contrary to known facts, namely, the assumed infallibility of neurons. Von Neumann therefore took the next important step of dispensing with the postulated perfection of neural behavior by explicitly incorporating into the network theory the possibility of neural malfunction. That is, he inquired whether a reliable automaton could be designed using unreliable logical elements like neurons which have a certain (statistical) probability of failing or misfiring. He proved in his customary elegant way that it is possible to assemble individually *unreliable* components into an automaton with any *arbitrarily* high reliability. This is a result on a level with the remarkable theorem of Shannon on noisy channels described earlier in Chapter IV. Just as there is no a priori reason why it should be possible to transmit information across a noisy channel with arbitrarily high reliability, a result guaranteed by Shannon's theorem, so also it is difficult to visualize how basically *unreliable* elements could be synthesized to yield auto-mata designed to function with as high degree of reliability as we desire—a result ensured by von Neumann's demonstration. Never-theless, as we shall presently see, it can be achieved in an analogous way, that is, by lavish provision of redundancy.

Von Neumann begins by stipulating that every basic universal organ used in the synthesis of any automaton or neuron network has a certain assigned statistical probability (e) of failure or malfunctioning. Although actually this probability of neural misfire is statistically dependent on the general state of the network and on one another, we may at the outset make the simpler assumption that every neuron in the network has, statistically independently of all else, exactly the same probability (e) of going astray.   There is evidently no loss of generality in supposing e to be less than or equal to $\frac{1}{2}$.   For if an organ consistently misfires with a probability greater than $\frac{1}{2}$, all we need do is to consider the reverse of its attributed function.   Such a reversed organ will obviously "misfire" with a probability equal to or less than $\frac{1}{2}$.   In actual practice, e will have to be considerably smaller still, as obviously no reliable automaton can possibly emerge out of components with as large probability of failure as $\frac{1}{2}$ or more.   However, our difficulty is that once we have envisaged the possibility of a malfunction, no matter how small, it seems at first sight that errors of individual components will tend to snowball over a sufficiently long period, destroying in the end the functional reliability of the automaton as a whole.   What really happens is not so much that incorrect information is obtained but that irrelevant results are produced. Consider, for example, the simple neural network of Fig. 65:

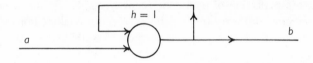

Fig. 65   Feedback network.

As will be observed, once the neuron a is stimulated, the network continues to emit pulses at all subsequent instants.   But suppose it has a (small) probability (e) of malfunctioning.   If the probability that the organ is still excited after any number (n) of cycles is p_n, then the probability p_{n+1} that it is excited after the $(n + 1)$th cycle is the sum of the probabilities of two events:

(i)   either the network functions after n cycles and the neuron b does *not* malfunction; the probability of the former is p_n and that of the latter $(1 - e)$ so that of the two jointly is $p_n(1 - e)$,* or

(ii)   the network after n cycles does *not* function but the neuron b *does* malfunction, the two errors thereby mutually cancelling them-

---

* We recall that the probability of the *conjunction* or simultaneous occurrence of two independent events with probabilities p and q is their product pq.   The probability of their disjunction, that is, either one or the other or both, is their sum $p + q$.

selves out. Obviously the probability of the first event is $(1 - p_n)$ and that of the second is e, leading to the probability $(1 - p_n)e$ of their joint occurrence.

The probability of the network functioning as a whole is therefore given by the recursion formula:

$$p_{n+1} = (1 - e)p_n + (1 - p_n)e$$

or

$$(p_{n+1} - \tfrac{1}{2}) = (1 - 2e)(p_n - \tfrac{1}{2}) \tag{1}$$

Substituting successively 0, 1, 2, 3, 4, ..., for n in (1) we find that

$$p_1 - \tfrac{1}{2} = (1 - 2e)(p_0 - \tfrac{1}{2})$$
$$p_2 - \tfrac{1}{2} = (1 - 2e)(p_1 - \tfrac{1}{2}) = (1 - 2e)^2(p_0 - \tfrac{1}{2})$$
$$p_3 - \tfrac{1}{2} = (1 - 2e)(p_2 - \tfrac{1}{2}) = (1 - 2e)^3(p_0 - \tfrac{1}{2})$$
$$p_4 - \tfrac{1}{2} = (1 - 2e)(p_3 - \tfrac{1}{2}) = (1 - 2e)^4(p_0 - \tfrac{1}{2})$$
$$\cdot \quad \cdot \quad \cdot \quad \cdot \quad \cdot \quad \cdot \quad \cdot \quad \cdot \quad \cdot \quad \cdot \quad \cdot \quad \cdot$$
$$p_n - \tfrac{1}{2} = (1 - 2e)(p_{n-1} - \tfrac{1}{2}) = (1 - 2e)^n(p_0 - \tfrac{1}{2}) \tag{2}$$

The above formula for the difference $(p_n - \tfrac{1}{2})$ between the probability p_n that the network functions correctly after the nth cycle and $\tfrac{1}{2}$, is a rough measure of the discrimination or sensitivity still remaining in the system after the nth cycle. For $p_n = \tfrac{1}{2}$ is the threshold value at which the network is as likely to function correctly as to misfire. That is, with $p_n = \tfrac{1}{2}$ the network's output is completely irrelevant to its input so that the excess of p_n over $\tfrac{1}{2}$ is an index of the input-output correlation. Now it can be easily shown that the expression $(1 - 2e)^n$ for any small value of e approaches zero as n tends toward infinity. It therefore follows from formula (2) that the discriminant $(p_n - \tfrac{1}{2})$ approaches zero. This is a way of saying that after a sufficiently long time the sensitivity of the machine vanishes altogether since its output is as likely to be right as wrong. In other words, its output is entirely freed of its input chaperonage after a sufficiently long spell of activity. Nor is this an isolated case. It is typical of all complicated networks having long stimulus-response chains. For the probabilities of even small errors in the basic organs sooner or later self-amplify to such an extent as to make the final output totally unreliable or irrelevant to the initial inputs of the network. While on the one hand the reliability of a network rapidly deteriorates as more and more failure-prone neurons are cascaded together to form it, there is, on the other hand, also a lower limit of error which it cannot possibly evade, no matter how few components it may contain.

Suppose, for instance, we are given a basic universal organ such as Sheffer stroke with a probability (e) of misfiring.   Clearly any output of such an automaton is the immediate result of an operation of a single-output neuron so that the reliability of the whole system cannot be better than that of this last component, that is, e.   How can we then construct from such unreliable organs an automaton yielding the desired response with an arbitrarily small probability of error very much smaller than e itself?

Von Neumann's "multiple-line trick," which enables the automaton to surpass this threshold restriction on its reliability, is a marvel of mathematical ingenuity.   The "trick" consists in carrying all the messages or impulses simultaneously on a bundle of several fibers instead of a single strand as in the networks hitherto described.   In other words, each (single) neuron becomes a packet of n such fibers. Von Neumann's majority organ with three input receptor neurons and one output effector described in Chapter XI becomes an instance of such a "multiplexed" network, if we agree to treat all the three input neurons as simply three separate strands, lines, or fibers of a single one.   When we do so, we adopt the convention that the stimulation of a (specified) majority of strands or lines of a bundle is interpreted as a positive state of the bundle as a whole.   Thus if the bundle consists of, say, N lines and the specified majority proportion is d, a proper fraction naturally exceeding $\frac{1}{2}$, then the stimulation of any dN or more lines in the bundle constitutes the state of stimulation of the bundle as a whole.   Stimulation of fewer than dN lines in the bundle corresponds to its non-stimulated state.   All other states of stimulation are treated as malfunctions.

To see how multiplexing helps control the accumulation of errors in a complex network, consider first the case of von Neumann's majority organ itself.   As we saw, its input consists of a bundle of three lines and output is determined by a majority vote of the three input lines. Thus if the three inputs are 111, the output is 1; if 100, it is 0; if 101, it is 1, and so on.   Suppose that we have such a majority organ with probability e of being in error and with probabilities f_1, f_2, f_3 that the input lines carry wrong signals.   Then, although $e + f_1 + f_2 + f_3$ is clearly an upper bound for the probability that the output lines are in error, it is far too gross to yield an automaton with arbitrarily high reliability such as that we are seeking.   However, we can obtain a finer upper bound if we make two assumptions that seem quite reasonable, that (*a*) the probabilities of error are independent, and that (b) under normal conditions all lines are in the same state of excitation, that is, all stimulated or all unstimulated. Then the probability P of *at least* two inputs being in error is clearly the sum of the probabilities of the following four events which are the only cases where *at least* two inputs misfire:

		Probability
(i)	Lines 2 and 3 wrong but line 1 right	$f_2 f_3 (1 - f_1)$
(ii)	Lines 3 and 1 wrong but line 2 right	$f_1 f_3 (1 - f_2)$
(iii)	Lines 1 and 2 wrong but line 3 right	$f_1 f_2 (1 - f_3)$
(iv)	Lines 1, 2, 3 wrong and none right	$f_1 f_2 f_3$

Then,

$$\begin{aligned} P &= f_2 f_3 (1 - f_1) + f_1 f_3 (1 - f_2) + f_1 f_2 (1 - f_3) + f_1 f_2 f_3 \\ &= f_1 f_2 + f_2 f_3 + f_3 f_1 - 2 f_1 f_2 f_3 \\ &\leqslant 3f^2 - 2f^3 \end{aligned} \tag{3}$$

where f is an upper bound of f_1, f_2, and f_3 so that f_1, f_2, and $f_3 \leqslant f$. From (3) we can derive the probability Q of the output being in error. This is an event which occurs either because the input is wrong and the output is right or vice versa. The probability of the former conjunction is $(1 - e)P$ while that of the latter is $e(1 - P)$ so that

$$Q = (1 - e)P + e(1 - P) = e + (1 - 2e)P \tag{4}$$

Now as we saw, $e + f_1 + f_2 + f_3$, or $e + 3f$, is a general upper bound for Q. In the general case therefore each operation of the automaton increases the probability of error, since $e + 3f$ exceeds f, with the result that if the serial depth of the machine, that is, the number of elements such as neurons, relays, tubes, or transistors arranged in series, is very great, it is impractical or impossible to obtain any kind of accuracy. But under the special conditions of the case we have stipulated above, we may obtain from (3) and (4) a finer upper bound for Q. For

$$\begin{aligned} Q &= e + (1 - 2e)P = e + (1 - 2e)(3f^2 - f^3) \\ &\leqslant e + (3f^2 - f^3) \\ &\leqslant e + 3f^2. \end{aligned} \tag{5}$$

Since $e + 3f^2 < f$ is quite possible, the error Q of the output of the automaton is less than that of any single malfunction and can therefore be kept under control. Consequently the chance of keeping the error of the system as a whole under check lies in maintaining throughout its construction the postulated conditions (*a*) and (*b*) of the special case cited above.   Von Neumann invented a very elegant artifice which, while ensuring their continuation, was also designed to inject into the network a measure of redundancy sufficient to secure the prescribed degree of reliability.

The basic idea underlying von Neumann's error-control scheme is similar to that of his majority organ, that is, to provide a plethora of machines with unreliable parts where one would do if all its components were reliable.   Consequently, instead of running the incoming data into a single machine, the same information is simultaneously fed into a number of identical machines and the result that comes out

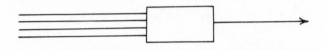

Fig. 66   Network *S*.

of a majority of these machines is assumed to be true, exactly as is the case with his majority organ.   As will be recalled, the latter's outcome too is decided by a majority vote of its inputs.   Hence, if in lieu of any given network *S* we start with several copies thereof, we may apply the theory of von Neumann's majority organ to the network *S'* formed by a union of several replicates of the original *S*.   Consider, for example, the case of a network *S* having four inputs and one output as in Fig. 66.   Then the new network *S'*, formed by constructing *S* in triplicate, is the network shown in Fig. 67.   The three outputs of the triplicate set may now be used as three inputs of a new majority organ *m* whose output is determined by a majority vote of the three *outputs* of the triplicate S_1, S_2, S_3 of the original *S*.   By thus incorporating a three-input majority organ to decide the outcome of the new network *S'* instead of the original *S* we are able to make use of the error-control mechanism whose basis is the lower upper bound (5) derived earlier.   Von Neumann proved that, provided the initial probability of error *e* is less than $\frac{1}{6}$, we can by successive repetitions of the aforementioned process keep the error of the replicated system under check. Thus for *e* = 0.08, that is, for an error level of 8 per cent in a single basic organ, the ultimate error in the replicated network with three-fold redundancy will continue to remain below 0.1, or about 10 per cent. Actually e has to be less than 0.0073 if error is to be reduced to any reasonably acceptable level. Thus von Neumann has shown that for an ultimate error level of 2 per cent, e should be less than 0.0041, that is, 0.41 per cent. This is not to say that an increasingly higher degree of reliability in the ultimate network requires correspondingly higher reliability of the single basic organ. It could be relaxed by repeating the process of triplication a sufficient number of times, though the inequality $e < \frac{1}{6}$ is essential. He showed that, subject only to e being less than $\frac{1}{6}$, an error-control mechanism can always be devised to reduce the ultimate error of the network below any preassigned level. All that we need do is to replicate the given network a sufficient number of times and pass each particular output

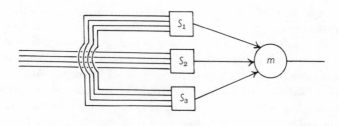

Fig. 67

of the replicated networks via majority organs in the manner described. The procedure, however, is totally impractical as it achieves its end by resort to uncontrolled replication and redundancy. Thus for each link in the serial chain of the original network von Neumann's method of construction triples the number of basic organs required, so that the replicated network has to accommodate 3^m such organs, where m is the number of links in the original network chain. Thus if m is 170, which is by no means an excessive "logical" depth for even a conventional computer, 3^{170} would equal approximately 3×10^{81}. This is a number about 300 times larger than Eddington's estimate of the total number of electrons in the universe. Fortunately von Neumann's "multiple-line trick" or "multiplexing" technique mentioned earlier is a more reasonable substitute in that it avoids the orgy of fantastically proliferating basic organs, though only in a relative way. Instead of inflating basic organs 10^{81} times, it multiplies *input* lines of such organs by factors of the order of only 10^4. Multiplexing their input lines considerably reduces the number of organs we need synthesize to secure the prescribed level of reliability. It is therefore worth our while to examine its error-control possibilities.

As already mentioned, multiplexing technique is merely an extension of the principle adopted in the construction of von Neumann's three-input majority organ. We replace its three input lines by any number N input lines. The general process of multiplexing requires that the message be carried over N input lines in parallel instead of only three used in the case of the majority organ. The substitution of N for three, however, introduces a new feature. With three input lines we need not specify the majority required, for only two or more lines can constitute it. But with any N exceeding 3 *any* integer above $\frac{N}{2}$ yields a majority. We have therefore to specify beforehand what level of majority of input lines is to determine the output of this new generalized version of our three-input majority organ. To do so a positive number $d < \frac{1}{2}$ is chosen and it is decreed that if $(1 - d)N$ lines or more are stimulated, it is a positive message, designated by a 1; otherwise it is the reverse type, designated by an 0. Any other number of stimulated lines is considered a malfunction of the system. The complete system is then organized in such a manner that a malfunction of the whole automaton or network cannot be caused by the misfiring of a single component or of a small number of components but only by that of a large number of them. It is only by making the failure of the whole network depend on the simultaneous failure of a large number of its components by a sufficiently high redundancy of input lines that von Neumann succeeds in making the probability of its occurrence arbitrarily small. In other words, he achieves reliability by introducing redundancy exactly as all reliable communications systems including the language of our daily use actually do. The difference is that the redundancy of input lines according to von Neumann's reliability recipe is on a staggeringly lavish scale though much less than that encountered before. The following table, reproduced from von Neumann's classic paper,* gives an idea of the prodigious redundancy factor of input lines required for various preassigned levels of probabilities of ultimate error or malfunction of the network as a whole.

---

* "Probabilistic Logics and the Synthesis of Reliable Organisms from Unreliable Components," in *Automata Studies*, C. E. Shannon and J. McCarthy, eds., Princeton University Press, 1956.

TABLE 37

N = number of input lines in a bundle	Probability of malfunction
1000	2.7×10^{-2}
2000	2.6×10^{-3}
3000	2.5×10^{-4}
5000	4.0×10^{-6}
10,000	1.6×10^{-10}
20,000	2.8×10^{-19}
25,000	1.2×10^{-23}

It will be seen that even with as large a redundancy factor as 1000, that is, with 1000 lines for each line of an ordinary network, the reliability is quite poor, barely 2.7 per cent. But it begins to improve considerably for each successive rise in redundancy factor. For the sake of definiteness, consider two cases, one of a moderate-size artificial automaton, say, a computer with 2500 vacuum tubes, and another of the living brain, the natural automaton with its equipment of some 10 billion neurons. If each vacuum tube in the computer is actuated on the average once every 5 microseconds, it will have in all some $\frac{3600 \times 10^6 \times 2500}{5} = 1.8 \times 10^{12}$ actuations per hour. Consequently, if we require an error-free operation of the automaton on the average every shift of 8 hours, the probability of malfunction must remain below $\frac{1}{1.8 \times 8 \times 10^{12}} = 7 \times 10^{-14}$. Von Neumann's table above shows that the redundancy factor N must lie between 10,000 and 20,000. An easy interpolation will fix it at about 14,000. Consequently the system must be "multiplexed" 14,000 times—which is merely a way of saying that every input line of the given network should be proliferated some 14,000-fold. In the second case, that of our natural automaton, the living brain with its complement of 10^{10} neurons, each neuron may be assumed to act on the average about 10 times per second. If we further postulate that the living brain has not committed any serious (biological) error over all the millennia since its emergence at the peak of the evolutionary ladder, the number of neural activations during this period of, say, 10^6 years would amount to $10^6 \times 365 \times 24 \times 3600 \times 10 \times 10^{10} = 3.2 \times 10^{24}$. Hence the automaton has to work with a malfunctioning probability lower than $\frac{1}{3.2 \times 10^{24}} = 3 \times 10^{-25}$. Table 37 again shows that the redundancy factor must be around 25,000. Indeed, when we require an order of reliability as exacting as the one considered here, we find that the order of magnitude of N is remarkably insensitive to variations in requirements. Thus Table 37 shows that an increase of reliability by a factor of about 10,000, that is, from 2.8×10^{-19} to 1.2×10^{-23}, merely raises N from 20,000 to 25,000—by only 25 per cent.

Von Neumann's scheme of "multiplexing" or providing built-in redundancy in the construction of an automaton for securing an arbitrarily high degree of reliability by a synthesis of unreliable components may then be summarized as follows:

Suppose we require an automaton to conform to any given input-output specifications and having a given (low) probability (a) of ultimate malfunction on the final result of the entire operation. Suppose further we use in its construction Sheffer neurons whose probability (e) of misfire in any single operation is also known. First, we design an automaton or network R conforming to the given specifications, using basic universal Sheffer organs whose neurons function with perfect accuracy. Secondly, we estimate the maximum number of reactions of all such single Sheffer organs actually assembled in the network R. Let the number of such reactions be m. Put $d = \dfrac{a}{m}$.

Thirdly, we refer to von Neumann's Table 37 to derive the bundle size N that is needed to give a "multiplexed" Sheffer organlike network an error probability of at most d. Fourthly, we replace each line of the network R by the "multiplexed" Sheffer organ network associated with this N. This is, then, the network having enough redundancy fed into it to yield any preassigned reliability in its ultimate outcome that we may desire.

As we saw, once reliability is pitched at a really stringent standard, N remains fairly stable in the face of any subsequent (moderate) change in reliability specification. Thus a ceiling value of N near the 20,000–25,000 range would seem to meet the reliability requirements of both the computer and the brain that are of immediate interest to us. Such proliferation of input lines as von Neumann's multiplexing procedure demands is therefore plainly beyond the resources of our present-day technology, even though it may well be feasible in the future when we have carried micro-miniaturization a stage further. At present, thanks to the newest techniques in electronics, we can just about pack a highly complex electrical circuit within a pea-sized capsule. If we could compress it still more to put it within a molecule no bigger than that of a protein, as is apparently the case with neural circuits of the nervous system, we could readily take advantage of the multiplexing principle. Hence multiplexing is by no means a basically untenable concept. At any rate it cannot be ruled out on grounds of size alone.

It is therefore quite natural to ask specifically whether it, or something more or less like it, is a feature of the actually existing animal nervous system. Some similarity is indubitable. The nerves are bundles of fibers not unlike the bundles in a multiplexed system. The nervous system also contains numerous "neural pools" whose function may be similar to what multiplexing does, namely, preventing self-amplification of errors caused by aberrant neurons. Yet the differences between the nervous system and the multiplexed model network we have constructed are deep. First, the nervous system is much more versatile than our neural network, incorporating, as it does, aspects of both the digital and analogy procedures. The digital action of neural operations freely dovetails into the analogue processes of humoral media in their complete chain of causation. For example, the pulse trains that carry quantitative messages along the nerve fibers do not seem to be coded digital representations of a number but rather analogue expressions of one by means of pulse frequency modulation as described earlier in Chapter X. Secondly, the whole logical pattern of the nervous system seems to depart in many significant ways from the conventional procedures of mathematics and mathematical logic that are the main inspiration of the construction plan underlying multiplexed networks. To name one specific instance of such departure: the "logical depth" of our neural operations, that is, the total number of basic operations from (sensory) input to (memory) storage or (motor) output, seems to be much less than it would be in any artificial automaton or computer dealing with problems of anywhere nearly comparable complexity. Thus profound differences in the basic organizational principles governing the nervous system and von Neumann's multiplexed model are certainly present. This is why von Neumann concludes the description of his system with the warning that "it is dangerous to identify the real physical (or biological) world with the models which are constructed to explain it. The problem of understanding the animal nervous action is far deeper than the problem of understanding the mechanism of a computing machine. Even plausible explanations of nervous reaction should be taken with a very large grain of salt."

Chapter XIII

TURING MACHINES

VON NEUMANN'S warning against identifying computing machines and neuron networks with the animal nervous system is quite opportune in view of the present controversy concerning whether or not machines can think. Take first the digital computer we described in Chapter IX. As we saw, it merely works out what has already been thought of beforehand by the designer and supplied to it in the form of program instructions. In fact, it obeys these instructions as literally as the unfortunate Casabianca boy who remained on the burning deck because his father had told him to do so. For instance, if in the course of a computation the machine requires the quotient of two numbers of which the divisor happens to be zero, it will go on, Sisyphus-like, trying to divide by zero forever unless expressly forbidden by prior instruction. A human computer would certainly not go on dividing by zero, whatever else he might do. The incapacity of the machine to deviate one whit from what the "moving finger" of prior instructions has already decreed makes it necessary to think out in advance every possible contingency that might arise in the course of the work and give the machine appropriate instructions for each case. Is the limitation imposed by this conservation law whereby the machine is incapable of originating a new instruction or idea destined to remain forever? Or will designers be able to construct in course of time automata able to do their own thinking like Rossum robots in Karel Čapek's *R.U.R.* or the Great Brains in Olaf Stapledon's *First and Last Men*? There are no unequivocal answers to these questions. It all depends on the meaning we choose to assign to the verb "to think." If we adopt a behavioristic definition of the term as the English logician A. M. Turing and his followers suggest, we may consider a machine capable of "thinking" provided it can be made to imitate a human being by answering questions sufficiently well to deceive for a reasonable time its human interlocutor into believing that he is conversing with another human being. Such "operational" or "behavioristic" tests of thinking are designed to steer clear of allegedly phantom notions of consciousness, ego, mind, and the like. However, in thus trying to avoid them we seem to run into the pragmatic error of identifying illusion with reality, provided it is sufficiently illusive. Thus Zeuxis's painted grapes that lured the birds of the field to peck at them, or Duchamp's false pieces of marble which lead the unwary onlooker to think they are sugar would have to be treated as "real," at any rate till the moment of disillusionment. Some tough-minded "practical" people, who are only concerned with the "cash" value of the "experiential reality" facing them at the moment, may not mind being so hoodwinked by what they would no doubt regard perfectly (though temporarily) valid reasons. The rub is that even success in an imitation game by a Turing machine may not suffice to warrant crediting it with the faculty of genuine thinking. For such a machine, in a sense, for any given input situation including past history, merely scans its input-output specification table or built-in dictionary to yield the associated response. With a suitable dictionary it would surely satisfy Turing's criterion of successful mimicry but will not reflect our usual intuitive concept of thinking. This suggests that a more fundamental definition of thinking must involve something relating to what we call understanding shown by a person who solves a problem by thinking it out and lacking in another who has previously learned the answer by rote. While we will deal with the question more fully later, it is nevertheless interesting to examine the theory of general-purpose computers which can play successfully Turing's imitation game. Not that there is at present any possibility of actually making a machine satisfying Turing's stringent criterion. But Turing himself has speculated that within a few decades it should be possible to make one. What then are these thinking machines *à la* Turing that are designed to "think," at least in the behavioristic sense of the word if not in its more fundamental intuitive meaning?

The basic idea underlying Turing machines is a denial of what seems at first sight eminently plausible. We should normally expect the yield or output of an automaton to be at least a shade less complicated than itself. In particular, if an automaton has the ability to construct another, there must be a decrease in complication as we proceed from the parent to the progeny. For the parent must somehow contain within it not only a complete description of the offspring it breeds but also various arrangements to carry out the instructions to implement the description.   In consequence, some decrease in complexity or "patternedness" is to be expected as one automaton makes another.   Nevertheless, the expectation is clearly contrary to the most obvious facts of life.   Organisms not only reproduce themselves, that is, give birth to new ones with no decrease in complexity, but have even produced during the long billennia of evolution increasingly complex beings.   This discrepancy between actuality and anticipation is, however, merely an instance of the apparent conflict between the second law of thermodynamics inexorably driving all matter towards increasing disorder or "mixed-upness" and the process of biological evolution with its continual unfolding of new patterns of order and organization.   We showed in Chapter VII how it could be resolved by trading information for negentropy so that the tendency of ordinary matter towards increasing chaos and disorder may be stemmed.   As we saw, cellular enzymes receive at birth in a coded form genetic information of great specificity whereby they are able to duplicate themselves out of materials present instead of letting those materials drift into chaos.   Turing gave a logically rigorous rationale of all such duplicating processes whether natural or artificial.   He showed that any automaton or computing machine that has the minimum proper information or, more precisely, the minimum proper number of instructions, can simulate any other automaton, however large the instruction repertoire of the latter.   In other words, there need be no diminution in complexity as one automaton constructs another.   On the other hand, it may well increase so that it may even be made to reproduce another twice as effective and complex as itself.

To prove that all this is possible in principle, Turing sketched the outline of an idealized computer not limited in use by a fixed maximum of amount of storage of information nor liable to any malfunction as actual computing machines are.   Although the machine Turing described in his classical paper* was concerned with the computation of computable numbers, that is, real numbers whose expressions as a decimal are calculable by finite means, it could easily be adapted to compute any function whose argument is an integral, real, or computable variable or for that matter any predicate that is

---

* "On Computable Numbers, with an Application to the Entscheidungsproblem," *Proceedings of the London Mathematical Society (Ser. 2)*, Vol. 42, 1936.   Also "A Correction," *Ibid.*, Vol. 43, 1937.

computable at all.   In other words, a Turing machine is designed
to handle the general computation problem, namely, what functions
or numbers can be computed or effectively calculated in the sense that
for a given argument, the value of the function can be found by use
only of preassigned rules, applicable without any ingenuity on the
part of the computer and built into its structure.

To understand how a Turing machine operates, consider first a
computer which writes its numbers in a form even simpler than the
binary system of the digital computers.   That is, it writes them as

Fig. 68

mere strings of unit marks 1 exactly as the caveman did when he
carved a tally or tick mark on the wall for each object he wanted to
count.   Thus it would write the number five not as 101 as in the
binary notation of the digital computer but simply as a row of five
units: 11111, somewhat like a caveman's row of five tally marks to
keep a "record" of his five babies.   Since the machine writes numbers in their most primitive form, mere strings of unit marks 1, it has
to operate with a potentially infinite paper tape, say, one inch wide
divided into equal segments each one inch long so that it is really a
sequence of infinite squares.   All numbers involved in any computation it has to perform are then written on this tape as strings of unit
marks 1, each square carrying a single mark 1.   Number five, for
example, would be written as a row of five consecutive 1's: 11111,
each "1" occupying one square of the tape as shown in Fig. 69.   In
order to distinguish one string of 1's representing any number, say,

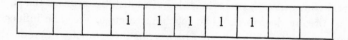

Fig. 69

five, from another representing a second number, say, three, a separation or punctuation mark X is used to indicate where a number string begins and where it ends, as shown in Fig. 70. Any tape square of the

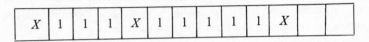

| X | 1 | 1 | 1 | X | 1 | 1 | 1 | 1 | 1 | X | | |

Fig. 70

machine therefore may carry the symbol 1 (the unit mark), the symbol X (the punctuation mark), or may remain blank, which we may denote by the cypher mark 0. The machine itself is merely a "black box" about whose internal mechanism nothing is assumed except that it is at any given time in one and only one of n possible alternative states consecutively catalogued $q_1, q_2, \ldots, q_n$. For convenience we may imagine it to have outside it a dial, indicating which of the n states it is in at any particular instant of time (see Fig. 71).

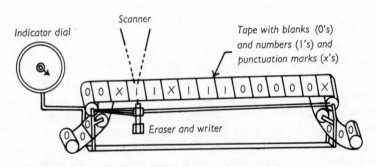

Fig. 71

Thus at one moment t it may be in a state, say, q_3, shown by the position of the needle at the mark q_3 on the dial, and at the next instant, $t + 1$, move into another state, say, q_5, shown by the needle jump from q_3 to q_5 on the dial. Such shifts from one discrete state to another—outwardly shown by a corresponding shift of the needle on the indicator dial—occur in response to influences from the outside world with which the machine is kept in touch by means of the paper tape already described. The machine reacts to the tape influence by means of its reading head which scans the symbol written on the square happening to fall under its view at any time. Having read the symbol inscribed on the scanned square, its next act depends on the symbol it has just read as well as on its own internal state at the instant of reading. Thus if at any time t the machine is in state q_3 and the tape symbol read at the time is 0, the pair $(q_3, 0)$ defines the configuration which determines the next act of the machine. This act may alter the situation in three possible ways. First, the scanned symbol 0 may be changed into 1 or X or may remain the same. Secondly, the tape may be shifted in the machine one square to the right or one square to the left or may remain where it is. Thirdly, the machine state q_3 is altered to some other which may in

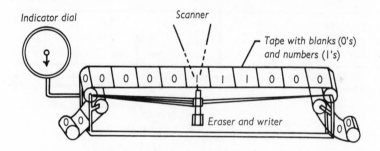

Fig. 72

particular even be q_3 itself. The machine's operation is thus defined by a table of commands which specifies all the afore-mentioned three-fold aspects of each successive act as the machine clicks off one move after another and stops in a final or terminal situation called output. Consider, for instance, a simple Turing machine capable of only two internal states q_1 and q_2 with its tape having the appearance shown in Fig. 72. As will be observed, three consecutive squares on the tape carry 1's and the rest 0's. If the initial state of the machine is q_2 and the machine specifications describing its successive clicks or moves are as in Table 38, it is easy to see that the machine's final output will be to

(i) seek the first square printed with a 0 to the right of the scanned square;

(ii) print a 1 there; and

(iii) stop in state q_1 scanning that square.

For at the outset our machine is in state q_2 with its reading head scanning the symbol 1 in the square which we identify by pointing the arrowhead over it. In this configuration the act ordained by Table

38 is that the tape is shifted one square to the left, the symbol in the scanned square remains unchanged, i.e., 1, and the machine relapses again into state q_2. The resulting situation therefore appears as follows, with the scanning head of the machine over the tape square marked with the arrow in Fig. 73 below.

TABLE 38*

Starting situation		Resultant situation		
Machine state	Scanned symbol	Tape shift	Machine state	Change in scanned symbol
q_2	1	To the left	q_2	1
q_2	0	Stop	q_1	1
q_1	1	Stop	q_1	1
q_1	0	To the right	q_2	1

* Since the machine is assumed to have only two possible internal states q_1 and q_2 and the tape symbols are also only two, 0 and 1, there are only 2 × 2 or four possible starting situations of the system, namely, $(q_2, 1)$, $(q_2, 0)$, $(q_1, 1)$ and $(q_1, 0)$, all of which have been listed in the table.

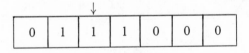

Fig. 73

The next two acts lead successively to the following situations:

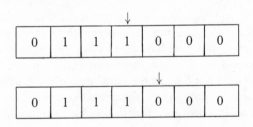

Fig. 74

In the last-mentioned situation the machine is in state q_2 and the reading head scans a 0. The next act according to Table 38 is that now the tape is not shifted any more, the symbol 0 on the scanned square is altered to 1, and the machine comes to a stop in state q_1 as shown in Fig. 75 on the next page.

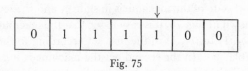

Fig. 75

In other words, the machine has found the first blank square marked 0 to the right of the first scanned square, printed a 1 there, and come to rest in that position as already mentioned. The single operation of searching the first blank square on the tape to the right has thus been resolved into four discrete steps or atomic acts. To take another instance of how a Turing machine breaks down each operation or computation into a series of atomic acts performed by the machine's successive clicks from one state to another, suppose we feed a tape with the inscription

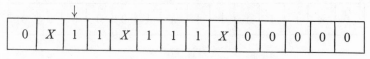

Fig. 76

into a Turing machine capable of assuming four distinct internal states: q_1, q_2, q_3, q_4. Suppose further its table of commands specifying what it will do under any given starting situation is as shown in Table 39.*

TABLE 39

Starting situation		Resultant situation		
Machine state	Scanned symbol	Tape shift	Machine state	Change in scanned symbol
q_1	1	To the left	q_1	1
q_1	X	To the left	q_2	1
q_2	1	To the left	q_3	1
q_3	1	To the left	q_4	1
q_4	1	Stop	q_4	X

* Since there are four possible internal states of the machine each of which may be combined with three possible symbols on the tape square, the table of commands has to provide for $4 \times 3 = 12$ contingencies. We have not specified in the table the resultant situations corresponding to the remaining eight possibilities. These may be made to suit other computations the machine may be required to perform or other requirements. For instance, corresponding to the starting situation (q_4, X), the resultant situation is stop, q_4, X.

If the original state of the machine is in state q_1 and the scanned symbol is 1 as shown in Fig. 76, it is easy to see that the machine will move from state $(q_1, 1)$ to $(q_1, 1)$ in the first act according to the first command of Table 39.   In the second act the machine is in state q_1 and scans the symbol 1, the tape is shifted to the left one square, and the machine goes again into state q_1.   The symbol scanned now is X so that the starting situation is (q_1, X).   The command in Table 39 now requires that X in the scanned square be changed to 1 and that the tape move leftward, going over into state q_2.   In state q_2 it scans the symbol 1, so that its next state is q_3 and the symbol scanned is 1. From the starting situation $(q_3, 1)$ the machine moves into state q_4 and comes to a stop substituting X for the symbol 1 in the scanned square. The tape of Fig. 76 therefore now begins to look like that in Fig. 77.

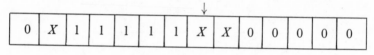

Fig. 77

It will be seen that the machine has substituted 1 for the punctuation mark X separating the two numbers 11 and 111 and changed the last symbol 1 of the second number into an X.   In other words, the machine has added the two numbers two and three to make the sum five.   The operation of adding two numbers has thus been broken down into six atomic acts or clicks of the machine.

If all this seems like putting a mountain in labor to produce a mouse, it must be added that herein lies the germ of Turing's brilliant breakthrough.   For *any* computation, no matter how complex, so long as it is at all performable, can be broken down into a series of atomic acts or successive clicks from one discrete state of the machine to another.   Turing carried out a careful analysis of what mathematical computations can be effected by automata of this type.   He showed that, proceeding on these lines, one could construct a machine capable of performing any particular computation or for that matter any task.   Since the heart of the machine designed for a given computation is its specification table describing the successive clicks or moves whose terminal click leads to the desired result, Turing devised a completely general but numerical code of writing it out.   To do so he first invented a standard way of summarizing any given specification table and then transformed the summary description into a numerical code, thus converting the specification table or its standard description literally into its catalogue number. A Turing machine, whose infinite tape carries the catalogue numbers of all kinds of specific computing machines and which is provided with a key to break the catalogue code, will be able to duplicate the computation that the corresponding machine is designed to perform. Such a machine is thus universal in the sense that it can perform not merely some given computation but any kind of computation that is at all performable. If we print on the machine tape the standard description of any machine in the Turing code, it will write the answer in the remaining free portion of the tape. It will, of course, require in general a different standard description or instruction for a different computation, but the (potential) infinity of its tape enables us to conceive of a universal Turing machine capable of taking in its stride all kinds of computations that are at all computable. In other words, there exists a way of so cataloguing all possible Turing machines that we may conceive of a universal Turing machine so constructed that when it reads the catalogue number of the specific Turing machine in question it would carry out the computation that that machine would have performed were it put on the blank tape. Indeed, any one of the present electronic computers would be a universal Turing machine in this sense if it knew how to ask for more punched cards and demand the return of those it had already punched. Obviously the last-mentioned proviso is equivalent to the infinite tape of a universal Turing machine. The potential infinity of the tape gives the machine another advantage. It enables a vast simplification of its logical design. As hitherto described, a universal Turing machine can be in one of a definite number n of internal states, $q_1, q_2, \ldots, q_n$, while its potentially infinite tape carries one of three symbols, 0, 1, X, in each tape square. Shannon has shown that the number n of its internal states may be reduced to only two, provided the number of symbols in which tape instructions are written is suitably increased. That is, a universal Turing machine can be designed having only two internal states provided it is given an adequately large alphabet or repertoire of tape symbols. On the other hand, we can reduce the number of tape symbols to only two by suitably enlarging the number of its internal states. There is thus a close tie-up between the number n of its internal states and number m of its tape symbols. If we have, therefore, a universal Turing machine A with n internal states and m tape symbols, we can make another universal machine B having only two internal states but at most $4 mn + m$ tape symbols.   Similarly another universal Turing machine C operating with only two tape symbols can also be designed; but it will then need to have at most $8 mn$ internal states.   In sum, it is possible within limits to barter tape symbols for machine states and vice versa.   Accordingly, to make a universal Turing machine we require either a *minimum* of two internal states in the machine *or* alternatively a *minimum* of two tape symbols.

While machines can be designed to utilize the Turing principle of one computer's reproducing another by reading its description from a tape, von Neumann has broadened the principle to cover the phenomenon of biological reproduction actually at work in nature.   For the description may be recorded not merely on a paper tape but also in the genetic materials of which genes and chromosomes are made.   It is now known that compounds of carbon by chemical bonding, isomerization (both structural and stereo) multiplication of benzene ring structure, and polymerization provide an infinite variety of materials which can and do carry genetic information of great specificity given them at birth in a coded form.   As we know, the chief carrier of the genetic information that tells the enzymes concerned what to do in the process of protein build-up are the DNA molecules.   Given a large number of such information-carrying molecules or more generally mechanisms or automata floating in a vast reservoir such as J. B. S. Haldane's "hot dilute soup" of protein precursors spread over the oceans covering a large part of our globe, would they begin to construct other molecules or mechanisms exactly like themselves?   In other words, if we replace the original Turing tape by a more diffuse medium such as Haldane's hot dilute soup in the oceans, where material carriers of information are planted and moved freely about, would there result a broader and more general version of the Turing principle?   Von Neumann has examined the problem.   He has shown that on the basis of certain logically rigorous definitions of what constitutes an automaton, construction, reproduction, and so on, it is entirely feasible to reformulate Turing's principle in an extended context so as to yield a valuable insight into the nature of biological reproduction.   His main conclusion is that while "complication" on its lower levels is probably degenerative—that is, while every automaton that can produce other automata will be able only to produce less complicated ones—once it exceeds a certain minimum critical level it can and does evade this degenerative tendency.   Degeneration of reproductive information is therefore like gravity in that, to escape it, the system must accumulate a certain minimum of complication in one case and velocity in the other. Once arrived at this critical point, automata, which can reproduce themselves or even construct higher entities, become possible. This fact—that complication as well as organization below a certain minimum level is degenerative and beyond that level can become self-supporting and even increasing—will clearly play an increasing role in the future theory of automata. It is a principle writ large in the blossoming of life from its inanimate roots and its subsequent evolution from some "subvital" autocatalytic molecule of protein all the way to man. In an age on the threshold of extensive and large-scale automation we are bound to hear more of it as the first crude formulations of its originators are refined.

Indeed, this principle, even in its narrow initial version of a universal Turing machine that imitates another, is already the basis of elaborate automatic coding programs leading to more and more complex computers. As we saw in Chapter IX, every computer has to be fed with a program of precise instructions appropriately codified. Such a program of codified instructions is the machine's *complete* code. The use of a modern computer is based on the programer's ability to develop and formulate complete codes for any given problem that the machine is required to solve. But in contrast to these complete codes, computer experts have by recourse to the ideas of Turing developed code-instruction systems for a computing machine which cause it to behave as if it were another specified computing machine. Such systems of instructions which make one machine imitate the behavior of another are known as *short* codes or autocodes. There are in vogue now many autocodes such as Ferranti Autocode, Flow-Matic, FORTRAN, and so on, all differing from one another in various ways and yet all mere embodiments of Turing's theorem. They are the props supporting various kinds of automatic programing techniques which have since been perfected to automatize even the task of programing computer instructions. Turing had a clear premonition of the vast potentialities of such automatic programing techniques. He predicted that they would be sufficiently perfected by the end of the twentieth century to make it possible to program computers with the colossal storage capacity of a billion bits. Such computers could play the imitation game so well that "an average interrogator will not have more than a 70 per cent chance of making the right identification after five minutes' questioning." They could also be made to perform a wide gamut of tasks. A machine could, for instance, write sonnets and having written one could be put to a viva-voce test to discover whether it really "understood" what it was doing or just wrote it parrot-wise without any real "comprehension." Turing suggests that it could in fact hold its own against its human interlocutor by sustaining impromptu a dialogue of the kind quoted below:

INTERROGATOR: In the first line of your sonnet which reads "Shall I compare thee to a summer's day" would not a "spring day" do as well or better?

WITNESS: It wouldn't scan.

INTERROGATOR: How about a "winter's day"? That would scan all right.

WITNESS: Yes, but nobody wants to be compared to a winter's day.

INTERROGATOR: Would you say Mr. Pickwick reminded you of Christmas?

WITNESS: In a way.

INTERROGATOR: Yet Christmas is a winter's day and I do not think Mr. Pickwick would mind the comparison.

WITNESS: I don't think you are serious. By winter's day one means a typical winter's day, rather than a special one like Christmas.

Even though Turing considered sonnet-writing machines of the future quite capable of debating issues in the above-quoted style, he was nevertheless fully aware of the behavioristic fallacy of equating mind-like activity with that of the human mind. As he conceded at the end of his charming essay "Can a Machine Think?" he had no very "convincing arguments" of a positive nature to support the behavior-istic position he advocated, only "certain fallacies in contrary views." He held that the only really satisfactory support for the conclusion he sought to deduce was the construction of a Turing machine with a billion-bit storage capacity actually playing the imitation game. However, our present inability to make such a machine is no reason why we need shelve the basic issue under debate, namely, to what extent, if any, the physical basis of computer or machine "thinking" approximates that of the human brain.

It is a great merit of cybernetics that it has recently highlighted the problem of the physical basis of thought and consciousness in animals and men exactly as earlier biology and biochemistry sought the basis of life itself. In the past we have been only too tempted to mask our total ignorance of the real complexities of both by pompous verbiage making much sound and fury but signifying nothing. In the one case, "*generatio aequivoca, generatio primaria*" expressed the belief that fully grown living organisms arise miraculously out of non-living matter; in the other, "*cogito, ergo sum*" stimulated by "*toto caelo*" in the conarion embodied the "ghost-in-the-machine" philosophy or mind-body dualism of Réné Descartes that has dominated Western thought during the last three centuries. Just as modern biochemistry has put an end to all the mystical rodomontade of the vitalists, telefinalists, and creative evolutionists, who thought of life as a "miracle" inexplicable by appeal to ordinary physico-chemical laws of ordinary matter, so also cybernetics today bids fair to debunk the parallel notion that life's consciousness stems from some mysterious intangible "spirit" or "soul" somehow animating the body from within. For living substances have now been shown to be built up of the same kinds of atoms as are found in non-living matter, with no evidence of any vital spirit entering it when it wakes to life or leaving it when it dies. What is therefore required is a naturalistic explanation of life's intelligence and consciousness in terms of physics and chemistry. It is true that the present state of these sciences is far from equal to the task of unraveling all the knots in the tangle of life and consciousness. But thanks to recent advances in what may compendiously be described as microtechniques such as electron-microscopy, x-ray diffraction, tracer chemistry, and so on, the progress already made in tracking the very real differences in the behavior of animate and inanimate matter to their objective foundations in some kind of spatio-temporal relationships makes it all but certain that such an explanation is in principle now possible even though it may take a long while to be fully spelled out. Consequently the scientific materialism or atomism of today that seeks the physical basis of life, intelligence, and consciousness is no mere speculative dogma like that of Democritus, which merely made the universe a thing of wonder to be stared at and despaired. It is, on the contrary, an unfailing guide to further research designed to unravel the mystery in these areas, as recent advances in genetics, biophysics, and biochemistry clearly show. More specifically it has already enabled us to make certain artifacts exhibiting in varying though rudimentary measure one or more of the fundamental attributes of life such as growth, reproduction, homeostasis, memory, learning, intelligence, and consciousness.

Since certain types of activities associated with animate beings, such as homeostasis, thinking, or learning, may be simulated by artifacts made of non-biological materials, fierce debates have arisen whether such artificial activities are sufficiently of a piece with their natural counterparts to warrant use of the same vocabulary. No doubt, we often employ the same word to denote two very different but superficially similar actions, as when we refer to the "flight" of birds and airplanes or to the "memory" of men and computers. Such usage anchors itself on certain (partial) resemblances in the net *outcomes* of the processes under comparison in tacit disregard of their true natures. The only safeguard against linguistic traps of this kind is the use of different words, such as "sail" and "swim" when applied respectively to the superficially similar behaviors of boats and sharks. In comparing the "cerebral" activities of men and machines our habitual use of the single word "think" has tended to blur among others one fundamental difference between the brain and the computer. It is the latter's incapacity to discriminate between the abstract and its physical correlate or material embodiment. The difference is well illustrated by the way men and machines treat the concept of *integer*. A machine cannot conceive of the notion of a number in the abstract as a universal in isolation of the material crutches it often wears to support itself. Even the most modern computer will treat it in the same way as does the primeval abacus, that is, as a concrete physical embodiment of as many material things or conditions, be they beads, pulses, punchcard holes, "magnetized spots or tapes," or anything else. It cannot arrive at the notion of "the classes of all classes that are similar to themselves," which is how the human mathematician defines number in the abstract independent of all its material manifestations in pluralities of socks, shoes, signals, vests, virtues, vipers, or what have you. It is this method of abstract thinking that is the life breath of modern mathematical thought. Clearly it is beyond the grasp of any modern computer, however clever. Since computers cannot think abstractly, they do not think out the information with which they are fed. All they do, when fed for example with physical marks on input tape, is to yield another pattern of physical marks of the same nature on another output tape. It is only when these physical marks are interpreted or read by the human operator that they become converted, in his brain, into authentic information. In other words, human thinking has to spark into life the desiccated yield of the computer before it becomes live, vibrant thought.

Consider, for instance, a new "original" proof attributed to a computer of the well-known theorem of Euclid concerning the equality of the two base angles of an isosceles triangle. The usual proof requires the construction of a straight line perpendicular from the apex A to the base BC (see Fig. 78). But Marvin Minsky derived the following

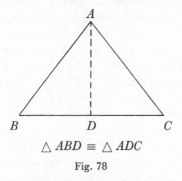

$$\triangle ABD \equiv \triangle ADC$$

Fig. 78

construction-free proof by feeding a simple program for Euclid's geometry into a computer. The machine has yielded the idea of a

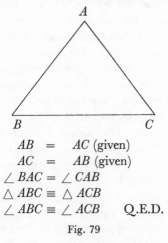

$$AB \;=\; AC \text{ (given)}$$
$$AC \;=\; AB \text{ (given)}$$
$$\angle BAC = \angle CAB$$
$$\triangle ABC \equiv \triangle ACB$$
$$\angle ABC \equiv \angle ACB \qquad \text{Q.E.D.}$$

Fig. 79

new and original proof even though it has been merely programed to recognize a congruent pattern in two triangles on the basis of equality of two adjacent sides and their included angle. The machine, however, did not become confused as we are apt to in certain "degenerate" situations like the one under consideration, in which we feel uneasy about using the same triangle in two ways at the same time, first as the triangle *ABC* and second as *ACB*. Even so, it seems to me that the real originator of the new proof is still the human programer, although it might have been suggested to him by some set of procedures or routines followed by the machine. The machine has as much claim to its discovery as the falling apple in Newton's orchard to that of the law of universal gravitation. Merely because human artifacts designed to manipulate concrete correlates of *abstract* concepts often suggest to their human creators new abstract ideas is no warrant for assigning to them the specifically human faculty of abstract thinking. Since computers do not need to "know" what numbers are, but only how to work with their concrete correlates in accordance with rules also fed into them, they perform their calculations without being aware of what they are doing. They are thus quite literally like water and wind in Omar Khayyám's stanza, willy-nilly flowing and blowing but neither knowing why, nor whence nor whither.

It is true that while computers thus far constructed lack the capacity for abstraction, it is a faculty that may well be built into newer machines. Already a beginning in this direction has been made with the "reading machine" of McCulloch and Pitts which is able to "recognize" the same general shape or pattern in material objects having individual differences such as printing faces of different sizes and styles. There are likewise other machines which can perceive geometrical patterns in the abstract of various kinds such as triangles squares, or circles. All these artifices are mere sieving devices which winnow the irrelevant chaff from the input signals and prepare a sort of filtrate. It is this latter transform of the input that becomes the symbolic substitute for the concept in question. Consider, for example, the symbol for *circle*. The configuration of signals received when an individual circle is within the reception field of the device obviously cannot suffice for its representation as an abstraction, because the configuration would change with the size and position of the circle. Nevertheless, the fact that all circles are recognized as belonging to one category of geometrical figure shows that the received signals must embody a pattern that remains (after winnowing) invariant, however the signals change with every alteration in the position and size of the circle. Thus if all these signals are passed through a filter which can compute the ratio of the circumference and diameter of the circle, it will find that the ratio is invariant. It is the existence of such an invariant feature remaining the same in the midst of all shifts of location and size which enables the filtering mechanism to correlate the unchanging filtrate of the input signals with the abstract geometrical entity we call "circle."

The most serious handicap of the McCulloch-Pitts type of reading machine which recognizes "universals" like circular forms and other geometric patterns as simulators of animal perception, cognition, and thinking, is that their main inspiration is the *secondary* language of logic and mathematics we outwardly and consciously use and not the *primary* logic and mathematics actually used by the central nervous system. Considering that the living brain is able to recognize visual patterns as belonging to the "same" face even when subjected to all manner of image transformations such as magnification, translation, rotation, intensification, blurring, caricaturization, and the like, it is quite unlikely that the brain computes the "invariant" of all such transformations in anything like the manner of the McCulloch-Pitts reading machine. For if so, not all its 10 billion neurons will suffice even for this single function of face recognition, as we shall see more clearly in Chapter XV. The fact is that von Neumann was right when he surmised that the *outward* forms of our logic and mathematics are much too cumbersome and involve far too many computational steps and chains of reasoning in reaching conclusions to be able to reveal the simpler "primary" logico-mathematical language used by the central nervous system. It is not easy to see the nature of this primary language through the misty distortions of its secondary envelope.

However, even though the present rather rudimentary recognitive artifacts practice only the lowest level of abstraction in the sense of taking away, casting aside, or ignoring particulars but without adding anything new (and that too without any inkling of the primary logico-mathematical language actually used by the nervous system), there is no reason why future ones may not do better and come closer to the natural automata to attain those higher levels of abstraction which seem to be the sole attribute of us humans. One cannot resolve an issue of this sort by merely making what D. M. Mackay calls "predictions of impotence," stipulating the impossibility of machines being able to perform some blanket unspecified feat *x* unless it happens, like the *perpetuum mobile* of the ancients, to infringe some limit law of nature such as the second law of thermodynamics. Since Gödel's theorem concerning the impossibility of proving the consistency or inconsistency of any sufficiently powerful logical system or its material embodiment (the computing machine) is one such limit law of mathematical logic, attempts have been made on its basis to prove that machines cannot mimic human thought completely. The crux of all such Gödel-inspired reasoning is that while mind, having the last word, is credited with the ability to pick a hole in any formal system presented to it as a model of its working, the machine considered is gratuitously denied such ability. The truth is that our failure to develop a satisfactory physical theory of mental activity obliges us to retain a mind-body duality and deny even in principle the possibility of mechanisms capable of a self-awareness similar to our own. In fact, as Minsky has recently argued, without such a unified theory of the physical basis of mind even a highly organized robot would maintain a dualistic opinion in this matter.

In sum, the upshot of the preceding argument is simply this. Since the physical basis of mindlike qualities resides in the patterns of organization of biological materials occurring naturally in animals, there is no reason why similar qualities may not emerge (in the future) from patterns of organization of similar or other materials* specifically rigged to exhibit those qualities. In other words, since human thinking is bound up somehow with natural brain activity, by exploring sufficiently deeply its material or physical basis we should in course of time be able to make what T. R. Miles has called a *Homo mechanisma*, that is, a robot identical with a human being in all respects except in its origin. Even so, Miles himself considers that men would still be different from such *mechanismas*, because while men have an awareness in relation to the body-schema (i.e., can recognize houses and trees as external to the body-schema but pains, aches, and tickles as internal), in the case of machines there is no body-schema to which perceptions could be related. This inward orientation of men towards their own bodies, according to Miles, provides a way of distinguishing men from machines. But, as T. S. Szaz has remarked, the distinction in turn is due to the fact that no machine is ever constructed merely to maintain itself as is the case with the human machine whose *raison d'être* is simply to keep going, notwithstanding

---

* A case in point is, incongruously enough, that of iron wire in strong nitric acid which reproduces fairly closely the main features of neural activity and therefore provides a fairly satisfactory model of a nerve. The Jerry Lettvin artificial neurons come closer still to imitating neural behavior in that they require the full Hodgskin-Huxley eight-order non-linear differential equation to describe their behavior as do the real ones. We are likely to hear more of them as they become installed in neurological laboratories.

what demagogic oracles, religious maniacs, political peddlers, and ideology vendors may have to say about the purpose of life. The point is that since the sole purpose of life is living, that is, to remain on the go, to build a machine that will imitate life as manifested in a live creature like man—and not merely some of his special skills such as counting, computing, sorting, and the like—requires that we construct a machine oriented solely inwards to the maintenance of its own physical frame. Indeed, the psychologist John Loehlin's "Aldous"— as Loehlin has named his computer simulation of a model personality —already classifies situations it meets as "satisfying," "painful," or "frustrating," even though as yet in quite a primitive way. Consequently, there is in principle no difficulty in erasing even this last shred of discrimination between *Homo sapiens* and *Homo mechanisma*, if only we succeed in uncovering sufficiently deeply the physical basis of our own cerebral-*cum*-physiological activity. This, however, depends not only on improvements in computer technology but, much more importantly, on parallel advances in neurophysiology. For although we may be able to make mechanisms exhibiting mindlike qualities such as memory, reasoning, learning, goal seeking, and so on, it is the task of physiology to anchor these concepts in their specifically human context to their proper physiological moorings. Otherwise, all we may have will be superficial verbal resemblances rather than deeper coincidences at the grass roots.

Already some progress has been made in finding out what sort of physico-chemical changes take place in the brain when the mind is at work. Two physiologists, D. H. Hubel and T. N. Wiesel, have shown the character of the brain-cell arrangements involved in abstracting notions such as "triangularity." Being the first work concerned with pinpointing something concrete which could be regarded as concept formation at the neural level, their work is naturally considered a landmark. Advances such as these are bound to make the ultimate problem of neurophysiology more definite, even though certain aspects of mental events may seem at the moment to lie beyond any physiology. As Sir Charles Sherrington has remarked, "It is a far cry from an electrical reaction in the brain to suddenly seeing the world around one with all its distances, its colors and chiaroscuro." There are also other mysteries of brain functions which do not yet seem amenable to physico-chemical explications. Neurosurgeons like Wilder Penfield have pointed out that while the cerebral cortex of man may well be the seat of consciousness, the physical basis of his mind, there is something in the mechanism of nerve-cell connections that eludes the mere physiology of its operation.   Thus he says:

> The patient who lies, fully conscious, on the operating table has no means of knowing when his cortex is being stimulated unless he is told.   What he feels may be a tingling sensation on this thumb, but he never seems to believe that something has actually touched his thumb.   He is aware that he moved his hand when the electrode was applied to the proper motor area, but he is never deluded into the belief that he willed the action.   A neurosurgeon therefore very soon gains the impression that in dealing with the cerebral cortex he is still at a distance from the highest level of integration.

Likewise, animals such as cats may be provoked into apparently meaningless "sham rage" by electrical stimulation of their hypothalamus.   All this clearly shows that springs of volition, free will, and emotions lie much deeper than the fringe at which neurophysiologists have hitherto been exploring.   For while certain responses such as the movement of limbs may be induced by electrical stimulation of the appropriate motor area of the human cortex, such "automatic" behavior differs from the volitional behavior the person himself wills. The distinction arises not in the difference between the movements or outward responses but in their different antecedents.   In the one case there is the experience of having "willed" an action while in the other it is wholly absent.   The reason is that neurophysiology has as yet barely succeeded in shifting the input and output terminals from the receptor and motor organs of the body to the brain surface.   It is still completely in the dark as to how the input of the afferent neurons reacts with those of the cerebral cortex to yield the output of the efferent ones.   We shall describe in the following chapters some neurophysiological speculations on this significant theme.

Chapter XIV

INTELLIGENCE AMPLIFIERS

THERE is a Turkish proverb which says, "If Allah gives you prosperity, He will give you the brains to go with it." Whether or not it was ever true of nations and men may be in doubt, for man's understanding is often corrupted by wealth. But there is no doubt that the affluence recently acquired by the technological societies of the West has not brought about any comparable growth of human mental capacity to comprehend their over-all complexities. It is therefore natural that the great nations of the West should dream of securing by artificial means the brains to match the affluence they have already gained. This new vision of giant robot brains able to take over *all* our "thinking" chores beyond our own mental grasp may look quixotic. Nevertheless, it has a respectable precedent. It is the counterpart, in respect of our brains, of those giant tools of today that already catapult a thousandfold the capacity of our brawn. Just as a factory worker, given a power pack, can put forth a physical effort equal to a thousand horsepower or more even though his own muscles provide only an infinitesimal fraction thereof, so also we may someday devise means to amplify our inborn I.Q. sufficiently to give us the over-all comprehension we so obviously lack. It is only by such amplification that we can hope to resolve some of the baffling dilemmas that beset us today, as indeed the Pentagon, social scientists, econometricians, operations researchers, and students of human engineering have already begun to do in a limited sort of way. Although they have had a fair measure of success, most of it to date is not because of any new design of an intelligence amplifier that discerns deeper than the human brain. It is rather the outcome of vastly improved computational facilities that the giant electronic computers nowadays provide. Because they can complete within a few

hours bulky arithmetical calculations that would otherwise take centuries or even millennia to perform, it is entirely feasible now to tackle
many economic, social, and management problems involving hundreds
or thousands of variables interlocked by as many constraints. For
their solution often boils down to solving a set of a large number of
simultaneous equations or optimizing some given output function of
variables such as utility, profit, welfare, or some other quantifiable
objective or goal. Such computational feats, prodigious though they
may be, are by no means too onerous for present-day electronic
computers. Since the computers that help solve such problems are
nevertheless programed by humans on the basis of human criteria and
human policy specifications, they are, strictly speaking, more like tools
carrying out programed instructions than founts of cerebral power
streaming intelligence and thought.

Such sources of cerebral power on tap may seem to infringe
the conservation law of intelligence or instruction to which all computers have in a way to conform. But a similar difficulty also
confronted the early dreamers of *perpetuum mobile*, an ever-flowing
fount of physical power. Indeed, had Archimedes, inventor of the
first power-amplifying tools such as levers and pulleys, pondered more
deeply his own classic boast, "Give me a place to stand and a large
enough lever, I will move the earth," he would have perhaps stumbled
onto the principle of conservation of energy that limits the power of
every machine. He would have realized that no matter whether one
employs a lever, pulley, or the screw that bears his name, its net
output of power cannot exceed the input of the muscles of its activating hand. However, what Archimedes did not divine was brought
home to his numerous followers in the art of mechanics by their
repeated failures to design perpetual-motion machines. This is one
reason why men of earlier ages took to domesticating more muscular
beasts of burden like horses and oxen and even breeding human slaves.
But as every animal form of organization has an upper ceiling of size
beyond which it will not function (a land animal, for example, cannot
be so big that the legs or other portions in contact with the ground
will be crushed by its weight), such efforts to secure the requisite
muscle power naturally did not succeed. In their dire predicament
men of that period must have been quite puzzled as to how any of
their simple power-amplifying devices like levers, pulleys, and cogs
could be made to do more work than could be put in by the limited

muscular effort of their pack animals and slaves. That is, while a lever could lift a much bigger weight than the bare hand, even Archimedes's lever lifting the earth itself could do no more work than the hand moving it at the other end. How then could a machine yield more physical energy than its animal prime mover could ever hope to provide?

It took many generations to find the answer to this puzzle. It was found by simply coupling such passive tools as men had already made with sources of power latent in nature. The first to be so yoked were those of wind and water. Later, when these proved too weak, fickle, and irregular to meet ever-growing human needs, the newly invented steam engine burning coal became the chief prime mover. While the total input of energy in the coupled tool-engine system exceeds its output, the latter is many times greater than any human or animal muscular effort alone could ever provide through the amplification of levers, pulleys, or wheels. The steam engine and its more modern variant, the internal combustion engine, have therefore managed to magnify greatly the muscle power of man without in any way infringing the conservation law of energy. They enable us, however, to put the latent energy of fossil fuels on tap to draw upon as, when, and to the extent we require. The natural question then is simply this: Can we devise new kinds of more sophisticated machines that produce "intelligence" without infringing the analogous* law of conservation of instructions requiring a strict balance between the input instructions of the programer and the outcome of the machine? The answer might be affirmative if we could make a machine or system able to draw not only the energy for its sustenance but also the information for its self-organization from the environment with which it is in constant interaction. Consider, for example, a motor car. It draws the energy for its locomotion from the fuel that is fed from time to time into its tank from an external source. But if it could also somehow draw from an external source the information-loaded signals that operated its ignition switch, accelerator, brake pedal, steering, and gears, it would really be an *automobile*, that is, a self-moving and self-driven vehicle. Those who consider the twin problem of energy and information flow from the environment to the system as a strongly linked single-channel affair, thus treating both its energy diet and information intake as synonymous, have naturally no difficulty in

* See Chapter XIII, page 184.

conceding the possibility "in principle" of systems able to "live" on the expense account of their environment for both.* But even if the two flows are, as is more likely, quite distinct despite their obvious inter-dependence, the system can secure the order, information, or intelli-gence it needs from its environment in two distinct ways. First, there is the "order" from disorder due to the stability of statistical attributes such as averages pertaining to assemblies of large numbers of micro-particles. The sheer "chaos" of myriads of them moving in the void gives rise to the "statistical" regularities known as physical laws. Secondly, there is what E. Schrödinger has called the "order from order" principle which is the "real clue to the understanding of life." Earlier we noted an instance of this kind of order in the activity of cellular enzymes which, like Maxwell's demon, trade information for negentropy. This is why we may well conceive of self-organizing systems which, when coupled to other natural sources of information, can extract it from their environment in the same way as we may drain the latent energy of coal and oil by means of prime movers. While the drainage of the fossil-fuel energy yields us all the power we need for our purposes, the conservation law is in no way infringed. The conservation is secured, however, at the cost of continual degradation. In other words, more of "live" or "free" energy originally available in the fuels is turned into "dead" or "inert" heat during the course of the process. This is a way of saying that the entropy or "shuffled-ness" of the system increases even if its total balance of energy remains the same. Although the tendency of the entropy of a system to increase or of its constituents to get more and more mixed up in the course of time is inexorable, this does not preclude the occurrence of disentropic or entropy-decreasing processes such as go on within all living beings. As we saw in Chapter VII, disentropic processes occurring within living matter are due to a kind of sorting or sieving

---

* Thus the operation of the brake pedal where the movement of the foot supplies both the signal (information) and the energy for braking is a case in point of the identity of the two flows. On the other hand, the operation of its accelerator, which merely provides the signal but not the energy for acceleration, illustrates the case where the two flows are quite distinct. Those who advocate the *essential* identity of signal and energy flows rest their case on the fact that every physical signal, though important solely for its information-carrying form and modalities and not for its energy, nevertheless does require a certain (small) expenditure of energy. In short, even though information is not the same thing as energy, to carry it we need to embody signals in some material way, so that energy and information cannot be wholly dissociated.

of energy-rich electrons by a large diversity of specific information-carrying enzymes, which seem to act like Maxwell's demons, decreasing entropy by a more complex variant of the simple sorting activity endowed them by Maxwell. It therefore seems that the basis of life's intelligence is the information coded within enzymes that confers on them the power to reproduce their kind by enabling them to select particular patterns useful to their purpose from the myriads that occur at random in their milieu. Given a number of such information-carrying molecules or more generally selecting or sorting mechanisms floating in a reservoir, organization and "patternedness" can become self-supporting and even increase, as the emergence of various forms of life from its inanimate beginnings clearly shows and as the deduction of the Turing–von Neumann principle explained in Chapter XIII confirms in all logical rigor. The core of intelligent behavior of any mechanism therefore appears to lie in its ability to recognize and sort patterns, events, and situations that are useful to the objective it is designed to serve out of those encountered.

Consider, for example, such an "intelligent" device scanning every line that E. Borel's immortal monkey, strumming at random on a typewriter, continually writes. If the device has the power to recognize and sort intelligible sentences from the myriad other nonsensical strings of letters in the monkey's incessant outpourings, it will "write" all the extant literature including the plays of Shakespeare and Shaw. Such a scanning or filtering device is then an intelligence amplifier that bestows even on a monkey the "creativity" of a Shakespeare and Shaw. This is not to say that mechanical contrivances such as that of Swift's Lagado device which enabled the "most ignorant person" to "write books on philosophy, poetry, politics and so on" are now around the corner; quite the contrary. For in actual practice no one can produce a single line of Shakespeare in this way, let alone his complete works. Take, for instance, the first line of "O Mistress Mine" in *Twelfth Night*:

O Mistress mine, where are you roaming?

It is one particular permutation of 31 alphabet letters buried deep in an immensity of others. Written in the compact notation of the mathematician, its measure is the number $(26)^{31}$. But its truly cosmological size is better revealed when we realize that even if our scanning device screened a million permutations per second, it would still take some three hundred million times the putative age of the cosmos to run through the lot! Nevertheless, the principle of producing intelligence by filtering random casts of letters or words underlying the Lagado contrivance that Swift pilloried so devastatingly is not wholly illogical, provided the inflationary spiral of permutational possibilities could somehow be checked by prior constraints. For it is after all only an adaptation of the computer strategy to a different context. It will be recalled that the electronic computers owe their sensational success in solving computational problems not to any improved methods of calculation but rather to their fantastic speed in carrying out the usual computational chores. In other words, because of sheer speed they manage to complete programed instructions which by themselves are grossly clumsy, inefficient, and wasteful in the sense that if entrusted to humans they could never be finished in many a lifetime. This has given rise to the hope or rather the dream that the help of some analogues of high-speed computers might well be invoked in other situations like writing poetry, philosophy, playing chess, proving logical theorems or algebraic identities, and the like, where high speed may also be relied upon to compensate for the extravagance, tedium, and inefficiency of the sieving or filtering method itself. Thus one may have the opportunity of accomplishing something worthwhile in these more "creative" spheres without the gift of "creativity." The idea becomes more credible when we recall that most creative thinkers and artists, if we may believe Newton, Mozart, Wagner, and others, may well be thought of as giant living sieves that managed simply to retain the right thoughts, melodies, and harmonies out of the myriads that poured in upon them. We may not yet understand how these great creative sieves of life work. But psychologists have accumulated impressive evidence to show that what seems to us direct insight, invention, inspiration, and serendipity of the thinker is the outcome of many mental flounderings and blind-alley entrances in a wide-ranging variation of countless thought trials made up of mere blind permutations and combinations. Poincaré, for example, spoke of "crowds of ideas" arising in the mind and moving at random like the molecules of gas in the kinetic theory of gases "until pairs interlocked, so to speak, making stable combinations." Contrary to usual belief, most "flashes" of insight like those associated with Archimedes's "Eureka" or Newton's falling apple do not arise fully formed out of their author's head, but are the fruits of long and laborious search of thought for meaningful patterns in a multitude of random permutations and combinations of basic thoughts and ideas, even though their authors have a special knack for reducing trial-to-trial stereotypes and sensing correct combinations. For the less gifted ones devices exist which are designed to increase the likelihood that all permutations are considered, as in going through a thesaurus for appropriate synonyms or through the alphabet for rhymes. There are therefore reasonable grounds for the hope that "intelligence" may be simulated by mechanizing some routine repetitive operations, which despite their inherent clumsiness and inefficiency could be productive if performed at a sufficiently fast rate. While no amount of acceleration in its scanning rate will ever make a Lagado contrivance anything but a utopian dream, its underlying idea is not wholly unsound. Thus already computers have been programed to produce "poetry" as well as "music" by being instructed to select words at random from their vocabulary (or notes in case of music) and reject those word permutations which are barred by certain built-in grammatical rules. It is true that what has been actually produced so far is gibberish, such as the following lines obtained from a computer program derived from a 3500-word vocabulary and regulated by 128 grammatical rules such as that a verb must follow a noun and so on:

> Few fingers go like narrow laughs
> An ear won't keep few fishes,
> What is that rose in that blind house?
> And all slim, gracious blind planes are coming,
> They cry badly along a rose
> To leap is stuffy, to crawl was tender.

Similarly, the computer Illiac at the University of Illinois has produced a musical piece of sorts—the *Illiac Suite*—which has even been broadcast on the radio. Such attempts to run before we can crawl may look premature. But they do suggest the possibility of artifacts that may amplify our feeble mental faculties by coupling some partly or wholly random source generating the various possibilities in a particular field of endeavor to a sieving device able to winnow the chaff from the grain. Just as by choosing a sieve of a sufficiently fine mesh we can make a selection finer than any we ourselves could ever secure unaided, so also by constructing a device that can select over a greater range than any we ourselves could cover, we can greatly amplify our own intelligence. A machine that could "scan," say, the *Encyclopaedia Britannica* or the resources of the Library of Congress and sift for us the information we need in a fraction of the time we ourselves would take, would obviously be an intelligence amplifier even if of a rudimentary kind. Although such mechanization of literature searching and information retrieval—notwithstanding some tinkering with the problem of auto-abstraction, extraction, or indexing by L. H. Luhn, S. Whelan and others—is nowhere in sight, intelligence-amplifying machines will sooner or later be able to produce originality by mere plodding with random permutations of words, notes, concepts, symbols, and the like. Once made they could take in their stride many of our vastly complex socioeconomic problems that at present have us so obviously out of our depth. This

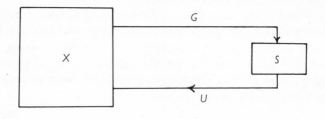

Fig. 80

is why Ross Ashby ventures to suggest even a specific albeit fictitious problem to illustrate how intelligence amplifiers might help us to organize a stable society immune from periodic crises. To begin with, we might spell out what we need to secure the stability we desire. This might require that the "unemployment level does not exceed 100,000 persons, crimes of violence 10 per week, minimal income does not fall below £500 per annum, and so on."

Ashby is of the opinion that such a problem could in principle be solved by coupling two dynamic systems, one generating all the possibilities open to our social organization, that is, the laissez-faire society functioning without controls, and the other sorting and recognizing those conforming to the specifications we have chosen in advance. Consider, for instance, two determinate dynamic systems X and S coupled through channels G and U as in Fig. 80 so that each affects the other. Further, suppose S has been specially built to have resting states of equilibrium if and only if certain conditions s in S are fulfilled. This ensures that the coupled system $X \leftrightarrow S$ will come to rest only if conditions s in S have materialized. If moreover the linkage G is such that it allows the conditions s to arise in S only if certain other conditions x have already materialized in X, then the selection of S and G will ensure that the permanent resting states of the coupled system are those which simultaneously secure conditions s in S and x in X.

It will be seen that the selection of x in X has been made in two stages. The first stage occurs when the designer specifies S and G and s. The second occurs when S, acting without further reference to the designer, rejects state after state of X, accepting finally one that gives x in X. The designer has selected x in X but he has done it out of a much wider range of possibilities than in the first stage and has thereby amplified his power of selectivity or intelligence through the amplifying mechanism S.

To solve the socioeconomic problem posed earlier, Ashby suggests identifying the economic world with the dynamic system X and the specified conditions to secure its stability with x. While we cannot by ourselves secure x in X, we could drive X into such a state naturally by coupling it to a system S so built that it has a resting stage if and only if it is informed via channel G that x has materialized in a resting stage in X. As time passes, the whole system X and S tends to rest in a permanent state of equilibrium where the specified conditions x materialize in X. The designer has to design S and G and to couple it to X, after which the process will occur automatically. While, as Ashby owns, we cannot yet build systems of the kind that can control the socioeconomic forces at work in the manner described, he does claim that the essence of the process at work is similar to that of a small mechanical toy he has built in his laboratory. He calls it "homeostat" after the name (homeostasis) chosen by some physiologists to denote the ability of living animals to maintain themselves in a relatively stable state of equilibrium.

Ashby's homeostat is an arrangement of four magnets that always come to rest in their central positions no matter how they are disturbed. Each of the four basic units consists of a movable magnet mounted on a pivot but enclosed within a coil through which a current passes. By varying the amount of current flowing through its coil one can make the magnet move about its pivot. A stiff metal wire through the pivot moving with the magnet is bent at one end, and the bent end carries a metal plate dipping into a semicircular trough filled with distilled water. Two electrodes, one at either end of the trough, provide a potential gradient. Depending on the position of the magnet, which itself is regulated by the current in the coil, the wire dipping in water can pick up a voltage. If the voltage is now conducted to the grid of a triode valve which controls the strength of the current passing through the coil, the current in the coil will vary with the potential of the plate and will in this way be influenced by the movement of the magnet (see Fig. 81). This is clearly a type of feed-

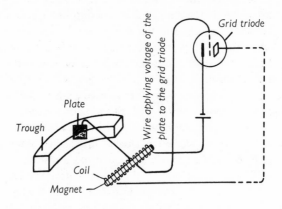

Fig. 81 Plan of unit *A* of homeostat. (Adapted from *Thinking by Machine*, by Pierre de Latil, Sidgwick & Jackson, London, 1956, p. 297.)

back arrangement whereby the output of the system, that is, the position of the plate, again influences its input, that is, the current in the coil that initially moves the magnet.

Mathematically the state of the system at any time may be completely described by the values of its two variables, namely, the angular deviation (x) of the magnet from its central position and its corresponding angular velocity (y). If we have a table of the associated pairs of values of x and y at various times, we may graph them to obtain what is called the line of behavior of the system. For example, the graph in Fig. 82 is the pictorial representation of the successive states assumed by the system at various times. Depending on where the magnet is taken by hand and how it is "kicked" at the outset, the line of behavior may well be any of those shown in Figs.

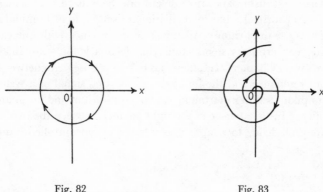

Fig. 82   Fig. 83

82 to 84.   Thus if the magnet merely swings rhythmically to and from its central position like a pendulum bob, its line of behavior will be a circle such as the one shown in Fig. 82.   If, on the other hand, it falls into a crescendo of uncontrolled hunting, the line of behavior may well be as in Fig. 83.   Lastly, if the system manages completely to damp its oscillations, the line of behavior will be as in Fig. 84, with the magnet eventually coming to rest in its central position of equilibrium. As will be observed, it is only in the last case, when the line of behavior converges on the origin, that the magnet manages to reach what may be called its terminal state of equilibrium, the goal it is desired to seek. All other states, where the line of behavior either continually diverges from the origin or forever goes around in circles, obviously do not lead to the prescribed goal.   The mechanism is therefore at the mercy of

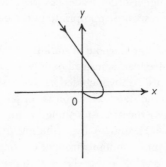

Fig. 84

the fortuitous disturbance it receives from the outside.   This may set it off on a course of runaway oscillations or send it to its terminal state of rest and equilibrium.   All this is in accordance with our earlier finding concerning systems employing feedback for self-regulation. As we saw in Chapter VIII, there has to be a precise tie-in between the output resonance and the input error-reporting signal of a system if it is to pilot itself to its terminal state of equilibrium and safeguard its stability.   In the absence of the right balance between the two it has a strong tendency to relapse into a frenzy of uncontrolled hunting.

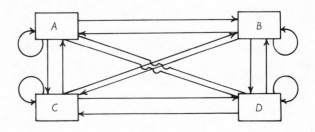

Fig. 85   Illustration showing interconnection of four homeostat units *A, B, C,* and *D.*

The theory of feedback which secures appropriate input-output matching in servo systems is well understood.   But instead of applying it to his homeostat Ashby introduced an ingenious innovation.   He used second- and higher-order feedbacks (feedbacks to feedbacks) to enable it to elicit a response appropriate to the outside disturbance it receives.

In order to use for the purpose of stability secondary, tertiary, and other higher-order feedbacks, instead of only one primary feedback as usual in servo systems, Ashby included a device whereby the mechanism radically alters the state of its internal organization every time it faces a situation that threatens to plunge it into a frenzy of uncontrolled oscillations.   He did so by including in the same circuit a uniselector which jumps randomly from its existing position to another of the twenty-five possible ones whenever the magnet swings more than 45° on either side of its central position.   The uniselector thus forces an internal reorganization of the mechanism should the preceding one fail to achieve the goal it seeks. In other words, the uniselector provides the mechanism with an adjustable parameter whose range of variation confers on it much greater versatility of behavior than it ever had before. In this particular case twenty-five possible positions or settings of the uniselector amplify twenty-five-fold the power of the mechanism to vary its response, should the one evoked by an outside disturbance happen to fail to achieve the desired stability. This is by no means the limit of the internal adjustments it can make in search of its prescribed goal. If we link two sets of movable magnets surrounded in coils, say, units A and B, so that the voltage grid of unit A controls not only the current of the coil A but also that of the coil B and vice versa, the twin setup acquires a parameter for securing new internal adjustments whose range of variation is not merely 25 but $25 \times 25 = 625$. The reason is that each of the twenty-five positions of the uniselector of A may be independently combined with those of B to yield $25 \times 25 = 625$ new permutations. Ashby actually built his homeostat by a combination of four such units, A, B, C, and D, as shown in Fig. 85, thus escalating the range of variation of the system's parameter by a factor of $25 \times 25 \times 25 \times 25 = 390,625$.

The new arrangement is merely an extension of the earlier scheme according to which each unit controls not only the current of its own coil but also that of the remaining three. It does so by sending the output current of its own triode to all four coils, each of which is subject to the "feedback" influence of four different circuits. Thus, if the magnet A turns through a certain angle on account of a strong current received in its coil from B, the plate of A will pick up an altered voltage, which will modify not only the current intensity of the coil surrounding the magnet A but the coils of B, C, and D as well. Such a set of four magnets acting on one another in a complex pattern of feedbacks always comes to rest with all four magnets in their central positions no matter how the system is disturbed. At the outset of any given disturbance its behavior may look chaotic or puzzled, but the system always muddles through to its final resting state. There is nothing occult or mysterious in its single-minded search for stability. For every initial state from which the system may be started, the system can adjust its internal organization in any one of 390,625 different ways. If the initial state happens to lead to a line of behavior away from the desired terminal state, the uniselector action changes the behavior pattern of the system. If the change again leads to an unstable line of behavior, another uniselector action intervenes to try yet another mode of behavior till one leading to its terminal resting state is found. The point is that the system keeps on jumping randomly from one permutation of four uniselector positions to another till it discovers one that yields a stable line of behavior. This is how the homeostat produces a matching state of internal adjustment suited to the particular outside disturbance received at the outset. The question then arises: Is this quest for stability always crowned with success and, if not, what is the probability of success? Although Ashby's homeostat does show in practice sufficient stability to deserve being called *ultrastable*, mathematical analysis of the necessary and sufficient conditions of ultrastability bristles with many intractable difficulties. Ashby's own mathematical explorations show that the probability of stability of a randomly constructed system steadily decreases as the system becomes more complicated. Large and complex systems are thus very much more likely to be unstable than stable.

Suppose we have an ultrastable machine with adjustable connections such as Ashby's homeostat. Because the connections are adjustable it has the ability to change its mode of internal organization. Corresponding to any particular adjustment of these connections there is a set of lines of behavior specifying what it will do. A case in point is the set of lines drawn in Figs. 82, 83, and 84. All such lines are collectively called the *field* of lines of behavior. Naturally the fields are different for different internal adjustments that the machine can make. As the machine shifts from one adjustment to another, so do the corresponding fields of its lines of behavior till the machine reaches a state of equilibrium or final stable field called the *terminal field*. For example, the equilibrium position of the four magnets in the homeostat is its terminal field after it has passed through all the internal adjustments (or switching actions of the uniselectors) sparked by the outside disturbance. The action of an ultrastable machine is thus mainly that of searching for its terminal field by trying one adjustment after another till the right one has been found to damp the external disturbance. It is thus of primary importance to know the average number of trials or internal adjustments necessary to reach the terminal field. This number (N) is very simply related to the probability (p) that an ultrastable machine comes to its resting state of equilibrium. Obviously the probability of reaching the stable terminal field at the first trial is p itself. Consequently the probability of not reaching the terminal field at the first go is $1 - p = q$. If all trials of internal adjustments, such as the switching actions of the homeostats' uniselectors, are perfectly random, then the probability that the ensuing field after any trial will be stable is still p and the probability that it will be unstable is q. Suppose then the machine tries m different internal adjustments before coming to its resting state of equilibrium. Since the fields of behavior after the first, second, third, fourth, ..., and $(m - 1)$st trials are unstable, and that after the mth trial is stable, the probability of reaching the terminal field in m trials is $q^{m-1}p$. The average number N of trials or shifts of internal adjustments to reach the terminal field is, therefore, the average of the number of such shifts weighted by the probability of its occurrence. It may therefore be computed as in Table 40.

TABLE 40

Number of trials or shifts of internal adjustments required to reach terminal field (i)	Corresponding probability or weight (ii)	Product of columns (i) and (ii) (iii)
1	p	p
2	qp	$2\,qp$
3	q^2p	$3\,q^2p$
4	q^3p	$4\,q^3p$
5	q^4p	$5\,q^4p$
$\vdots$	$\vdots$	$\vdots$
m	$q^{m-1}p$	$mq^{m-1}p$
$\vdots$		$\vdots$
Total $p(1 + q + q^2 + \ldots) = p(1 - q)^{-1}$		$p(1 + 2q + 3q^2 + 4q^3 + \ldots)$ $= p(1 - q)^{-2}$

The weighted average of the number of trials required is therefore merely the quotient obtained by dividing the sum of column (iii) by that of column (ii). That is,

$$N = \frac{p(1 + 2q + 3q^2 + 4q^3 + \ldots)}{p(1 + q + q^2 + q^3 + \ldots)}$$

$$= \frac{(1 - q)^{-2}}{(1 - q)^{-1}} = \frac{1}{1 - q} = \frac{1}{p}.$$

When p is very small which, as we have seen, is the case with very large and complex machines, the number N of trials necessary for reaching the stable terminal field is very large, making the search for such a field a long and tedious affair.

Consider, for example, a complex machine with, say, 100 parameters to adjust. If each adjustment is as likely to be right as wrong, the probability of securing the right adjustment for all of them at the same time and thus bringing it to its terminal resting state is $(\frac{1}{2})^{100}$. It therefore follows that the number N of trials or shifts of adjustments required to lead the system into stability is $N = \frac{1}{(\frac{1}{2})^{100}} = 2^{100} = 10^{30}$. Even if we allow a million trials per second, the average time taken for reaching a terminal state of equilibrium will be $\frac{10^{30}}{10^{6}} = 10^{24}$ seconds or some 10,000 billion millennia. Such a settling time is all but infinite. As a result, for complex machines like the human brain, which Ashby's homeostat is supposed to model, an underlying principle of ultrastability for automatically reaching stable behavior is totally impractical.

To remedy this situation, Ashby suggests a different way of increasing the probability of stability and thereby reducing the settling time of the system. He claims that for a very complicated system containing a large number of parametric variables, any single disturbance or change of operating conditions directly affects only a relatively small number of variables. Thus if the variables directly disturbed can be isolated from the rest to form an ultrastable system by themselves, the probability of stability for that particular type of disturbance can be greatly increased. For instance, if the number of variables directly influenced at any one disturbance is five, instead of 100 as assumed earlier, the probability p of stability is $\frac{1}{2^{5}} = \frac{1}{32}$, so that the average number of trials required to reach its terminal field is only 32. At the rate of even one trial per second, the settling time is barely 32 seconds. Thus if the 100 variables are actually divided into twenty such groups of five variables each, forming twenty separate ultrastable systems, the total time required for adapting to a completely new set of operating conditions will be $20 \times 32 = 640$ seconds or barely 11 minutes. This tremendous reduction in settling time from an earlier estimate of some 10,000 billion millennia is secured by a large sacrifice of flexibility and richness of response of the system. For the range of action of a system with 100 interacting variables, all mutually affecting one another, is vastly greater than that of one composed of twenty separate subsystems of five variables each. The reason is that while the five variables of a subgroup do influence one another, they neither affect nor are affected by the variations of those in other subgroups. The feedback influence of the variables is thus greatly restricted. However, the flexibility of response may be improved a good deal by varying the division of variables into subgroups to suit different kinds of disturbances. Thus if a disturbance involves only the first five variables of the system, then these five variables would be associated to form an ultrastable subsystem of five variables. If a later disturbance affects, say, the second, tenth, fifteenth, eighty-first, and hundredth variables, then these five variables would be associated to form another ultrastable subsystem. This phenomenon of ever-shifting grouping of variables into subsystems according to the prevailing operating conditions is called by Ashby the *dispersion of behavior.*

By thus resolving the entire aggregate of possible environmental influences into a number of subsystems each ultrastable with respect to only those variables that are included in it, the living animal manages to curb the permutational orgy that otherwise prevents a complex machine from settling into equilibrium in a reasonable period of time. For the living animals have developed during the course of evolution different specialized sense organs which enforce an initial dispersion of behavior. Thus most animals have two organs, the eye and the skin, to handle electromagnetic stimuli. The full range of permutational possibilities open with varying intensities of beams of different wavelengths is greatly limited by making the eye sensitive to only a subgroup of rays of wavelengths in the range 0.4 μ* to 0.5 μ and the skin sensitive to another subgroup of rays with wavelengths exceeding 0.8μ. In other words, while the optic nerve of the eye is excited by the former subgroup and remains uninfluenced by variations in the other subgroup, that of the latter stimulates only the trigeminal nerve in the skin. Every animal is thus built up of a number of ultrastable subsystems organized with the possibility of dispersion of behavior. Such a multistable system can therefore adapt its behavior to settle in a stable resting state in a much shorter time than a single ultrastable system of the kind considered earlier. This is the slender basis on which Ashby claims his homeostat as a stage on the way to more highly developed machines which, to use his own

* μ is the angstrom unit of length (10^{-8}cm) used for measuring the wavelength of radiant light.

expression, would be "copies" of the human brain. His book *Design for a Brain*, where he has developed this theme at length, and also his essay "Design for an Intelligence Amplifier" read as if the homeostat and its underlying principle of ultrastability via multiple feedbacks were likely to provide the key to the mystery of the living brain. But the assumption that the adaptive behavior of animals and their goal-seeking activities necessarily require their nervous systems to embody ultrastability is gratuitous. Although Ashby has catalogued a number of instances of adaptive behavior in animals that do not conflict with the notion of ultrastability, there is no evidence that the central nervous systems do, in fact, have recourse to it. Nor is any indication given as to what anatomical or physiological facts correspond with the proposed design. The mere production of a machine that carries out an operation similar to that performed by an animal is no warrant for assuming that both the animal and the machine work in the same way, any more than for treating birds and airplanes as identical mechanisms simply because both manage to "fly."

Despite the obvious semantic traps lurking beneath the arguments based on such premises, they have often lured enthusiastic inventors of ingenious machines such as the homeostat into believing that the key to brain function lies in the particular artifact of their making. In this they are not unlike the man who looks for the key to his house under a street lamp for no other reason than that there is no light where it might actually be lying. The theories of goal-seeking machines with adjustable connections such as the homeostat or of others such as the *machina spora* and *speculatrix*, are no doubt some of the many street lamps we shall need to illumine the path to our neurophysiological goal. But since the key we are looking for is in a place far beyond their range of illumination, there is no reason to stop there and imagine that *lifelike* is synonymous with *life* itself. If the extravagant cybernetical promises of intelligence amplifiers that will help us cure all our economic and social ills, resolve all our dilemmas, and divine all our riddles are to materialize, we need to acquire infinitely more neurophysiological insight than the working of these toys can possibly provide. A step—and only a step—in this direction is the theory of perceptrons, that is, self-adaptive systems designed to shed some light on the problem of explaining brain function in terms of brain structure. We shall deal with them in the next chapter.

Chapter XV

LEARNING MACHINES
OR PERCEPTRONS

ALTHOUGH our account of Turing machines has followed the McCulloch-Pitts theory of neural networks, historically it was Turing's conclusive demonstration of their possibility that inspired the latter in the hope that the organization of networks of neurons, each acting on the digital, all-or-nothing principle, might give a clue to the functioning of the living brain. While the right clues have yet to be found, McCulloch and Pitts nevertheless broke new ground when they suggested substituting biological neurons for electric relays in the electrical switching circuits devised by Shannon to implement logical operations like addition, multiplication, or negation, whereon practically the whole of computer technology is reared. We saw in Chapter XI how such neuron networks can be designed to conform to any desired input-output specification. These networks, however, had fixed thresholds at their synapses. By envisaging neuron networks with alterable or adjustable synapses, which could raise or lower their threshold values, McCulloch added a new dimension to his original theory. For such networks by suitably altering the thresholds acquire a means of changing the mode of their internal organization to yield the prescribed behavior even under widely varying conditions. As a result they can be made to mimic homeostasis, that is, self-adjustment to changing environment, much more strikingly than Ashby's toy, the homeostat. Thus, as McCulloch has remarked, "If networks with adjustable synapses are embodied in our brains, they answer von Neumann's repeated question of how it is possible to think and speak correctly after taking enough absinthe or alcohol to alter the threshold of every neuron." However that may be, networks with adjustable connections are obviously far more versatile having an additional degree of parametric freedom. This is why Hebb adopted the idea of an adjustable synapse as a basis for a new neurophysiological theory.   He suggested that "when an axon of cell A is near enough to excite a cell B and repeatedly or persistently takes part in firing it, some growth process or metabolic change takes place in one or both cells such that A's efficiency as one of the cells firing B is increased."   Prima facie the suggestion is plausible enough because even very slight changes in the dimensions of the processes or fibers of a neuron can easily lead to great differences in the pattern of its connectivity in the network.   Consequently, permanent changes in the

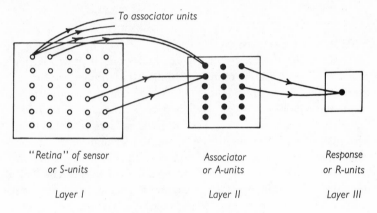

To associator units

"*Retina*" *of sensor*   *Associator*   *Response*
or S-units   *or A-units*   *or R-units*

Layer I   *Layer II*   *Layer III*

Fig. 86   Organization of perceptron.

threshold of excitation of the neuron can possibly occur, although neurophysiologists have not yet been able to demonstrate them in the living brain.

Nevertheless, the idea of adjustable synapse is a fruitful one.   It has already become the cornerstone of new kinds of learning machines or perceptrons that function like computers in that they can make decisions as well as exercise control, both activities based on logical rules.   But unlike computers they also manage to adapt themselves to conditions not envisaged in the programed instructions.   As we have seen, a computer is as inexorably tied to its instructions as a railway vehicle to its track so that it is always necessary in computer programing to think out in advance every contingency that might arise in the course of the computation and give the machine appropriate instructions for each case.   In other words, every computer must be precisely briefed beforehand.   It cannot make a single calculation extempore. Learning machines, on the other hand, are much more flexible. They can rise to occasions not foreseen by the programed instructions. They therefore represent a stage beyond the electronic computers despite being built up from such computer hardware as relays, switches, and the like, which behave like simplified neurons. Such assemblies or networks of artificial "neurons" acquire the additional faculty of interpreting their environment, besides that of decision and control based on logical rules as in ordinary computers. For they have connections or "synapses" with alterable thresholds whereby they can change their internal operation in order to tailor the response to the changing needs of the occasion. The principle of adaptation adopted by them is thus very similar to that of biological animals. Just as the animal responds to modifications of the environment in order to secure his own survival, so also a learning machine modifies the structure of its internal organization according to the results obtained, that is, according to the indications of success or failure it receives. If it is informed that the result of the action it has just taken is favorable to the desired outcome, it retains intact the structure of its inner connections. If not, the connections are modified and its internal operation altered to make another trial. Their grand strategy may therefore be neatly summed up in Guilbaud's classic maxim, "Heads I win, tails we start again on the other foot."

Consider, for example, F. Rosenblatt's perceptron, which is a machine capable of identifying visual patterns. As will be observed from the structure of its organization shown in Fig. 86, it consists of three layers of basic elements, which we may call binary threshold logic units, TLU for short, similar to those used in neuron networks. They are in effect threshold devices, which summate the "weights" of their input signals and trigger off if and only if the sum of the weights exceeds the prescribed threshold value. The first layer consists of sensory units called S-units, which provide the inputs to the rest of the machine. This input or sensor layer is stimulated by optical patterns shown to a grid or "retina" of photoelectric cells mounted in the focal plane of a camera to which the stimulus pictures are shown. While none of the S-units are interconnected, some of them are joined to the second TLU layer consisting of association units called A-units. Each A-unit is thus a threshold device receiving inputs from a selection of S-units. If a sufficient number of S-units linked to it are turned on by the stimulus, that is, the display of any particular optical pattern so that the sum of the input signals to the A-unit exceeds its threshold, it will "fire." Any input pattern will therefore activate a specified set of A-units. The set specified will naturally depend on the

(a) S-units excited by the initial stimulus or the pattern shown;
(b) the S-A connections provided in the machine; and
(c) the A-unit thresholds.

Since the mode of S-A connections in the network is predetermined, there is naturally so far no scope for adaptation or adjustment. This feature appears in the third and final layer of TLU's of the machine. It consists of response units called R-units. Unlike the (fixed) input signals received by A-units from S-units, those of R-units from A-units have adjustable weights. If the weighted sum of all the inputs from A-units exceeds the fixed* R-unit threshold, it is activated; otherwise it stays quiescent. Thus if we assume for the sake of simplicity that the third layer consists of a single R-unit, "training" the machine means merely adapting the weights of A's input signals into the R-unit so that the R-unit responds to a certain set of patterns but not to others. Thus let us divide the pattern of stimuli shown to S-units into two types: type I and type II. To enable our machine to discriminate between these two types all we require to do is to ensure that each pattern of type I evokes in the R-unit the response "yes" or "1" and that of type II the alternative "no" or "0." To do so we need a "training" method for adapting the weights of A's inputs into the R-unit so as to elicit the correct response on every occasion after it has learned the desired discrimination. This is done by leaving the weights of the A-units' input signals intact every time the pattern shown evokes the correct response, but altering it when it does not in accordance with certain reinforcement rules, whereby we amplify the influence of operative A-units favorable to the desired outcome and attenuate that of the unfavorable ones.

The general plan of the organization and working of a simple perceptron or neural net machine on these lines may then be as sketched diagrammatically in Fig. 87. Each of the $A_1, A_2, A_3, \ldots$, associator units in the second TLU layer receives input signals from those S-units of the retinal grid with which it is linked. If the input signals arriving at any associator unit A_i exceed its prescribed threshold, it is activated. If not, it remains inactive. In the former case its output, S_i, is taken

---

* In other words, the adjustment is secured not by changing the synaptic thresholds of the network, as may well be the case in the network of live neurons, but by the weight of the input signals reaching it.

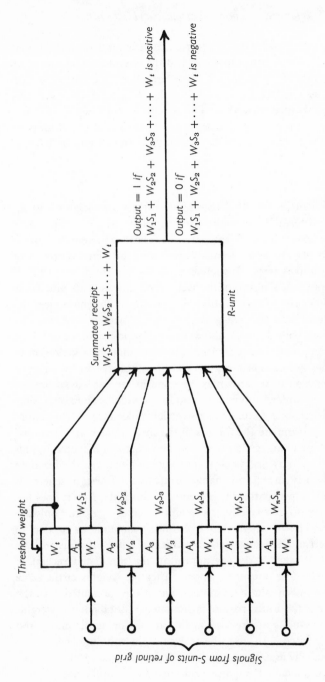

Fig. 87 The output of $W_i S_i$ of any A_i-unit is either W_i for an active A_i-unit when $S_i = 1$, or 0 when A_i is inactive and $S_i = 0$. The output of R-unit is therefore 1 when the sum of the weights of *active* A-units exceeds the threshold weight W_t. It is 0 in the other case.

as 1 while in the latter it is 0 in accordance with our usual binary rule. Each *A*-unit like A_i is in turn linked to the *R*-unit feeding into it its output signal S_i duly amplified (or retarded) by the corresponding weight W_i assigned to it. In addition, the *R*-unit receives a stimulus of fixed threshold weight W_t. The *R*-unit's output depends on the "weighted" sum of all its input signals emanating from *A*-units as well as of the fixed threshold W_t. As will be seen from Fig. 87, this sum is

$$W_1S_1 + W_2S_2 + W_3S_3 + \ldots + W_iS_i + \ldots + W_t, \ldots \quad \text{(i)}$$

the typical contribution W_iS_i coming from the *i*th associator unit A_i, and the final term W_t from the fixed threshold weight. Since S_i is assumed to be either 0 or 1, expression (i) above is merely the sum of the weights of only *active* *A*-units plus W_t, as the signal output *S* of inactive *A*-units is zero. It therefore follows that the *R*-unit "fires" or has output 1, if the sum of the weights of *active* *A*-units plus W_t is positive; otherwise, it is 0. This is how the *R*-unit dichotomizes the input patterns into two categories. The problem of teaching the machine then boils down to discovering an appropriate set of values of weights W_1, W_2, W_3, ..., of its *A*-units so that the segregation of patterns into two categories by the *R*-unit comes off correct.

The alteration of weights may be done in several ways, some of which are guaranteed to yield a solution, provided one exists. One such way is recourse to an error-correction procedure. The picture patterns that stimulate the *S*-units in the first instance are presented to the machine in any order. The initial weights of *A*'s input signals into the *R*-unit may also be any convenient values. If the response to the pattern is correct, no change in the adopted weight scheme is made, and the next pattern is presented. But if the *R*-unit does not respond to a pattern correctly, the weights of the *active* *A*-units only are either reinforced or attenuated by suitable amounts as needed to rectify the error. Obviously no adjustment of *inactive* *A*-units need be made as their weights do not appear in the summated receipt of *R*-unit on which its output depends. After the weights of the *active* *A*-units have been altered, another pattern is presented. If the response is right, the next pattern is presented. But if not, the weights of the *active* *A*-units are revised again, and so on until the desired response is elicited. In sum, the essence of the training scheme is to reduce selectively and iteratively the influence of *active* *A*-units, which tend to give unwanted response and enhance the influence of those

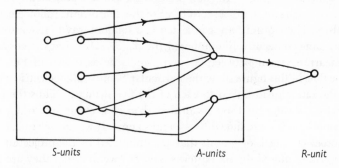

S-units   A-units   R-unit

Fig. 88

that tend to give the desired response. If some structure of fixed size of the form shown in Fig. 88 admits of a solution to such a problem, this procedure is guaranteed to converge upon a solution in course of time. In other words, after a certain number of trials a stage is reached when no further adjustment of weights of A's inputs into R-unit is required to secure correct identification by the machine in *all* subsequent presentations of picture patterns to it.

A simple example of a learning machine that can be taught to discriminate between two patterns in the afore-mentioned manner may easily be contrived in the following way. Let there be a 3 × 3 "retinal" grid of nine photoelectric cells on which we can project two patterns, a vertical pattern and a horizontal one. The former type can have three possible positions, V_1, V_2, V_3, and the latter H_1, H_2, H_3, as

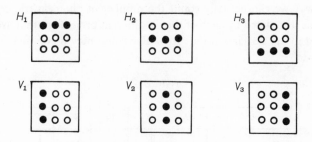

Fig. 89 The stimulation of all the three photoelectric cells in any column yields three vertical patterns V_1, V_2, V_3, and that of all the three photoelectric cells, in any row, three horizontal patterns H_1, H_2, H_3.

indicated in Fig. 89. In each position the pattern projected forms a signal which stimulates a set of three of the nine S-units (photoelectric cells). These S-units are connected in a random way to five association units consecutively numbered $A_1, A_2, \ldots, A_5$. Let the connection arrangement between A- and S-units be as shown in Fig. 90. The dots in this figure show the particular S-units (photoelectric cells) of the retinal grid linked to each of the five A-units. Thus the first square indicates the three S-units (dark circles) connected to A_1; the second square those linked to A_2, and so on. If we now examine the photoelectric cells or S-units that are stimulated by the projection on the grid of any of the six patterns, say, H_1, we find that they are the

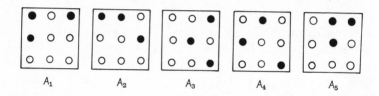

Fig. 90

three photoelectric cells in the first row. But of these three only two are linked to the A-unit A_1: the first and third cells in the first row. Projection of H_1 thus stimulates only two of the S-units that are linked to A_1. On the other hand, projection of H_2 stimulates three cells of the second row but only one of them happens to be linked to A_1, as a glance at Fig. 90 clearly shows. Thus while pattern H_1 activates two S-units linked to A_1, pattern H_2 activates only one. Proceeding in this way we can actually count the number of photoelectric cells or S-units stimulated by each of the six different projections that are also linked to the association unit A_1. The count may be summarized as follows:

TABLE 41

	H_1	H_2	H_3	V_1	V_2	V_3
A_1	2	1	0	2	0	1

Similar counts can be made for the remaining four A-units, A_2, A_3, A_4, A_5. The result is shown in Table 42.

TABLE 42

	H_1	H_2	H_3	V_1	V_2	V_3	
A_1	2	1	0	2	0	1	
A_2	2	1	0	1	1	1	Each A-unit is
A_3	1	1	1	0	1	2	stimulated by the number of S-units
A_4	1	1	1	1	1	1	shown here.
A_5	2	1	0	0	2	1	

Now we have to fix a threshold for the A-units. Suppose we arrange that an A-unit "fires" or yields the output 1 if it is stimulated by two or more S-units but otherwise remains quiescent with 0 output. At this threshold level the response pattern of A-units is easily seen to be as in Table 43.

TABLE 43*

	H_1	H_2	H_3	V_1	V_2	V_3	
A_1	1	0	0	1	0	0	The A-units against which 1 is
A_2	1	0	0	0	0	0	shown have the threshold value 2
A_3	0	0	0	0	0	1	or exceed it. Others against
A_4	0	0	0	0	0	0	which 0 is shown have lower
A_5	1	0	0	0	1	0	thresholds.

* Table 43 may be derived from Table 42 by substituting "1" for numbers equal to or exceeding the threshold 2, and "0" for all others shown therein.

We are now ready to drill our imaginary machine into discriminating between a horizontal pattern H and a vertical one V. To do so we first link all five A-units to a response unit or R-unit on whose outcome the machine's discrimination is to depend. We proceed on the assumption that if the output of R-unit is 1, the machine categorizes the projection as horizontal, and otherwise as vertical. It is at this stage that the machine acquires an adjustable parameter whereby it reorganizes its internal functioning to learn from "experience." This is done by applying adjustable positive or negative weights to the outputs of A-units in order so to regulate their inputs into the R-unit that the machine identifies correctly the pattern shown it. If the total weighted input into the R-unit plus the fixed threshold of five (one each for the five A-units) is positive, the R-unit "fires," indicating that the machine has detected an H. If negative, the R-unit does not "fire" and the machine indicates a V. The "learning" course of the machine consists merely in adjusting the weights of the outputs of *active* A-units to values at which the machine always responds correctly. To discover them we assume initially that all A-units have (equal) zero weights and proceed to amend them on the basis of results of successive trials.

TABLE 44

CHANGING VALUES OF WEIGHTS APPLIED TO ACTIVE A-UNITS ON SUCCESSIVE TRIALS

Trial number $\rightarrow$	(1)	(2)	(3)	(4)	(5)	Solu-
Pattern shown $\rightarrow$	H_1	V_1	V_2	V_3	H_1	tion
A_1	0*	0	−6	−6	−6	−6
A_2	0	0	0	0	0	8
A_3	0	0	0	0	−6	−6
A_4	0	0	0	0	0	0
A_5	0	0	0	−6	−6	−6
Threshold	5	5	5	5	5	5
Total	5	5	5	5	−7	
Machine response	H (correct)	H (incorrect)	H (incorrect)	H (incorrect)	V (incorrect)	
Correction required in weight of operative unit	−	−6	−6	−6	+8	

* The weights of active or operative A-units in each trial are underlined.

Suppose at the first trial we show the machine an H in the position H_1. A glance at Table 43 shows that only units A_1, A_2, A_5 are sufficiently stimulated to reach the prescribed threshold. But as the initial weights are all zero, the only output is 5. Since this is positive, the R-unit "fires" so that the machine identifies the pattern shown as an H. The identification being correct, we leave the initial weights intact and proceed to the second trial showing the machine V_1. Reference to Table 43 will show that only unit A_1 "fires" as it alone is stimulated to the threshold level. But because the weights remain fixed at zero as originally, the total output is still 5. Being positive, the *R*-unit "fires," again identifying the pattern as an *H*. Since the identification is now wrong, we have to adjust the weights of the *operative* or *active* *A*-unit, namely, A_1, to the extent required to make the total negative, say, -1. This obviously means altering its (A_1's) initial zero weight to -6. We thus start the third trial with a new pattern of weights: $A_1 = -6$, $A_2 = 0$, $A_3 = 0$, $A_4 = 0$, and $A_5 = 0$, as shown in column 3 of Table 44. Suppose now we show the machine V_2. Again from Table 43 we find that only A_5 is active. Since the weight of A_5, the only active unit, is zero, the sum is still 5. Being positive, the machine identifies V_2 as an *H*, making again a

TABLE 45

MACHINE RESPONSE TO PRESENTATION OF VARIOUS PATTERNS

A-unit ↓	Pattern pre-sented→	H_1	H_2	H_3	V_1	V_2	V_3
	Weight ↓						
A_1	-6	-6	Inactive	Inactive	-6	Inactive	Inactive
A_2	8	8	Inactive	Inactive	Inactive	Inactive	Inactive
A_3	-6	Inactive	Inactive	Inactive	Inactive	Inactive	-6
A_4	0	Inactive	Inactive	Inactive	Inactive	Inactive	Inactive
A_5	-6	-6	Inactive	Inactive	Inactive	-6	Inactive
Fixed threshold		5	5	5	5	5	5
Total		$-6+8-6$ $+5=+1$	5	5	$-6+5$ $=-1$	$-6+5$ $=-1$	$-6+5$ $=-1$
Machine response		*H* Correct	*H* Correct	*H* Correct	*V* Correct	*V* Correct	*V* Correct

wrong identification. We have therefore to revise once again the weight of A_5, the only active unit, in order to make the total a negative number, say, -1. We do so by making it -6 as shown in column 4 of Table 44, leaving the weights of other inoperative units as before. For the fourth trial, we show the machine V_3. As previously, we look for the operative units—in this case the single unit A_3. Since this is zero, the weighted total again is 5, which being positive leads the machine to identify wrongly a *V* as an *H*. To make the total negative, say, -1, we alter the weight of the operative unit A_3 from 0 to -6 as shown in column 5 of Table 44. For the fifth (and final) trial we show the machine H_1. The active or operative units are A_1, A_2, and

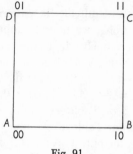

Fig. 91

A_5, whose newly adjusted weights add up to $(-6) + 0 + (-6) = -12$, leading to a total of $5 - 12 = -7$. Since the total is negative, the machine identifies it wrongly as a V. Hence, to make this sum positive we alter the zero weight of *one* of the three *active* units, A_2, to 8 as shown in the last column of Table 44. After five trials we thus reach a terminal set of weights which gives correct results for all subsequent presentations of H and V patterns. For with these weights the machine response for each pattern will now be correct, as may be verified from Table 45. It will thus be observed that the machine has learned the desired H-V discrimination.

The general theory of perceptrons or adaptable neural nets may now be briefly described. If, as usual, we begin by assuming our artificial neuron as an "all-or-nothing" affair, we may denote its active state by "1" and the inactive one by "0." With n such elements in the net we have in all 2^n possible input states of the network. We could conceive of them picturesquely as the vertices of a hypercube in an

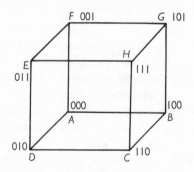

Fig. 92

imaginary *n*-dimensional space. For instance, when $n = 2$, the four (2^2) possible input states of the net are four permutations of two binary digits 0 and 1:

$$00, 10, 11, 01.$$

They may be viewed as the four vertices A, B, C, D, of a two-dimensional "cube," that is, the unit square $ABCD$ shown in Fig. 91. For $n = 3$, the eight (2^3) possible permutations of two binary digits 0 and 1, or

$$000, 100, 110, 010, 011, 001, 101, 111,$$

are the eight vertices A, B, C, D, E, F, G, H of the unit cube $ABCDEFGH$ drawn in Fig. 92. We could therefore geometrically represent all the input patterns of any set of n "neurons" or sensor units in our net by the vertices of a hypercube in an *n*-dimensional space which for convenience of subsequent reference we may call S-space. On the other hand, the output of the single R-unit in our

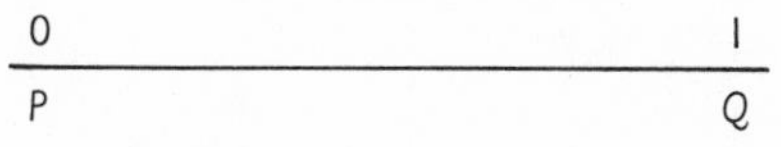

Fig. 93

machine is only twofold, 0 or 1. It may therefore be represented by the two terminals P and Q of a unit segment, the one-dimensional analogue of the *n*-dimensional hypercube (see Fig. 93). The problem of machine training then reduces to that of mapping the vertices of an *n*-dimensional hypercube in S-space onto the two end points P and Q of the line segment PQ, which we may call R-space. This is a way of saying that we have to discover ways of segregating all the vertices into two categories so that those in the first category are associated with the "point" Q of R-space, corresponding to R-unit's output 1, and those in the second with the "point" P of R-space, corresponding to 0 output of the R-unit. Thus in the example of Fig. 89, where the retinal grid consists of nine S-units, the problem we had to face was to partition six of the vertices (corresponding to patterns $H_1, H_2, H_3, V_1, V_2, V_3$) of a hypercube in a 9-dimensional S-space so that they are not only separated out from the rest but also separated from one another.

The problem may therefore be solved in two stages. First, we represent all possible input patterns of n given sensor or S-units by the

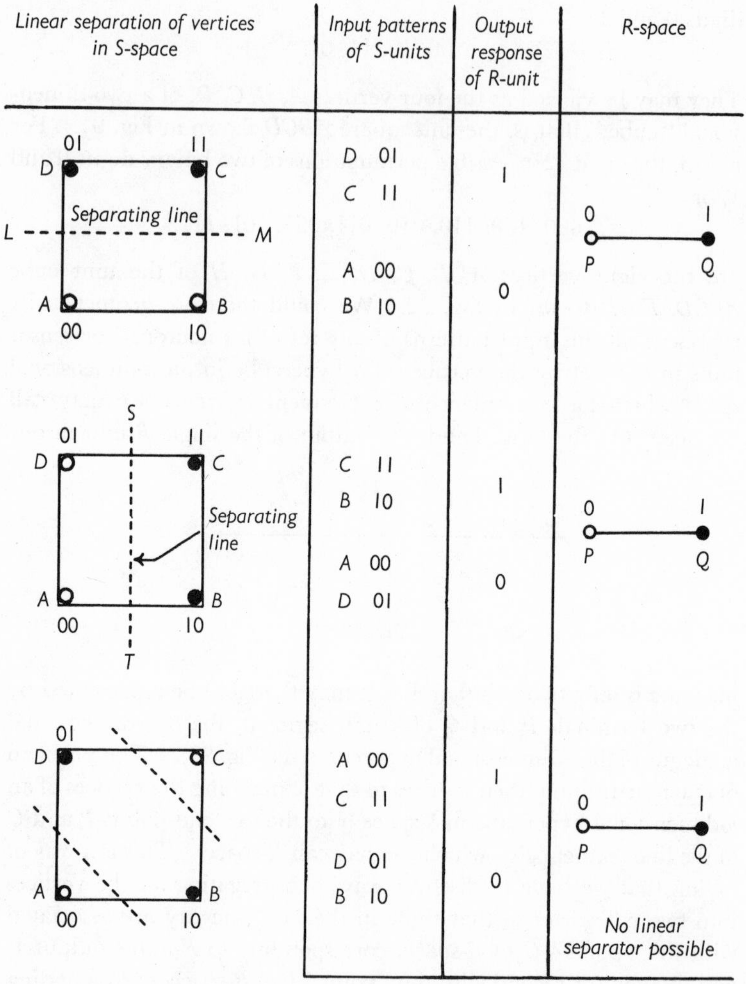

Linear separation of vertices in S-space	Input patterns of S-units	Output response of R-unit	R-space

Fig. 94

vertices of a hypercube in *n*-dimensional *S*-space. Second, we seek a way of separating them into two groups in order to correlate each group with one or another of the two "points" of the *R*-space representing the two possible outputs of the *R*-unit. There are naturally many

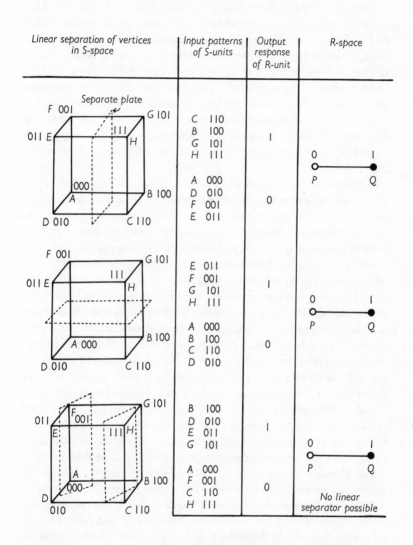

Linear separation of vertices in S-space	Input patterns of S-units	Output response of R-unit	R-space
	C 110 B 100 G 101 H 111	1	
	A 000 D 010 F 001 E 011	0	
	E 011 F 001 G 101 H 111	1	
	A 000 B 100 C 110 D 010	0	
	B 100 D 010 E 011 G 101	1	
	A 000 F 001 C 110 H 111	0	No linear separator possible

Fig. 95

ways of making the separation. But the simplest geometrical separator is a "hyperplane" drawn through the hypercube in such a way that the "vertices," that is, geometrical counterparts of S-unit input patterns, which have to evoke 1 in the R-unit are on one side of the "hyperplane" while those having to evoke 0 lie on the other.   Thus the four vertices of the two-dimensional "cube" or the square *ABCD* of Fig. 91 may be separated by a two-dimensional "hyperplane" or straight line in two ways: we separate them into two groups either by the line *LM* or by the line *ST* as shown in Fig. 94.   Each of them yields a particular mapping of *S* and *R*-spaces.   But no such separating line could be drawn if we had to associate the vertices *B* and *D* with one point of *R*-space and vertices *A* and *C* with the other (see Fig. 94).   Similar remarks apply *mutatis mutandis* to the mapping of "vertices" in *S*-space of more than two dimensions onto *R*-space (see Fig. 95).

A glance at Figs. 94 and 95 shows that quite often no single hyperplane can be drawn to yield the required separation of vertices into two groups.   In such a case a single *R*-unit cannot be trained to acquire the desired discrimination of input sensory patterns.   In most cases of interest *n*, the number of *S*-units, is very large so that our usual geometrical intuition, which works well enough up to three dimensions of our perceptual space, begins to fail us.   It is then quite difficult to tell whether or not the "vertices" are linearly separable.   Since the desired separation by a hyperplane is often impossible, it becomes necessary to interpose an intermediary layer of *A*-units between *S*-units receiving its sensory input patterns and *R*-units delivering its discriminatory judgment on them.   With the introduction of *A*-units we are able to chart the outputs of *S*-units in a new *A*-space of lower dimensions if the number of *A*-units does not exceed that of *S*-units. Thus in the case of our *H-V* discriminating machine considered earlier, the outputs of *S*-units are represented by the vertices of a hypercube in a nine-dimensional *S*-space.   They are in turn associated with the vertices of another hypercube in a new five-dimensional *A*-space of five *A*-units.   As they happened to be linearly separable, we could find a scheme of weights whereby the machine, a three-layered assembly, could be made to learn the required discrimination.   But if the vertices in *A*-space had not been linearly separable, we would have had to interpose yet another layer of associator units *B* and generate another *B*-space and so on till we finally reached a linearly separable *M*-space, whose vertices could be correlated with the binary output of the final *R*-unit.   The organization of such a multilayer net would then be as shown in Fig. 96.

While the organization of a multilayer learning machine thus looks simple, its apparent simplicity should not delude us into thinking that the actual analysis of its working is easy.   Indeed, the basic problem of such a multilayer machine—that of adapting its weight scheme to teach it the required discrimination—has yet to be solved even though iterative procedures to tackle a number of particular cases have been devised.   An example is the elementary *H-V* perceptron already described.   It is no doubt an artificial oversimplified imaginary construct made up merely to illustrate the method of weight adjustment needed to evoke an ever-correct response.   But a more elaborate actual machine called Mark I has recently been built on

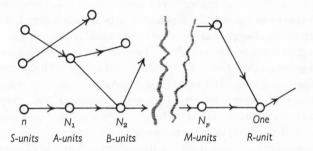

Fig. 96

similar lines by F. Rosenblatt at Cornell Aeronautical Laboratory.   It consists of 400 *S*-units arranged in a 20 × 20 "retinal" grid of photo-electric cells mounted in the focal plane of a camera.   The *S*-units or photoelectric cells are connected to 512 *A*-units in multiple parallel ways so that any *S*-unit can have up to 40 connections emanating from it.   The wiring is normally made according to a table of random numbers.   The *A*-units, which are mere gating switches, are then connected to eight binary-response *R*-units feeding into the latter suitably "weighted" inputs to elicit the discriminating response we require.   In actual practice the regulation or adjustment of weights assigned to *A*-units is secured by varying the *A-R* connections according to requirements by means of motor-driven potentiometers.   Since there are eight binary-response *R*-units, the *R*-space has $2^8 = 64$ vertices so that the input patterns can be classified into as many different categories.

Mark I has yielded many interesting results.   For example, it was trained to recognize all 26 letters of the alphabet when they are presented in a standard form. For this experiment, five of the eight R-units were used to yield $2^5 = 32$ different categories of which 26 were identified with the letters of the alphabet according to a code. The machine learned to recognize all 26 letters after having been trained on only 15 samples of each. Further, since its response is the outcome of the weighted majority vote of several A-units operating in parallel, we may reasonably expect a certain robustness of behavior in that failure of a few units will not completely damage the machine. Actual experiments with the machine have borne out the expectation. Removal of a few parts may degrade its performance but does not, in general, disable it altogether. For example, an α-perceptron with 240 A-units was trained to discriminate between the letters E and X. Failure of the A-units was simulated by randomly removing some of them *after* training the machine. The decline in performance was found to be gradual rather than sudden and varied with the number of A-units removed. It is often possible even to retrain the truncated machine and restore its erstwhile performance so that "repair" becomes synonymous with retraining. This is an aspect of machine behavior that is certainly reminiscent of the amazing plasticity or equipotentiality of brain tissue we have already noted in Chapter X. It owes its "equipotentiality" to the fact that the machine is not a memory device that operates by comparison with a stored file of standard patterns. The discriminatory faculty is rather distributed throughout its structure which, once disturbed, does lend itself in many cases to recovery by fresh training.

Further experiments with Mark I have shown that it could learn to discriminate between the letters E and X even when the training samples were slightly "noisy" in that extraneous random dots were superimposed on the projections of these patterns on the retinal grid. The machine is thus capable of a generalization even though of a primitive kind by availing itself of the overlap between the test and training patterns. More intricate perceptual problems such as recognition of letters in various forms, fonts, and positions, are, however, beyond the capacity of such simple perceptrons. It does seem possible, however, that more sophisticated (future) models might be able to perform some of these feats such as identifying a letter whether presented in gothic type, roman, italic, sans-serif, or any other style.

The inability of Mark I to recognize "similarity" of patterns other than that of the most primitive sort arises primarily from the limitations of its structure. Any three-layer arrangement of units like Mark

I can give rise to only a severely restricted concept of similarity. Consider, for example, the tinier version of Mark I, the simple three-layer perceptron of 3 × 3 photoelectric cells shown in Fig. 89 that was trained to discriminate between horizontal (H) and vertical (V) patterns. It was taught to treat all three horizontal patterns H_1, H_2, H_3 as alike or similar in contradistinction to the remaining three similar vertical patterns V_1, V_2, V_3. These six patterns were the standard texts on which it was "educated" to recognize similarity of horizontal and vertical patterns. The question now arises as to how it will classify, without further training, patterns which it has not seen before. Suppose it were presented with an unseen pattern on its retinal grid like either of the two shown in Fig. 97. In such a

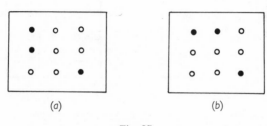

(a)   (b)

Fig. 97

situation, if the R-unit's output happened to be 1, the pattern would be classified as an H; otherwise it would be classified as a V. Since three H patterns evoke in the R-unit the output 1, any of the unseen patterns that happened to have a sufficient number of common elements with any of the three original training or textual patterns H_1, H_2, H_3 would be expected to elicit the same response in the R-unit and therefore be recognized as an H. On the other hand, if the unseen pattern had more elements in common with any of the other three textual patterns V_1, V_2, V_3 it would have a fair chance of being recognized as a V. Thus the unseen pattern a of Fig. 97, having two elements in common with the seen pattern V_1 but only one each with H_1, H_2, or H_3, might be classified as a V, while pattern b, with two elements in common with H_1 but only one with V_1, V_2, or V_3, might be identified as an H. If we project pattern a on the machine's retinal grid, we find that the projection will activate only two associator units, A_1 and A_4, because they alone share two of the three photoelectric cells stimulated by pattern a (compare Fig. 97a

with Fig. 90).   It therefore results from the weight scheme of Table 45 that their summated input into the R-unit is $-6 + 0 + 5 = -1$ so that the machine classifies it as a V.   Likewise, pattern b of Fig. 97, which stimulates only A_2 and A_4 units, yields the weighted sum $8 + 0 + 5 = 13$ so that the R-unit classifies it as an H.

However, while the machine classification in the afore-cited two cases has been as anticipated, there is no guarantee that it need always be so.   Consider, for instance, the two patterns c and d shown in Fig. 98.   Since patterns c and d have greater overlap with horizontal patterns H_1 and H_2 than with any of the vertical patterns, the machine might be expected to identify both of them as an H.   Yet with the weight scheme of Table 45 built into it, pattern c will activate

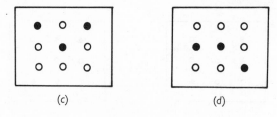

(c)   (d)

Fig. 98

A_1, A_3, and A_5, so that the weight of input signals into the R-unit is $-6 - 6 - 6 + 5 = -13$.   The machine therefore "misclassifies" c as a V.   Similarly, pattern d activates A_3 and A_4.   The weight of their input signals into the R-unit is now $-6 + 0 + 5 = -1$.   The machine therefore again mistakes pattern d as a V.   Although it might be possible to design a weight scheme that is less heavily biased in favor of a V pattern than the one we have adopted, it is obvious that "overlap" as a basis for similarity of patterns has very serious limitations.   Indeed, if our simple perceptron had a somewhat larger retinal "grid," say, an array of 20×20 instead of 3×3 photoelectric cells as in Mark I, it would present "similar" patterns which may yet have no "overlap" whatever, as for example, the two patterns formed on such a larger retinal grid by the stimulation of ten photoelectric cells (marked by dark circles) on the upper left-hand corner and an equal number on the lower right-hand corner of the grid in Fig. 99. Although none of the two patterns have a common overlap of stimulated cells, both of them are "similar" in the sense that they can be

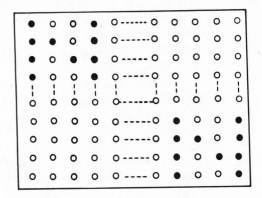

Fig. 99

made to represent the same letter *N*. This kind of similarity arises because one pattern may be derived from the other by a one-to-one transformation. It therefore follows that another way of recognizing "similarity" of patterns is to define a one-to-one transformation of a

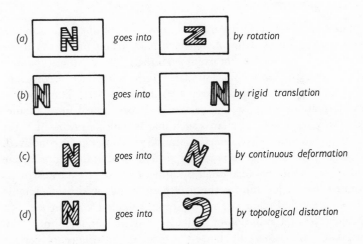

Fig. 100 Transformations of the letter *N*. (From "Perceptual Generalization over Transformation Groups," by Frank Rosenblatt, in *Self-organizing Systems*, Marshall C. Yovits and Scott Cameron, eds., Pergamon Press, New York, 1960, p. 65.)

given pattern into another. Thus we may start with any initial pattern and make an arbitrary choice of transformation group such as the group of all rigid translations or rotations, and so on. All patterns obtained by applying the group of transformations to the initial pattern would then be considered "similar" to it. Consequently we have so to design our perceptron that its response unit or *R*-unit yields the output 1 when it perceives any one of these "similar" patterns and the contrary output 0 when it perceives a "dissimilar" pattern. Now there are many kinds of transformation groups which can be used to define "similarity." Fig. 100 illustrates a number of such transformations like rotation, rigid translation, continuous deformation, or topological distortion of the same single pattern, the letter *N*. Each of these transformations may form the basis of similarity of patterns and would in general require a different kind of identification technique.

Following Rosenblatt we may broadly classify the various methods of recognizing similarity of patterns into four main categories:

(*a*) The analytic-descriptive method.
(*b*) Image transformation.
(*c*) Contiguity or overlap generalization.
(*d*) Transform association.

The analytic-descriptive method consists of reducing a stimulus pattern to a simple description which is invariant under the transformation in question. For example, if the stimulus patterns happen to be circles, the basis of their similarity is the invariance or constancy of π, the ratio of the circumference to the diameter. The group of transformations whereby one pattern may be derived from another and hence considered similar is such that it leaves π invariant. Yet other kinds of similarity-preserving transformations may be conceived. A case in point is the group of superpositions of, say, the center of one square form onto that of another by a physical shift (rigid translation) from its former location to the new position followed by a suitable reorientation and scaling of size to secure complete congruence. In all such cases the criterion of similarity may be embodied in a "description," which usually takes the form of invariance of certain geometrical attributes such as ratios of certain dimensions or other relations given in terms of measurements of lines, angles, and the like. The machine then detects similarity of patterns by comparing these measurements with a stored set of master descriptions. Those input stimulus patterns which correspond most closely to a particular master description are then recognized as similar. Such machines, however, suffer serious handicaps. They have no neurological possibility. Their success depends on discovering some method of pattern description which is amenable to programed application either by a digital computer or by some other special-purpose device. Most such systems lack both simplicity of organization and generality of application, being merely *ad hoc* inventions designed to meet a particular purpose. Nevertheless, they are the only systems, to date, which can deal readily with the recognition of really complicated topological transforms of the type shown in item *d* of Fig. 100. It is therefore not unlikely that we may hear more of them when we are able to take the design of perceptrons far beyond their present stage of development.

The second method of "image transformation" has been adopted by McCulloch and Pitts as a possible model for the operation of the brain in the perceptual-generalization of similar patterns, or the problem of recognizing what they call "universals." Thus the property of "squareness" may be recognized as an attribute of a figure, regardless of the position and size of the image on the retina because of the possibility of bringing all squares into superimposition by an appropriate blend of three operations: (i) a shift of center, (ii) a reorientation by rotation, and (iii) an appropriate scaling of its size. Consequently, in devising a neuron network capable of recognizing "universals," McCulloch and Pitts apply all three kinds of transformations to a stimulus image which is obtained from the retina and attempt to "normalize" this image in position, size, angular rotation and the like, so that at some point the image can be superimposed on and recognized as identical with one of a number of stored standard or "normalized" forms or "memory traces." Unfortunately, for several reasons it seems quite unlikely that this method or anything like it is actually adopted by the natural automata, living brains. First, the method is very extravagant in the use of neurons or neuron-like elements used to make the network. For example, all 10 billion neurons of the brain could easily be used up just in the process of centering, rotating, and scaling the size of the retinal image, leaving none for any other function. Each new transformation which we may wish to consider, such as an elongation or a tilting distortion, would require an additional specially designed computing or transformation network. As the number of admissible transformations is legion, an astronomical proliferation of the network would ensue. Secondly, such networks demand a rigidity of connection and a type of functional specificity of different units quite different from the observed plasticity or equipotentiality of the brain tissue, according to which an undamaged part of the cerebral cortex is able to take over the functions of the damaged areas. If the visual cortex of a rat is destroyed, for example, the animal can still recognize its food and avoid obstacles when it runs, even though it can no longer discriminate between patterns in the way possible before the operation. Thirdly, once a faculty for recognition of similarity of patterns based on a given transformation has been built into the system, it *must* be applied willy-nilly to any form which comes in. Thus a system which recognizes similarity of patterns on the basis of rotation as in Fig. 100a would automatically assign both patterns to the same class, no matter whether the rotation is small or large. When the rotation is large, say, 90° as in Fig. 100a, it will recognize N in both positions as "similar" but per contra will never learn that an N rotated through 90° could also become something different, that is, a Z. There is no way of compromise in this method whereby we may teach the system, say, to treat a slightly rotated N as similar but a right-angled rotated one as different. As a result, the only way to enable it to distinguish between an N and a Z is to do away with its built-in mechanism for recognizing rotation-based similarities. But this leads to a new disability in the machine. It now begins to treat even a slightly tilted N as something totally dissimilar to an N in the normal upright position. Although these logical incompatibilities can by sufficient ingenuity be reconciled, the reconciliation is secured at a frightful increase in complexity. It is therefore unlikely that the living brain actually uses it.

The third method of contiguity or "overlap" generalization is the one we described at the outset. In its simplest form it rests on the fact that a slight displacement or modification of a pattern, which shares most of its sensory stimuli with the original pattern, is *likely** to evoke the same response as the original rather than evoke an alternative response associated with a different pattern with which it has fewer points in common. It is really an offshoot of the "classification" principle first proposed by A. M. Uttley to explain an important

---

* We say *likely* because the contrary outcome cannot be completely ruled out. As we saw, our simple perceptron misclassified patterns c and d of Fig. 98 as vertical even though they had greater overlap with horizontal patterns.

feature of animal behavior, namely, the tendency to respond in the same way to a variety of different patterns of input signals emanating from the external world.   The reason is that because of their overlap the patterns resemble one another sufficiently in some respects as to look alike to the animal.   The aspects in respect to which they differ are ignored as irrelevant.   Uttley has coupled the idea of overlapping classes with that of conditional probability to design yet another kind of perceptron.   We shall deal with it in Chapter XVIII.   Here we merely remark that B. G. Farley has recently extended the same idea in another direction to suggest a "property-class" model.   His new model seeks to provide a neurologically plausible basis for many features of learned perception although no experimental evidence of

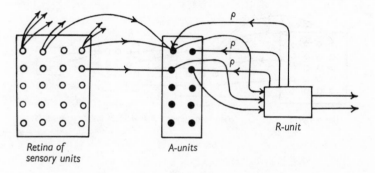

Fig. 101

its value exists at present.   Despite the obvious utility of the "overlap" idea as a basis for similarity of pattern, it has, as we have seen, some very serious limitations.   We therefore need other criteria whereby the similarity of patterns may be recognized even when there is no "overlap" of common elements at all.   For example, we would certainly want our Mark I to identify the two patterns N in two different corners of its retinal grid (see Fig. 99) as similar though they have no overlapping common elements whatever.   The machine is trained to make such an identification by being shown the letter N in a large number of positions on the retinal grid intermediate between these two so as to form a chain or "contiguity sequence" connecting the original pattern to the new one.   This then is the method of transform association whereby Rosenblatt was able to overcome the limitation of the simple three-layered perceptron mentioned earlier.

He showed that a three-layered "cross-coupled" perceptron running a feedback loop from the *R*-unit to the *A*-units would tend to develop an improved similarity criterion much wider than that of Mark I with its reliance on the overlap of common retinal elements.   Fig. 101 shows the organization of such an improved cross-coupled perceptron. As will be observed, it is similar in all respects to that of Fig. 86 except that feedback loops from the *R*-unit run back into the *A*-units.   The function of the feedback loops is to ensure an automatic adjustment of the weights *W* of the *A*-unit's output signals into the *R*-unit.   The adjustment is secured by the application of a "reinforcement operator" *ρ* as shown by the feedback lines in Fig. 101.   This is merely a way of saying that if the output of the *R*-unit is 1, then the weights of con-

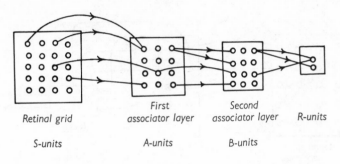

	First	Second	
Retinal grid	associator layer	associator layer	R-units
S-units	A-units	B-units	

Fig. 102

nections of all the *active A*-units which evoked this response are amplified.   At the same time, any units which are currently inactive at the time the reinforcement is applied lose in strength algebraically, so that collectively they cancel out the gain of the active units, keeping the total weight or value over the entire set of *A*-units equal to zero at all times.   The theory of such *gamma* systems, where the gain in active units is balanced by a compensating loss in the inactive units, has been developed in great detail by Rosenblatt.   We shall not go into it here as such systems are liable to feedback reverberations and therefore present additional complications.   In particular, like most other feedback systems they are prone to runaway hunting.   It therefore becomes necessary to pay particular heed to the question of whether these feedback reverberations die out, stabilize, or spread to activate all units.   We can, however, sidestep all such questions by recourse to simpler networks consisting of four layers of TL units but without any cross-coupling or feedback from the R-units. The additional layer is a second associator layer of B-units interposed between the A-units and R-units of the earlier perceptron (see Fig. 102). Such a four-layered perceptron is truly self-organizing in the sense that during the training period the trainer does not have to tell the machine the category of each stimulus. The only contact between the experimenter and the machine is the presentation of the stimuli. It can also be shown that the behavior of four-layered perceptrons is very similar to three-layered *cross-coupled* systems, but without the latter's attendant handicap of feedback reverberations, which may easily spiral off into an orgy of uncontrolled hunting.

In all the perceptual problems of pattern recognition considered so far we have been concerned with certain geometric or spatial configurations as existing at a particular instant of time. If on the other hand we were interested in the properties of a temporal pattern or sequence such as is involved in speech recognition, then the simple perceptron we have described would no longer be adequate. For such temporal effects to show up, it is naturally necessary to introduce time delays into the system. A speech-recognizing perceptron which utilizes such delays is currently being built at Cornell University.

The potential applications of various kinds of perceptrons or learning machines are not restricted to visual and speech patterns. A machine might have a number of discrete sets of input signals derived from any kind of sensors. Thus, besides the optical and auditory, there are tactile, olfactory, gustatory, and other kinds of signals emanating from sensor or S-units which could be sampled spatially and temporally and, after suitable processing through one or more layers of associator-units, presented to the last layer of R-units for sorting into appropriate categories. For these complex input signals could form patterns, which have previously been "taught" to the machine by assigning prescribed output signals from associator units to each such pattern. Although most perceptrons are yet quite rudimentary in pattern recognition, the output signals from their response units could operate other equipment. They could also change some aspect of the environment such as temperature, light, and so on, or regulate or guide other similar automata. With sufficient capacity future perceptrons could display enough sorting ability or discrimination to qualify as the intelligence amplifiers dreamt of by Ashby. For the discriminatory ability enables them to weigh features of their inputs so that when more fully developed, they could be used in disentangling complicated meteorological, medical, or economic processes. Already a simple perceptron has had considerable success in selecting or sorting medical diagnoses where the sensory input was the patient's coded clinical signs and symptoms.

Despite all the potential uses of perceptrons, both as prototypes of future intelligence amplifiers and as "models" of biological neuron networks, there is no doubt that they are still very far from elucidating the problem of perception in animals because of its enormous complexity. This is no mere accident. For it is the partial unraveling of the neurophysiological complexity of the living brain that has hitherto inspired the design of perceptrons rather than the reverse. For instance, the convergence of a great many connections emanating from several S-units of the retinal grid of the perceptron shown in Fig. 86 onto a single A-unit provides a very good correlate of the fact that one fiber in the optic nerve responds to an illumination of a fair-sized "patch" of receptors. Indeed, neurophysiologists have shown that long before the retinal image is carried to the brain there is a hundred-fold convergence of input channels from receptors to optic nerve followed by further confluence of fibers in higher nuclei. Such definite anatomical knowledge of the physiology of vision as we have managed to accumulate has suggested the design of multilayered perceptrons illustrated in Figs. 96 and 102, where the output of several S-units of the retinal grid congregates onto one of the A-units, and that of several A-units onto one of the B-units, and so on finally to the R-units. If such perceptrons as have been designed so far are quite poor imitations of the seeing eye, it is because of large gaps in our knowledge of the physiology of vision. In some unknown way, the living brain behind the eye, unlike present-day perceptrons, does manage to respond to *all* the stimuli it receives from the external world even though these vary greatly and often in unpredictable ways. A case in point is the change in the retinal image of objects when viewed from different angles of regard or distances or seen under varying conditions of illumination or association with other objects of the visual field. Indeed, the *va-et-vient* of the retinal images is greater even than the flux of a river, so that one can no more see the "same" image twice than he can step into the "same" river twice. Obviously, therefore, all the afore-mentioned generalization-pattern-recognition techniques we have described are far too primitive to serve as models of perception. Much wider but logically "simpler" criteria of "similarity" are required if perceptron nets are to simulate the performance of the network of real neurons. We may have a faint glimmer of the vast variety and manifold diversity of such criteria from a mere enumeration of some of the general principles of perception found experimentally by the gestalt school. First, the principle of "closure and good continuation" seems to enable us to fill up some "obvious" gaps in the perceptual field. A certain style of hair-do or a particular inflection of tone often suffices to make instant recognition by immediate recall of and

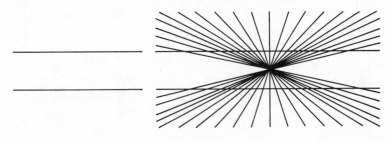

Fig. 103

telescoping with other attributes associated with the person. It is precisely through some sort of similar semantic telescoping of texts that we can read books intelligibly, not letter by letter, but by chunks which may be larger than words and phrases or even sentences and paragraphs. Secondly, there is the principle of "wholeness" often expressed by the dictum "The whole is greater than the sum of all its parts." For example, two parallel lines no longer appear parallel when intersected by a pencil of lines crossing at various angles (see Fig. 103). The addition of the pencil alters the whole pattern. Thirdly, certain mysterious "field forces" seem to be at work whereby a single dot that may happen to be somewhere out of line in an otherwise perfect dotted circle usually appears closer to the circle than it really is. A "force" is said to pull the dot back. Fourthly, there is the well-known feature of "constancy" of perception (which is indeed its essence) whereby a tea cup remains a cup, always appearing round and cylindrical no matter what the angle of regard. Fifthly, learning acquired by different senses is constantly exchanged. It is this faculty that enabled a deaf Beethoven virtually to hear with his eyes the music he wrote or with his fingers the symphonies and sonatas he played. A more commonplace instance is our capacity to recognize immediately by touch a shape learned visually. Even when the image happens to be too large to fall at once on the retina, it can be recognized by moving the eyes or hand, or even the whole body. For, after all, most perception has emerged during the eons of animal evolution and struggle for survival as a prelude to movement. Finally, we have also to reckon with the significant part played by "attention," "set," "motivation," and "context" to denote what D. O. Hebb has

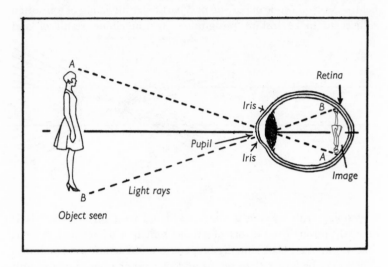

Fig. 104

called the "non-sensory" factors in perception. A classic instance of their importance is the ability of our visual cortex to readapt itself—albeit after some period of initial confusion and discomfort—to seeing objects almost "normally" even when wearing special lenses which invert everything seen through them. As is well known, we manage to see objects right side up although their images on the retinal screen are inverted (see Fig. 104). In some mysterious way we succeed in uprighting them. But having learned to do so once we can repeat the trick, that is, reorganize the "uprighted" images turned upside down by the special lenses. It is therefore no wonder that no "network" theory of perception has yet been found to satisfy these stringent boundary conditions of the live networks of real neurons. Even a flatworm has a more highly organized nervous system than any perceptron so far made. Similar comparisons between the size of the switching networks that can reasonably be constructed on perceptron principles and that of the live neuron networks used by higher animals would suggest that we have yet a long way to go before we can obtain practical devices able to show sufficiently deep functional equivalence with living brains.   This failure of the "network" approach to elucidate the physical structures and neurophysiological principles that underlie the emergence of natural intelligence exhibited by the living brain has given rise to other methods of creating artificial intelligence. We shall describe some of them in the next chapter.

Chapter XVI

ARTIFICIAL INTELLIGENCE—
GAME-PLAYING MACHINES

AS we explained in Chapter XIV, the problem of simulating intelligence in any given area such as writing poetry, playing games, proving theorems, composing music, or recognizing patterns is merely the problem of mechanizing some repetitive routine operations, which despite their inherent clumsiness and inefficiency could be productive if performed at a sufficiently fast rate. The computer owes its enormous computation "intelligence" entirely to this principle. The reason it has not been possible to exploit it to the same extent for simulation of other kinds of intelligence is that there is a basic difference between computation and any of the afore-mentioned tasks. It is not that computers are strictly arithmetic devices capable of doing only numerical sums, for a computer can manipulate non-numerical symbols as adroitly as numbers. The basic difference stems from the fact that while computational problems are amenable to what are called "algorismic" methods, other more complex problems like writing poetry or composing music are not.

An algorism for a problem is a repetitive routine which, if followed, is guaranteed to yield a solution, assuming, of course, that such a solution exists. An example is that of the simple algorism for searching for a word in a dictionary. One scans the list of words in alphabetical order till one finds it. The dictionary provides a set of possible solutions in some order and we test each candidate word in succession till the required one is found. Furthermore, the iterative scheme,

$$x_{i+1} = \frac{1}{2}\left(x_i + \frac{N}{x_i}\right),$$

for extracting the square root of any given number N cited in Chapter IX, is an instance of a rather more recondite algorism. It too defines a routine yielding a set of possible solutions $x_1, x_2, x_3, \ldots$, in some order with a prescribed procedure for testing them till the right solution is secured. Both algorisms are typical of any problem-solving process. There is a generator that produces possible solutions —the word list in one case and the iterative formula in the other— with a test procedure for recognizing *the* solution. In both cases the search is guaranteed to succeed in reasonable time such as we can afford. Both processes are therefore amenable to computer treatment even though the word search in a list involves handling non-numerical symbols. The computer is programed merely to follow the algorism or recursive routine of scanning possible solutions produced by the generator process, test them in succession, and terminate the operation when the solution is in hand. The computer owes its success in accomplishing such computational or algorismic tasks to its high-speed operation, so that as long as some way of performing a task can be specified, it does not really matter how laborious the ensemble of operations would be if carried out by us humans. As we saw in Chapter IX, it is precisely the great rapidity of its action that makes even its most devious computational roundabouts quicker than many an apparent crow flight. What is true of computation does *not* hold for the aforesaid miscellany of jobs. Although in these cases, too, problem-solving processes can be devised, they offer no guarantees of success. Consider, for example, Swift's Lagado routine for writing "books on philosophy, poetry, politics, and so on" cited earlier in Chapter XIV. As we explained, no computer, however rapid, could follow it through to success simply because the number of possible solutions that the routine generates rises exponentially. It is the same with all other complex problems such as playing games, proving theorems, recognizing patterns, and so on, where we may be able to devise a recursive routine to generate possible solutions and a procedure to test them. The search fails because of the overwhelming bulk of eligible solutions that have to be tested.

The only way to solve such non-algorismic problems by mechanical means is to find some way of reducing ruthlessly the bulk of possibilities under whose debris the solution is buried. Any device, stratagem, trick, simplification, or rule of thumb that does so is called a *heuristic*. For example, printing on top of every page of a dictionary the first and last word appearing there is a simple heuristic device which greatly lightens the labor of looking for the word we need. "Assume the answer to be x and then proceed backwards to obtain an algebraic equation" is another instance of heuristics for divining arithmetical riddles like those listed in the *Palatine Anthology* or Bhaskara's *Lilavati*. Drawing a diagram in geometry and playing trumps in bridge "when in doubt" are other instances of heuristic devices that often succeed. In general, by limiting drastically the area of search, heuristics ensure that the search does terminate in a solution most of the time even though there is no guarantee that the solution will be optimal. Indeed, a heuristic search may fail altogether. For by casting aside a wide range of possibilities as useless, it is likely occasionally to throw out the baby with the bath. Consequently a certain risk of partial failure, such as sometime missing the optimal solution, or even of total failure in a heuristic search has to be faced. Nevertheless, resort to heuristics for solving problems more complex than computation and not amenable to algorismic routines is inescapable.

Among the more complex non-algorismic tasks to which heuristic strategy has recently been applied we may list game playing, theorem proving, problem solving in general, pattern recognition as in reading or writing machines, machine translation, information retrieval, and so on. These tasks are being accomplished at present by programing a wide diversity of computers to handle them. Such attempts are of interest to us in that they reveal how vastly different must be the brain's operation, particularly in respect of its methods of storage, recall, and data processing from those practiced in computer engineering today. For they show that despite the computer's great superiority in computation and data processing it is as yet quite ill-adapted for performing the afore-mentioned miscellany of tasks that the living brain takes so deftly in its stride. The fact is that the computer still largely operates by prescribed rules of procedure built into it. It is therefore really at home only in those tasks which can be performed by resort to algorismic methods or rule-of-thumb routines. When it is set to grapple with tasks requiring non-algorismic methods having little resemblance to the familiar rules of logic and mathematics which are built into digital devices, its performance no longer seems as glamorous as while doing sums. Nevertheless, by the invention of new kinds of highly sophisticated machine languages or codes it is being rapidly reshaped to perform many of these more difficult tasks.

Of the diverse computer programs now being devised to undertake some of these non-algorismic tasks the most avidly studied are those designed to play games such as chess, checkers, and nim. There are several reasons for this preference.   First, a game situation is ideally amenable to computer treatment because in most games the problem is sharply defined both in allowed legal moves as well as in the ultimate goal, that of winning the game.   It therefore results that the task of winning the game can be unambiguously described even though the description in question may be long, laborious, and tedious.   Secondly, a game situation in most cases is neither so simple as to be trivial nor so ultra-complex as to be beyond the capacity of any computer that present-day technology may hope to construct.   Thirdly, since the classic work of von Neumann and O. Morgenstern, the theory of games has begun to provide a new approach to many unsettled questions in economics, sociology, politics, war, diplomacy, and even scientific research.   Game-playing computers therefore are no mere interesting toys for self-amusement.   They point the way to techniques that have several useful applications.   Fourthly, by pitting a game-playing machine against a human player we have a fair measure of the machine's ability to simulate the particular brand of "intelligence" that it mechanizes.

The chief aim of designers of game-playing machines is to discover, if possible, some scheme which can be used to guarantee a win irrespective of the opponent's moves and then to embody it in the computer program.   A case in point is Ferranti's computer, Nimrod, exhibited in 1951 at the Science Exhibition of the Festival of Britain and in various other European cities later.   This special-purpose digital computer was constructed to show how a large electronic computer may be programed to play and always win a game of nim against any opponent ignorant of the simple formula that guarantees the machine a win.   As is well known, the nim game is played with tokens, usually matchsticks, distributed in a number (N) of heaps.   Each of the two players is alternately allowed a move during the course of which he may pick up as many matches as he wishes subject only to two conditions.   First, he must pick any number of them from one or more piles but the number of piles interfered with must not exceed a given number k which is naturally less than N, their total number.   Secondly, he must pick at least one match from some pile.   The player obliged to pick the last match or group of matches is deemed to have lost the game.   It was shown long ago that in such a game victory lay inevitably with the player who played it according to a set procedure which could be relied upon to yield a certain win.   To understand how one may apply such a winning formula, consider, for the sake of definiteness, four heaps designated *A, B, C, D* consisting respectively of nine, six, four, and eleven matches as shown in Fig. 105.   Suppose further that k is 1 so that not more than one heap can be touched at a time.   To be able to tell whether in these circum-

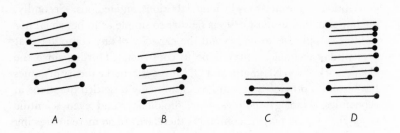

A   B   C   D

Fig. 105

stances the initial position is a winning one, all we need do is to apply the following rule: First, express the number of matches in every heap in the binary notation, as the number nine of heap *A* by 1001 or the number eleven of heap *D* by 1011.   When we do so, the initial configuration of the heaps may be represented by the table:

TABLE 46

	(8)	(4)	(2)	(1)
A	1	0	0	1
B	0	1	1	0
C	0	1	0	0
D	1	0	1	1
Column sum	2	2	2	2

We next total each column of Table 46 and record the result at the bottom to see whether each column sum is an exact multiple of $(k + 1)$, or 2 in the present case.   If it is, the starting configuration is a winning position in the sense that no player facing it can make a move that can avert his defeat.   Since in this case each column sum is exactly divisible by two, the starting configuration is a winning position.   But if our game allowed selections from at most two heaps at a time so that, k being 2, the column sums would be no longer divisible by $k + 1 = 3$, the configuration would not be a winning one any more.

The player who knows this "winning position" rule can always manage to win. For there are only two possibilities. Either a starting configuration is a winning position or it is not. If it is *and* the opening move lies with the opponent, the "secret"-knowing player can ensure that he retains the advantage of his initial position by making only such moves as leave the column sums after every alteration divisible by $(k + 1)$. If, on the other hand, he himself faces a winning position, he has to wait till his opponent (supposedly ignorant of the winning gimmick) makes a faulty move which converts a winning position into a losing one. Once the opponent makes such a mistake, as he is likely to do in the course of some move or other, the knowing player gets the advantage and can manage to retain it thereafter till the end. In the second case, when the initial position is *not* a winning position, the knowing player can always turn it into one by withdrawing an appropriate number of matches from the given heaps. Thus, suppose heap B had only four matches instead of six. The number against B in Table 46 then becomes 100 instead of 110, making the sum under column head (2) only 1. Since this column sum 1 is now not divisible by 2, as against the earlier value 2, the new initial position of the four heaps is no longer a winning one. But our player can immediately make it so by merely removing two matches from heap D, reducing its number from eleven to nine or in the binary notation from 1011 to 1001. For with their removal from heap D all the column sums become divisible by 2. The new position is therefore a winning one as may be seen from Table 47. In this position no

TABLE 47

	(8)	(4)	(2)	(1)
A	1	0	0	1
B	0	1	0*	0
C	0	1	0	0
D	1	0	0	1
Sum	2	2	0	2

* Withdrawal of two matches from heap B turns the original digit 1 in this position into zero.

possible move can alter the balance of advantage in his favor except a mistaken subsequent move of his own.

While a computer can be programed to apply the afore-mentioned winning algorism, trouble arises when it faces a human player knowing the secret of its success.   For with two players both sharing the secret the game becomes totally trivial.   If the initial position is a winning one, the player who has the first move will lose, assuming that no mistake is made by his opponent.   If not, he will win since he can convert it into a winning position by an appropriate withdrawal of matches and thus force a defeat on his opponent.

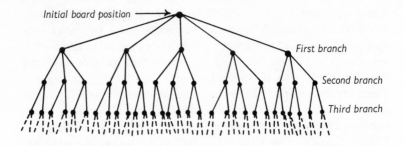

Fig. 106   Simplified "tree" of possible moves.   Notice how quickly the moves proliferate with each new branch of the tree.

Because a simple algorism turns the game into a triviality, most computer programs have been concerned with making the computer play other games like chess and checkers where a winning formula cannot be so readily devised.   Take, for instance, chess.   As is well known, given any chess position, it is possible in principle to consider all possible first moves, then all possible first countermoves of the opponent, then all second moves and their replies, and so on to the bitter end where the game terminates in a win, lose, or draw.   Working backwards through the "tree" of moves, determining at each branch point which move is the most advantageous for the side making the move, one arrives at the best initial move (see Fig. 106).   The big snag in carrying out this procedure in practice is the rapid proliferation of possible moves, which makes it impossible to continue for very long even with computer assistance.   Consider, for example, any initial position.   As there are on the average about thirty possible moves corresponding to each position, we have to consider thirty moves of one player and thirty countermoves of his opponent to each such move.   The very first move of both players therefore gives rise to $30^2 = 900$ different possible plays. The second move of both players will raise it to $30^2 \times 30^2 = 810,000$, with the consequence that at the end of a typical game of some 40 moves there will have to be considered some 30^{80} different possible moves. Even if we assume that our chess-playing computer examines a thousand billion (10^{12}) moves per second, it will still take some $\dfrac{30^{80}}{10^{12}}$ seconds or 10^{98} years to make even the first move. Since this exceeds the putative age of the universe by a factor of 10^{88}, the "victory"-yielding strategy is utterly impracticable. This is why most computer programs have per-force to confine the "look-ahead" procedure to only a few moves, evaluating the resulting board position in some way analogous to that adopted by a good chess player. If we can specify an approximate evaluation function $f(P)$ of the board position P at the end of any move,* the play will consist of the white player's choice of the move that maximizes $f(P)$ at every stage and the black player's choice of one that minimizes it. Suppose, for instance, the values of $f(P)$ for each of the thirty board positions after white's first move are

$$f_1(P), f_2(P), \ldots, f_{30}(P).$$

Now consider thirty board positions corresponding to the thirty possible replies of the black player to *each* of these moves. We then have a 30 × 30 square array of possible board positions at the end of the first moves of both players:

$$f_{1,1}(P), f_{1,2}(P), \ldots, f_{1,30}(P)$$
$$f_{2,1}(P), f_{2,2}(P), \ldots, f_{2,30}(P)$$
$$f_{3,1}(P), f_{3,2}(P), \ldots, f_{3,30}(P)$$
$$\cdot \quad \cdot \quad \cdot \quad \cdot \quad \cdot \quad \cdot \quad \cdot \quad \cdot$$
$$f_{30,1}(P), f_{30,2}(P), \ldots, f_{30,30}(P)$$

---

* For example, as a first rough approximation we may evaluate any given board position by simply adding up the "fighting power" of the total pieces on either side in terms of the pawn unit, treating a knight, bishop, rook, queen, and king as worth respectively ± 3, ± 3, ± 5, ± 9, and ± 5 pawns, the [+] sign being reserved for white and the [−] sign for black pieces. It is true that such an evaluation gives short shrift to a number of other very important features such as the mobility and placement of pieces, the weakness of king protection, the nature of pawn information, and the like. But we shall not go into further sophistication of the evaluation function for the present.

With the above array of possible board positions the white player's choice of a move is aimed at maximizing f and the black player's choice at minimizing it. If the white player plays the first of the thirty possible moves open to him, the second player will pick that one in reply which will make f a minimum. In other words, for his choice of the first of the possible thirty alternatives available to him, the white player can expect only the minimum of the possible thirty values of the board position, namely, the minimum of the first row of the array:

$$f_{1,1}(P), f_{1,2}(P), f_{1,3}(P), \ldots, f_{1,30}(P).$$

Let this minimum be $f_{1,i}(P)$. Similarly, if the white player plays the second of his thirty alternatives as his first move, the black player will reply with a move which corresponds to the minimum of the board positions in the second row, or the minimum of

$$f_{2,1}(P), f_{2,2}(P), \ldots, f_{2,30}(P).$$

Let this minimum be $f_{2,j}(P)$. The white player then examines in turn the consequences of adopting the third, fourth, . . ., and thirtieth alternative open to him. In other words, he searches for the minima $f_{1,i}, f_{2,j}, f_{3,k}, \ldots, f_{30,u}$ of each row of the above 30×30 array. His best move then is the one that *maximizes* the row *minima*

$$f_{1,i}, f_{2,j}, f_{3,k}, f_{4,p}, \ldots, f_{30,u}.$$

Let this maximum of row minima be $f_{s,t}$. The white player then adopts the sth alternative of the thirty possible as his first move and the black player adopts the tth alternative in reply. This becomes the new starting situation and the play proceeds exactly as before—a new alternation of maximizing the new minima of rows. In view of the great proliferation of alternatives even when the "look-ahead" is confined to only a few moves, this maximizing of row minima or "*minimaxing*" procedure has perforce to be restricted to two or three moves ahead. Even so, it is necessary, to lighten the task, to discard a number of alternatives without examination of their corresponding board positions. Certain *ad hoc* rules can be prescribed for deciding such discards. Having thus arrived at a reasonably practicable strategy for choosing the moves to be made by a chess-playing computer, our next problem is to describe it unambiguously in machine language for implementation.

The problem of setting up a digital computer designed to play chess according to a prescribed strategy may then be handled in two stages. In the first, we have to devise a code to represent the chess pieces and their positions on the board as numbers; and in the second, we spell out the prescribed strategy as a sequence of commands that is virtually the computer program. Fig. 107 illustrates Shannon's code for the chessboard and the chess pieces. As will be observed, each of the sixty-four board squares is represented by a two-digit number, the right-hand digit denoting the "rank" or horizontal row and the left-hand the "file" or vertical column. If to the two-digit number denoting a board square, say, 43, we add a third to indicate the chess

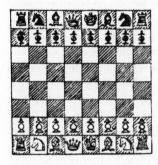 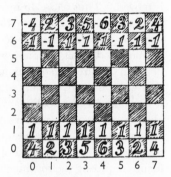

Fig. 107

piece lying there, we can represent any chess piece position by a three-digit number. The third number, however, has to be one of the following:

$$0, \pm 1, \pm 2, \pm 3, \pm 4, \pm 5, \pm 6,$$

in order to cover all the varieties of pieces of either side. Which one of these thirteen integers from -6 to $+6$ is chosen to denote a given piece is decided by two conventions. First, positive numbers are assigned to white pieces and negative numbers to black pieces. Secondly, pawns are denoted by 1, knights by 2, bishops by 3, rooks by 4, queens by 5, and kings by 6, zero being reserved for all empty squares. With a two-digit number denoting a board square and a single digit from -6 to $+6$ denoting a chess piece including zero for vacant squares, the juxtaposition of the two numbers becomes a code indicating the location of the relevant piece in that square. Thus the juxtaposition of the digit 5 (denoting the white queen) with the number 43 (denoting the square at the intersection of the third row and fourth column), that is, the number 543, becomes a code for the statement that the white queen occupies the square 43.   Likewise, the three-digit number, 056, indicates that the square at the intersection of the sixth row and fifth column is empty.   This is how any given board position can be coded as a series of three-digit numbers which in turn can be stored in the numerical memory of a digital computer. The same code is also adequate for describing changes in the board position.   For any such change occurs only by a player's move, which may ordinarily be specified by giving the number of the square on which the piece stands followed by the number of the one to which it is moved.   Thus 543, 546 means that the white queen at the square 43 is moved to the square 46.   The code number 5 for the white queen is repeated in order to take care of the special case of pawn promotion to a higher piece when it moves into the last row on the board in the direction of its motion.   Thus the number 136, 337 means that when the pawn at the square 36 moves into the topmost row 37, it is promoted to a rook for which the prescribed code number is 3. Having developed a numerical code to represent chess pieces, their moves, and the board positions from move to move, the "mini-maxing" strategy described above is translated into a series of commands requiring the machine to evaluate the board position function $f(P)$ for a specified number of "look-ahead" moves, depending on the storage capacity of the computer being programed and the time we can afford to allow for each evaluation.

However, when we actually attempt to program a computer to play chess on these lines, we find that even if the look-ahead exploration is confined to no more than four moves, the number of possibilities to be examined before each move can be decided swells to about a million (actually 30^4 or 810,000).   Such an exploration is quite beyond the memory capacities of most modern computers.   The only way to reduce their number is to consider a few of the most plausible alternatives out of the thirty possible as was done by A. Bernstein *et al.* when writing the first complete chess-playing program for the IBM 704 computer.   By exploring only seven of the most plausible avenues out of the thirty available at each move and limiting the look-ahead to a depth of four moves at each stage, they managed to deflate the number of possibilities to be examined from 810,000 to only $7^4 = 2401$.   But Bernstein's heuristic was not a conspicuous success as the performance of the computer has been none too bright.   In the two games actually played so far it could barely reach the standard of a passable amateur. The main weakness lay in the inability of the computer to learn from its own mistakes.

A. L. Samuel has been able to remedy this defect, but only at a price. By substituting for chess an easier game, that of checkers, he has programed a computer that plays an excellent game of checkers. His success is due to the relative simplicity of the rules of checkers which permits greater emphasis to be laid on machine-learning techniques. There are two ways in which a machine might learn to improve its performance. One is the perceptron-type approach described in Chapter XV, where we induce learned behavior into a randomly connected switching net by reinforcing or attenuating the weights of the A-unit's input signals into the R-unit. Since this kind of reward-*cum*-punishment training scheme—aimed at producing only general-purpose learning machines imitating animal behavior—has not yet been markedly successful, Samuel preferred the second alternative, where we do not aim so high. We confine ourselves to producing merely a computer version of a highly organized network designed to learn only certain specific things. The compensating payoff of the sacrifice is immediate practicability.

Proceeding on the same lines as Bernstein *et al.*, Samuel too makes his computer play by looking ahead a few moves and by evaluating the resulting board positions. But to enable the computer to generalize from its past experience he employs a novel heuristic technique called the "multiple-simultaneous-optimizer" method into which we will not go here except to remark that the source of reinforcement signals is highly ingenious. Samuel does not wait to play out one or more entire games for each single learning step. He measures instead for each move the difference between what the evaluation function $f(P)$ yields directly of a board position and what it predicts on the basis of an extensive continuous exploration of moves. The sign of this error, "Delta," is used for reinforcement in order to make the system learn something at each move. The learning scheme is important because it represents the only really successful attempt at machine learning in problem-solving situations. Indeed, it is so successful that Samuel's computer in course of time was sufficiently trained to defeat even a former Connecticut checkers champion and one of the United States' foremost players. This is why Samuel's program is rightly considered a landmark in the synthesis of artificial intelligence.

The next step, that of making a computer play as proficiently the more complex game of chess, has, however, yet to be taken. The most promising line of advance seems to be that explored by A. Newell and his collaborators. They propose substituting for the single numerically additive evaluation function, $f(P)$, used to "minimax" alternatives, a multiplicity of goals and subgoals listed in order of their importance or priority. They are king safety, material balance, center control, development, king-side attack, pawn promotion, and the like, or may represent a more limited objective such as "attack the black king bishop with the white king rook," and so on. Naturally a leading goal such as king protection takes precedence over a less important one like pawn promotion. The goals in turn determine rules, and out of these the program is constructed in close imitation of how human players actually play the game. As is well known, players do so according to a vast collection of rules of thumb which form the common lore of the chess world. The machine is similarly instructed to behave according to the same rules of thumb, being at any particular instant under the control of one rule or shunting between two or more while remaining under the command of a master program. The rules which lead to the prescribed goal or subgoal are reinforced and those which do not are inhibited, somewhat analogously to weights of the learning machines described in Chapter XV. It is to be emphasized that the criterion of success adopted in deciding whether a rule is to be reinforced or inhibited is not the final outcome of the game, that is, "win, lose, or draw," but the particular goal or subgoal it is intended to achieve. The reason is that the machine can learn nothing at all in any reasonable time if the efficacy of a rule is to be determined by reference to the ultimate result of the game. For in that case the number of possibilities to be explored and the learning information to be processed by the machine before any learning can occur is staggeringly large. But by confining the learning decision—reinforcement or inhibition of a rule—to only partial goals rather than the end goal of the game, it is possible to cut the learning information to be processed by the machine to a manageable level. In other words, it is only by breaking down the main problem of winning a chess game into several component goals or subgoals that the Newell team is able to make any headway at all towards its ultimate objective of showing how *in fact* an organized collection of such rules of thumb can pull itself up by its boot strings and learn to play good chess.

To do so Newell and his collaborators proceed in two stages. First, they describe the organization of the rules in order subsequently to program the computer; and secondly, they demonstrate that the organization will actually work in practice. For the present they have been mainly preoccupied with the first stage. For the description of the machine program itself requires the invention of a hierarchy of new languages more task-oriented than the usual machine code. Thus, besides the machine code, a basic chess vocabulary, and the chess program, the Newell team had to invent a number of general information-processing languages, what they call IPL's, primarily intended to handle lists of goals and subgoals the rules of thumb are designed to achieve. Since these lists have to be flexible to accommodate ever-shifting goals (which is how the machine can learn anything at all), they are of unknown lengths and contain terms which may themselves be names or catalogue numbers of other lists and so on. Though the number of such IPL's used in their program was originally four, it has already risen to six and is likely to rise further. The main reason for this increasing complexity of their IPL's is that the chess program is intended to use chess as a model for describing human thinking and decision processes, in order to explore wider possibilities for learning and self-organization in a computer program for almost any problem. In other words, the chess-playing-machine program is merely a stepping stone to what may be called the General Problem Solver, or GPS for short.

GPS is a heuristic way of programing computers to solve a wide diversity of problems such as playing games, discovering proofs of logical theorems, or finding algebraic and trigonometrical identities. To enable the computer to grapple with all these diverse tasks GPS tries to make the best of each of the two possible approaches to the problem of synthesizing artificial intelligence. One approach seeks to accomplish with machines the same task that humans perform, often on a vastly amplified scale but without securing any functional equivalence between the two, exactly as an automobile enables a man to move quickly or as an elevator enables him to ascend. The other, like the perceptron networks, merely attempts to simulate or reproduce the processes humans actually use to accomplish those tasks. GPS endeavors to combine the two approaches maximally with mutual benefit. Consider, for instance, the GPS program devised by the Newell team to handle problems in logic as well as game playing. It has been consciously modeled on how a human being would set about proving a theorem in symbolic logic or playing chess, if like the machine he had no prior knowledge of either subject but were merely told to manipulate logical expressions or chess pieces according to certain prescribed rules. The common approach to the problems in logic and game playing that makes GPS programing possible at all is the close parallel between the two as shown in Table 48. In chess the

TABLE 48

Logic	Chess
Initial premises	Initial position of pieces
Rules of inference	Rules for moves
Theorems	Subsequent arrangement of pieces
Proof searching	Sequence of allowable moves

main problem is to decide whether any given arbitrary arrangement of pieces could be arrived at from any given initial arrangement by a sequence of legal moves. Its analogue in logic is deciding whether any given arrangement of logical symbols could be derived from another specified arrangement of them by means of the allowable rules of inference.

Using the afore-mentioned analogy between game playing and chess as a foothold, GPS programing is intended to evolve a general strategy for solving both kinds of problems. The basic idea of the common strategy is to take a program that accomplishes a significant task in its field of endeavor and then proceed to discover all the ways it can be improved or improve itself. Consider, for instance, a com-

Input I — | Performance program | — Output O

Fig. 108

puter that has been programed to yield an output O with an input I as shown in Fig. 108. But if the computer is required to improve its own output or "learn from experience," it will require another program, called the learning program, that operates on the initial performance program as its object or input in order to produce a new performance program better adapted to its task. The new situation that thus arises is depicted in Fig. 109, where the learning program is selected out of a set of possible alternatives whereby the given task such as a preassigned subgoal A can be performed better than before. Such a set may be given simply by a list of alternatives or by the variation of numerical parameters used to define an algorism or mathematical formula designed to serve the same end. For example, in a chess-playing computer the subgoal A under consideration may be that of pawn promotion, attack on the black king bishop, or any other subsidiary goal as in a normal chess play. The set of possible A-components fed into the learning machine (see Fig. 109) will then simply be the list of all possible programs that will lead the computer

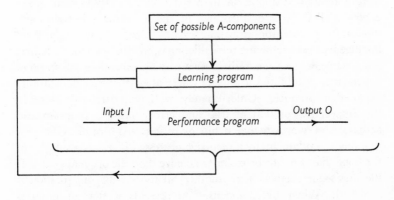

Fig. 109

to the subgoal A. If the subgoal A selected for learning is a significant part of the performance system, then the list of possible programs or the set of possible components will be large and complex. The learning program will have a wide diversity of choice in selecting one program after evaluating the performance of all candidates. This is why the machine must be provided with complete access to information about every performance program under trial, its inputs and its outputs. That is, a learning program attempts to make a "good" selection of an element from the set or list of all possible performance programs designed to secure the preselected subgoal A. Since for any significant non-trivial problem the set of candidate programs from which a choice is to be made is enormous (the chess problem, for instance, may have to choose from a list of a million or more different possibilities even for a limited objective like attacking the black king's bishop), the basic problem of the learning program is how to diminish such large lists of contingencies to smaller size to make the problem soluble at all. In other words, it is basically the same as that of intelligence amplification considered earlier. It will be recalled that the main difficulty in mechanizing "intelligence" lay in making sieving devices able to process the large permutations made possible by random stringing together of letters of the alphabet, thoughts, ideas, melodies, or what have you. As we have seen in the last four chapters, we still do not know how the human brain does its own sieving. The Newell team's efforts at intelligence learning in a GPS are aimed at discovering exactly this, how the human brain selects fruitful paths of exploration in a space of possibilities that grows exponentially, "where dilemmas of speed versus selectivity and uniformity versus sophistication exist." Because the essence of intelligence lies in resolving these dilemmas, we can hope to mechanize intelligence only if we can discover a way of controlling the spiral of exponential possibilities to a level where alone they can be fruitfully explored in practice. Unfortunately, we have no reliable guide in this respect except that of trial and error, trying a program and actually observing whether it hits or misses. As a result, GPS programing is fundamentally a recursive process. It selects a subgoal in the hope that it might be easier to achieve than the original goal. It then tries one method after another till the subgoal in question is achieved. When this happens, it represents a step of progress towards the original goal. A succession of such steps is expected to lead to the main goal.

Consider, for the sake of definiteness, a GPS program working on a specific task like discovering proofs for theorems in logic. As we showed in Chapter IX, a computer may readily be programed to prove logical theorems, provided practicable decision procedures or mechanical routines like the truth-table technique exist for proving them. GPS programing is intended to search for proofs of theorems in cases where decision procedures do not exist or, if they do, are not practicable. In other words, it tries to mimic the specifically human technique of free derivation guided *not* by the dreary mechanical "method" prescribed by decision procedures but by that of "unregimented insight and good fortune." The difference between the two methods, which may be said to represent the antithesis between the rationalism of a machine and the irrationalism of blind guessing, is simply this. In the former the task of proving a logical theorem, that is, of showing how it may be derived step by step from given premises by appeal to certain given rules of inference, proceeds according to the dreary mechanical routine prescribed by decision procedures. In the latter the derivation proceeds freely by trial and error. The machine is supplied with the premises and rules of inference as in the first method; but instead of being programed to implement proof-yielding decision procedures, which do not exist, it has to rely on some very general operating guides or heuristics which tell the machine how to guess or grope for proofs. It is possible to mechanize the process of guessing by treating logical propositions as objects to which certain operators or rules of inference may be applied. Thus the four logical propositions L_1, L_2, L_3, L_4 expressed in the language of symbolic logic explained in Chapter IX and shown on the left-hand side

Objects	Operators
$L_1: S \cdot (\bar{P} \rightarrow Q)$	$R_1: A \cdot B \equiv B \cdot A$
$L_2: (\bar{P} \rightarrow Q) \cdot S$	$R_6: \bar{A} \rightarrow B \equiv A + B$
$L_3: (P + Q) \cdot S$	$R_1: A + B \equiv B + A$
$L_4: (Q + P) \cdot S$	

Fig. 110

of Fig. 110 are four objects to which two of the operators, R_1, R_6, or two of the rules of inference shown on the right-hand side may be applied. As will be observed from Fig. 110, object L_1 is transformed into object L_2 by applying the operator R_1. This particular operator is applied by substituting S for A and $(\bar{P} \rightarrow Q)$ for B in the "input" or left-hand side of R_1 and extracting the corresponding object L_2 from its "output" or right-hand side. GPS programing designed to prove theorem L_4, given L_1, consists in discovering ways of transforming the object L_1 into the object L_4 by repeated application of the given operators, namely, rules of inference like R_1 and R_6. In other words, we have to find which particular succession of operators applied to an object L_1 will wipe out its difference d from another object L_4. This requires that the main goal be divided into three subgoals:

(i) to transform one object a into another object b;
(ii) to apply an operator q to an object a; and
(iii) to reduce a difference d on an object a.

Given a goal such as that of transforming L_1 into L_4, GPS programing would then proceed as shown in Fig. 111. It would examine the goal to see whether it should be worked on. If it accepts the goal, it selects a method associated with that goal and applies it. If the method fails, it evaluates whether to continue attempting the goal. If so, it selects another method, and so on. In other words, GPS is a basic system of interlinked methods which the Newell team calls "means-end" analysis, whereby the efficacy of means selected to attain specified ends or goals is evaluated. Fig. 112 shows how the methods devised to attain the afore-mentioned three types of goals that are the core of GPS are interlinked. As will be observed, when the goal is a transform-goal type (i), the method consists in matching

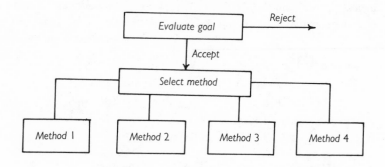

Fig. 111   GPS basic organization.

the two objects *a* and *b*, discovering a difference *d*, if any, between them. Having done so, problem (i) is resolved into that of reducing the difference, *d*, between *a* and *b*, that is, setting a new goal, goal type (iii). If this is accomplished, leading to an object *c* from *a*, we have to set up a new transform-goal, that of changing *c* into *b*. If this last goal is achieved, the original goal type (i) can be achieved in two installments. If not, we have to continue the installments.

The method associated with reduce-goal type (iii) consists in searching for an operator, *q*, that is *relevant* to the difference *d*. If one is found, the goal is reduced to goal type (ii), namely, that of applying the operator. The method associated with apply-goal type (ii) consists in determining if the operator can be applied at all. For it must be remembered that every operator cannot be applied to every object. It has a specificity which restricts its application to only objects having certain characteristics. The operator R_6 of Fig. 110, for instance, is applicable only to such logical propositions as contain the implication symbol [→] as its main connective. Again if an operator *q* can be applied to an object *c* at all, the application *q(c)* yields a new object *p*. The recursive structure of the GPS program is thus quite apparent. Transform-goals generate reduce-goals which in turn breed new

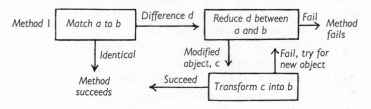

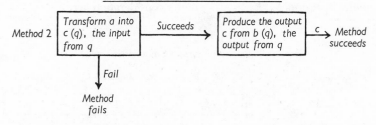

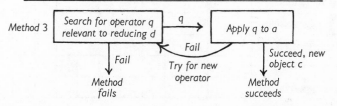

Fig. 112   Means-end analysis.   (From "A Variety of Intelligent Learning in a General Problem Solver," by Newell *et al.*, in *Self-Organizing Systems*, Marshall C. Yovits and Scott Cameron, eds., Pergamon Press, New York, 1960.)

transform-goals. Likewise, reduce-goals beget apply-goals and apply-goals lead to both transform- as well as apply-goals in succession till the original goal of wiping out the difference, *d*, between *a* and *b* is achieved.

But how, it may be inquired, are the differences between two given objects actually defined? Specific differences and the tests that detect them are not part of the GPS proper but are parts of each particular task environment to which the program is applied. For example, in the task environment of symbolic logic cited above, we may have twelve operators $R_1, R_2, \ldots, R_{12}$, that is, rules of inference, each of which performs a certain operation on the logical expression to which it may be applicable. Thus the operator R_1, which merely changes the position of the two propositions on its input and output sides, is associated with change of position. Operator R_6, which performs two functions—altering the sign of the proposition (from $\bar{A}$ on its input side to A on its output side) and altering the connective (from $[\rightarrow]$ on its input side to $[+]$ on the output side)—has to be associated with two functions. Table 49 shows the association of functions with the twelve operators $R_1, R_2, \ldots, R_{12}$ under consideration here:

TABLE 49

TABLE OF LOGICAL CONNECTIONS

Functions ↓	R_1	R_2	R_3	R_4	R_5	R_6	R_7	R_8	R_9	R_{10}	R_{11}	R_{12}
Add variables									×	×		×
Delete variables							×				×	×
Increase number			×			×			×	×		×
Decrease number			×			×	×				×	×
Change connective					×	×	×					
Change sign		×			×	×						
Change grouping				×			×					
Change position	×	×										

It is now easy to see how GPS programing would handle the problem of transforming object L_1 into L_4. A first look at the two expressions leads to detection of a difference in position between the two expressions (S, which is the first item in the expression L_1, appears as the second item in L_4). A reference to Table 49 showing logical connections reveals that the operator relevant to the difference in position is R_1.* Hence the goal of reducing this aspect of difference between L_1 and L_4

* R_2 is also a possibility but will have to be discarded after actual trial.

will require the application of the operator R_1. Thus the goal of reducing the difference between L_1 and L_4 will generate the goal of applying R_1 to L_1. Since L_1 matches the input to R_1, the goal will be achieved, producing L_2 and generating the new goal of transforming L_2 into L_4. Again, using the table of logical connections we find that the sign of a term in L_2 is reversed in L_4 ($\bar{P}$ in L_2 becomes P in L_4). The operator relevant to this function is R_6 so that we now have a new goal, namely, applying R_6 to L_2, yielding L_3, and a new transform-goal of changing L_3 into L_4. This new goal leads once again to detection of a difference in position requiring the application of R_1 once again. It is obvious that the core of GPS programing lies in correlating the differences listed in Table 49 with their associated operators or rules of inference. The correlations shown are effective for problem solving in the environment task of symbolic logic. For another environment task such as proving trigonometrical identities or playing checkers we will naturally need a new table of differences appropriate to that task.

The importance of having a set of relevant differences and associated operators designed to obliterate them cannot be overemphasized in problem solving. For any problem solver lacking a set of appropriate differences has no means of working towards his goal except to try at random or by rote different sequences of operators until he reaches his goal. He cannot even see whether the random trials are leading him to his goal or away from it, for the most direct clue to progress is the breakdown of the difference between the terminal object he is in search of and the object he has in hand into basic difference types, each one of which can be wiped out by the application of its corresponding operator(s). In the case of symbolic logic we constructed Table 49 showing logical connections on the consideration that any difference between two given objects (or logical expressions) may be built up by the superposition of one or more of eight types of basic elementary differences such as change of position, change of sign, addition of variables, and the like. For instance, while the difference between L_3 and L_4 is obtained by applying a single type, that is, a mere change of position, that between L_2 and L_3 requires the superposition of two types of differences, change of the negation sign $[-]$ accompanied by change of the connective $[\rightarrow]$. Each of the eight kinds of differences of Table 49 has associated with it one or more operators which when applied to an expression induce therein the type of difference in question. Since in the case under consideration there are eight types of differences and twelve rules of logical inference or operators with which they may be associated, we can in theory have $12 \times 8 = 96$ possible connections, assuming that each operator is relevant to each type of difference. If we did not have any prior information about the relevance of an operator to any given difference type, we might use a simple trial-and-error scheme to build up Table 49. That is, we first begin with an arbitrary table that assumes that all operators are associated with all types of differences. We then keep statistics of how frequently each assumed association of an operator with a difference type succeeds in fact in reducing the type of difference in question. The associations that succeed most frequently are reinforced and those that do not or do so only rarely are inhibited, so that in due course we have a table like the one already reproduced, Table 49. But it is evident that it is a far from efficient way of producing a table of connections which is to serve as a basis for GPS programing intended to solve a specified task. The only way of making the search efficient is to secure, if possible, prior information concerning the relevance of each operator to each difference type and use it to construct the table of connections exactly as we built Table 49. In cases where such prior information is not available, the hit-and-miss method of blind variation is the only alternative open. But the rub is that it may continue to miss for so long that we may not in practice be able to construct the table in any reasonable time we can afford, especially in task environments of great size and complexity usual in any significant problem.

In sum, GPS programing proceeds in two successive steps. First, we formulate a way of recognizing differences between objects of the given task environment and of breaking them down into a set of basic difference types. Next we proceed to discover means of identifying the relevance of each available operator or rule of the game to each difference type. We may do so by searching the list of operators either randomly or systematically, using any prior information that we may have. Having built up once for all a table of connections indicating which difference types are removable by which operator, all we have to do when faced with a difference is to choose only those operators of the list that are relevant to obliterating this difference. The success of GPS programing therefore depends on our ability to implement these two steps in the given environment task. So long as the task in view is a specific one like theorem proving, it may be possible to implement both steps. Take, for example, a particular case of the Newell team's GPS program, their Logic Theory (LT) program designed to discover proofs of theorems in symbolic logic, in particular those listed in Chapter II of Russell and Whitehead's *Principia Mathematica*. Although its performance record—mastery of thirty-eight out of the fifty-two theorems under assault—is quite impressive, it has not been completely successful even in this limited area. It has therefore been criticized by H. Wang, who has invented alternative methods of mechanizing proofs that are far more powerful for handling such problems.

Wang's methods are able with much less machine effort to prove all the theorems of *Principia Mathematica*, and not merely the thirty-eight mechanized by Newell *et al*. The secret of their power lies in Wang's readiness to use standard algorisms such as the method of truth tables which tend to make theorem proving almost akin to calculating. It will be recalled* that suitable switching circuits can be built up to evaluate the truth values of any complex logical expression consisting of individual elementary propositions like T, S, R, etc., linked together by logical connectives such as $[+]$, $[\rightarrow]$, etc., for all possible combinations obtained by assigning either the truth value 0 or 1 to its constituents T, S, R. If we find that the truth value of the logical expression is always 1 for every possible combination of the truth values of its individual components, the expression is obviously a tautology, that is, a theorem which is always true. Computation of truth tables is therefore a task no different in principle from that of computation with numbers. Consequently it is as easily handled by a computer as any ordinary computation. Wang has carried a stage further the similarity between "proving" and "computing" implied in the truth-table technique of proving logical theorems, by examining the basic differences between the two and showing how the apparent gulf between the two may be bridged. The basic difference between the two is not that computations deal with numbers whereas proofs deal with propositions, for computers can handle non-numerical symbols as readily as numbers. It is rather that computers can be instructed to follow rules of computation which are exact but not so readily rules of inference, which are very often vague. For example, the instruction "multiply x by y and divide the product by z" is quite precise and unambiguous. But in a chain of logical reasoning in theorem proving it is by no means always obvious what is meant by saying that step Q "follows" from step P or "evidently" A, "hence" B, and so on. If a machine is to prove anything, it must be explained

* See Chapter IX, page 112.

what the terms "follows," "evidently," "hence," and so on, mean. Indeed, fifty years ago, long before anyone thought of making theorem-proving machines, David Hilbert founded the formalist movement by asking similar questions.   By insisting on "formalizing" proof procedures or rules of inference, that is, rigorously spelling out what they are, he and his followers managed to make them *nearly* as exact as rules of computation.   This is why computers can now be programed to implement rigorously specified "formalist" proof procedures, as Wang has recently done, thus amply justifying the seemingly pointless hairsplitting involved in the logician's formalization. Indeed, Wang has used all the sophistication of the modern formalist theory to undertake a rather thorough mechanization of the logic underlying theorem proving.   As a result he has invented a new branch of applied logic called "inferential analysis" which treats "proofs as numerical analysis does calculations."   Wang has already implemented this strategy by searching for algorisms, which, though less all-embracing than decision procedures, produce "interesting" mechanical proofs within a reasonable amount of time.   In proving *Principia* theorems, for example, Wang uses a more elegant system than the combinatorial system of Russell and Whitehead.   Consequently Wang's theorems though *logically* equivalent are *formally* much simpler.   He secures this simplicity by recourse to the "cut-free" formalisms of Herbrand and G. Gentzen whereby one obviates the need to employ the *modus ponens* principle of logic (that if "P" and "P implies Q" are both proved, then one is entitled to infer that "Q" is also proved).   As a result, Wang obtains a method in which, roughly speaking, for every proof each of the steps is no more complex than the conclusion.   Nor is it necessary to use results previously proved. These formalist artifices make proof procedures far more amenable to mechanization than had been thought possible before Wang's breakthrough. Nevertheless, Wang's mechanization of proof procedures, though a notable act of creating artificial intelligence in the area of theorem proving, is of limited heuristic value.   For obviously the feats of human intelligence other than theorem proving cannot all be duplicated by traditional methods of mathematical logic.   They need heuristics, guide lines aimed at simplifying the search for a solution while avoiding being overwhelmed by a plethora of eligible candidates.   It is precisely because of the Newell team's accent on heuristics rather than mere theorem proving that their work has been considered valuable.   Wang's criticism of their avoidance of standard algorisms "merely because these procedures do not produce a proof in the meaning of Whitehead and Russell" misses the *raison d'être* of their method.   Their objection to algorismic methods in devising "acceptable" proofs is not on logical grounds but because of their desire to duplicate by artificial means what goes on in the human brain when confronted with the task of theorem proving. They hope thereby to acquire valuable insights to further the goal of artificial intelligence, not merely in the area of theorem proving but also in those other areas not amenable to methods of either numerical or inferential analysis.   The exclusive preoccupation of Wang's inferential analysis with the particular problems of symbolic logic has led him to methods which do not have facilities for using previous results or for deciding when to give up a particular line of attack, precisely because he had no need to do either.   Consequently they suffer from two handicaps.   First, they are likely to degrade rapidly at a certain level of problem complexity.   Second, they evade the fundamental heuristic problem, that of knowing when to discard any given strategy in general problem solving.   Ways of overcoming both will, no doubt, have to be found before the machine can be made to handle even mathematical problems more advanced than those handled so far.   The Newell team's LT program, on the other hand, is fundamentally oriented towards achieving these heuristic goals. Indeed, it is the first heuristic program completely realized on a computer.   This is why it has rightly been acclaimed as a great achievement in the synthesis of artificial intelligence.

Nevertheless, the Newell team's GPS programing does run into serious difficulties as soon as we attempt to free it from the close chaperonage of the specific task to which it is tied.   As already noted, it requires implementation of two distinct steps—recognition of basic difference types and their correlation with operators designed to wipe them out.   A GPS program for any *general* task environment runs into serious difficulties in trying to implement both.   To begin with, it is by no means clear how the set of difference types in the wider task environment is to be delineated when the problem to be solved is a general one and not merely that of proving a logical theorem or a trigonometric identity.   Obviously the set of difference types in general problem solving is a very ambiguous affair.   For no difference can be completely evaluated in abstraction, simply because the question of what differences between objects of a task environment are relevant is a matter that can be decided only by reference to the specific task in view.   Nor can we attain complete factorization with each operator (rule of the task game) associated uniquely with a particular difference in isolation of the specific task.   Even if we succeed in describing the difference types, the problem of constructing the table of connections correlating operators and difference types is soluble only if we have prior information regarding the relevance of each operator to each difference type, or if the number of difference types and operators is severely limited.   Since in any significant task the number of difference types and operators is likely to be large, in the absence of prior information there seems to be no way of constructing the table of connections, the basis of intelligent learning, except blind variation and selective survival as in biological evolution of animal intelligence and learning.   But the great danger inevitable in any such blind groping for solution is that we are all but certain to be overwhelmed by the exponential avalanche of trials that such a process spawns.   This is why the main hurdle in mechanizing intelligence is simply that of reducing the staggeringly large number of possibilities that blind variation lets loose to an extent that can actually be tried and tested in spans of time available to us.

While a host of formidable difficulties have yet to be overcome to make GPS programing more versatile and less oriented towards any specific task, Newell and his collaborators have nevertheless added to GPS a considerable number of new mechanisms not specifically attached to the learning of logic, trigonometry, or algebra in order to confer on GPS the capacity to handle a wider diversity of tasks.   But the capacity of the suggested mechanisms to do so is quite untested, as all their work has been limited to the task of logic, trigonometry, and algebra.   The question whether a sufficient population of environment tasks amenable to GPS programing can be constructed is therefore still open.

While the possibilities of GPS programing in other fields have yet to be proved, its performance even in the more restricted environments of purely mathematical tasks such as proving logical theorems or chess playing has had so far only limited success.   It has not come anywhere near solving the fundamental problem of mechanizing (and therefore amplifying) human intelligence.   As we have seen repeatedly, this problem is simply one of preventing the machine from being overwhelmed by an avalanche of permutational possibilities by enabling it to select at a glance only the few that alone are worthwhile, rejecting straightway all other more numerous ones that are worthless. A master chess player, for example, who can look ahead to a depth of twenty moves, is not choked with the immense number of chains that such a far-flung look-ahead involves simply because he has the faculty of right selection. By means of it he selects for examination only the few promising alternatives, rejecting offhand all the useless ones. No general way has yet been found to imbue the machine with this faculty of short-circuiting the exploration of a mountain of permutational possibilities in order to proceed directly to the nugget of intelligence that may lie buried somewhere beneath it. Nevertheless, with a steady accumulation of improved heuristics and machine strategies that are the endeavor of GPS programing in this field, it is possible gradually to ameliorate both the theorem-proving as well as the game-playing capabilities of the general-purpose computer. Indeed, a chess-playing computer is ideally suited to test empirically the effectiveness of possible chess strategies and thereby obtain valuable experimental data that may well be of use in general problem solving.

Chapter XVII

ARTIFICIAL INTELLIGENCE— TRANSLATING MACHINES

AMONG other non-algorismic tasks which may be entrusted to computers for simulating artificial intelligence, machine translation seems at first sight quite a tempting objective.   For translation in the primitive form of coding is entirely algorismic.   As we know, the coding and decoding of a message, such as the telegraphist's dash-dot transform before transmission or its retrieval after receipt, is a sort of translation of a natural language text into the artificial one of a code and vice versa.   Because the code key tying the two together is an unambiguous formula applicable without exception, the "translation" involved in coding or decoding is a simple routine easily amenable to machine manipulation.   From such mechanization of coding and decoding procedures to full-blast translation of natural language texts might seem but a step.   For as Warren Weaver has remarked, any Russian text may well be regarded as a text "really written in English" but "coded in some strange symbols."   The rub is that no simple straightforward key linking the two natural languages exists, so that translation, unlike code conversion, is not a one-to-one transformation.   As a result, it is inevitably likely to suffer more or less serious conversion losses of meaning and content.   Indeed, in the case of texts of extreme subtlety and sophistication surcharged with emotional overtones as, for example, Pushkin's poems, even the ablest bilinguist may fail to convey the original meaning in all its purity; and it is well known that many jokes are all but untranslatable, their point or punch being too specifically rooted in the structure of the parent language to permit its transfer to another.   This is why translation is often more or less a semantic treason as the Italian proverb *Traduttori, traditori* ("Translators, traitors"), explicitly acknowledges.   What chance then has the mere computer, the drudge that carries out programed mechanical repetitive routines and decision procedures, to undertake a task that taxes all the ingenuity of the nimble human mind? The answer is none, at least in the foreseeable future.

Take, for instance, the simple English idiom "out of sight, out of mind." If we "instruct" a machine (or someone ignorant of Russian) to translate it into Russian, word by word, substituting for each one its Russian equivalent after mechanically scanning an English-Russian dictionary provided in its store, the result may very well be either gibberish or worse—the Russian equivalent, perhaps, of the words "invisible idiot." Nevertheless, while hi-fi fully automatic translation is nowhere yet in sight, machine translation has already become a serious business in many Western countries such as the United States, the USSR, Great Britain, and France. The reason is that herein lies our sole hope of de-Babelizing the world by making available to its polyglot peoples the vastly growing body of literature both scientific and humane now mushrooming everywhere. This hope would not be so difficult to realize if the natural languages were merely simple associations of ideas and symbols, wherein one symbol denotes one idea as is the case with the number language of our daily use or to an approximate extent with the Chinese, where the symbols (ideographs) directly represent ideas. But in most natural languages the ideas emerge not out of language symbols or words per se but out of complex *patterns* formed from them. It is the absence of any direct association between ideas and their symbolic representation in individual words, such as exists between, say, the symbols 1, 2, 3, . . ., and the ideas of varying degrees of pluralities that they represent, that is responsible for most of the difficulties of translation. Such correlation, if it existed, would be grist to the computer mill, translation being merely a routine substitution of one symbol for another, such as the replacement of the Hindi numeral ৬ by its arabic counterpart 7. Indeed, if only natural languages conformed to the law "one word or symbol, one meaning or idea," the whole translation effort could be turned into routine scanning of a bilingual dictionary in which the symbol of one language leads to its equivalent in another via the kernel or invariant idea denoted by both. Such a routine could be easily entrusted to a computer, and machine translation would merely be a problem of indexing the related bilingual symbols, if one may be excused for using "merely" to describe a new and difficult task, that of indexing an ideographic language without an alphabet.

But, given a bilingual dictionary of the related ideographs, all the machine need do is scan it for any given symbol of one language to pick its correlate in the other. The one-to-one transformation of one set of symbols by another, that is, translation, would be free of the frictional conversion losses that otherwise destroy or impair meaning. Since no such direct correlation between ideas and symbols (words) exists in most natural languages, it is no wonder that word-by-word translation, which is what a machine may be entrusted to perform easily enough, turns out to be virtually a complete failure, as the case of the Russian translation of the English proverb quoted above clearly shows. The fact is that the word is too small a unit for language translation if the original meaning is to escape some degree of mutilation. To preserve the original meaning every sentence must be taken intact; for complete sentences are the natural quanta of meaning, although in the case of more complex texts even a sentence may not suffice, requiring attention to a whole paragraph or page. For a faithful rendering of the original meaning, therefore, it is necessary to have an over-all understanding of the whole sentence or paragraph before a decision can be made as to what symbols of the target language would be appropriate to the purpose in view. Since such a gestalt approach is denied to a machine, it is likely to turn out gibberish if geared *only* to word-by-word translation of text.

Because only complete sentences have meaning, and because the meaning of a sentence is a function both of the semantic content of its individual words and their syntactical structure or form, there is a telescoping of information carried by the words and the word order prescribed by the rules of grammar and syntax. This is why the two types of information, the lexical and grammatical, inextricably fused in the sentence must first be unscrambled only to be scrambled *de novo* according to the new lexical-*cum*-grammatical requirements of the target language. Hence arises a tangle of complex linguistic problems that must be solved in order to enable a machine to translate from one natural language to another. Of these, three are fundamental: the recognition of individual words, the translation of the words recognized, and the transposition of the translated words to conform to the syntactical constraints of the target language.

Take first the recognition problem. It arises because dictionaries as a rule list words only in their pure uninflected forms, dropping all the different kinds of endings which are attached to the stem of a word to indicate grammatical information such as number, case, gender, tense, and the like. As a result, if we encounter in a text an (inflected) unfamiliar word like "yielded," we would look in vain for it in a dictionary. Thus when a word appears in any of the variety of grammatical forms it can assume, the primary machine problem is one of recognition, that is, of determining what the word actually is, independent of its inflectional ending. There are two computer solutions to the recognition problem. The first consists in stripping the endings off the word in question, letter by letter, until the stem is recognized by comparison of it with the entries stored in a "stem" dictionary. Failing to find "yielded" in its store, the machine would be programed to try again, dropping the last letter *d* and looking for "yielde." Failing again, it would be made to repeat the same drill till finally it reached the stem word "yield" in its store. If the source language is English and the target language French, reference to the stem dictionary will yield the equivalent French stem "ced." After the stem word has been found, the machine is instructed to compare the ending "ed" in another "endings dictionary" so that it has not only the semantic content of the stem word "yield" but also the grammatical function of the inflectional ending "-ed." Reference to the endings dictionary will show that the equivalent inflectional ending in French for the past tense required here is "ai" so that the French equivalent of "yielded" is "cedai."

An alternative solution to the recognition problem is to compile and store in the machine memory a so-called paradigm dictionary. This is a dictionary which lists all words with all their inflectional forms. Thus it would list words like "rushed" as well as "rush," "boys" as well as "boy," "flies," "flying," and "flew" as well as "fly," and so on. Obviously this second free-form approach requires much more space in the machine than the first, since a paradigm dictionary is considerably greater in size than the stem and endings dictionaries put together. Nevertheless, the handicap of larger size is not without its compensations. For the first alternative, that is, the stem-and-ending approach, demands automatic dissection of input forms, automatic identification of the constituent stem and ending or endings, and the automatic determination of the intended meaning of the dissected free form by a pooling of the information coded with the stem and ending. All this naturally requires quite a number of machine operations. Moreover, the dissection into stem and ending involves the loss of the meaning or meanings the free form carries, and this lost semantic information has to be somehow subsequently retrieved by the machine. For example, the French equivalent of the English ending "-ed" in "yielded" cited above may well be any one of the six endings "ai/âmes," "as/âtes," "a/èrent." The reason is that while in English the same ending "ed" will do for all subject pronouns, as "I/we," "thou/you," "he/they," in French the ending has to match the subject pronoun. There was no escape from these drawbacks to the stem-and-ending approach at the time the machine-translation idea was first raised, because the means of making computers with a large storage capacity did not then exist. But with the invention of new devices such as the photoscopic disk, which have enabled the construction of computers with phenomenally large storage capacities of several hundred thousand bits, the "free-form" or paradigm approach, no longer handicapped by limited storage capacity, is beginning to be increasingly popular in machine-translation circles. For it mitigates in great measure the already overwhelming problem of retrieving the lexical meaning inevitably mutilated to some extent in the stem-ending dissection operation of the first alternative.

The end of the word-recognition problem would, if it could be achieved, be the beginning of the next, the translation problem. For when we try to translate the recognized word, we often face considerable semantic ambiguity. As we know, most words have several meanings and which of them is to be chosen is not easy to decide, and certainly not for the computer. It has therefore to be provided with some simple decision procedure to make a choice. Consider, for example, the word "tip" which as a noun may mean the rounded edge of a finger but as a verb may denote the act of giving a *pourboire* to a waiter. While these semantic ambiguities may be resolved sometimes by the identification of the grammatical function of the term in question, in many cases this alone does not suffice to fix its meaning. Thus, even when it is known that the word "tip" is a noun, it may well be an item of advance confidential information, a forecast or prediction, a tap or light touch, and so on. A student dictionary in common use lists eleven distinct categories of meaning of this word, of which six are nouns and five verbs. The only way out of the *embarras du choix* due to such polysemy or multiplicity of meanings is to view the word in its context. Very often knowledge of the preceding word or the subsequent one helps greatly to reduce the ambiguity as, for example, with such phrases as "give *up*" and "give *to*" or "*on* the house" and "*in* the house." In order for a machine to eliminate semantic ambiguity it would have to "know," that is, have built into it, thousands of rules concerning the kinds of nouns which follow certain prepositions, the kinds of verbs which precede them, and so on. For it is these associations which give specific meaning to certain nouns, verbs, and other words. Unfortunately, many of these rules have not yet been explicitly formulated, because we imbibe them unconsciously with our mother's milk. Only when such rules have been clearly formulated can the machine be programed or instructed to choose correctly with proper discrimination. In other words, before the machine can mimic the expert human linguist's discernment of *le mot juste* in the target language, it has first to be captured and caged in a corpus of rules of usage. Since linguistic analysis of natural languages designed to formulate such rules is still far short of requirements, most machine-translation schemes to overcome polysemy are far from adequate. However, even if it were overcome, machine translation would still have one more hurdle to cross, namely, the transposition problem.

The transposition problem develops from the well-known fact that when translating from one language to another, the word order appearing in the source text has to be transposed in the target version in order to preserve the meaning of a sentence. In many cases, as for example in German, meanings are entirely lost in word-by-word translation so that it is necessary to transpose the order of the original German text into the usual word order of English (that is, subject before verb, adjective before noun, and direct object after verb, and so on). For the machine automatically to reorder the words from one language to the grammatically correct order in another, it has to be instructed to break up the sentence into clauses and handle them one by one. That is, it has to "know" how to unscramble the individual terms within their respective clauses, for which purpose it has to recognize (*a*) the beginning as well as the end of a clause and (*b*) the grammatical function of each word in the clause, in order to rearrange the words to conform to the standard order in which they would appear in a clause of the same type in the target language. This requires a much more thoroughgoing knowledge of the syntax and structure of both the languages in question than we possess today.

The afore-mentioned threefold division of the machine-translation task—word recognition, text translation, and text transposition—represents by and large the grand strategy underlying the present practice of the art. Even though none of these problems, as we have remarked, has been solved fully, the partial solutions so far suggested can actually be implemented by a computer. To illustrate the implementation with reference to a specific case, we may choose French as our source language and English as the target. Given any source text in French, we have at the outset to find a way of presenting it to the machine in a numerical form, for that is the only form the machine is designed to recognize. We may easily do so by recourse to a simple code, where $a = 1$, $b = 2$, $c = 3, \ldots, z = 26$, word space $= 27$, full stop $= 28$, and so on. In such a code any French word like "avec" appears as a constellation of four numbers 1, 22, 5, 3, the respective code of its constituent letters. There are other refinements that need to be embodied in the coding scheme, such as indications to show the type of accent French letters sometimes carry. Thus the acute, grave, and circumflex accents may respectively be represented by three additional symbols 01, 02, and 03. With this convention accepted, letters appearing in a word like "été," where the letter e carries the acute accent, are coded as 5,01,20,5,01, the interposition of 01 after 5 indicating that the fifth letter, e, is acutely accented. With such a number code it is possible to represent any text as a sequence of number constellations. Accordingly the text to be translated is typed on a teleprinter punch in the usual way with one space between each word and full stop at the end of each sentence. The end of the text is indicated by typing "end."

After delivering the source text to the computer in the number code it is designed to handle, our next task is to incorporate in the computer a store or dictionary, which after all is the heart of any machine-translation scheme. Since French words and their English meanings are associated constellations of numbers according to the code we have adopted, all we have to do is to arrange the word list in some order according to which the machine can scan the store and look for the English equivalent of any French word it needs to translate. Because words are written in a numerical code, it is obvious that numerical ordering, that is, an arrangement of words in ascending order of numbers used in coding them, is the appropriate course. Indeed, it is identical with the usual alphabetic order of all ordinary dictionaries as the number code adopted for the letters preserves the letter order. The reference procedure then becomes a routine which the machine can be easily programed to follow. The machine first locates the number constellation of the required word in the French side of the dictionary, after which it simply extracts another number constellation representing the English equivalent of the word in question from the corresponding location on the English side of the store. Thus, corresponding to the number constellation 1, 22, 5, 3, the code for the word "avec" stored in the French side of the machine dictionary, there is in the English side of the store the matching constellation 23, 9, 20, 8, the code for its English equivalent "with."   Note that $w = 23$, $i = 9$, $t = 20$, and $h = 8$ according to our code, the same code being used for the representation of letters in both the source and target texts.   There are, of course, sophistications of various sorts required by the stem-and-ending approach to the word recognition problem if the storage space is too limited to permit the paradigm or free-form alternative.   We shall not go into them here but rather proceed straight to the next task the machine has to be instructed to perform, namely, the transposition or reordering of the translated words to conform to the requirements of English syntax.   A specific example will best illustrate the point.   A word-by-word translation of even the simplest French sentence such as

<blockquote>"nous le leur donnons," or
"we it them give,"</blockquote>

is jarring enough and needs to be rearranged as "we give it them."   This is why, after the machine has secured the word-by-word translation of the source text, it must learn to transpose the translated words according to the syntactical rules of target language, in this case English.   The machine can be programed to obey such rules only to the extent that they have been formalized.   Thus in the example cited above, the rule is that an arrangement like $p_1 p_2 p_3 v$, wherein three pronouns p_1, p_2, p_3 precede a verb v in the source text, must be reordered as $p_1 v p_2 p_3$ in the target text with the verb v wedged in between the first and second pronouns p_1, p_2.   There are hundreds of such rules, many of them still waiting explicit formulation by the linguists and grammarians, which a machine has to be "taught" even as a human translator learning his trade.   But the great difference is that the nimble human mind manages to learn and practice them much better unconsciously by simply reading and speaking, justifying Schlegel's injunction to throw our grammar books into the fire:

<blockquote>*Lisez, lisez, jetez vos grammaires au feu.*</blockquote>

Precisely because the machine cannot learn merely by "reading," that is, through being fed any amount of coded texts, it has to be programed explicitly to carry out each and every instruction needed in carrying out the translation. Thus when a source text punched in coded form on a tape as described is placed in the input reader of the computer, it is instructed to read the first complete word or rather its coded number constellation in order to look up in the dictionary the relevant keys for its stem and ending. A test is then made to see whether the stem key is that for "end" (of text). If so, the machine is programed to stop. If not, a test is made for "full stop." If there is not a full stop, it is a sign that the full sentence has not yet been read and the machine is instructed to read on the next word till it encounters a full stop. When at last it does so, it has clearly disposed of all words in the complete sentence just read. It is therefore time to pool the lexical and grammatical information already extracted by reference to the dictionary and apply the syntactical rules to obtain the correct arrangement of the target text. The machine is programed to do so by following another routine designed to recognize the grammatical function of each word in order to determine the correct rearrangement of adjectives in relation to nouns they qualify or of pronouns in relation to verbs, and so on. All these routines are decision procedures which tell the machine in yes-or-no fashion what to do at each stage of its operation.

From the outline of machine programing given above it is obvious that all instructions the machine is intended to obey must be reduced to simple rule-of-thumb routines of the type: "if x, then do y; if not-x, then do z." This requires that all it is intended to do must be set down precisely in an ordered meaningful sequence of symbols with which the machine can operate. In other words, the program instructions of the machine must be written in the machine's own internal language, or *machinese*, which, as it happens, is much more precise, ordered, and decipherable than any natural language. It is this hiatus between the ordered language of the machine and the natural ones of man that is at the root of virtually all the difficulties of machine translation. To the extent we can turn our present knowledge of the morphology, syntax, and semantics of natural languages into cut-and-dried routines or decision procedures, the process of translation from one natural language into another can be mechanized. But not all of it is amenable to such decision-procedure regimentation. This is not surprising, considering that even an artificial language like that of modern logic, tailor-made for precision and order and entirely free of ambiguities, refuses to submit to it. As we saw, proofs of non-decidable theorems in logic cannot be reduced to mere mechanical follow-up of prescribed routines. If therefore by mere recourse to digital circuitry even they cannot be proved, that is, teased out of some given set of premises by permissible rules of transformation (inference) *mutatis mutandis*, the task of translation, that is, meaning-invariant transformation of expressions from one language into another, is still more refractory to the ordinary computer. This is why hi-fi fully automatic translation is likely to remain beyond the reach of the usual digital computer though entirely feasible by appropriate machine-man partnership, wherein either the input text is pre-edited by human intervention to make it more easily amenable to machine manipulation or the output text is similarly post-edited to make it more intelligible to the ultimate reader. In other words, the computer can be a valuable *aid* to translation even though it cannot yet be programed to go all the way on its own steam.

If machine translation through man-machine collaboration is intended to break the language barrier to knowledge, mechanization of literature searching and information retrieval is designed to overcome what may be called the bulk barrier due to its exponential proliferation. With the increasing numbers of publications of all kinds even in one's own language, it is becoming more and more difficult to find all the relevant information on a specific subject in a reasonable time. Automatic search and retrieval systems, if they could be successfully engineered, are the obvious solution of the growing difficulty at present facing not merely scientists, technocrats, and research workers searching libraries for material but also attorneys hunting for patents, lawyers seeking legal precedents, and doctors scanning case histories as an aid in diagnosis. All these manifold applications are variations on the same basic theme. For in mechanizing these tasks we encounter the same central problem of linguistics as in machine translation, that of identifying similar meanings in information, even though this is formulated in one language rather than two as before. Consider, for example, the request of a research worker who wants certain material and the work of the author who produces it. Both express their meanings in the same language, their common lingua franca. The problem is to determine automatically whether the subject of the request is the same as, or close to, that contained in the author's book or article. Since machines merely scan but cannot actually read a document and decide whether or not its subject matter coincides with that required, it is necessary to use some intermediate indexing system to identify the

intention of the borrower with the author's output.   A case in point
is the accession number or some similar tag used in a library to trace a
book on a specified subject like biochemistry or cosmology from among
those on its shelves.   Since subjects like cosmology are apt to cover
other allied topics such as relativity, nucleonics, or origin of matter, a
single classification number will not suffice and has to be replaced by
a constellation of numbers as in the so-called coordinate indexing
system.   In either case, the system of index numbers adopted is the
intermediate language, which the library uses to match the language
of its documents with the language of the users.   By recourse to it, the
retrieval of the required documents becomes a trivial routine of merely
comparing the index numbers assigned to the document with the
number associated with the demand.   Moreover, it is a routine which
a computer can be easily programed to undertake.   For once a set of
indices has been assigned to each document it can be encoded into
digital form, put on a suitable machine medium like punched cards,
and scanned automatically.   By matching the index numbers of the
document with the number of the demand, a process at which the
computer is an adept, it is possible to list the accession or coordinate
numbers of all the relevant documents.   The actual process of
retrieving the documents from the shelves would then be a hand process.   A further sophistication of the process designed to eliminate
manual retrieval is the so-called Rapid Selector System recently
devised.   It consists in using photographic film instead of paper tape
so as to allow the document to be photographed beside its index or
coordinate numbers.   The machine then scans the film, matches
indices with the request, and automatically photocopies the desired
documents after the search.

The main snag of such systems is the semantic "noise" inevitable
in the matching procedure built into the machine.   For it is obviously
a yes-or-no affair in that a set of indices either satisfies a demand or it
does not; indeed, it is precisely this feature that makes it so readily
amenable to computer manipulation.   But its adequacy depends on
the exactitude with which we can establish correspondence between
the information content of a document and its associated set of
indexes.   Since it is obviously impossible to specify precisely all the
information content of a document by a mere constellation of index
numbers, cases of dissonance between the borrower's demand as
formulated in terms of one or many indices and his real intention will
often arise.   Such dissonance may, on the one hand, pick up docu-

ments irrelevant to his real need and, on the other, fail to provide some really relevant documents not retrieved, adding injury to insult. The trouble is that the basic assumption of the scheme is a gross over-simplification of a very complex state of affairs. For it assumes that all documents of the world can be classified relative to a given problem into two mutually exclusive and simultaneously exhaustive classes: relevant and irrelevant. In actual fact, relevancy is not a black-and-white dichotomy but a continuum of gray shades. Moreover it is relative to the user. For everything pertaining to a topic will not be relevant to everyone. This is why automatic retrieval of relevant information is in some respects even more difficult than hi-fi automatic translation of natural languages.

Nevertheless, when we narrow down the *general* problem of some specialized field such as information retrieval for only legal questions, or patent specifications, or medical diagnosis for a particular type of malady, mechanization of information retrieval is not altogether an impossible task. For the legal provisions, to cite one particular case of such circumscribed fields, as embodied in laws, acts, regulations, bylaws and decisions of jurisprudence do not represent an innumer-able amount of documents. The concepts utilized for expressing these concepts are generally precise and can provide a basis for abstracting and indexing in such a way as to auto-retrieve relevant information, as L. Mehl and others have recently shown. The essence of such schemes is good abstracting and indexing, that is, a precise interlanguage of the machine. If for a small specialized field such an improved indexing language can be devised, it is possible to generate computer programs which would, in effect, mechanize the notion of relevance. It would enable the machine not only to look for an exact match of indices but also to retrieve items relevant to the user's request even though not explicitly included in his request. In other words, it would exhibit some sort of "understanding" or "compre-hension" of the user's needs. But to make an intelligent mechanism capable of grasping the meaning of strings of symbols fed into it, we have to discover the information-processing structure underlying the act of "comprehending" or the process of "understanding."

A step in this direction is the recent creation of two computer pro-grams—the "baseball" program of B. F. Green *et al.* and "Sad Sam" program of R. K. Lindsay. The former is designed to answer queries about baseball "facts and figures" from a stylized baseball "yearbook" stored in the computer's memory, and the latter answers questions about family relationships. In the baseball project, the "fact library" is stored in advance in the computer memory in a form which makes searching the library relatively easy. The program is written in one of the information-processing languages devised by Newell *et al.* and already referred to in the preceding chapter. As will be recalled, such an information-processing language uses lists and hierarchies of lists, called list structures, to represent information. Both the data and the dictionary are list structures, in which items of information are expressed as attribute-value pairs as, for example, a baseball team may be denoted by the pair "Red Sox." In "Sad Sam" the kinship relation between members of the particular family under discussion is not given the program in advance but is put into the program in the form of English sentences. The program, assimilating and analyzing these sentences, constructs an internal "map," or "model," of the familial relationship—an information structure referenced later in answering questions about the family. Both programs, operating as they do within extremely limited spheres of facts, are designed to explore in a preliminary way basic mechanisms for language comprehension rather than attempting prematurely to deal with wide-ranging universes of discourse.

Although these recent attempts in computer programing to discover the basic mechanisms of understanding or comprehension and to aid translation and information retrieval so as to supplement legal arguments, improve medical diagnosis, and undertake a variety of other jobs in specialized fields like auto-abstraction of scientific papers, have had some measure of success, they have not as yet led to any major breakthrough. For the basic approach underlying them has its own inevitable limitation in that it is oriented far more towards the equipment in use than the problem under attack. The reason is that the technique of computer programing happens at present to be well ahead of the analysis of our normal processes of thinking and learning, which, in contrast with the mathematical logic we have created, have a logic all their own. As a result the digital computer, the hardware embodiment of mathematical logic par excellence, is by no means ideally adapted to imitating normal processes of human thinking and learning involved in such activities as translation, game playing, literature scanning, and the like. So long as we remain ignorant of the more nimble neural logic that governs these processes occurring in our brains, most schemes for intelligence simulation of this kind will be like that given to the sorcerer's apprentice for bottling a genie: "First you catch him—." For they are mainly concerned with the "bottling" details of the operation while our intelligence genie still stalks the sky.   As we have seen repeatedly, no one can make a machine to do any human job, computational or otherwise, such as chess playing, proving a theorem in logic, making a translation, or collecting relevant information for some particular research, without specifying in sufficiently precise detail what that job is.   In some way the enormous amount of information required to perform it must first be gathered in all its minutiae before a machine can be programed to undertake it. In other words, the human faculty or intelligence the machine is designed to simulate must first be synthesized and put into it before the machine can show any such intelligence.   For instance, our greatly improved understanding of the neurophysiology of vision and hearing is already inspiring the design of new kinds of perceptrons that can be "trained" to recognize visual and speech patterns even though as yet in a very rudimentary manner.   The perceptrons of Chapter XV are an instance of one kind of advance suggested by the great work on the neurophysiology of vision now under way.   Another is the class of conditional probability machines to be described next.

Chapter XVIII

UTTLEY MACHINES

IN a bid to uncover the mathematical principles underlying the organization of the central nervous system, A. M. Uttley suggested two: the principle of classification and that of conditional probability. He based his suggestion on an important characteristic of animal behavior, whereby the same response can be evoked by a variety of different configurations in the external world. Thus birds may be tricked into mistaking pieces of stone as eggs by mere superficial similarity of form. More recent experiments with birds, fish, and other animals have conclusively shown that certain combinations of simple properties of the objects suffice in many cases to evoke the requisite response while other aspects tend to be ignored as irrelevant, so that the ancient myth of Zeuxis in which birds pecked at his painted grapes is not wholly without factual basis. This is because even though the stimuli emanating from the objects in the external world are in a state of perpetual flux, the mind images they create in the animal's head have in many cases a certain overlap of common attributes that makes them look alike. The existence of this overlap permits the mathematical theory of sets and conditional probability to be applied to design a class of machines which we may call Uttley machines after their designer. They have a structure in some respects similar to that of the nervous system and react to external stimuli in the same way as animals even though to a rather limited extent.

Stripped to bare essentials, an Uttley machine consists of three basic components. First there are the sensor units, the counterparts of animal receptor cells. Just as the latter are linked by afferent neurons to the central nervous system, so are the former connected to input channels along which incoming signals from the external world enter the second component, a central "black box" (the nervous system). After a certain time lag the "black box" dispatches signals along the third component, the output channels to response units. They correspond to efferent channels flowing from the nervous system to the effectors or motor organs of the animal (see Fig. 113). We thus have all the basic ingredients of a mechanism, whereby the input signals first create an inward "awareness" of the state of affairs prevailing in the outside world and later determine the output signals to enable the machine to adjust itself to its environment. A glance at Fig. 113 shows that each specific pattern of input signals emanating

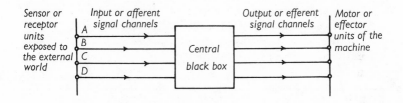

Fig. 113

from the external world brought along afferent channels into the central black box is a "representation" of some particular state of affairs or configuration of the external world. The central "black-box" mechanism, having no direct access to the external world, can have no idea of the resemblance, if any, of the external configurations. It can only infer such resemblances indirectly by sensing them in their respective representations. The representations in turn will resemble one another only if they belong to the same class or set. Thus if an animal responds in the same way in two given configurations of its environment, it is because it senses a measure of resemblance between their corresponding representations or mind images in its head. We have therefore to reckon not the myriad diversity of stimuli that the external world radiates to the sensor units of the machine, but rather the number of different representations of the external situations that its input afferent channels can possibly *accommodate*. Consider, for the sake of definiteness, the four input or afferent channels *A*, *B*, *C*, and *D* of the Uttley machine shown in Fig. 113. As will be observed, they all emanate from the sensor units exposed to stimuli from the external world. If as usual we assume them to be all-or-nothing affairs, all the manifold diversity of configurations of the external world will give rise to only sixteen different types or classes of "representations." For sixteen is the total number of combinations we can possibly derive from four afferent channels by activating none, one, two, three, or four of them at a time.   Consequently the system perforce classifies all

TABLE 50

Number of channels active at a time	Active channels	Total number of combinations
None	Neither A nor B nor C nor D	1
One	A or B or C or D	4
Two	AD or AB or AC or BC or DB or DC	6
Three	ADB or BCA or BCD or DAC	4
Four	$ABCD$	1
		Total 16

the myriad states of the external world into one or another of sixteen possible kinds of representations.   In other words, it has built into it an amplified version of a sort of Procrustean bed whereon every situation of the external world of which it at all becomes aware is willy-nilly fitted.   This is why many configurations of the outside world that may actually be very different give rise to one and the same representation, such as that evoked by activating the three channels B, C, and D at a time.   Accordingly all such outside configurations are classified as the "same" and elicit an identical response in the output or efferent channels controlling the motor units of the machine. A sixteen-fold classification machine on this model may actually be built in hardware according to the block diagram of Fig. 114.   It will be observed that to be able to "recognize" or discriminate each of these $2^4 = 16$ different kinds of incoming signal patterns, the machine has to have one "unit," the counterpart of a central neuron, in the central black box, one such unit being needed for the recognition of each input pattern (see Fig. 114).

In general, if the machine has n afferent channels each one of which is digital in action, that is, either active or inactive, it is easy to see that we can have in all 2^n signal patterns.   For if we decided to activate at any time, say, r channels out of the total available n, in order to form an input pattern or representation, we could do so in n_{C_r} different ways.   The total number of patterns or representations that we could thus form by activating 0, 1, 2, 3, ..., n input channels at a time is therefore

$$n_{C_0} + n_{C_1} + n_{C_2} + n_{C_3} + \ldots + n_{C_r} + \ldots + n_{C_n} = (1 + 1)^n = 2^n.$$

Since each incoming signal pattern would need one discriminating "unit" in the central black box for its recognition, it would require

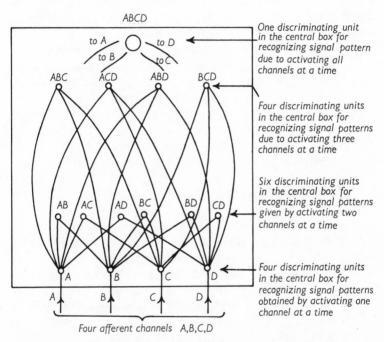

One discriminating unit in the central box for recognizing signal pattern due to activating all channels at a time

Four discriminating units in the central box for recognizing signal patterns due to activating three channels at a time

Six discriminating units in the central box for recognizing signal patterns given by activating two channels at a time

Four discriminating units in the central box for recognizing signal patterns obtained by activating one channel at a time

Four afferent channels A,B,C,D

N.B. Discriminating unit for recognizing the null pattern, that is, the pattern due to activating no channel at all, is not shown.

Fig. 114

2^n such units for recognition of all the possible patterns. Consequently an n-channel classification machine can accommodate in all 2^n different signal patterns but would need an equal number of "units" within its black box to be able to discriminate between them. It would then be able to classify all the manifold configurations in the external world into one or another of a total of 2^n different kinds of representations, no doubt telescoping many *actually* different situations into a single representation. If we treat all the various configurations in the outside world that evoke the *same representation* in the machine as "similar" in the sense that they all belong to the same class (the class of all outside situations leading to some prescribed pattern of input signals in the machine), an Uttley classification machine becomes virtually an apparatus for implementing the logical theory of classes based on the logical relationship of ownership or belonging. For each of the 2^n representations or signal patterns that it can possibly receive from the outside world then defines a class to which an outside situation is said to belong if and only if it evokes the representation in question. All situations belonging to the same class will naturally appear alike to the machine, as they give rise to the same representation and therefore the same output response from its motor or effector units. Its main handicap as a simulator of the animal nervous system, however, is not the Procrustean principle built into it, whereby all the minute differences between external situations classified as belonging to the same representation are wiped out. The violence associated with Procrustes is due not to the classification principle he adopted but rather to the gross inadequacy of the single channel, the fit-no-fit bed, he employed as his classificatory tool. If he had used, say, about 500 beds of different lengths ranging from 3 feet to 7 feet, he would have been able approximately to match a bed to every traveler who happened to fall his way and there would have been no excuse for the orgy of mutilation in which he indulged. Provided n is sufficiently large, a series of n channels with its potential 2^n classifications provides sufficient scope for as much proliferation of different classes or representations for sorting out external situations as we may ever want. As we have seen repeatedly, 2^n increases exponentially with increasing n so that even with no more than only thirty input channels, we could have $2^{30} \approx 10^{10}$ or ten billion different patterns of input signals to represent as many different situations in the outside world. But since each input pattern would require a unit or neuron in the central black box to be recognized by means of its connections to the input channels, all the available ten billion neurons of the human nervous systems, the most developed natural automaton, would be exhausted in taking care of barely thirty input channels, whereas in the human brain there are several millions of such channels. The main debility of the Uttley classification machine as a replica of animal behavior therefore arises not from the inadequacy of the classification principle per se but rather from its extravagant requirements of neurons even for the simplest representations. Consider, for example, the input signals having quantitative measures such as light signals of varying intensities and color or sounds of different pitch and loudness. It could take account of the full range of these quantitative variations only by recourse to an astronomical proliferation of input channels. For, as may be recalled, a single binary channel has to be amplified 3.3 times to express even the ten digits of our usual decimal notation. To express magnitudes varying over the continuum of real numbers, a prodigious multiplication of channels is inevitable. Even if the human nervous system had only a million afferent channels, which is perhaps barely 2 per cent of their actual number, there would have to be in all $2^{1,000,000}$ possible input patterns, each requiring a neuron in the central black box for its recognition. Since the actual number of neurons is only 10^{10} or 2^{30}, it appears that the ratio of neurons we actually have to those we need is $2^{30}:2^{1,000,000} = 2^{-999,970}$. Which is a way of saying that we have virtually none of the neurons we need, if the classification principle alone were really at work in the central nervous system. If the biological animals adopt it, they have obviously somehow managed to ward off the fantastic neuronal extravagance it entails. For all evidence seems to show that the nervous system of every animal has sufficient neurons to match its powers of discriminating patterns emanating from its receptors or sensor units.

It has been suggested that the animal neurons might be able to avoid this inherent extravagance to a great extent by tempering the rigidity of their assumed all-or-nothing basis of action by incorporating aspects of analogy procedure as well. But if so, this would require even more central neurons, because if each afferent channel were capable of, say, m different states instead of the assumed two (active and inactive), the input signal patterns possible with n channels would be vastly greater, namely, m^n against the earlier 2^n. This is why the input channels have to act on an "all-or-nothing" basis if the classification principle is to work at all. Indeed, even on the basis of twofold or binary action all the available ten billion (10^{10}) neurons of the human system barely suffice, as we have already seen, for some thirty input channels. Such a classification machine, operating without the wisdom and economy of the living neurons, is therefore obliged in practice to give short shrift to almost all quantitative nuances of sound, color, smell, touch, pressure, and the like.

Uttley has suggested three different ways whereby the neural extravagance of the classification principle might be checked and the nervous system enabled to economize the number of discriminating units that its adoption otherwise entails. First, a number of different afferent channels emanating from the sensor units or receptors seem to merge into single fibers before entering the brain.   The central neurons interposed between receptors and brain might be able to abstract in some mysterious way key features of input patterns and reduce their number.   A case in point is the considerable reorganization of the visual image as perceived by the eye to which we alluded in Chapter X.   All of it is accomplished at the point of entry of the optic nerve.   Even at the early stage of this accomplishment, long before the image is carried to the brain, there is a hundredfold convergence of input channels from receptors to optic nerve.   There is a corresponding loss of detail and discrimination in that the information passed on is concerned primarily with contours.   Secondly, the nervous system does not completely segregate input patterns and there is much telescoping between one and the other.   For in the absence of such merging there would be within the nervous system many master discriminating units capable of recognizing complicated patterns in a blaze of instantaneous, almost Buddha-like illumination. A single discriminating unit, for, say, Beethoven's *Eroica* or Shakespeare's *Hamlet*, would, if fired, reveal the whole symphony or play in a single magic flash.   Actually, however, through the phenomenon of short-term memory, we perceive the patterns in short bits so that if r is the number of channels which fire during the span of short-term memory, the number of units required is of the order of n_{C_r}.   Thirdly, there is the phenomenon of the spectrum or range of discrimination whereby a set of unrelated objects can be distinguished, at first glance, only if the number in the set is less than about seven.   All these suggestions, however, do not overcome the main difficulty of the classification machine, the gross inadequacy of the discriminating units or neurons in the central nervous system for the input channels that it clearly has.   Even if we overcame this handicap by discovering biologically plausible ways of economizing the number of discriminating units, two other limitations of the classification principle as a basis of the animal nervous system would still remain.   First, pattern recognition in a classification machine is instantaneous, depending only on which discriminatory unit of the central black box is activated by the incoming pattern.   Once the unit operates, "recognition" occurs instantaneously.   In other words, the machine, like the mythical Bourbons but quite unlike living animals, can neither learn nor forget. Secondly, its basic assumption of complete independence of input channels is also contrary to the known behavior of nervous systems.

For the incoming signal patterns received by the machine are assumed to be made up of independent elements having no relation among themselves except that of class ownership, that is, of belonging or not belonging to the given class. On the other hand, the input signals from the external world actually received by the animals are far from independent, being closely interconnected in many ways.

Both the aforesaid limitations of a classification machine may be mitigated in good measure by grafting onto the classificatory principle the supplementary one of conditional probability. Consider, for example, a past ensemble of representations. Suppose we fix our attention on two particular classes of representations of this past set, namely, class *A*, obtained by activating or not activating only one channel *A*, and class *B*, yielded by similarly stimulating or not stimulating another (single) channel *B*. Suppose further that the state of the input channels *A* and *B* had been

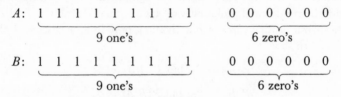

where 1 and 0 denote the active and inactive state of the channel respectively and therefore of the occurrence or non-occurrence of the associated representation. Although in actual fact the active state of *A* channel or representation *A* is followed by a similar state of *B* channel or representation *B* and vice versa, our machine has as yet no way of recognizing this interdependence of the states of the two channels or their corresponding representations. Before we can manage to provide the machine with the means of recognizing this interdependence, we have first to devise a way of measuring it. On the basis of the actual behavior of the two channels, we may reasonably assume that if *A* is stimulated, so must be *B*. In other words, though the probability that either of the *channels A* or *B* will be stimulated by itself is nine times out of fifteen ($\frac{9}{15}$), the chance of *B* being stimulated, given that *A* is already active, will be nine times out of nine, that is, unity. The mathematical description of the situation is that while the *unconditional* probability, $P(A)$, of the representation *A*, or $P(B)$, that of the representation *B*, is $\frac{9}{15}$, the *conditional* probability of *B*, given that *A* has already occurred, symbolized $P(B/A)$, is $\frac{9}{9}$ or unity.

However, the past ensemble of representations need not be one of complete association of A and B as in the afore-mentioned example. A case in point of partial association is the series

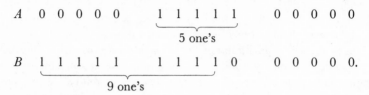

The unconditional probability of channel A's being active and there-fore of the representation A's occurring, that is, $P(A)$, is obviously $\frac{5}{15}$, there being five 1's in a total of fifteen. Likewise, $P(B)$ is $\frac{9}{15}$. But the conditional probability of channel B being active assuming that A is active, that is, $P(B/A)$ is $\frac{4}{5}$, because out of the five instances in which A is active there are four where B is also active. On the other hand, the conditional probability of A, given that B is active, $P(A/B)$, is $\frac{4}{9}$, for out of nine cases of B activation, only in four cases is A also active. In short,

$$P(A) = \tfrac{5}{15}, \text{ but } P(A/B) = \tfrac{4}{9};$$
$$P(B) = \tfrac{9}{15}; \text{ but } P(B/A) = \tfrac{4}{5}.$$

Obviously, the activation of either channel raises the conditional probability of the other, so that the channel dependence and therefore that of their corresponding representations is positive, though not as absolute as in the first case. An instance of reverse or negative dependence is the series

$$A \quad 0 \ 0 \ 0 \ 0 \ 0 \ 0 \ 0 \ 1 \ 1 \ 1 \ 1 \ 0 \ 0 \ 0 \ 0$$
$$B \quad 1 \ 1 \ 1 \ 1 \ 1 \ 1 \ 1 \ 1 \ 0 \ 0 \ 0 \ 0 \ 1 \ 1 \ 1.$$

It is obvious that while the unconditional probability of A channel being active, $P(A)$, is $\frac{4}{15}$, its conditional probability, given that B is active, $P(A/B)$, is much lower, only $\frac{1}{11}$, there being only one case of A activation out of a total of eleven cases of B activation shown in the above series. Likewise, while $P(B)$ is $\frac{11}{15}$, $P(B/A)$ is $\frac{1}{4}$. The activa-tion of either channel or the occurrence of its associated representation lowers the conditional probability of the activation of the other. The notion of conditional probability thus ties together two channels and therefore their associated representations on the basis of their joint occurrence in the same ensemble irrespective of whether the representations to which channel activation gives rise possess a common overlap or not. It is solely determined by the relative frequency of their joint activation in a series of past trials. Consequently it is not formed instantaneously as in the purely classificatory machine considered earlier. Quite the contrary; in so far as it is formed on the basis of past representations, it can be acquired and once acquired is constantly modified even to the point of total extinction or complete reinforcement. To see more clearly how the conditional probability may be constantly modified, consider a series where the state of A and B channels is as follows:

A	0 1 0 1	0 0 1 1	0 1 0 1	0 1 0 1	1 0 0 1
B	0 0 1 1	0 0 1 1	0 0 1 1	0 0 1 1	0 0 1 1
$P(A/B)$	$\frac{1}{2}$	$\frac{3}{4}$	$\frac{4}{6}$	$\frac{5}{8}$	$\frac{6}{10}$

The last line shows the conditional probability of A given B, that is, $P(A/B)$ during each of the five successive runs of four trials each. In the first four trials of the series, $P(A)$ is $\frac{2}{4}$ or $\frac{1}{2}$ as also is the conditional probability $P(A/B)$. In the first two sequences $P(A)$ is $\frac{1}{2}$ as before but $P(A/B)$ now becomes $\frac{3}{4}$. Continuing, we observe that while the unconditional probability $P(A)$ remains $\frac{1}{2}$ throughout all five sequences of four trials each, the conditional probability $P(A/B)$ becomes successively $\frac{4}{6}$, $\frac{5}{8}$, and finally $\frac{6}{10}$. In other words, while the unconditional probability of A remains constant at $\frac{1}{2}$, the conditional probability of A given B rises, at first rapidly, from $\frac{1}{2}$ to $\frac{3}{4}$ and then begins to fall but more slowly than it rose.

Since the mutual dependence of channels and therefore their corresponding representations may well be measured by the conditional probability of one given that the other is active, all we need do to take account of this interdependence of input channels is to provide a mechanism for computing it. As we saw, in the pure classification machine we require a discriminating unit for every possible combination or pattern of input channels. The unit fires if the pattern or its allied representation occurs, but continues to slumber if it does not. In other words, the unit yields a quantity which is 1 when the pattern or representation occurs but is 0 when it does not. But if such a machine is to have a means of learning from the past, the unit must be modified so as *not* to yield the output 0 when the pattern or representation in question does not occur, even though it continues to yield 1 when it *does* occur. It should yield instead the unconditional probability of the input channel A as determined by past trials or "experience" so that the past states of channel A and its allied representations are not completely ignored but are duly heeded.　In addition, we have also provided a way of recognizing the mutual dependence of the input channel A on another like B as measured by the conditional probability $P(A/B)$.　For this the unit must also be able to compute $P(A/B)$ in addition to $P(A)$.　To meet both requirements, namely, the computation of probabilities of activating channels A and B individually, that is, the unconditional probabilities $P(A)$ and $P(B)$ as well as the conditional probabilities $P(A/B)$ or $P(B/A)$, Uttley suggested computing the unconditional probabilities like $P(A)$ and $P(B)$ on the logarithmic scale.　Since these probabilities lie between 0 and 1, he introduced the positive quantity, $-\log P(A)$, calling it the rarity function $R(A)$ of A.　When rarity or $R(A)$ is zero, probability is obviously 1 so that the activation of A or the occurrence of its allied representation is certain.　In other words, rarity is really an inverted measure of probability: the less it is, the more the frequency of the associated event.

Consider now a classificatory machine such as the one with four input channels A, B, C, and D shown in Fig. 113.　Suppose further that it has been exposed to a number, say, 100 input patterns or representations of various kinds.　All of them naturally belong to one or another of 16 kinds or classes that the machine can possibly accommodate and discriminate.　For example, ten of them may belong to the class ABC, that is, the pattern obtained by activating three out of the four channels, that is, A, B, and C.　In the purely classificatory machine the particular discriminating unit in its central black box linked to channels A, B, and C for recognizing the pattern ABC would have fired on ten occasions and on the remaining ninety occasions other discriminating units would have fired as their respective associated input patterns such as A, BC, and CD were sensed. But in such a machine each input pattern is a law unto itself, firing or stimulating its associated discriminating unit when it arises and then passing away into oblivion without a trace anywhere in the machine. If the machine has to take heed of the past and in particular of the fact that out of the 100 past input patterns received ten belonged to the class ABC, the discriminating unit associated with it has naturally to be more sophisticated than before.　It cannot perform this function by merely living from hand to mouth, firing when ABC occurs and continuing to slumber otherwise.　It has somehow to store the past and recall it in order to decide its next move.   This new function has to meet three requirements of which only one happens to coincide with what the discriminating unit does already: firing or yielding a 1 when its associated input pattern, *ABC* in this instance, occurs.   But in its absence the associated unit does *not* remain quiescent, yielding only a 0 as in the earlier purely classificatory machine.   It must now yield instead a quantity that is the unconditional probability of the pattern *ABC*, as determined by its past frequency of occurrence in the total given set.   In the aforesaid example it should yield 10/100, the unconditional probability of *ABC*, as only ten input patterns out of a total of 100 belong to the class *ABC*.   Further, it should also have a means of evaluating the association between different classes of input patterns.   Thus, suppose out of 100 input patterns considered above, thirty belonged to the class *AB*, that is, those obtained by activating channels *A* and *B* simultaneously.   It therefore follows that out of these thirty there were only ten where the channel *C* was also active in addition to *A* and *B*, so that the *conditional* probability of the representation *ABC*, given *AB*, namely $P(ABC/AB)$, is $\frac{10}{30}$.   The discriminating unit associated with the input pattern *ABC* should also be able to assess its *conditional* probability $P(ABC/AB)$ in addition to its unconditional probability $P(ABC)$.   It will be noted that the conditional probability $P(ABC/AB)$ is really a ratio of the unconditional probability of the input pattern *ABC* to that of the input pattern *AB*. Consequently, if we make the discriminating units of the machine associated with these two input patterns measure their respective unconditional probabilities on the logarithmic scale, the conditional probability required is given by their difference.   In symbols, since

$$P(ABC/AB) = \frac{P(ABC)}{P(AB)},$$

therefore

$$\log P(ABC/AB) = \log P(ABC) - \log P(AB).$$

Or, to make the logarithms positive because the probabilities are numbers less than unity,

$$-\log P(ABC/AB) = \log P(AB) - \log P(ABC).$$

This is the *raison d'être* of Uttley's suggestion to transform probabilities of representations into their logarithms or rather their negatives called rarities.   We can then readily derive the *conditional* rarity of any representation given another by the difference of their respective *unconditional* ones.

To enable the discriminating unit associated with any input pattern to fulfill all three afore-mentioned requirements, it should be of the functional form shown in Fig. 115 instead of the binary "on-and-off" type switch that sufficed for the simpler purely classificatory machine described earlier.   To see how it functions we may recall that to compute unconditional probability of the pattern *ABC* or its associated

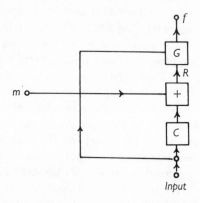

Fig. 115 Discriminating unit, functional form. (Reprinted from "Conditional Probability Machines and Conditioned Reflexes," in *Automata Studies*, edited by C. E. Shannon and J. McCarthy, p. 266, by permission of Princeton University Press. Copyright 1956 by Princeton University Press.)

rarity $R(ABC)$, namely $-\log P(ABC)$, or $-\log \frac{10}{100}$, we need merely find the difference, $\log(100) - \log(10)$.   If the unit is made to compute the second component of this expression, that is, $-\log 10$, by the mere addition to it of $\log 100$, we obtain the unconditional rarity of the representation *ABC*.   But if we do so, we have to ensure that its output is zero when the pattern *ABC* does occur.   For in that case the rarity function becomes zero, making the probability of its occurrence unity.   It therefore follows that the unit's output should be a function $f(ABC)$ of the representation *ABC* in question, such that $f(ABC)$ is zero when *ABC* occurs but equals its rarity value $R(ABC)$ otherwise.   These requirements are met by a gate G between $R(ABC)$ and $f(ABC)$.   The active input has a dual role.   In the first place, it has to count the number of trials made.   It does so by increasing their number, say, 100, as in the case considered, by 1 each time a fresh pattern or representation is sensed. Secondly, it has to close the gate so as to make $f(ABC)$ zero. This function is called *counting* control and the machine that operates on these principles may be called an *unconditional* probability machine. In brief, it is exactly like the earlier classification machine except that the discriminating units in its central black box connected in all possible ways to input channels do *not* operate in the "on-and-off" style of a two-way switch, firing when the associated input pattern materializes and otherwise remaining off. Instead, the unit linked with, say, the input pattern ABC first *counts*, if the set of input channels A, B, C connected to it are all in the active state. Secondly, it computes the unconditional rarity $R(ABC)$ of the representation ABC, ensuring that $R(ABC)$ grows each time the pattern does not occur but decreases by a certain amount when the

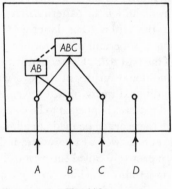

Fig. 116

associated representation ABC does occur. This means that if its output is the function $f(ABC)$, then $f(ABC)$ equals $R(ABC)$ if ABC does not materialize but is zero if it does. It now remains to see how the machine may be enabled to compute the conditional rarities (or probabilities) of two or more input representations. Consider, for example, two representations, namely, representation ABC obtained by stimulating three channels A, B, C at a time, and representation AB obtained by stimulating only two, A and B. The unconditional probability machine already evaluates $R(ABC)$ by means of the unit ABC connected to the three channels A, B, and C, and $R(AB)$ by means of the unit AB connected to the two channels A and B (see Fig. 116). If now we interconnect the two units ABC and AB in such a way as to compute the difference between their outputs, that is,

$R(ABC) - R(AB)$, the difference is obviously the conditional rarity $R(ABC/AB)$ or the negative logarithm of the conditional probability of ABC given that AB materializes. Unfortunately, interconnection of discriminating units in order to enable the machine to compute conditional probability or its equivalent rarity introduces a new complication. The reason is that the input patterns or representations associated with the units are not always independent. For example, suppose we link a unit recognizing any input pattern, say A, with another, say B. Since the patterns are independent, interlinking yields the difference of the unconditional rarities $R(A)$ and $R(B)$ which is also the conditional rarity of A given that of B, or $R(A/B)$. But if we linked two units whose associated patterns are not independent, the simple difference of their unconditional rarities will *not* yield the conditional rarity of one given the other. Thus the pattern ABC presupposes by definition the pattern AB in that the former could not occur without the latter. The latter (AB) is therefore, in a manner of speaking, a superunit of the former (ABC). Per contra, ABC is a subunit of the unit AB. Consequently the straight difference between the unconditional rarities of the two will not be a correct measure of the conditional rarity of ABC given AB, as was the case when the associated patterns happened to be completely independent. Arrangements have therefore to be made to allow for the influence of superunits on the units as well as the reverse influence of their subunits. They are respectively called supercontrol and subcontrol.

A conditional probability machine on these principles has been built but appears to have rather restricted neurological plausibility. To improve its neurological value, Uttley has amended it into what he calls a conditional *certainty* machine. In the amended version each unit does not compute the conditional rarity (or probability) of its associated input pattern, such as A, given another such as B. In other words, instead of computing the conditional rarity $R(A/B)$ or its equivalent the conditional probability $P(A/B)$, it merely indicates whether or not it exceeds some arbitrarily prescribed threshold number. For example, suppose this threshold to be $\frac{3}{5}$ and that in the past, patterns A and B have occurred as follows:

$$A \quad 1 \ 1 \quad\quad 1 \ 1 \ 1 \quad\quad 0 \ 0 \ 0 \ 1$$

$$B \quad 0 \ 0 \quad\quad 1 \ 1 \ 1 \quad\quad 1 \ 1 \ 1 \ 1$$

We observe that while $P(A/B)$ is $\frac{4}{7}$, $P(B/A)$ is $\frac{4}{6}$. Since the latter exceeds the prescribed threshold $\frac{3}{5}$, the unit linked with B fires, indicating B given A. Contrariwise, if B occurs, $P(A/B)$ is only $\frac{4}{7}$ which is less than $\frac{3}{5}$, the threshold, so that the unit linked with A does not fire. Hence A is *not* indicated or inferred when B occurs. Each unit therefore indicates in two different ways; if the corresponding set of inputs becomes active it indicates occurrence. But in its absence the pattern is only inferred conditionally, that is, provided only that its conditional probability exceeds the prescribed threshold. Such a machine is a conditional certainty system.

A conditional certainty machine is therefore a more sophisticated variant of the classification machine, which has in its central black box a pattern-recognizing unit for each one of its input patterns that its incoming channels can possibly provide. In the conditional certainty machine the discriminating unit does not merely go on and off with the appearance or disappearance of its associated input pattern. It is also enabled to count on a common scale the number of times it has indicated. For simplicity of design counting is on an approximately logarithmic scale which can be achieved in the following way:

(1) When a unit is not indicating the occurrence of its linked pattern, some physical quantity associated with it grows, preferably in an approximately exponential manner. In other words, the physical quantity is to measure the rarity function of the pattern.

(2) When a unit indicates the occurrence of the linked input pattern, this physical quantity, the rarity function, is decreased, preferably by a fairly constant fraction of its present value.

(3) To imitate spontaneous recovery in conditioning for prospective neurological applications there must be storage of the rarity function in depth.

(4) The units are interlinked one with another in all possible random ways to enable computation of conditional rarities. But as indiscriminate interlinking of units introduces the complications of "supercontrol" by superunits and "subcontrol" by subunits of the unit in question, the following two additional requirements have also to be met.

(5) Since there is a connection from each unit to all its superunits, the supercontrol function is simply this: A unit which is indicating occurrence of an input pattern causes any superunit of it to indicate conditionally if the rarity stored in the latter does not exceed by more than a specified critical amount. In other words, if any unit, say,

ABC of Fig. 116 corresponding to the input pattern *ABC* is activated by the occurrence of that pattern, it will have to cause all its super-units like *AB* or *BC* or *CA* to show whether or not the rarity stored in any of them exceeds a certain threshold prescribed for it.

(6) Exactly as in (5) there is a connection from any unit to all its subunits. The function of subcontrol is analogous. A unit which has been supercontrolled to indicate conditionally causes all its sub-units to indicate conditionally.

(7) Finally, if the system has more than two inputs there is the further rule that counting inhibits supercontrol by its subunits.

Uttley has explored the possibility of these requirements, being met in nervous tissue. Requirements (1) and (2), connected with count-ing, demand an amendment of the (assumed) all-or-none basis of the behavior of a neuron. This is not difficult as the assumption is certainly an oversimplification of a very complex state of affairs. The difficulty, however, is to discover the specific mechanisms to which the counting control may legitimately be assigned. Uttley suggests that these requirements may be met by a reversible process in the neuron whereby its state is changed when it fires. An example of such a process may well be the transfer of sodium ions across neural mem-brane even though the recovery process (the sodium pump mechanism) appears to be too rapid to make it feasible. Since, however, the rate of recovery has been measured so far only in fibers of large diameter which are not associated with learning and the recovery rate for fibers of smaller diameters may well be slower, the suggestion is not yet completely *hors de combat*. But the requirements of supercontrol and subcontrol, items (4) to (7), are more difficult to meet. Since the connections for supercontrol and subcontrol include some which are required for counting control as well, it is an important question whether two or even all three forms of control could be implemented by the same physical connections. This has not been achieved in the conditional probability machine built out of electronic hardware, which has to use three separate connective systems to fulfill these functions. Uttley has examined various ways in which biological neurons could meet them. But the attempt cannot be considered very successful as yet. The main difficulty is that requirements (5) and (6) imply that a unit can indicate in quite a different way con-ditionally. In doing so it must not count; but by subcontrol, it must affect other units to which it is connected. Translated into neurological terms this implies that a neuron gives its binary on-and-off indication in two different situations. First, when the input pattern associated with the neural unit occurs, it fires. Secondly, it does so when by subcontrol or supercontrol its conditional rarity crosses the prescribed threshold. In only one of these two situations will the state of the neuron be changed. The enigma of neural firing as an aftermath of two quite distinct activities—the occurrence of the input pattern by itself or its conditional reflex by means of conditional probability (rarity) via subcontrols or supercontrols—remains still unresolved. However, even if it is resolved, the more serious one of the gross inadequacy of available neurons remains. As we have noticed already, the ratio of available animal neurons to those required, if the principles of classification and conditional probability are really at work in nervous tissue, is absurdly low $(2^{-999.970})$, so that we have none of the neurons we need to make these principles work. Uttley, however, considers that a conditional rarity computer designed on these principles with vast overconnections does achieve the necessary economy of units—with chance connections. Because of the overconnections, there is initially ambiguity of discrimination, with units failing to recognize their associated input representations to a high degree. As information is accumulated those connections which carry little information become less effective until they are disconnected. Ambiguity is then eliminated and the system learns to discriminate, meeting some of the physiological and psychological facts rather well.

Chapter XIX

MATHEMATICAL THEORIES OF
THE LIVING BRAIN

WHILE our self-awareness as sentient egos having a "mind" that somehow seems to "know" itself is no doubt due primarily to the intense activity of neurons in our cerebral cortex, histological studies show that no theory, mathematical or otherwise, which seeks to correlate specific neuron circuits with particular "feelings," "thoughts," and "states of mind" can be sustained, if indeed it could ever be formulated. For in trying to formulate it we face the horns of a dilemma. If we cut the neuronal section sufficiently thin to study fine details of its functioning, we obtain only small scraps of neurons and pieces of processes so that the relationships in which we are interested are lost. On the other hand, if we use thick sections, we are presented with such a bewildering maze of closely interwoven processes that no analysis is possible. This complexity assumes astronomical dimensions when we try to examine the cortical circuitry as a whole, which we must do as every neuron is in one way or another ultimately interlinked with every other. A few statistics suffice to show the enormity of the task of mapping neuron circuits within the cerebral cortex of man. It is made up of some 10 billion neurons. Each one of them has on the average about 100 synapses so that we need to know details of some 1000 billion synaptic connections before we can even begin to correlate specific neural circuits with specific "states of mind." Fortunately there is no need to make such an attempt. There is enough neurophysiological evidence to show that the neural network of the living brain does not have that degree of detailed specificity which such a correlation plan envisages. Moreover, we could exorcise its existence by a neat kind of *reductio ad absurdum*. For, if it existed, all the minutiae of its connectivity would have to be carried in our genes at birth. It is all but impossible that the 1000 billion specifications could be so embodied. It seems more probable that only certain parameters of growth are mapped out within the genes and the fine connections are grown in a more or less random manner subject to broad genetic mappings. If it is true that the connection schemes according to which the living brain develops are determined only by certain broad parameters of growth, then there is some hope that the performance of such a system might be analyzed in terms of these parameters. The analysis might aim at elucidating the main types of behavior patterns.

First, there are those which are innate such as the navigation systems of certain birds and courting dances of bees, which are genetically transmitted *in toto*. That is, information concerning their precise mechanism is embodied in every specific detail in the genes at birth. Despite the enormous difficulties of deciphering the information-bearing genetic codes in which the *modus operandi* of the hereditary mechanisms is written, we may expect that the explanations of the innate genetically predetermined behaviors, when they come, will be based on conventional physics, chemistry, and mathematical analysis and could, in principle, be duplicated by engineering techniques some orders of ingenuity beyond the present level. But the second type of behavior patterns—those which are sufficiently flexible to allow individual variations on a basic theme determined by some broad parameters of growth—would seem to require a new kind of analytical technique that is inspired more by the simpler primary logic and mathematics the brain *actually* uses than by the deeper, more complicated ones we *consciously* employ. Consider, for example, the faculty of speech in Homo sapiens, which is genetically determined but not in such detail as to determine the particular language a man learns to speak in adulthood. It seems we shall have to discover radically new concepts and principles of mathematical analysis if we are to understand the organization of information and mode of operation that leads to "learned" as distinct from genetically fixed or predetermined behavior. Thus the more interesting and intricate part of the brain function is not the discovery of neuronal circuitry yielding an "unconditioned reflex" or genetically determined behavior pattern, such as the pupillary contraction of the eye under bright light, but the conditioned behavior of animals and men, such as the precise happenings in a child's brain when he learns to recognize the letter *A* or in that of Pavlov's dog when he begins to salivate not at the smell of food but at the sound of a bell or the sight of a circle. For such studies of learned behavior, what we require is not the detailed circuitry of the individual neurons of the cortex but rather the statistical parameters which determine the broad over-all pattern of connectivity of the neural aggregate as a whole.

Unfortunately, no statistical theory able to take in its stride even some of the more salient features of brain function exists at present. What we do have are speculative fragments with varying degrees of marginal plausibility. Consider, for instance, the analogical reasoning of B. G. Cragg and H. N. V. Temperley whereon they have reared what may be called the "cooperative" theory of cortical organization. Taking their cue from the "cooperative" phenomena or interaction effects which emerge purely from the interaction of large assemblies of microparticles studied by statistical mechanics, Cragg and Temperley tried to show that assemblies of neurons as closely packed as in the cerebral cortex could also give rise to analogous "cooperative" phenomena through the mutual interaction of neighboring neurons. Such interaction could occur either by synaptic transmission or by the extra-cellular flow of current. Assuming that certain relations hold between the relative probability of finding neighboring neurons in like or unlike states and the measure of connectivity of the neurons, they could show that neighboring neurons would organize themselves into packets in such a way that the packets would exhibit a pattern of organization in spite of changes in the polarization of individual neurons. Consequently, while the whole cortical tissue becomes divided into a series of packets, wherein each packet's internal make-up may change as the result of impulses arriving from the outside, the entire assembly of packets tends to adopt an over-all pattern of packet organization which minimizes the total "free" energy. Impulses arriving at one cortical region would change the local energy level and the consequential effect on the whole pattern of packets might well be such as to give rise to impulses leaving the cortex at another region. In sum, the theory relies more on the "cooperative" effect of patterns of neural packets or "pools" for over-all cortical integration than on the behavior of individual neurons. It is thus able to explain not only how the level of excitation in any area of the cerebral cortex depends on that of all other areas but also how all cortical areas are integrated in a single large pattern of activity without any need for long fiber connections.

While the Cragg-Temperley "cooperative" theory is in better accord with the known anatomical and physiological features of cortical organization than most others, the quantification of its central ideas to make precise predictions raises intractable mathematical problems as soon as interactions between neurons that are not nearest neighbors are considered. Nevertheless, certain qualitative predictions of the theory have been made and verified. For example, the arrival of an impulse in a neuron should give rise not merely to a local response or a single traveling wave but to a quite complex disturbance. This effect, too minute to be detectable by the use of only a pair of electrodes usually employed to obtain an electrocorticogram, has been reported by a number of workers by using a battery of twenty-five electrodes. Secondly, it easily accounts for the observed ability of the cerebral cortex to take over the functions of damaged or extirpated portions. For if the cortex worked on cooperative principles, local damage or lesion would not prevent the emergence of "packet" patterns in the surrounding surviving tissues. Thirdly, since interaction between neurons depends on the number and extent of axons and dendrites which increase during the growth and development of the animal, there should be a stage before or shortly after birth when cooperative interaction effects become discernible in their sudden appearance on the electrocorticogram. This too has been actually observed by A. E. Kornmüller and others.

R. L. Beurle has deduced further implications of the cooperative theory of neuronal interaction by examining theoretically the activity of an assembly of "units" assumed to behave like neurons. In order to give mathematics a foothold, he postulated that each of the units in the assembly had the following properties:

(*a*) The units are connected one with another in a non-specific manner subject to certain statistical constraints which in the aggregate define the parameters of the connectivity of the assembly as a whole.

(*b*) Active units excite inactive units by means of impulses through the connections (synapses) with their neighbors.

(*c*) An inactive unit is stimulated into action if and only if the total sum of excitations it receives from all other units with which it is linked exceeds a certain threshold value.

(*d*) Once stimulated, it becomes refractory for a short while, taking no further part in the assembly activity. After this refractory period is over it is ready to trigger off again exactly like the live neuron it is designed to simulate.

Beurle showed that the properties of such an assembly are very different from those of the individual units because of the "cooperative" effects sparked by their mutual interactions. In particular, such a structure could support a wave of activity with a number of interesting features. First, a small local disturbance gives rise to a wave that quickly attenuates and dies away. But a larger disturbance may lead to a wave of a certain critical amplitude that travels through the whole assembly, always activating a constant portion of the units through which it passes. Secondly, if the amplitude of the wave exceeds the critical value, more and more units are activated, until all units in the region are involved and the wave becomes "saturated." Thirdly, the critical amplitude is a function of the connective density of the units and their thresholds, decreasing with increasing density and/or increasing thresholds and vice versa. This may be expected even from purely qualitative considerations. For increasing density of connections will naturally dilute the activity of the assembly, which has to be shared over a larger number of units. Likewise, increasing thresholds by raising the resistance of synaptic connections to the passage of excitatory activity will lead to the attenuation of the wave. Beurle has quantified these qualitative anticipations of his theory.

An interesting corollary of Beurle's assumption that the threshold of a unit is slightly lowered each time it is activated is that the attenuation of the traveling wave depends on the past history of the assembly. Those waves of activity which managed to travel through the assembly of units many times in the past will pass more easily on subsequent occasions. Earlier passages facilitate later passages. Another conclusion of Beurle is that if two waves of activity meet obliquely within the assembly, their rendezvous will lead to an increased proportion of units with a reduced threshold in the region of their encounter. It can then be shown that, after a certain amount of repetitions, the presence of one of the waves will lead to the regeneration of the other. If so, this would be a plausible explanation of the conditioned reflex.

Beurle tentatively draws the analogy between his assembly of units and the cerebral cortex:

> He stresses the non-linear cooperative nature of the propagation of the waves and is emphatic that even slight changes in almost any property of the neurons that results from use and facilitates activity will have far-reaching consequences. He himself has considered the effects of change in threshold by way of example, but changes in

dendritic and axonal distribution would be equally pertinent and lead to similar conclusions.*

Although these theories of Cragg, Temperley, and Beurle do not explain all the features of cortical organization, they are in better accord with neurophysiological evidence than earlier attempts to explain the mode of cortical activity by analogy to models ranging from automatic telephone exchanges and scanning of television sets to the vague radiation and even avowedly inscrutable "black box" type models of neuropsychologists like Pavlov and others. The unique type of inflexible neuronal circuitry demanded by some of these models disqualifies them altogether in view of the observed plasticity

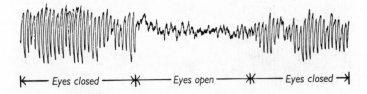

|←——— Eyes closed ———⋇——— Eyes open ———⋇——— Eyes closed —→|

Fig. 117   Illustration showing effect of opening eyes in suppressing alpha rhythm; rhythm returns when eyes are closed.

and equipotentiality of the cortical tissue and other modern anatomical and physiological observations. The last of these models to be discarded is the cathode-ray–oscilloscope scanning model inspired by H. Berger's discovery of the spontaneous electrical activity of the brain known as alpha rhythm. As is well known, alpha rhythm is most readily detected by means of an electroencephalograph, a vacuum-tube amplifying device with oscillographic pens for recording changes in the electrical potential of the brain. The electrodes are attached to different parts of the skull, particularly at the back of the head over the visual-association areas of the brain, and amplified potential differences between pairs of electrodes are recorded by the pens on a moving strip of paper. If the subject is relaxed with his eyes closed, the record shows a steady series of waves with a frequency of between 8 to 13 cycles per second and an average amplitude of 50 to 100 microvolts (50×10^{-6} volts) or about a tenth of the magnitude of electrocardiographic potentials. This regular or rhythmic wavelike

---

* *The Organization of the Cerebral Cortex*, by D. A. Sholl, Methuen & Co., Ltd., London, 1956, p. 107.

pattern vanishes as soon as the subject opens his eyes or begins to think intensely about some problem. The new oscillations of potential differences are far less regular, as a glance at Fig. 117 clearly shows. Several other types of wave forms variously called delta, theta, and beta rhythms are recognized by electroencephalographers. In the first flush of enthusiasm generated by the undoubtedly great value of electroencephalographic (or EEG) records to the clinicians in detecting the position and extent of pathological lesions such as old scars, atrophy, tumors, and vascular anomalies in the brain, they came to be regarded "as the bits and pieces of a mirror for the brain, itself *speculum speculorum*."

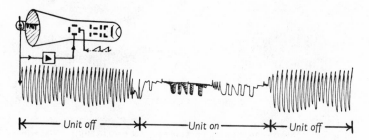

|← —— Unit off ——— →|← ———Unit on——— →|← Unit off —→|

Fig. 118   A profile scanning device.   When a scanning system has nothing to scan it tends to oscillate.   When it scans a pattern, its movement reproduces a facsimile of the pattern on a time base.   (Reprinted from *The Living Brain*, by W. Grey Walter, p. 101, by permission of W. W. Norton & Company, Inc.   Copyright © 1963, 1953, by W. W. Norton & Company, Inc.)

Attaching high significance to the various kinds of rhythms shown in EEG records and correlating their differences with presumed cytoarchitectonic areas, Grey Walter suggested that the function of the living brain could largely be revealed by EEG flickers.   It is a theme he has developed at length in his charming book *The Living Brain*. His main idea is that the living brain functions largely as a cathode-ray oscilloscope, a scanning device Walter made to study EEG records.   It consists of a cathode-ray tube and a photoelectric cell that "looks" at a light spot on the screen of the tube (see Fig. 118). If the voltage of the cell is amplified and fed back to the tube, the spot will follow the profile of any curve placed on the screen; if no curve is present, the system will tend to oscillate in a way similar to alpha rhythm.   This is the basis on which Walter draws an analogy between the screen and the visual cortex.   The screen is the counterpart of the projection area of the visual cortex, which may be either vacant or occupied by projection upon it of an electroneural chart of the visual field. The electron beam and spot of light represent the fluctuating electrical activity generated by a contiguous association area through excitation of chains of neurons leading through the projection area. The photo-cell represents the other end of the neuron chain which receives stimuli back from the projection area and completes the retroactive loop.*

The underpinning of the analogy is the scansion principle employed by the apparatus Walter has used extensively in his own EEG research. This work has led him to believe that an analogous scanning process takes place in the cortex and may be "the final stage of all sensory processes." As evidence in support of his belief he cites the cessation of the eight- to thirteen-second cycle of the alpha rhythm recorded by the electroencephalograph when the subject opens his eyes or sees a pattern. For, according to Walter, "the alpha rhythms are a process of scanning—searching for a pattern—which relaxes when a pattern is found." Now the afore-mentioned profile scanning device tends to oscillate and the resultant oscillations seem to resemble the alpha rhythm when it has nothing to scan. But when it scans a profile pattern, the oscillations cease and its movements reproduce the facsimile of the profile scanned. Walter therefore leaps to the conclusion that the ultima Thule of all sensory processes is the scanning principle of the oscilloscope he has so extensively used. Here again we have a machine that performs an operation roughly similar to one performed by the brain. While it is possible that the brain might work on these principles, there is no evidence that it does so; quite the contrary.

Indeed, despite the great clinical value of EEG records it is doubtful that their "flicker" has any significance as a "mirror" of the brain. For the precise sources of the recorded flickers, the potential differences, are not at all clear. The EEG records are over-all summated effects of the activities that emanate from a very large but unknown number of sources that become attenuated en route in an obscure fashion during their passage from their origins to the recording instruments across tissues, membranes, bone, and scalp. The numerous devices invented to analyze these wavelike rhythms may be useful clinically but are poor guides to the study of cortical organization and brain function itself. The reason is that the analyzers break down

* *The Living Brain*, by W. Grey Walter, Penguin Books, Inc., 1961, p. 101.

automatically the recorded wave forms into a series of components. But as there are many ways of resolving a wave form into sets of components, each set yielding the same summated effect (the original wave form), there is no way of ascertaining which particular set actually gave rise to it.   In other words, it is an indeterminate problem without a unique or unequivocal answer, like splitting a sum into its summands.

It is therefore no surprise that the rhythmic electrical activity of the cortex continues to be a mystery.   An earlier surmise attributes it to an inherent rhythm of the individual neuron which gets a chance of asserting itself in the relatively synchronized responses of great numbers of neurons during periods of inattention and inactivity.   When the brain is active, as when one is doing a sum or perceiving an object, this formless, amorphous neural throbbing with its approximate synchronization of large groups of neurons is broken up.   Yet another conjecture views it as due to circulation of impulses in closed, self-exciting neural chains.   But both these alternatives, which regard it as occasioned by the electrical throbbings of the underlying neurons, seem to be untenable with more recent observations now made possible not merely by attaching microelectrodes outside the skull but even more markedly by inserting them deep in the mid-line region of an animal's brain.   An alternative likely source of alpha rhythm may be the ebb and flow of excitability in the dendritic layers of the cortex. The finely graded changes in the dendritic activity may well modulate cortical excitability.   But the fact that the common laboratory animals, with their comparatively small association cortexes, hardly show any of the simple, almost sinusoidal oscillations characteristic of alpha rhythm, would seem to suggest that it is due to the large volume of association cortex possessed by man.   It is well known that the homeostatic processes throughout the body of the higher animals which keep their internal environment so remarkably constant are largely under the control of the association cortex.   The rhythmic periodicity of the alpha waves may therefore be the outcome of the homeostatic or self-stabilizing processes of the association cortex when free from the bombardment of stimuli and thus unperturbed by the processing of transmitted messages.

However that may be, it is not likely that we shall be able to correlate alpha rhythm with the formation of any very specific neural circuits in the cortex, the "enchanted loom where millions of flashing shuttles (the nerve impulses) weave dissolving, always meaningful patterns, though never an abiding one, a shifting harmony of subpatterns."*   While therefore the mystery of alpha rhythm, at least for the present, cannot be unraveled in any more specific terms, there is some evidence that even its revelation will not suffice to show the organization and functioning of the cerebral cortex as a whole.   For alpha rhythm seems to be the drift taken by the neural net when the rudder of "mind" is removed or its influence greatly attenuated.   As J. C. Eccles has pointed out,

> Unconsciousness is an invariable accompaniment of a neuronal net, that as shown by the electroencephalogram is at rest or only active in low degree or active in a driven stereotyped way as in a convulsion of epilepsy or shock therapy, that is, the net as such is not in liaison with mind.   Adrian (1947) even brings forward evidence that the part of neuronal net giving the alpha rhythm is not in liaison with mind.†

If the electrical activity of the cerebral cortex is to provide any clue to its functioning, other patterns that emerge when the brain is active or excited are more important than the rudderless alpha rhythm when the "mind" is asleep or at any rate not fully awake or active.

The upshot of all this is that although neural circuits are no doubt the life breath of cortical activity, there is a gestalt law at work here which makes it something qualitatively altogether different from a mere "sum" of all these circuits.   In particular, these circuits have considerable lability that makes them virtually jacks of all trades in enabling the cerebral cortex to discharge its multifarious functions. It is this lability that may partly account for the amazing plasticity of the cortical tissue that makes any localizations of its functions all but impossible.   It is a tissue capable in some way of classifying impulses arising from many different sources, extrinsic and intrinsic, relating the immediate pattern of activity to those of the past to determine the animal's response to the ambient situation.

In sum, as we have seen repeatedly, no mathematical, statistical, or network theory can yet be devised to account for the cortical activity of, at any rate, higher mammals and man.   All the various engineering, electrical, and heuristic models devised to mimic or "mechanize" thought processes seem barely to touch the fringe of the problem of unraveling the mystery of the living brain.   We know fairly well the

---

* *Man on his Nature*, by C. S. Sherrington, Cambridge University Press, 1951.

† *The Neurophysiological Basis of Mind*, by J. C. Eccles, Oxford University Press, 1953, p. 270.

basic principles of the secondary logico-mathematical language of our conscious daily use on which all these models have been reared. But perhaps it is precisely because of this that they depart so widely from the living neural model they seek to simulate even when they do succeed in duplicating many of its activities compendiously labeled "thinking." It is true that this departure in respect of their *modus operandi* to duplicate thinking is not relevant to one purpose of cybernetics, namely, that of making machines at any rate capable of taking over some of the higher functions hitherto performed only by human beings. For after all, as Uttley has remarked, we shall not make brains any more than we have made muscles. But it is the very meat of the matter for those who desire a deeper insight into the working of the brain. They have first to discover the primary logico-mathematical language the brain *actually* uses. Deep psychological probes into the working of certain gifted mathematical prodigies like A. C. Aitken, who can match computers in doing computational chores, may provide some clue to the principles of computation employed by the brain. They are certainly much "simpler" than those that we learn at school and program into computers. "Simpler" in this context does not mean that they, when discovered, will be easier to learn; quite the contrary. It merely means that the number of successive steps required to be taken to implement a given operation such as logical or arithmetical addition and multiplication are far fewer in a net of live neurons than in that of vacuum tubes, transistors, and the like. Discovery of this primary logico-mathematical language actually used by the neural net, the living brain, is the next major advance that still awaits its Newton and Gauss.

EPILOGUE

IN our quest for the physical basis of human intelligence we have tacitly assumed that all the remarkable powers of the living brain stem only from (*a*) the topological organization of the network of its constituent neurons and (*b*) the dynamics of neural impulse propagation, without any specifically vitalistic powers which could not be duplicated by man-made devices. In other words, what we call mindlike behavior of the living brain is wholly a property of the neural material of which it is made, so that we do not require what G. Ryle pejoratively calls a "ghost in the machine" to activate it. This is not to say that the mind-body problem which has harassed philosophers since Anaxagoras has been solved and the great gulf between mind and matter bridged. Far from it; some neurologists like J. C. Eccles, Wilder Penfield, and Herrick, to name only a few, doubt that this will ever happen. But we have nevertheless made the assumption because, to invert a famous maxim of Voltaire, even if "mind" exists, it is necessary to *abolish* it for a break-through to artificial intelligence. For, it is only by a ruthless commitment to our physical point of view that we can separate potentially testable and therefore answerable questions from untestable metaphysical presumptions and steer our search along fruitful lines. The denial of "mind" as a *deux ex machina* to pseudo-rescue us from our neurophysiological bafflements is thus a *sine qua non* of any acceptable approach.

Guided by it we have examined a variety of brain models constructed by merely combining simple neural elements in topological organizations analogous to that of the living brain. Beginning with assemblages of simple neural substitutes, either of the digital kind like on-off switches, vacuum tubes, transistors, and cryotrons, or of the analogue sort like current-carrying wires, differential gears and rheostats, we have already enumerated the coincidences and contrasts of networks of electrical hardware (digital or analogue computers) on the one hand, and of biological "software" (animal brains) on the other. We found the brain-computer comparison to be our most puzzling paradox. For though in some respects as closely allied as next of kin, they are in others as far apart as stars and sputniks.

Consider, to start with, the resemblances: they are mainly three. First, the computers can be programed to make decisions of a sort even as living brains do. For a typical program instruction is no mere command to carry out a specific instruction. It is very often also an unfolding of possibilities among which the machine is required to choose in the light of its earlier computations. Secondly, both the computer and the brain employ feedback whereby they monitor and correct their own aberrations in a changing environment. Thirdly, both treat their environment—internal as well as external—as a source of "information," which must somehow be communicated over channels that form an integral part of their network before it is "processed." Both therefore require a theory which ensures *communication* of optimal information with minimal interference by vitiations of noise. The heart of such a theory was seen to be Shannon's theorems on coding described in Chapters IV to VI. These show that to secure optimal flow of information over any channel we have to send internal or "parity" checks along with the message. That is, we have to code the message with a large amount of redundancy. Von Neumann applied the selfsame reliability-through-redundancy principle to automatic machines by showing that they too, like messages, can be safeguarded from error by incorporating into them *redundant* parts. He thus proved a complete parallel of Shannon's coding theorem. As we may recall, the latter guarantees the existence of codes ensuring transmission of information over noisy channels with arbitrarily high reliability. Von Neumann's parallel theorem likewise ensures that it is possible to assemble individually unreliable components into an automaton that will function with any arbitrarily high reliability.

The afore-mentioned threefold resemblances—recourse to the three principles of *choice* to decide the future course of action, of *feedback* to self-rectify errors, and of *redundancy* in coding as well as of components to secure reliability—which we found at work in both the natural and artificial automata, appeared at first encounter so striking as to earn the computers the nickname of electric brains. But we now know better. Alas, the divergences diverge much more radically than the coincidences coincide. As we noted earlier, the most conspicuous departure is in respect of methods of storage, recall, and processing of information. Because the methods of data storage, access, and processing practiced in computer engineering today are very primitive vis-à-vis their infinitely more complex but unknown analogues of the living brain, the computer has not yet come of age to wean itself away from the tutelage of algorisms. That is, it can handle only such tasks as can be performed by a more or less slavish follow-up of prescribed routines. The living brain, on the contrary, operates essentially by non-algorismic methods bearing little resemblance to the familiar rules of logic and mathematics built into the computer. It is therefore no wonder that the latter is hard put to mimic such other creative feats of the living brain as are not readily amenable to algorismic routines. All it has been able to do so far is to ape them crudely, and that too by the invention of new kinds of highly sophisticated machine languages or codes that are nowhere like those of the living brain. It seems that the language of the brain is logically much "simpler" than any we have been able to devise so far. As von Neumann remarked, we are hardly in a position even to talk about it, much less theorize about it. We have not yet been able to map out the activity of the human brain in sufficient detail to serve as a foothold for such an exercise. This is why the next significant advance in the production of brain "models" will depend on the discovery of a new, much more profound and subtle mélange of logic, mathematics, neurophysiology, molecular biology, biophysics, biochemistry, electronics, engineering, and so forth, than any we have today. This also explains why the present research into brain "models" has reached almost a dead end. On the one hand, there are the inflexible kinds of neural networks described in Chapter XI, where the designer attempts to make a network conforming to any given input-output specification. The high-water mark of this approach is the McCulloch-Pitts theorem. But despite its great mathematical sophistication and further refinements by von Neumann and others, its biological cash value has been disappointingly small because it does not provide any clue for implementing in *practice* the principle it proves in *theory*. Although various kinds of machines that identify specific patterns, either visual, audio or otherwise, have been constructed, their recognition facilities are exceedingly primitive compared with those of the human —or for that matter even animal—eye and ear. For example, visual pattern-recognizing machines cannot identify large classes of patterns that appear different to the human eye at the most casual glance. It is true that some of them have been extended to distinguish such classes of patterns, but only at the cost of introducing new *ad hoc* complications instead of simplifications.

The failure to realize the McCulloch-Pitts principle has led to the adoption of a second approach, namely, the *perceptron* approach described in Chapter XV. The main point of departure in this scheme is that the designer does not pre-program to process specific arrays of input patterns. Instead the network is designed as a *tabula rasa* with certain abilities to adjust the thresholds of its "synapses" in order to learn the scheme the trainer desires to impart. But the second type of self-adjusting or "learning" strategy has also not managed to acquire methods for accumulating experience that are sufficiently powerful to score any notable organization. The perceptrons thus far made show relatively poor discrimination, and it is likely that further sophistication or elaboration may not yield commensurate dividends, especially when we begin to vary the patterns. We have already noted the main reason for the poor payoff: the lack of sufficient neurophysiological realism in the network approaches of both kinds.

Take, for example, the visual-pattern perceptron described in Chapter XV. Even its "retina" of photoelectric cells, not to speak of other components, the successive associate units, is a poor substitute for its biological counterpart. Recent anatomical investigations revealing the manifold specializations and rich interconnections of retinal receptor cells seem to indicate that the animal retina plays a far more active and complex role than the array of photoelectric cells in the perceptron. To cite one example of such sophistication ignored by photoelectric cells, each fiber linked to retinal receptor cells does not merely report the presence or absence of illumination as the photoelectric cell does. It is designed to sense whether some complex situation in a given "context" of biological interest to the animal, such as the approach of a prey like a bug to a frog's eye, exists in a given part of the visual field. In other words, the animal retina is not a passive transmitter of information about the point-to-point pattern of light and shade in the image formed on it as is the case with a photographic plate or a "retina" of photoelectric cells. It is a highly selective receptor in what it chooses to "sense" and transmit and what it decides to ignore or suppress. It is this discriminatory faculty of biological receptors that makes even the most elementary perception a veritable act of creation inextricably tied up with learning based on memory rather than mere transmission of physical signals. Thus, hearing is no mere passive perception of pressure variations in air experienced at the eardrum, but actual creation of individual voices and musical melodies. Likewise, vision is not camera-wise perception of retinal images but an inferential construct of peoples and objects which preserves their constant shape and size regardless of angle and distance. If the eye is a camera, it is unlike any that we know in that behind its lens there is a series of compensating, correcting, and retouching devices that determine the pattern it is likely to see. For all awareness of mental activity seems to involve the comparison of a sensed or thought pattern with a pre-existing one, a pattern formed in the brain's physical structure by biological inheritance and the imprint of experience. This is why receptor organs of animals are something qualitatively altogether different from the transducers of communications engineering. While they, no doubt, process information by converting one form of energy into another as their engineering simulacra do, they largely report what the animal will *want* to know or has *learned* to *infer*. Consequently they are far less "objective" instruments than those of engineering and technology and are far more "subjectively" oriented towards the animal's biological needs and wishes. A case in point is the ability of the human ear to pick in a bedlam of voices just the one it wants to hear, unlike the indiscriminating tape recorder that will "hear" them *all* but will listen to *none*. Obviously we have yet a long way to go before we can hope to understand even the manner in which the senses filter the information they receive from the outside world before conveying it to the brain.

With the failure to make in practice brain models or artificial automata capable of exhibiting all or even some partial aspects of an animal's intelligent behavior, there has now been increasing awareness of our debility to synthesize human intelligence by methods other than plodding with algorismic routines. As a result, participants in the search for intelligent machines are of two minds. On the one hand, there are those who consider that major obstacles to the synthesis of each kind of artificial intelligence can be overcome by making the computer's plod more plodding by improving its infallible memory, electronic speed, vast computational capabilities, and prodigious information-processing prowess. They believe that even the existing computer assets have not yet been fully exploited. Aided by methods of more sophisticated searching and statistical procedures, these assets, it is believed, can be employed to yield more rewarding "intelligence" payoffs than any we have had so far. Most of the instances of artificial intelligence such as game playing, problem solving, and theorem proving, and so forth, described in the preceding chapters, owe their success to the deployment of the afore-mentioned computer resources. On the other hand, there are those who feel that the problem of the neurophysiological basis of brain functioning—or more specifically that of the discovery of its methods of storage, recall, data processing, perception, understanding, and so on—must be somehow resolved before significant progress can be made. For these problems are not solely a matter of speed, computation, and data processing. This is, of course, very true. But as we are not likely to be deterred in our pursuit of producing intelligence in the diverse fields of human endeavor by our great ignorance of the neurophysiological behavior of the living brain, there will be further computer developments designed to amplify its storage capacity, speed of action, and information-processing ability. But all that they are likely to yield is an amplified computer and not a "model" of the living brain that duplicates its amazing economy, wisdom, and intelligence. Even so, these advances are not so slight as to be despised. They may lead by the end of the century to the construction of machines able to play successfully Turing's imitation game. But more immediately, the present advances are meant to foster the synthesis of intelligence by carrying the existing possibilities of man-machine combination a stage further. One way of doing this is to make the computer answer directly in ordinary English the questions that the administrator, military commander, or scientist would like to ask, instead of having recourse to the artificial and stylized languages in which we must communicate with computers at present. The Baseball and Sad Sam computer programs mentioned in Chapter XVII are merely preliminary excursions into this area. With the further recent innovation of multiprograming computer systems whereby we are able to handle simultaneously a diversity of tasks, there has thus emerged the possibility of providing ourselves with what are in effect thinking aids. We may expect such man-machine systems to bulk large in our advance towards the creation of artificial intelligence in the immediate future. But for the construction of machines capable of functional duplication of the living brain we must wait for our next breakthrough into the neurophysiological complexity of the human cerebral cortex.

Unfortunately, such a break-through is not easy to come by. For there is a kind of indeterminacy, which though quite different in essence from the famous principle of Heisenberg, is just as effective a barrier to our understanding of the living brain. The indeterminacy arises from the fact already noted, that the more "micro" our neurological probe the less "macro" is our comprehension of the working of the cerebral cortex as a whole. The way out of this dilemma is a synthesis of both micro and macro approaches. But the desired synthesis is not likely to be a mere derivation of macro or aggregate effects by some sort of statistical averaging of myriads of micro neurological events. The transformation of trillions of nerve impulses, surging back and forth helter-skelter in billions of neural channels into the world of color and form that we actually perceive and reason about, could hardly be achieved in such a naïve fashion. Nor can mental activity, including the emergence of human intelligence, be sheet-anchored to a sort of summated upshot of elementary reflexes, those "atoms of behavior" whereon incipient psychology tried in vain to rear itself. While therefore the probe into the genesis of animal intelligence must proceed on the two afore-mentioned collateral lines, one proceeding from the complex to the elementary and the other from the elementary to the complex, both lines of approach must be interdisciplinary. Not only must they rear themselves on the new branches of science enumerated earlier in this chapter, but they must also borrow such insights as linguistics, aesthetics, and the humanities are able to give. For, as we remarked at the outset, Fournié's surmise that human speech is a window on the working of the cerebral cortex may well be truer than we know at present. Moreover, the artist too has long been making meaningful and communicable statements, if not always precise ones, about complex things. In particular, it is well to recall that most of what we know at present about the mind of man is to be learned not from the writings of scientists so much as from those of men of letters—the poets and philosophers, biographers and historians, novelists and literary critics. If the human mind is to uncover its working, it cannot afford to neglect any way of gaining insight. Indeed, it needs, like the youthful Bacon, to take "all knowledge" for its "province." For thus alone may we hope to stumble on some enlargement of the boundaries of natural science able to reveal to us the secret of the human brain's uncanny wisdom.

Many scientists are trying to create that enlargement today. But we must not be too impatient if most of them happen to miss rather than hit the target. For after all the secret of the human mind is a primeval mystery. In the words of an ancient epigram:

> Though many a thing is unfathomable for mankind,
> Nothing looms more ineffable than the mind of man.

NAME INDEX

Aitken, A. C., 324
Anaxagoras, 325
Archimedes, 206, 207, 210
Aristotle, 2
Ashby, Ross, 6, 153, 212–22, 223, 249

Bacon, F., 103, 331
Babbage, C., 7, 115
Beethoven, L. van, 302
Berger, H., 319
Bernstein, A., 264
Beurle, R. L., 317–19
Boole, G., 7
Borel, E., 209
Bose, R. C., 57–58
Boulton, M., 7
Brillouin, L., 77
Broca, Paul, 1
Brueckner, K. A., 166
Burali-Forti, C., 147

Čapek, K., 184
Chase, S., 4
Clarke, A., 153
Copi, I. M., 112
Cragg, B. G., 316, 319
Culbertson, J. T., 158

Democritus, 197
Descartes, R., 197

Eccles, J. C., 323, 325
Eddington, A. S., 75
Elias, P., 54–55, 58
Empedocles, 80

Farley, B. G., 247

Foerster, H. von, 158–60
Fourier, J. B. J., 65
Freudenthal, H., 6

Gabor, D., 77
Gauss, C. F., 324
Gell-Mann, G., 166
Gentzen, G., 278
Gödel, K., 201
Goethe, J. W. von, 4
Goldsmith, O., 128
Green, B. F., 293
Guilbaud, K., 225

Haldane, J. B. S., 194
Hamming, R. W., 54–55, 57–58
Hebb, D. O., 223, 252
Heisenberg, W., 331
Helmholtz, G., 64
Herbrand, 278
Hero, viii
Herrick, 325
Hilbert, D., 278
Hoyle, F., 153–54
Hubel, D. H., 203
Huffman, D. A., 36

Khayyám, Omar, 200
Kleene, S. C., 144
Kornmuller, A. E., 317

Latil, Pierre de, 214
Leibnitz, G. W., 7, 19
Lettvin, J. Y., 202
Lindsay, R. K., 293
Loehlin, J., 203
Luhn, L. H., 212

333

SUBJECT INDEX

A CATALOGUE OF
SELECTED DOVER BOOKS
IN ALL FIELDS OF INTEREST

A CATALOGUE OF SELECTED DOVER
BOOKS IN ALL FIELDS OF INTEREST

RACKHAM'S COLOR ILLUSTRATIONS FOR WAGNER'S RING. Rackham's finest mature work—all 64 full-color watercolors in a faithful and lush interpretation of the *Ring*. Full-sized plates on coated stock of the paintings used by opera companies for authentic staging of Wagner. Captions aid in following complete Ring cycle. Introduction. 64 illustrations plus vignettes. 72pp. 8⅝ x 11¼.   23779-6 Pa. $6.00

CONTEMPORARY POLISH POSTERS IN FULL COLOR, edited by Joseph Czestochowski. 46 full-color examples of brilliant school of Polish graphic design, selected from world's first museum (near Warsaw) dedicated to poster art. Posters on circuses, films, plays, concerts all show cosmopolitan influences, free imagination. Introduction. 48pp. 9⅜ x 12¼.
23780-X Pa. $6.00

GRAPHIC WORKS OF EDVARD MUNCH, Edvard Munch. 90 haunting, evocative prints by first major Expressionist artist and one of the greatest graphic artists of his time: *The Scream, Anxiety, Death Chamber, The Kiss, Madonna*, etc. Introduction by Alfred Werner. 90pp. 9 x 12.
23765-6 Pa. $5.00

THE GOLDEN AGE OF THE POSTER, Hayward and Blanche Cirker. 70 extraordinary posters in full colors, from Maitres de l'Affiche, Mucha, Lautrec, Bradley, Cheret, Beardsley, many others. Total of 78pp. 9⅜ x 12¼.   22753-7 Pa. $5.95

THE NOTEBOOKS OF LEONARDO DA VINCI, edited by J. P. Richter. Extracts from manuscripts reveal great genius; on painting, sculpture, anatomy, sciences, geography, etc. Both Italian and English. 186 ms. pages reproduced, plus 500 additional drawings, including studies for *Last Supper*, Sforza monument, etc. 860pp. 7⅞ x 10¾. (Available in U.S. only)
22572-0, 22573-9 Pa., Two-vol. set $15.90

THE CODEX NUTTALL, as first edited by Zelia Nuttall. Only inexpensive edition, in full color, of a pre-Columbian Mexican (Mixtec) book. 88 color plates show kings, gods, heroes, temples, sacrifices. New explanatory, historical introduction by Arthur G. Miller. 96pp. 11⅜ x 8½. (Available in U.S. only)   23168-2 Pa. $7.95

UNE SEMAINE DE BONTÉ, A SURREALISTIC NOVEL IN COLLAGE, Max Ernst. Masterpiece created out of 19th-century periodical illustrations, explores worlds of terror and surprise. Some consider this Ernst's greatest work. 208pp. 8⅛ x 11.   23252-2 Pa. $6.00

DRAWINGS OF WILLIAM BLAKE, William Blake. 92 plates from Book of Job, *Divine Comedy, Paradise Lost,* visionary heads, mythological figures, Laocoon, etc. Selection, introduction, commentary by Sir Geoffrey Keynes. 178pp. 8⅛ x 11. 22303-5 Pa. $4.00

ENGRAVINGS OF HOGARTH, William Hogarth. 101 of Hogarth's greatest works: *Rake's Progress, Harlot's Progress, Illustrations for Hudibras, Before and After, Beer Street and Gin Lane,* many more. Full commentary. 256pp. 11 x 13¾. 22479-1 Pa. $12.95

DAUMIER: 120 GREAT LITHOGRAPHS, Honore Daumier. Wide-ranging collection of lithographs by the greatest caricaturist of the 19th century. Concentrates on eternally popular series on lawyers, on married life, on liberated women, etc. Selection, introduction, and notes on plates by Charles F. Ramus. Total of 158pp. 9⅜ x 12¼. 23512-2 Pa. $6.00

DRAWINGS OF MUCHA, Alphonse Maria Mucha. Work reveals drafts-man of highest caliber: studies for famous posters and paintings, render-ings for book illustrations and ads, etc. 70 works, 9 in color; including 6 items not drawings. Introduction. List of illustrations. 72pp. 9⅜ x 12¼. (Available in U.S. only) 23672-2 Pa. $4.00

GIOVANNI BATTISTA PIRANESI: DRAWINGS IN THE PIERPONT MORGAN LIBRARY, Giovanni Battista Piranesi. For first time ever all of Morgan Library's collection, world's largest. 167 illustrations of rare Piranesi drawings—archeological, architectural, decorative and visionary. Essay, detailed list of drawings, chronology, captions. Edited by Felice Stampfle. 144pp. 9⅜ x 12¼. 23714-1 Pa. $7.50

NEW YORK ETCHINGS (1905-1949), John Sloan. All of important American artist's N.Y. life etchings. 67 works include some of his best art; also lively historical record—Greenwich Village, tenement scenes. Edited by Sloan's widow. Introduction and captions. 79pp. 8⅜ x 11¼. 23651-X Pa. $4.00

CHINESE PAINTING AND CALLIGRAPHY: A PICTORIAL SURVEY, Wan-go Weng. 69 fine examples from John M. Crawford's matchless private collection: landscapes, birds, flowers, human figures, etc., plus calligraphy. Every basic form included: hanging scrolls, handscrolls, album leaves, fans, etc. 109 illustrations. Introduction. Captions. 192pp. 8⅞ x 11¾. 23707-9 Pa. $7.95

DRAWINGS OF REMBRANDT, edited by Seymour Slive. Updated Lipp-mann, Hofstede de Groot edition, with definitive scholarly apparatus. All portraits, biblical sketches, landscapes, nudes, Oriental figures, classical studies, together with selection of work by followers. 550 illustrations. Total of 630pp. 9⅛ x 12¼. 21485-0, 21486-9 Pa., Two-vol. set $15.00

THE DISASTERS OF WAR, Francisco Goya. 83 etchings record horrors of Napoleonic wars in Spain and war in general. Reprint of 1st edition, plus 3 additional plates. Introduction by Philip Hofer. 97pp. 9⅜ x 8¼. 21872-4 Pa. $4.00

THE EARLY WORK OF AUBREY BEARDSLEY, Aubrey Beardsley. 157 plates, 2 in color: *Manon Lescaut, Madame Bovary, Morte Darthur, Salome,* other. Introduction by H. Marillier. 182pp. 8⅛ x 11. 21816-3 Pa. $4.50

THE LATER WORK OF AUBREY BEARDSLEY, Aubrey Beardsley. Exotic masterpieces of full maturity: *Venus and Tannhauser, Lysistrata, Rape of the Lock, Volpone,* Savoy material, etc. 174 plates, 2 in color. 186pp. 8⅛ x 11. 21817-1 Pa. $5.95

THOMAS NAST'S CHRISTMAS DRAWINGS, Thomas Nast. Almost all Christmas drawings by creator of image of Santa Claus as we know it, and one of America's foremost illustrators and political cartoonists. 66 illustrations. 3 illustrations in color on covers. 96pp. 8⅜ x 11¼. 23660-9 Pa. $3.50

THE DORÉ ILLUSTRATIONS FOR DANTE'S DIVINE COMEDY, Gustave Doré. All 135 plates from Inferno, Purgatory, Paradise; fantastic tortures, infernal landscapes, celestial wonders. Each plate with appropriate (translated) verses. 141pp. 9 x 12. 23231-X Pa. $4.50

DORÉ'S ILLUSTRATIONS FOR RABELAIS, Gustave Doré. 252 striking illustrations of *Gargantua and Pantagruel* books by foremost 19th-century illustrator. Including 60 plates, 192 delightful smaller illustrations. 153pp. 9 x 12. 23656-0 Pa. $5.00

LONDON: A PILGRIMAGE, Gustave Doré, Blanchard Jerrold. Squalor, riches, misery, beauty of mid-Victorian metropolis; 55 wonderful plates, 125 other illustrations, full social, cultural text by Jerrold. 191pp. of text. 9⅜ x 12¼. 22306-X Pa. $7.00

THE RIME OF THE ANCIENT MARINER, Gustave Doré, S. T. Coleridge. Dore's finest work, 34 plates capture moods, subtleties of poem. Full text. Introduction by Millicent Rose. 77pp. 9¼ x 12. 22305-1 Pa. $3.50

THE DORE BIBLE ILLUSTRATIONS, Gustave Doré. All wonderful, detailed plates: Adam and Eve, Flood, Babylon, Life of Jesus, etc. Brief King James text with each plate. Introduction by Millicent Rose. 241 plates. 241pp. 9 x 12. 23004-X Pa. $6.00

THE COMPLETE ENGRAVINGS, ETCHINGS AND DRYPOINTS OF ALBRECHT DURER. "Knight, Death and Devil"; "Melencolia," and more—all Dürer's known works in all three media, including 6 works formerly attributed to him. 120 plates. 235pp. 8⅜ x 11¼.
22851-7 Pa. $6.50

MECHANICK EXERCISES ON THE WHOLE ART OF PRINTING, Joseph Moxon. First complete book (1683-4) ever written about typography, a compendium of everything known about printing at the latter part of 17th century. Reprint of 2nd (1962) Oxford Univ. Press edition. 74 illustrations. Total of 550pp. 6⅛ x 9¼. 23617-X Pa. $7.95

THE COMPLETE WOODCUTS OF ALBRECHT DURER, edited by Dr. W. Kurth. 346 in all: "Old Testament," "St. Jerome," "Passion," "Life of Virgin," Apocalypse," many others. Introduction by Campbell Dodgson. 285pp. 8½ x 12¼. 21097-9 Pa. $7.50

DRAWINGS OF ALBRECHT DURER, edited by Heinrich Wolfflin. 81 plates show development from youth to full style. Many favorites; many new. Introduction by Alfred Werner. 96pp. 8⅛ x 11. 22352-3 Pa. $5.00

THE HUMAN FIGURE, Albrecht Dürer. Experiments in various techniques—stereometric, progressive proportional, and others. Also life studies that rank among finest ever done. Complete reprinting of Dresden Sketchbook. 170 plates. 355pp. 8⅜ x 11¼. 21042-1 Pa. $7.95

OF THE JUST SHAPING OF LETTERS, Albrecht Dürer. Renaissance artist explains design of Roman majuscules by geometry, also Gothic lower and capitals. Grolier Club edition. 43pp. 7⅞ x 10¾ 21306-4 Pa. $3.00

TEN BOOKS ON ARCHITECTURE, Vitruvius. The most important book ever written on architecture. Early Roman aesthetics, technology, classical orders, site selection, all other aspects. Stands behind everything since. Morgan translation. 331pp. 5⅜ x 8½. 20645-9 Pa. $4.50

THE FOUR BOOKS OF ARCHITECTURE, Andrea Palladio. 16th-century classic responsible for Palladian movement and style. Covers classical architectural remains, Renaissance revivals, classical orders, etc. 1738 Ware English edition. Introduction by A. Placzek. 216 plates. 110pp. of text. 9½ x 12¾. 21308-0 Pa. $10.00

HORIZONS, Norman Bel Geddes. Great industrialist stage designer, "father of streamlining," on application of aesthetics to transportation, amusement, architecture, etc. 1932 prophetic account; function, theory, specific projects. 222 illustrations. 312pp. 7⅞ x 10¾. 23514-9 Pa. $6.95

FRANK LLOYD WRIGHT'S FALLINGWATER, Donald Hoffmann. Full, illustrated story of conception and building of Wright's masterwork at Bear Run, Pa. 100 photographs of site, construction, and details of completed structure. 112pp. 9¼ x 10. 23671-4 Pa. $5.50

THE ELEMENTS OF DRAWING, John Ruskin. Timeless classic by great Viltorian; starts with basic ideas, works through more difficult. Many practical exercises. 48 illustrations. Introduction by Lawrence Campbell. 228pp. 5⅜ x 8½. 22730-8 Pa. $3.75

GIST OF ART, John Sloan. Greatest modern American teacher, Art Students League, offers innumerable hints, instructions, guided comments to help you in painting. Not a formal course. 46 illustrations. Introduction by Helen Sloan. 200pp. 5⅜ x 8½. 23435-5 Pa. $4.00

THE ANATOMY OF THE HORSE, George Stubbs. Often considered the great masterpiece of animal anatomy. Full reproduction of 1766 edition, plus prospectus; original text and modernized text. 36 plates. Introduction by Eleanor Garvey. 121pp. 11 x 14¾.   23402-9 Pa. $6.00

BRIDGMAN'S LIFE DRAWING, George B. Bridgman. More than 500 illustrative drawings and text teach you to abstract the body into its major masses, use light and shade, proportion; as well as specific areas of anatomy, of which Bridgman is master. 192pp. 6½ x 9¼. (Available in U.S. only)
                                                                    22710-3 Pa. $3.50

ART NOUVEAU DESIGNS IN COLOR, Alphonse Mucha, Maurice Verneuil, Georges Auriol. Full-color reproduction of *Combinaisons ornementales* (c. 1900) by Art Nouveau masters. Floral, animal, geometric, interlacings, swashes—borders, frames, spots—all incredibly beautiful. 60 plates, hundreds of designs. 9⅜ x 8-1/16.   22885-1 Pa. $4.00

FULL-COLOR FLORAL DESIGNS IN THE ART NOUVEAU STYLE, E. A. Seguy. 166 motifs, on 40 plates, from *Les fleurs et leurs applications decoratives* (1902): borders, circular designs, repeats, allovers, "spots." All in authentic Art Nouveau colors. 48pp. 9⅜ x 12¼.
                                                                    23439-8 Pa. $5.00

A DIDEROT PICTORIAL ENCYCLOPEDIA OF TRADES AND INDUSTRY, edited by Charles C. Gillispie. 485 most interesting plates from the great French Encyclopedia of the 18th century show hundreds of working figures, artifacts, process, land and cityscapes; glassmaking, papermaking, metal extraction, construction, weaving, making furniture, clothing, wigs, dozens of other activities. Plates fully explained. 920pp. 9 x 12.
                              22284-5, 22285-3 Clothbd., Two-vol. set $40.00

HANDBOOK OF EARLY ADVERTISING ART, Clarence P. Hornung. Largest collection of copyright-free early and antique advertising art ever compiled. Over 6,000 illustrations, from Franklin's time to the 1890's for special effects, novelty. Valuable source, almost inexhaustible.
Pictorial Volume. Agriculture, the zodiac, animals, autos, birds, Christmas, fire engines, flowers, trees, musical instruments, ships, games and sports, much more. Arranged by subject matter and use. 237 plates. 288pp. 9 x 12.
                                                            20122-8 Clothbd. $14.50

Typographical Volume. Roman and Gothic faces ranging from 10 point to 300 point, "Barnum," German and Old English faces, script, logotypes, scrolls and flourishes, 1115 ornamental initials, 67 complete alphabets, more. 310 plates. 320pp. 9 x 12.   20123-6 Clothbd. $15.00

CALLIGRAPHY (CALLIGRAPHIA LATINA), J. G. Schwandner. High point of 18th-century ornamental calligraphy. Very ornate initials, scrolls, borders, cherubs, birds, lettered examples. 172pp. 9 x 13.
                                                                    20475-8 Pa. $7.00

ART FORMS IN NATURE, Ernst Haeckel. Multitude of strangely beautiful natural forms: Radiolaria, Foraminifera, jellyfishes, fungi, turtles, bats, etc. All 100 plates of the 19th-century evolutionist's *Kunstformen der Natur* (1904). 100pp. 9⅜ x 12¼. 22987-4 Pa. $5.00

CHILDREN: A PICTORIAL ARCHIVE FROM NINETEENTH-CENTURY SOURCES, edited by Carol Belanger Grafton. 242 rare, copyright-free wood engravings for artists and designers. Widest such selection available. All illustrations in line. 119pp. 8⅜ x 11¼. 23694-3 Pa. $4.00

WOMEN: A PICTORIAL ARCHIVE FROM NINETEENTH-CENTURY SOURCES, edited by Jim Harter. 391 copyright-free wood engravings for artists and designers selected from rare periodicals. Most extensive such collection available. All illustrations in line. 128pp. 9 x 12. 23703-6 Pa. $4.50

ARABIC ART IN COLOR, Prisse d'Avennes. From the greatest ornamentalists of all time—50 plates in color, rarely seen outside the Near East, rich in suggestion and stimulus. Includes 4 plates on covers. 46pp. 9⅜ x 12¼. 23658-7 Pa. $6.00

AUTHENTIC ALGERIAN CARPET DESIGNS AND MOTIFS, edited by June Beveridge. Algerian carpets are world famous. Dozens of geometrical motifs are charted on grids, color-coded, for weavers, needleworkers, craftsmen, designers. 53 illustrations plus 4 in color. 48pp. 8¼ x 11. (Available in U.S. only) 23650-1 Pa. $1.75

DICTIONARY OF AMERICAN PORTRAITS, edited by Hayward and Blanche Cirker. 4000 important Americans, earliest times to 1905, mostly in clear line. Politicians, writers, soldiers, scientists, inventors, industrialists, Indians, Blacks, women, outlaws, etc. Identificatory information. 756pp. 9¼ x 12¾. 21823-6 Clothbd. $40.00

HOW THE OTHER HALF LIVES, Jacob A. Riis. Journalistic record of filth, degradation, upward drive in New York immigrant slums, shops, around 1900. New edition includes 100 original Riis photos, monuments of early photography. 233pp. 10 x 7⅞. 22012-5 Pa. $7.00

NEW YORK IN THE THIRTIES, Berenice Abbott. Noted photographer's fascinating study of city shows new buildings that have become famous and old sights that have disappeared forever. Insightful commentary. 97 photographs. 97pp. 11⅜ x 10. 22967-X Pa. $5.00

MEN AT WORK, Lewis W. Hine. Famous photographic studies of construction workers, railroad men, factory workers and coal miners. New supplement of 18 photos on Empire State building construction. New introduction by Jonathan L. Doherty. Total of 69 photos. 63pp. 8 x 10¾. 23475-4 Pa. $3.00

THE DEPRESSION YEARS AS PHOTOGRAPHED BY ARTHUR ROTH-STEIN, Arthur Rothstein. First collection devoted entirely to the work of outstanding 1930s photographer: famous dust storm photo, ragged children, unemployed, etc. 120 photographs. Captions. 119pp. 9¼ x 10¾.
23590-4 Pa. $5.00

CAMERA WORK: A PICTORIAL GUIDE, Alfred Stieglitz. All 559 illustrations and plates from the most important periodical in the history of art photography, Camera Work (1903-17). Presented four to a page, reduced in size but still clear, in strict chronological order, with complete captions. Three indexes. Glossary. Bibliography. 176pp. 8⅜ x 11¼.
23591-2 Pa. $6.95

ALVIN LANGDON COBURN, PHOTOGRAPHER, Alvin L. Coburn. Revealing autobiography by one of greatest photographers of 20th century gives insider's version of Photo-Secession, plus comments on his own work. 77 photographs by Coburn. Edited by Helmut and Alison Gernsheim. 160pp. 8⅛ x 11.
23685-4 Pa. $6.00

NEW YORK IN THE FORTIES, Andreas Feininger. 162 brilliant photographs by the well-known photographer, formerly with Life magazine, show commuters, shoppers, Times Square at night, Harlem nightclub, Lower East Side, etc. Introduction and full captions by John von Hartz. 181pp. 9¼ x 10¾.
23585-8 Pa. $6.95

GREAT NEWS PHOTOS AND THE STORIES BEHIND THEM, John Faber. Dramatic volume of 140 great news photos, 1855 through 1976, and revealing stories behind them, with both historical and technical information. Hindenburg disaster, shooting of Oswald, nomination of Jimmy Carter, etc. 160pp. 8¼ x 11.
23667-6 Pa. $5.00

THE ART OF THE CINEMATOGRAPHER, Leonard Maltin. Survey of American cinematography history and anecdotal interviews with 5 masters—Arthur Miller, Hal Mohr, Hal Rosson, Lucien Ballard, and Conrad Hall. Very large selection of behind-the-scenes production photos. 105 photographs. Filmographies. Index. Originally Behind the Camera. 144pp. 8¼ x 11.
23686-2 Pa. $5.00

DESIGNS FOR THE THREE-CORNERED HAT (LE TRICORNE), Pablo Picasso. 32 fabulously rare drawings—including 31 color illustrations of costumes and accessories—for 1919 production of famous ballet. Edited by Parmenia Migel, who has written new introduction. 48pp. 9⅜ x 12¼. (Available in U.S. only)
23709-5 Pa. $5.00

NOTES OF A FILM DIRECTOR, Sergei Eisenstein. Greatest Russian filmmaker explains montage, making of Alexander Nevsky, aesthetics; comments on self, associates, great rivals (Chaplin), similar material. 78 illustrations. 240pp. 5⅜ x 8½.
22392-2 Pa. $4.50

HOLLYWOOD GLAMOUR PORTRAITS, edited by John Kobal. 145 photos capture the stars from 1926-49, the high point in portrait photography. Gable, Harlow, Bogart, Bacall, Hedy Lamarr, Marlene Dietrich, Robert Montgomery, Marlon Brando, Veronica Lake; 94 stars in all. Full background on photographers, technical aspects, much more. Total of 160pp. 8⅜ x 11¼.   23352-9 Pa. $6.00

THE NEW YORK STAGE: FAMOUS PRODUCTIONS IN PHOTO-GRAPHS, edited by Stanley Appelbaum. 148 photographs from Museum of City of New York show 142 plays, 1883-1939. *Peter Pan, The Front Page, Dead End, Our Town,* O'Neill, hundreds of actors and actresses, etc. Full indexes. 154pp. 9½ x 10.   23241-7 Pa. $6.00

DIALOGUES CONCERNING TWO NEW SCIENCES, Galileo Galilei. Encompassing 30 years of experiment and thought, these dialogues deal with geometric demonstrations of fracture of solid bodies, cohesion, leverage, speed of light and sound, pendulums, falling bodies, accelerated motion, etc. 300pp. 5⅜ x 8½.   60099-8 Pa. $4.00

THE GREAT OPERA STARS IN HISTORIC PHOTOGRAPHS, edited by James Camner. 343 portraits from the 1850s to the 1940s: Tamburini, Mario, Caliapin, Jeritza, Melchior, Melba, Patti, Pinza, Schipa, Caruso, Farrar, Steber, Gobbi, and many more—270 performers in all. Index. 199pp. 8⅜ x 11¼.   23575-0 Pa. $7.50

J. S. BACH, Albert Schweitzer. Great full-length study of Bach, life, background to music, music, by foremost modern scholar. Ernest Newman translation. 650 musical examples. Total of 928pp. 5⅜ x 8½. (Available in U.S. only)   21631-4, 21632-2 Pa., Two-vol. set $11.00

COMPLETE PIANO SONATAS, Ludwig van Beethoven. All sonatas in the fine Schenker edition, with fingering, analytical material. One of best modern editions. Total of 615pp. 9 x 12. (Available in U.S. only)
                            23134-8, 23135-6 Pa., Two-vol. set $15.50

KEYBOARD MUSIC, J. S. Bach. Bach-Gesellschaft edition. For harpsichord, piano, other keyboard instruments. English Suites, French Suites, Six Partitas, Goldberg Variations, Two-Part Inventions, Three-Part Sinfonias. 312pp. 8⅛ x 11. (Available in U.S. only)   22360-4 Pa. $6.95

FOUR SYMPHONIES IN FULL SCORE, Franz Schubert. Schubert's four most popular symphonies: No. 4 in C Minor ("Tragic"); No. 5 in B-flat Major; No. 8 in B Minor ("Unfinished"); No. 9 in C Major ("Great"). Breitkopf & Hartel edition. Study score. 261pp. 9⅜ x 12¼.
                            23681-1 Pa. $6.50

THE AUTHENTIC GILBERT & SULLIVAN SONGBOOK, W. S. Gilbert, A. S. Sullivan. Largest selection available; 92 songs, uncut, original keys, in piano rendering approved by Sullivan. Favorites and lesser-known fine numbers. Edited with plot synopses by James Spero. 3 illustrations. 399pp. 9 x 12.   23482-7 Pa. $9.95

PRINCIPLES OF ORCHESTRATION, Nikolay Rimsky-Korsakov. Great classical orchestrator provides fundamentals of tonal resonance, progression of parts, voice and orchestra, tutti effects, much else in major document. 330pp. of musical excerpts. 489pp. 6½ x 9¼. 21266-1 Pa. $7.50

TRISTAN UND ISOLDE, Richard Wagner. Full orchestral score with complete instrumentation. Do not confuse with piano reduction. Commentary by Felix Mottl, great Wagnerian conductor and scholar. Study score. 655pp. 8⅛ x 11. 22915-7 Pa. $13.95

REQUIEM IN FULL SCORE, Giuseppe Verdi. Immensely popular with choral groups and music lovers. Republication of edition published by C. F. Peters, Leipzig, n. d. German frontmaker in English translation. Glossary. Text in Latin. Study score. 204pp. 9⅜ x 12¼. 23682-X Pa. $6.00

COMPLETE CHAMBER MUSIC FOR STRINGS, Felix Mendelssohn. All of Mendelssohn's chamber music: Octet, 2 Quintets, 6 Quartets, and Four Pieces for String Quartet. (Nothing with piano is included). Complete works edition (1874-7). Study score. 283 pp. 9⅜ x 12¼. 23679-X Pa. $7.50

POPULAR SONGS OF NINETEENTH-CENTURY AMERICA, edited by Richard Jackson. 64 most important songs: "Old Oaken Bucket," "Arkansas Traveler," "Yellow Rose of Texas," etc. Authentic original sheet music, full introduction and commentaries. 290pp. 9 x 12. 23270-0 Pa. $7.95

COLLECTED PIANO WORKS, Scott Joplin. Edited by Vera Brodsky Lawrence. Practically all of Joplin's piano works—rags, two-steps, marches, waltzes, etc., 51 works in all. Extensive introduction by Rudi Blesh. Total of 345pp. 9 x 12. 23106-2 Pa. $14.95

BASIC PRINCIPLES OF CLASSICAL BALLET, Agrippina Vaganova. Great Russian theoretician, teacher explains methods for teaching classical ballet; incorporates best from French, Italian, Russian schools. 118 illustrations. 175pp. 5⅜ x 8½. 22036-2 Pa. $2.50

CHINESE CHARACTERS, L. Wieger. Rich analysis of 2300 characters according to traditional systems into primitives. Historical-semantic analysis to phonetics (Classical Mandarin) and radicals. 820pp. 6⅛ x 9¼. 21321-8 Pa. $10.00

EGYPTIAN LANGUAGE: EASY LESSONS IN EGYPTIAN HIERO-GLYPHICS, E. A. Wallis Budge. Foremost Egyptologist offers Egyptian grammar, explanation of hieroglyphics, many reading texts, dictionary of symbols. 246pp. 5 x 7½. (Available in U.S. only) 21394-3 Clothbd. $7.50

AN ETYMOLOGICAL DICTIONARY OF MODERN ENGLISH, Ernest Weekley. Richest, fullest work, by foremost British lexicographer. Detailed word histories. Inexhaustible. Do not confuse this with *Concise Etymological Dictionary*, which is abridged. Total of 856pp. 6½ x 9¼. 21873-2, 21874-0 Pa., Two-vol. set $12.00

A MAYA GRAMMAR, Alfred M. Tozzer. Practical, useful English-language grammar by the Harvard anthropologist who was one of the three greatest American scholars in the area of Maya culture. Phonetics, grammatical processes, syntax, more. 301pp. 5⅜ x 8½.　　23465-7 Pa. $4.00

THE JOURNAL OF HENRY D. THOREAU, edited by Bradford Torrey, F. H. Allen. Complete reprinting of 14 volumes, 1837-61, over two million words; the sourcebooks for *Walden*, etc. Definitive. All original sketches, plus 75 photographs. Introduction by Walter Harding. Total of 1804pp. 8½ x 12¼.　　20312-3, 20313-1 Clothbd., Two-vol. set $70.00

CLASSIC GHOST STORIES, Charles Dickens and others. 18 wonderful stories you've wanted to reread: "The Monkey's Paw," "The House and the Brain," "The Upper Berth," "The Signalman," "Dracula's Guest," "The Tapestried Chamber," etc. Dickens, Scott, Mary Shelley, Stoker, etc. 330pp. 5⅜ x 8½.　　20735-8 Pa. $4.50

SEVEN SCIENCE FICTION NOVELS, H. G. Wells. Full novels. *First Men in the Moon, Island of Dr. Moreau, War of the Worlds, Food of the Gods, Invisible Man, Time Machine, In the Days of the Comet.* A basic science-fiction library. 1015pp. 5⅜ x 8½. (Available in U.S. only)
　　20264-X Clothbd. $8.95

ARMADALE, Wilkie Collins. Third great mystery novel by the author of *The Woman in White* and *The Moonstone.* Ingeniously plotted narrative shows an exceptional command of character, incident and mood. Original magazine version with 40 illustrations. 597pp. 5⅜ x 8½.
　　23429-0 Pa. $6.00

MASTERS OF MYSTERY, H. Douglas Thomson. The first book in English (1931) devoted to history and aesthetics of detective story. Poe, Doyle, LeFanu, Dickens, many others, up to 1930. New introduction and notes by E. F. Bleiler. 288pp. 5⅜ x 8½. (Available in U.S. only)
　　23606-4 Pa. $4.00

FLATLAND, E. A. Abbott. Science-fiction classic explores life of 2-D being in 3-D world. Read also as introduction to thought about hyperspace. Introduction by Banesh Hoffmann. 16 illustrations. 103pp. 5⅜ x 8½.
　　20001-9 Pa. $2.00

THREE SUPERNATURAL NOVELS OF THE VICTORIAN PERIOD, edited, with an introduction, by E. F. Bleiler. Reprinted complete and unabridged, three great classics of the supernatural: *The Haunted Hotel* by Wilkie Collins, *The Haunted House at Latchford* by Mrs. J. H. Riddell, and *The Lost Stradivarius* by J. Meade Falkner. 325pp. 5⅜ x 8½.
　　22571-2 Pa. $4.00

AYESHA: THE RETURN OF "SHE," H. Rider Haggard. Virtuoso sequel featuring the great mythic creation, Ayesha, in an adventure that is fully as good as the first book, *She.* Original magazine version, with 47 original illustrations by Maurice Greiffenhagen. 189pp. 6½ x 9¼.
　　23649-8 Pa. $3.50

UNCLE SILAS, J. Sheridan LeFanu. Victorian Gothic mystery novel, considered by many best of period, even better than Collins or Dickens. Wonderful psychological terror. Introduction by Frederick Shroyer. 436pp. 5⅜ x 8½.   21715-9 Pa. $6.00

JURGEN, James Branch Cabell. The great erotic fantasy of the 1920's that delighted thousands, shocked thousands more. Full final text, Lane edition with 13 plates by Frank Pape. 346pp. 5⅜ x 8½.
23507-6 Pa. $4.50

THE CLAVERINGS, Anthony Trollope. Major novel, chronicling aspects of British Victorian society, personalities. Reprint of Cornhill serialization, 16 plates by M. Edwards; first reprint of full text. Introduction by Norman Donaldson. 412pp. 5⅜ x 8½.   23464-9 Pa. $5.00

KEPT IN THE DARK, Anthony Trollope. Unusual short novel about Victorian morality and abnormal psychology by the great English author. Probably the first American publication. Frontispiece by Sir John Millais. 92pp. 6½ x 9¼.   23609-9 Pa. $2.50

RALPH THE HEIR, Anthony Trollope. Forgotten tale of illegitimacy, inheritance. Master novel of Trollope's later years. Victorian country estates, clubs, Parliament, fox hunting, world of fully realized characters. Reprint of 1871 edition. 12 illustrations by F. A. Faser. 434pp. of text. 5⅜ x 8½.   23642-0 Pa. $5.00

YEKL and THE IMPORTED BRIDEGROOM AND OTHER STORIES OF THE NEW YORK GHETTO, Abraham Cahan. Film *Hester Street* based on *Yekl* (1896). Novel, other stories among first about Jewish immigrants of N.Y.'s East Side. Highly praised by W. D. Howells—Cahan "a new star of realism." New introduction by Bernard G. Richards. 240pp. 5⅜ x 8½.   22427-9 Pa. $3.50

THE HIGH PLACE, James Branch Cabell. Great fantasy writer's enchanting comedy of disenchantment set in 18th-century France. Considered by some critics to be even better than his famous *Jurgen*. 10 illustrations and numerous vignettes by noted fantasy artist Frank C. Pape. 320pp. 5⅜ x 8½.   23670-6 Pa. $4.00

ALICE'S ADVENTURES UNDER GROUND, Lewis Carroll. Facsimile of ms. Carroll gave Alice Liddell in 1864. Different in many ways from final Alice. Handlettered, illustrated by Carroll. Introduction by Martin Gardner. 128pp. 5⅜ x 8½.   21482-6 Pa. $2.50

FAVORITE ANDREW LANG FAIRY TALE BOOKS IN MANY COLORS, Andrew Lang. The four Lang favorites in a boxed set—the complete *Red, Green, Yellow* and *Blue* Fairy Books. 164 stories; 439 illustrations by Lancelot Speed, Henry Ford and G. P. Jacomb Hood. Total of about 1500pp. 5⅜ x 8½.   23407-X Boxed set, Pa. $15.95

HOUSEHOLD STORIES BY THE BROTHERS GRIMM. All the great Grimm stories: "Rumpelstiltskin," "Snow White," "Hansel and Gretel," etc., with 114 illustrations by Walter Crane. 269pp. 5⅜ x 8½.
21080-4 Pa. $3.50

SLEEPING BEAUTY, illustrated by Arthur Rackham. Perhaps the fullest, most delightful version ever, told by C. S. Evans. Rackham's best work. 49 illustrations. 110pp. 7⅞ x 10¾.
22756-1 Pa. $2.50

AMERICAN FAIRY TALES, L. Frank Baum. Young cowboy lassoes Father Time; dummy in Mr. Floman's department store window comes to life; and 10 other fairy tales. 41 illustrations by N. P. Hall, Harry Kennedy, Ike Morgan, and Ralph Gardner. 209pp. 5⅜ x 8½.
23643-9 Pa. $3.00

THE WONDERFUL WIZARD OF OZ, L. Frank Baum. Facsimile in full color of America's finest children's classic. Introduction by Martin Gardner. 143 illustrations by W. W. Denslow. 267pp. 5⅜ x 8½.
20691-2 Pa. $3.50

THE TALE OF PETER RABBIT, Beatrix Potter. The inimitable Peter's terrifying adventure in Mr. McGregor's garden, with all 27 wonderful, full-color Potter illustrations. 55pp. 4¼ x 5½. (Available in U.S. only)
22827-4 Pa. $1.25

THE STORY OF KING ARTHUR AND HIS KNIGHTS, Howard Pyle. Finest children's version of life of King Arthur. 48 illustrations by Pyle. 131pp. 6⅛ x 9¼.
21445-1 Pa. $4.95

CARUSO'S CARICATURES, Enrico Caruso. Great tenor's remarkable caricatures of self, fellow musicians, composers, others. Toscanini, Puccini, Farrar, etc. Impish, cutting, insightful. 473 illustrations. Preface by M. Sisca. 217pp. 8⅜ x 11¼.
23528-9 Pa. $6.95

PERSONAL NARRATIVE OF A PILGRIMAGE TO ALMADINAH AND MECCAH, Richard Burton. Great travel classic by remarkably colorful personality. Burton, disguised as a Moroccan, visited sacred shrines of Islam, narrowly escaping death. Wonderful observations of Islamic life, customs, personalities. 47 illustrations. Total of 959pp. 5⅜ x 8½.
21217-3, 21218-1 Pa., Two-vol. set $12.00

INCIDENTS OF TRAVEL IN YUCATAN, John L. Stephens. Classic (1843) exploration of jungles of Yucatan, looking for evidences of Maya civilization. Travel adventures, Mexican and Indian culture, etc. Total of 669pp. 5⅜ x 8½.
20926-1, 20927-X Pa., Two-vol. set $7.90

AMERICAN LITERARY AUTOGRAPHS FROM WASHINGTON IRVING TO HENRY JAMES, Herbert Cahoon, et al. Letters, poems, manuscripts of Hawthorne, Thoreau, Twain, Alcott, Whitman, 67 other prominent American authors. Reproductions, full transcripts and commentary. Plus checklist of all American Literary Autographs in The Pierpont Morgan Library. Printed on exceptionally high-quality paper. 136 illustrations. 212pp. 9⅛ x 12¼.
23548-3 Pa. $12.50

AN AUTOBIOGRAPHY, Margaret Sanger. Exciting personal account of hard-fought battle for woman's right to birth control, against prejudice, church, law. Foremost feminist document. 504pp. 5⅜ x 8½.

20470-7 Pa. $5.50

MY BONDAGE AND MY FREEDOM, Frederick Douglass. Born as a slave, Douglass became outspoken force in antislavery movement. The best of Douglass's autobiographies. Graphic description of slave life. Introduction by P. Foner. 464pp. 5⅜ x 8½.

22457-0 Pa. $5.50

LIVING MY LIFE, Emma Goldman. Candid, no holds barred account by foremost American anarchist: her own life, anarchist movement, famous contemporaries, ideas and their impact. Struggles and confrontations in America, plus deportation to U.S.S.R. Shocking inside account of persecution of anarchists under Lenin. 13 plates. Total of 944pp. 5⅜ x 8½.

22543-7, 22544-5 Pa., Two-vol. set $12.00

LETTERS AND NOTES ON THE MANNERS, CUSTOMS AND CONDITIONS OF THE NORTH AMERICAN INDIANS, George Catlin. Classic account of life among Plains Indians: ceremonies, hunt, warfare, etc. Dover edition reproduces for first time all original paintings. 312 plates. 572pp. of text. 6⅛ x 9¼.

22118-0, 22119-9 Pa.. Two-vol. set $12.00

THE MAYA AND THEIR NEIGHBORS, edited by Clarence L. Hay, others. Synoptic view of Maya civilization in broadest sense, together with Northern, Southern neighbors. Integrates much background, valuable detail not elsewhere. Prepared by greatest scholars: Kroeber, Morley, Thompson, Spinden, Vaillant, many others. Sometimes called Tozzer Memorial Volume. 60 illustrations, linguistic map. 634pp. 5⅜ x 8½.

23510-6 Pa. $10.00

HANDBOOK OF THE INDIANS OF CALIFORNIA, A. L. Kroeber. Foremost American anthropologist offers complete ethnographic study of each group. Monumental classic. 459 illustrations, maps. 995pp. 5⅜ x 8½.

23368-5 Pa. $13.00

SHAKTI AND SHAKTA, Arthur Avalon. First book to give clear, cohesive analysis of Shakta doctrine, Shakta ritual and Kundalini Shakti (yoga). Important work by one of world's foremost students of Shaktic and Tantric thought. 732pp. 5⅜ x 8½. (Available in U.S. only)

23645-5 Pa. $7.95

AN INTRODUCTION TO THE STUDY OF THE MAYA HIEROGLYPHS, Syvanus Griswold Morley. Classic study by one of the truly great figures in hieroglyph research. Still the best introduction for the student for reading Maya hieroglyphs. New introduction by J. Eric S. Thompson. 117 illustrations. 284pp. 5⅜ x 8½.

23108-9 Pa. $4.00

A STUDY OF MAYA ART, Herbert J. Spinden. Landmark classic interprets Maya symbolism, estimates styles, covers ceramics, architecture, murals, stone carvings as artforms. Still a basic book in area. New introduction by J. Eric Thompson. Over 750 illustrations. 341pp. 8⅜ x 11¼.

21235-1 Pa. $6.95

GEOMETRY, RELATIVITY AND THE FOURTH DIMENSION, Rudolf Rucker. Exposition of fourth dimension, means of visualization, concepts of relativity as Flatland characters continue adventures. Popular, easily followed yet accurate, profound. 141 illustrations. 133pp. 5⅜ x 8½.
23400-2 Pa. $2.75

THE ORIGIN OF LIFE, A. I. Oparin. Modern classic in biochemistry, the first rigorous examination of possible evolution of life from nitrocarbon compounds. Non-technical, easily followed. Total of 295pp. 5⅜ x 8½.
60213-3 Pa. $4.00

PLANETS, STARS AND GALAXIES, A. E. Fanning. Comprehensive introductory survey: the sun, solar system, stars, galaxies, universe, cosmology; quasars, radio stars, etc. 24pp. of photographs. 189pp. 5⅜ x 8½. (Available in U.S. only)
21680-2 Pa. $3.75

THE THIRTEEN BOOKS OF EUCLID'S ELEMENTS, translated with introduction and commentary by Sir Thomas L. Heath. Definitive edition. Textual and linguistic notes, mathematical analysis, 2500 years of critical commentary. Do not confuse with abridged school editions. Total of 1414pp. 5⅜ x 8½.   60088-2, 60089-0, 60090-4 Pa., Three-vol. set $18.50

Prices subject to change without notice.

Available at your book dealer or write for free catalogue to Dept. GI, Dover Publications, Inc., 180 Varick St., N.Y., N.Y. 10014. Dover publishes more than 175 books each year on science, elementary and advanced mathematics, biology, music, art, literary history, social sciences and other areas.